SPECULATORS AND SLAVES

"Selling Females by the Pound." From G. Bourne, *Picture of Slavery in the United States.* Reproduced from copy at Wilberforce House, Kingston upon Hull City Museums, High Street, Hull, Humberside, U.K.

SPECULATORS AND SLAVES

Masters, Traders, and Slaves in the Old South

MICHAEL TADMAN

The University of Wisconsin Press

The University of Wisconsin Press
114 North Murray Street
Madison, Wisconsin 53715

3 Henrietta Street
London WC2E 8LU, England

5 4 3 2 1

Printed in the United States of America

Library of Congress Cataloging-in-Publication Data
Tadman, Michael, 1946–
Speculators and slaves: masters, traders, and slaves in the Old South / Michael Tadman.
336 pp. cm.
Includes bibliographical references.
1. Slave-trade—United States—History—19th century. 2. Slave traders—United States—History—19th century. 3. Slaves—United States—Social conditions. 4. Slaveholders—Southern States—History—19th century. 5. Southern States—History—1775–1865. 6. Slave-trade—Southern States—History—19th century. 7. Slave traders—Southern States—History—19th century. I. Title.
F442.T33 1989
975'.00496—dc20 89-40269
ISBN 0-299-11850-9 CIP

To my parents

Pre-eminence in villainy and a greedy love of filthy lucre stands the hard-hearted Negro Trader, who is in every respect as unconscionable a dog of a Southern Shylock as ever drank raw brandy by the glassful, or chewed Virginia tobacco, or used New England cowskins to lacerate the back of a slave. . . . The miserly Negro Trader . . . is, outwardly, a coarse, ill-bred person, provincial in speech and manners, with cross-looking eyes, a dirty tobacco stained mouth, and shabby dress. . . . He is not troubled evidently by a conscience, for although he habitually separates parent from child, brother from sister, and husband from wife, he is yet one of the jolliest dogs alive and never evinces the least sign of remorse.

—D. R. Hundley, *Social Relations in our Southern States* (1860)

[*The interregional slave trade*] *is a sore subject with the defenders of slavery. It is difficult to weave it handsomely among the amenities of the patriarchal institution. They fain would make a scapegoat of the "Trader," and load all the iniquities of the system on his unlucky back.*

—James Stirling, *Letters from the Slave States* (1857)

Contents

Illustrations

Figures

Tables

Preface

THIS study is partly a reconstruction of the scale and organization of the interregional slave trade which operated before the Civil War. Much more importantly, though, it is an attempt to establish the significance of slave sales and forcible family separations for the values and cultures of masters and slaves. Indeed, it is argued that a strong sense of family was central to the lives of antebellum slaves, and that sales and forcible separations formed a crucial yardstick by which slaves were able to judge their masters and find them wanting. Slave trading or, as it was popularly called by contemporaries, "Negro speculation," clearly raises questions about "paternalism," "dependency," and the world views of masters and slaves. It seems, however, that, for masters, the fundamental assumptions of racism generally made it possible to reconcile notions of paternalism and the family with the realities of a social system based upon trading in slaves, and upon the routine destruction of black families. The crucial justificatory myths were that blacks benefitted from almost any contacts with the "more advanced" white civilization, that black attachments to family were temporary and easily forgotten, and that even where forcible separations occurred, proximity to the industrious, white "leadership group" would inevitably tend to produce the best long-term results for blacks. The domestic slave trade, in fact, bears upon the most fundamental values and attitudes of slaves and masters and yields extensive evidence, both quantitative and qualitative, from which we can seek to delineate the leading characteristics of the antebellum system. It suggests, not a rather smooth process of accommodation, but a situation of essentially segregated and conflicting worlds of slaves and masters.

In examining the interregional slave trade and the sort of issues which have just been indicated, this study takes advantage of numerous slave traders' correspondence collections and account books. These records represent immensely rich sources of information which have previously received very little attention from historians. They detail every aspect of the trader and his world, revealing, for example, the personal lives of speculators; their means of disciplining slaves and preparing them for the market; attitudes of traders, masters, and slaves toward sales and separations; the social position of traders; trading tactics; and the traders' often anxious experiences in extracting high profits from their slave property. This study draws upon records of probate, sheriffs', and other sales of slaves (these sources revealing much about prices, demographic structure, and separations). The study makes extensive use of manuscript court records concerning traders (such documents often give very valuable insights into business and personal lives). It draws, too, upon a great many newspaper files (which include hundreds of advertisements by speculators). Other important record groups include ships' manifests (documenting the coastal traffic in slaves), census records (which allow interregional slave movements to be calculated), and abolitionist and proslavery publications.

I should like to thank Dr. William Dusinberre of Warwick University, Dr. John White of Hull University, Dr. Stanley Engerman of the University of Rochester, and Dr. Sheila Blackburn of Liverpool University for comments on early drafts of this study. I am particularly indebted to Dr. Allan Kulikoff for his painstaking and invaluable comments. I am grateful, too, for the assistance of the Twenty-Seven Foundation, and for the expert editorial work of Ms. Jan Blakeslee.

Finally, a note about the citation of certain source materials. In many of the primary sources cited, especially slave traders' letters, the approach of correspondents to spelling and punctuation was casual in the extreme. Basic punctuation has, therefore, without acknowledgment, been added to some of the passages of correspondence quoted, and generally where misspellings occur I have omitted *sic* unless it has seemed to be especially required for clarity.

Abbreviations

ARCHIVES

AAS	American Antiquities Society, Worcester, Massachusetts
AU	Atlanta University, Georgia
BL	British Newspaper Library, Colindale, London
BPL	Boston Public Library
CHS	Chicago Historical Society
DU	Duke University, Durham, North Carolina
HLH	Houghton Library, Harvard University, Cambridge, Massachusetts
JCL	Jefferson County Library, Louisville, Georgia
LC	Library of Congress, Washington, D.C.
MHS	Missouri Historical Society, St. Louis
NA	National Archives, Washington, D.C.
NCA	North Carolina Department of Archives, Raleigh
NYHS	New York Historical Society
NYPL	New York Public Library
SCA	South Carolina Department of Archives, Columbia
SCHS	South Carolina Historical Society, Charleston
SCL	South Caroliniana Library, University of South Carolina, Columbia
SHC	Southern Historical Collection, University of North Carolina, Chapel Hill
SCSO	Sumter County Sheriff's Office, Sumter, South Carolina
UL	Brynmor Jones Library, University of Hull, England
UVA	University of Virginia, Charlottesville
VSL	Virginia State Library, Richmond

DISTRICTS

South Carolina districts are often referred to by abbreviations which employ the first four letters of the district concerned (but in the case of

Chesterfield the abbreviation Chesf is used, thus distinguishing that district from Chester district). The districts are listed in full in Table 2.3.

APPEALS COURT CASES

The following abbreviations are used in reference to published digests of Appeals Court cases:

Richardson	Richardson, J.S.G., *Reports of Cases at Law Argued and Determined in the Court of Appeals and Court of Errors of South Carolina* (Columbia, 1867).
Rich Eq	Richardson, J.S.G., *Reports of Cases in Equity Argued and Determined in the Court of Appeals in Equity and Court Errors of South Carolina* (Columbia, 1868).
Strobhart	Strobhart, James A., *Reports of Cases Argued and Determined in the Court of Appeals and Errors of South Carolina on Appeal from the Courts of Law* (Columbia, 1850).
Strob Eq	Strobhart, James A., *Reports of Cases in Equity Argued and Determined in the Court of Appeals and in the Court of Errors of South Carolina* (Columbia, 1850).

Part One

An Almost Endless Outgoing of Slaves: The Extent and Character of the Trading Business

1

Masters, Traders, and Slaves: An Introduction

THE interregional slave trade has always raised awkward questions about the character of slavery in the antebellum South. At the very core of the proslavery ideology was the insistence that masters sponsored and encouraged the family institution among slaves—but, for the abolitionists, the wrecking of families through trade and sale was central to the indictment of the whole system of human bondage. And, of course, the attitudes of masters and slaves toward the family have seldom been far from the center of the unending scholarly debates on the character of slavery in the South. Indeed, no general theoretical interpretation of American slavery can, without risking serious error, afford to ignore the scale and character of slave trading, the forcible family separations it produced, and the impact of these processes upon the mentalities of masters and slaves. Whatever theories of slavery we develop, whether of conflict or of accommodation, we must seek to define the role of "Negro speculation"—that is to say, the economic and psychological impact of the South's traffic in slaves.

In *Slavery Unmasked,* Philo Tower, typical of his antislavery collegues of the 1850s, cursed those "miserable anti-human critters, walking on two legs, . . . looking like men, [and] called nigger drovers." Tower and other nineteenth-century abolitionists, however, did not simply condemn the trader, but the whole system which allowed him to flourish. With telling effect, the critics of slavery pointed to the embarrassment with which Southerners squirmed when forced to make some reference to the internal slave trade in their otherwise flowing eulogies of the "paternal" institution. As James Stirling, a Scottish visitor, observed, the slave traffic "was a sore subject with the defenders of slavery. . . . They fain would . . . load all the iniquities of the system on [the trader's] unlucky back." Much the same point was made by Harriet Beecher Stowe when, in her *Key to Uncle Tom's Cabin,* she wrote:

> If there is an ill-used class of men in the world it is certainly the slave-traders: for if there is no harm in the institution of slavery . . . then there is no earthly reason why a man may not as innocently be a slave-trader as any other kind of trader.[1]

The abolitionists, then, took a broad view of the trade, and, we should note, their analysis to a great extent set the terms of both the contemporary and much of the academic debate on antebellum slavery. To the abolitionists, slave trafficking seemed to be at the very core of the slavery system. Their economic analysis was striking and provocative. Slave agriculture, they argued, had become highly unprofitable in the Upper South, where plantation monocultures had "exhausted" the soil. Instead of "running itself out" through unprofitability, however, slavery was "kept alive by . . . [the] unnatural process" of interregional slavemongering. Thus, the planters of the Upper South (the slave "exporting states") were seen as becoming economically dependent upon selling a substantial proportion of their bondsmen to the new and expanding cotton regions of the Lower South.[2] In this way, an internal trade of vast proportions was said to have developed and, furthermore, to have brought about the wholesale separation of black families. And even worse, the rich prospects of the internal slave market—according, for example, to Robert Finley of the American Colonization Society—turned the exporting states into "stud farms" where blacks were "bred like other livestock for the more southern states."[3] Such arguments, we shall

1. Philo Tower, *Slavery Unmasked: Being a Truthful Narrative of Three Years' Residence and Journeying in Eleven Southern States* (Rochester, 1856), p. 249; James Stirling, *Letters from the Slave States* (London, 1857), pp. 292–93; and Harriet B. Stowe, *The Key to Uncle Tom's Cabin; Presenting the Original Facts and Documents Upon Which the Story is Founded* (London, 1853), p. 9.

2. The terms Upper and Lower South are used in this study not as descriptions of fixed geographic areas but as convenient labels for constantly changing and expanding regions of, respectively, net exportation and net importation of slaves.

3. Stowe, *The Key,* p. 279; Finley cited in D. L. Dumond, *Antislavery: The Crusade for Freedom in America* (New York, 1961), p. 68. For a detailed contemporary exposition of the abolitionist position on the trade see Executive Committee of the American Anti-Slavery Society (eds.), *Slavery and the Internal Slave Trade . . . Being Replies to Questions Transmitted by the British and Foreign Anti-Slavery Society* (London, 1841), especially reply to seventh question. An important statement on the economic arguments relating to the trade appeared in John E. Cairnes, *The Slave Power: Its Character, Career and Probable Designs* (London, 1862).

see, occur again and again in the literature on North American slavery.

Note, too, the fundamentals of the proslavery formulation regarding the place of the trade in antebellum slavery. Because the proslavery school found the direct defence of the trade hard going, they tended, where possible, to bypass that issue in their propaganda. Their inclination was instead, while praising the benefits which the black population supposedly enjoyed under slavery, to concentrate upon attacking the evils of northern industrial "wage slavery."[4] When challenged point-blank, however, they routinely dismissed the trader as an outcast who could gain little or no foothold in the economy and society of the South. Typical of this school was the proslavery clergyman N. L. Rice who, in 1845, at a public debate on slavery, assured his adversary that "the slave trader was looked upon . . . with disgust" by all decent men in the slaveholding states, for "none but a monster could inflict anguish upon unoffending men for the sake of accumulating wealth."[5]

Because they feed into so much of the literature on slavery and the domestic slave trade, the essentials of the proslavery and abolitionist propaganda positions on the trade have been outlined. We shall see that highly resilient legends were generated by both sides—for example, the largely mythical "stud-farm" system of the abolitionist school, and the misleading proslavery claims about the "disgust" with which the trader was viewed. Before pursuing such issues, though, we should establish something of the context of the trade.

We should note, first, that there has never been any real doubt that the antebellum period saw a massive interregional movement of slaves. In fact, between 1820 and 1860 that movement averaged, each decade, some 200,000 slaves (or fully 10 percent of the Upper South's slave population). The years covered by this study (approximately 1790 to 1860 and, more especially, 1820 to 1860) were indeed the classic years of the Cotton Kingdom. In those years, as a result of European demand

4. See, for example, the major defenses of slavery edited by E. N. Elliot and published as *Cotton is King, and Pro-Slavery Arguments: Comprising the Writings of Hammond, Harper, Christie, Stringfellow, Hodge, Bledsoe, and Cartwright* (Augusta, 1860). For an interesting recent investigation of the South on "wage slavery," see Allen Kaufman, *Capitalism, Slavery, and Republican Values: American Political Economists, 1819–1848* (Austin, 1982). Kaufman argues that political economists, North as well as South, had a dread of creating a disaffected white proletariat; but the South also wrung full value from the proletarian issue for sectional propaganda purposes.

5. J. Blanchard and N. L. Rice, *A Debate on Slavery Held in the City of Cincinnati on the First, Second and Sixth days of October 1845, Upon the Question Is Slaveholding in Itself Sinful, and the Relation between Master and Slave, a Sinful Relation?* (Cincinnati, 1846; New York, 1969), p. 28.

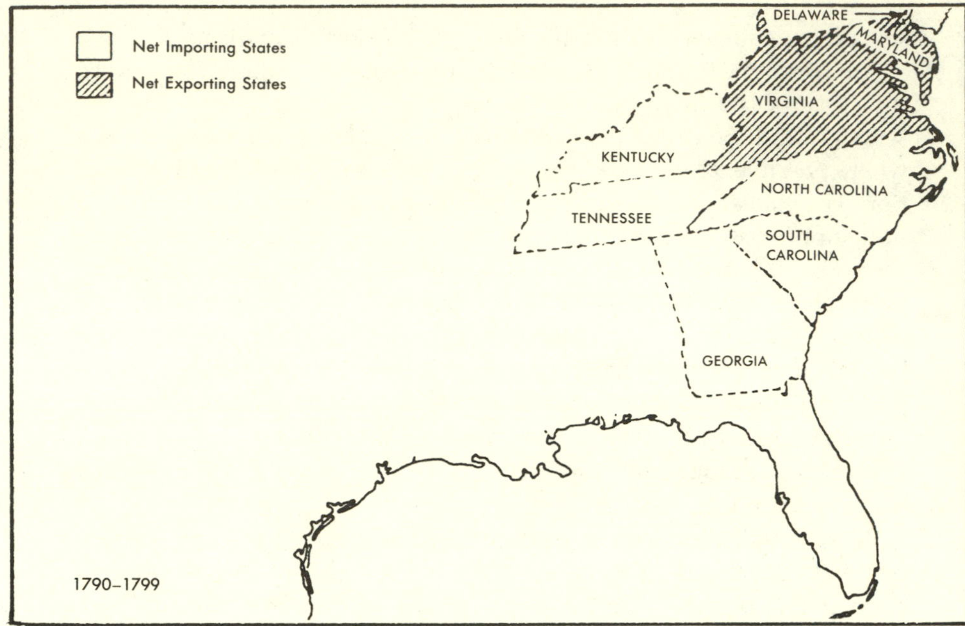
Net Importing States
Net Exporting States
DELAWARE
MARYLAND
VIRGINIA
KENTUCKY
NORTH CAROLINA
TENNESSEE
SOUTH CAROLINA
GEORGIA
1790–1799

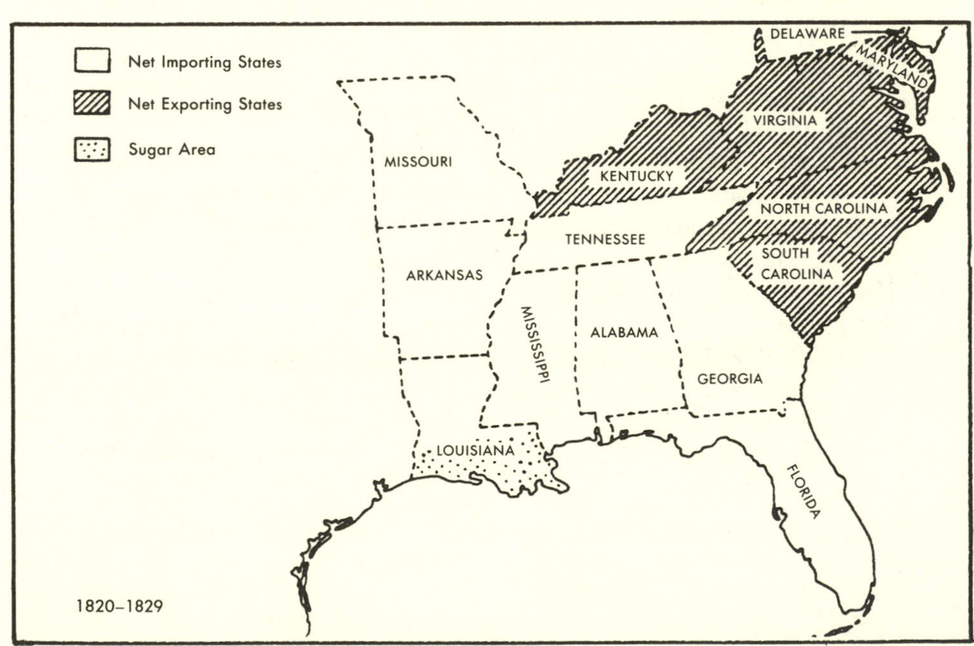
Net Importing States
Net Exporting States
Sugar Area
DELAWARE
MARYLAND
VIRGINIA
MISSOURI
KENTUCKY
NORTH CAROLINA
TENNESSEE
SOUTH CAROLINA
ARKANSAS
MISSISSIPPI
ALABAMA
GEORGIA
LOUISIANA
FLORIDA
1820–1829

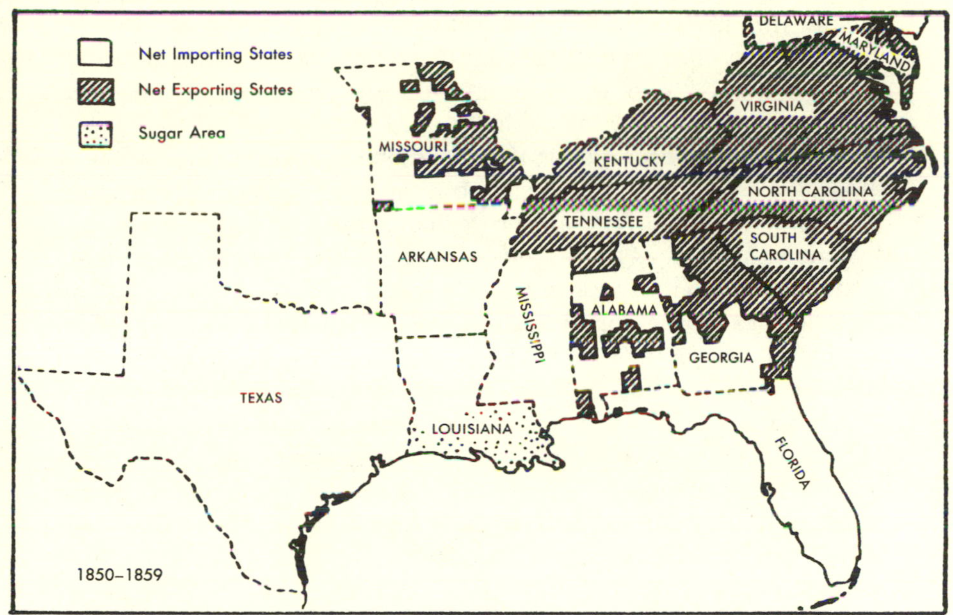

Figure 1.1. Principal slave exporting and importing areas. Source: Data from federal censuses (discussed in Chapter 2).

and of the suitability of the southern interior to large-scale cotton production, American slavery broke loose from the eastern seaboard and rapidly established its domain over vast regions extending as far west as Texas (see Figure 1.1). But although there has been no serious dispute about the massive expansion of slavery in this period, there has always been sharp debate over the composition of that movement. Slave movement combined two elements—*slave trading* on the one hand and *planter migrations* on the other. It will be a vital part of our task, then, to break down the overall movement into its trade and planter-migration components, and from this to find some way of quantifying these separate elements.

In broad terms, we can now sketch the kind of traffic with which we are concerned. This traffic was internal, distributing slaves from the relatively thickly populated Upper South (including Delaware, Maryland, Kentucky, Virginia, Tennessee, and North Carolina) to the expanding cotton and sugar regions of the Lower South (states such as Alabama, Mississippi, Louisiana, and Texas). The trade began to draw comment in the last decades of the slave trade from Africa to North America. It grew to maturity, however, after about 1807, when the African slave trade to the United States was officially ended.

Being internal, the trade was overwhelmingly concerned with American-born slaves. In part it was conducted by a well-organized coastal shipping link between the Chesapeake ports and New Orleans (and this branch of the trade has usually attracted the bulk of historians' attention). It will become clear, though, that the great preponderance of the traffic was in fact conducted by overland traders. These latter "speculators" drove "coffles" of perhaps thirty or forty slaves (but sometimes as many as a hundred or more) on long treks to the markets of the Lower South. To a great extent the trade was conducted by professionals whose part-time, and very often full-time, occupation was the conduct of the interregional traffic. A further part of the trade, however, was pursued by those slaveowners who themselves made trips to the Upper South in order to buy slaves or, much less commonly, set out to the Lower South to sell some of their own slaves.

Planter migrations, as I have said, lay outside the trade. They are taken, basically, to be occasions where a planter, usually from a well-established slaveholding area, decided to set out (with the gang of slaves he already owned) and follow the attractions of newer lands further to the south and west of his old home. Such migrations, of course, did cause separations of slave families. Indeed, where the ownership of family members was split between neighboring planters, separations could be extensive. But the trade was a far more nakedly commercial activity, and one where, it seems, there was little question of slaveowners taking care of their "people."

The present study takes up an interrelated series of themes. It starts by addressing the fundamental question of the scale of the trade and argues that trading substantially outweighed planter migrations in numerical importance. After that, very extensive collections of slave traders' accounts and correspondence are exploited in order to detail the pattern of slave trading routes, business practices, and the experiences of slaves caught up in the interregional traffic. With this basis, it is possible to turn to much wider questions relating to the mentalities of masters and slaves, and to the broad tendencies of antebellum slavery.

At a whole series of points, evidence from the trade offers opportunities to gain insights into the mental world of masters. For example, did masters show reluctance in dealing with the trader? Did they sell to him simply for profit or, instead, under the pressure of economic distress and in circumstances where inherited estates were unavoidably to be divided among heirs? To understand the world of slaveowners, we need to know the slaveholders' attitudes toward separating families, and we need to know something of the scale of such separations. Evidence on the trade provides invaluable insights into these areas. The position of the trader in southern society, again, offers the possibility of important insights into slaveholder mentalities. Was the trader a marginal figure, shunned as a southern "Yankie," disloyal to southern traditions, or was he a figure of respectability and influence? Certainly ambiguities run through many aspects of relations between traders and southern society at large; but the ordering of such inconsistencies was vital to the whole process of rationalizing slaveholding in the minds of white southerners.

"Negro speculation," it will be argued, unlocks much of the mental world of masters, but seems to be equally important in penetrating the world of slaves. The family was at the very heart of slave culture, at the core of their web of ideas and understandings—so that, it seems, family separations formed a vital yardstick by which to judge masters and, indeed, to reckon with the whole relation between slave and slaveholder. Sales to the trade, it will be argued, brought a very high risk of family breakups; and these dealings would have brutally jarred and affronted the slave's sense of family and pattern of beliefs. So crucial, it seems, were such disruptions that, where they occurred, they almost inevitably resulted in a bitter distancing of slaves from the ideology of slavery and of white supremacy. And beyond that, as we shall see, was the interlinked and almost universal legacy of distrust which stemmed from the constant *fear* of separation.

This study, then, is ultimately concerned with the significance of the slave trade for the mentalities of masters and slaves. The trade developed and flourished at the very time when, as Willie Lee Rose has written, contemporaries thought more and more in terms of the "domesticating" of their "domestic institution." Instead of portraying slaves as outsiders, as "barbarian Africans," travellers, planters, and writers in the nineteenth century seem increasingly to have portrayed them as a settled population of permanent children. The defense and rationalizing of slavery turned, it appears, increasingly on the notion that the planter had a domesticating mission to sponsor among slaves the virtues of the "Victorian family," encouraging cheerful obedience and gratitude in return for "paternalistic wisdom, protection, and discipline on the part of the father [read 'master']."[6] Such domestication involved both the encouragement of the black family and the guidance of slaves within the "family" of the plantation.

6. See Willie Lee Rose's essay "The Domestication of Domestic Slavery," pp. 18–36 in W. L. Rose, *Slavery and Freedom* (New York, 1982), ed. and with preface by William W. Freehling. Quotations pp. 20 and 21.

The conjunction of a vigorous, brutal, domestic slave trade with the rise of the ideal of "domestication" is important and puzzling. With the growth of an increasingly American-born slave population, the general increase in the size of slaveholding units, and the spread of the plantation system into vast new areas, we are apparently observing a significant trend in the ideology of slavery. But such a tendency seems in most cases to have been confined precisely to ideology, to rationalizing the unreconcilable, to generating comfortable, self-serving, defensive images.

Slaveholders might perhaps rest easily within their world view of domestication, but the worlds of slave and master seem ultimately to have been as far apart in the nineteenth century as in earlier centuries. It will be important, later in this study, to point to variations according to time and place and between different slave–master patterns. But cutting across the South was the slave trade—and with it both the forcible separation of families and repeated affronts to the most dearly cherished of slave values and attachments. Such circumstances, it will be argued, meant that masters and slaves lived in separate worlds. Segregation did not begin with the "Jim Crow" experience of the postslavery period: it was fundamental to antebellum practice and, if not to the ideological pretensions of whites, then to the values of most slaves.

Masters, by separating families and by all of their involvements with the business of "Negro speculation," demonstrated that they could not truly enter the mental worlds of their slaves. And slaves, not least by the experience of the family and the trade, seem, in most cases, unlikely to have entered into the ideology of slavery and white supremacy. "Accommodation," of course, occurred under slavery, and was vital to its operation, as I shall repeatedly note later; but (although a range of slave responses existed), the dominant tendency seems to have been an adjustment to power relationships rather than a basic accommodation of ideas and values.

2

The Scale of Negro Speculation

THIS study will concentrate on the operations of the domestic slave trade from about 1808, that is, from the time when importations from Africa finally became illegal and, it seems clear, very few in number. Because age structures will be important in tracing the extent of the domestic traffic in slaves (and because federal censuses did not enumerate slaves by age until 1820), detailed statistical work will concentrate on the period from 1820 until the Civil War. From general census data, it is clear, nevertheless, that extensive interregional slave movements occurred from at least the 1790s; the broad outlines of these movements are suggested in Table 2.1.[1]

Careful analysis is necessary in order to separate interregional movements into their planter migration and domestic slave trade components (and for the early years, as Appendix 1.3 shows, we must make allowance for the impact of African arrivals). But let me, for the moment, merely indicate the broad pattern of movements across the South. Over the antebellum period, the divide between the slave-importing and slave-exporting states pushed steadily further westward and southward, and the division was never at all sharply defined (see Figure 1.1). As states evolved, subregions within them gradually passed (see Alabama, Georgia, and Missouri in Figure 1.1) from being net importers into becoming net exporters of slaves. As early as the 1790s, Virginia, Maryland, and Delaware were already net exporters, and shortly afterwards North Carolina and the District of Columbia

1. On slave movements in the period up to about 1820, valuable evidence and suggestions are provided by two articles in Ira Berlin and Ronald Hoffman (eds), *Slavery and Freedom in the Age of the American Revolution* (Charlottesville, Va., 1983): Phillip D. Morgan, "Black Society in the Low Country, 1760–1810," and Allan Kulikoff, "Uprooted Peoples: Black Migrants in the Age of the American Revolution, 1790–1820."

Table 2.1. Estimates of net interregional slave movements according to state, 1790–1859

	1790–99	1800–09	1810–19	1820–29	1830–39	1840–49	1850–59
Natural growth rate of whole slave population (%)	27.0	27.0	30.5	31.2	23.8	27.8	23.4
Alabama			+35,500	+54,156	+96,520	+16,532	+10,752
Arkansas			+1,000	+2,123	+12,752	+18,984	+47,443
Delaware	-4,523	-3,204	- 817	-2,270	-1,314	- 912	- 920
Dist. of Columbia		-1,123	- 576	-1,944	-2,575	-2,030	-1,222
Florida			+1,000	+2,627	+5,833	+5,657	+11,850
Georgia	+6,095	+11,231	+10,713	+18,324	+10,403	+19,873	-7,876
Kentucky	+21.636	+25,837	+18,742	- 916	-19,907	-19,266	-31,215
Louisiana		+1,159	+20,679	+16,415	+29,296	+29,924	+26,528
Maryland	-22,221	-19,960	-33,070	-32,795	-33,753	-21,348	-21,777
Mississippi		+2,152	+9,123	+19,556	+101,810	+53,028	+48,560
Missouri			+5,460	+10,104	+24,287	+11,406	+6,314
North Carolina	+3,671	- 407	-13,361	-20,113	-52,044	-22,481	-22,390
South Carolina	+4,435	+6,474	+1,925	-20,517	-56,683	-28,947	-65,053
Tennessee	+6,645	+21,788	+19,079	+31,577	+6,930	+4,837	-17,702
Texas						+28,622	+99,190
Virginia	-22,767	-41,097	-75,562	-76,157	-118,474	-88,918	-82,573
Total est. exportations	49,511	65,791	123,386	154,712	284,750	183,902	250,728
Total est. importations	42,482	68,641	123,221	154,882	287,831	188,863	250,637

Note: Basic population evidence is derived from federal censuses. The method used is the comparison of decennial growth rates. For an explanation of procedures involved and for adjustments made to cancel out importations from the African slave trade, 1790–1809, see Appendix 1.

were added to the heartland of exportation. By the 1820s, South Carolina and Kentucky (while still containing subregions of importation) joined the ranks of net exporters, and eventually in the 1850s Georgia and Tennessee also became net exporters (again with subregions of importation). By that last decade Missouri and Alabama, although still net importers, had come to contain substantial exporting enclaves. Whereas certain states, then, completed the transition from importation to exportation, the importing section from 1820 to 1860 was dominated by Alabama, Arkansas, Louisiana, Mississippi, Florida, and, eventually, Texas.

A VIGOROUS EARLY TRADE?

Although our prime concern will be the period after 1807, it is clear from scattered, unsystematic evidence that a professional domestic traffic in slaves dated back to at least the 1780s. Ulrich B. Phillips noted that "the internal traffic at the South began to be noticeable about the end of the eighteenth century." Indeed, members of the Constitutional Convention were fully aware of the rationale for an extensive interregional trade and, in the early years of the Republic, Americans were already taking up sectional and moral positions on the trade. At the Philadelphia Convention of 1787, Charles C. Pinckney observed:

> South Carolina and Georgia cannot do without slaves. As to Virginia she will gain by stopping the importations [from Africa]. Her slaves will rise in value, and she has more than she wants. It would be unequal to require South Carolina and Georgia to confederate on such unequal terms.

In 1787, too, Delaware passed legislation aimed at regulating slave trading from that state, in particular the trade in kidnapped free blacks. And two years later, trading from Maryland was clearly in operation, for in 1789 Quakers and their allies urged that state's legislature to prohibit the exportation of her slaves. This proposal and a similar one of 1791 were, however, turned down on the grounds that such schemes would interfere with the rights of property, would restrain the "desirable" diminution in the state's black population, and would prevent slaves "from moving to a warmer and more congenial climate." In these years the Maryland reformers also sought, unsuccessfully, to prohibit the selling south of those who were slaves for fixed periods of years rather than for life; and in 1801, again without success, they attempted to protect against separation from their parents those slave children who were caught up in the export trade.[2]

An exceptional branch of the early domestic slave trade often attracted particular attention and criticism—that from the northern and middle states to the South. From the 1770s to 1820—a period when these northerly states were steadily dismantling the institution of slavery—Robert Fogel and Stanley Engerman have found a significant, though probably not massive, unloading of slaves upon the southern states. Such slaves—connected with the troublesome idea of freedom, and indeed sometimes kidnapped freedmen, or those officially enslaved for a fixed period only—caused alarm in the South. Protests

2. Ulrich B. Phillips, *American Negro Slavery: A Survey of the Supply, Employment and Control of Negro Labor as Determined by the Plantation Regime* (New York, 1918; Baton Rouge, 1966), p. 188; Pinckney in Max Ferrand (ed.), *The Records of the Federal Convention of 1787* (New Haven, 1911), vol. 2, p. 371; 1787 legislation in Winfield H. Collins, *The Domestic Slave Trade of the Southern States* (New York, 1904), p. 125; Jeffrey R. Brackett, *The Negro in Maryland: A Study of the Institution of Slavery* (Johns Hopkins University Studies in Historical and Political Science, Extra vol. 6, Baltimore, 1889), pp. 58–61.

were common, as when in 1792 the inhabitants of Beaufort, South Carolina, petitioned their legislature against the "notorious" practice of northerners who "have for a number of years past been in the habit of shipping to these Southern States, slaves, who are scandalously infamous and incorrigible." The practices of kidnapping blacks from northerly states and trading in slaves from that area were still being lamented in 1815 when Jesse Torrey compiled his *American Slave Trade.*[3]

At the real focus of the early domestic trade (the southern states themselves), essays in financial stringency sometimes resulted in curbs on trading. Thus in 1787, the year in which her representatives had defended at Philadelphia the right, in principle, to import slaves from whatever source, South Carolina prohibited both the African and the domestic trades. The legislation, entitled "An Act to Regulate the Recovery and Payment of Debts and for Prohibiting the Importation of Negroes," reflected the state's debts from war years, a postwar surge in spending, and a series of bad harvests. As Winthrop Jordan was noted, the prohibition (running from 1787 to 1803) was "a matter of men denying themselves what they wanted [slave importation] but could not afford."[4] But the ban became more than that: it became a sectional conflict of interests within the state. The politically dominant seaboard counties, relatively well stocked with slaves, repeatedly clashed with the expanding upcountry, starved of slaves. Petitions for the reopening of the domestic trade, for example by Abbeville district in 1802, were repeatedly outvoted by the seaboard, keen to protect the prices of slaves, to discourage both overproduction of crops and excessive financial speculation, and to limit the size of the state's black population. Such sectional divisions within states were probably long-run affairs, and certainly we shall find that within Georgia clashes of regional interest on the trade ran over several decades. In South Carolina in the 1790s and early 1800s, the low country, then, used its political power to ban importation by the domestic trade. How effective such restrictions were is far from clear; already in December 1795 the state senate was

3. Robert W. Fogel and Stanley L. Engerman, "Philanthropy at Bargain Prices: Notes on the Economics of Gradual Emancipation," *The Journal of Legal Studies,* 3 (1974), esp. pp. 381–83; Morgan, "Black Society," pp. 84–85; Jesse Torrey, *The American Slave Trade; or An Account of the Manner in which the Slave Dealers take Free People from Some of the United States of America, and Carry them Away, and Sell them as Slaves in Other of the States . . .* (London, 1822, with preface by William Cobbett; reprinted Negro University Press, Westport, Conn., 1971, and originally published as *A Portraiture of Slavery in the United States,* Philadelphia, 1817).

4. Winthrop D. Jordan, *White over Black: American Attitudes Towards the Negro, 1550–1812* (Chapel Hill, 1968; Baltimore, 1969), p. 318.

informed that over the previous six months or so, "Those slaves brought in [illegally] by land I have not been able to procure any accounting of, although I have reason to believe there have been many."[5]

Certainly, the period from 1787 to the African ban of 1807 yields significant glimpses of direct evidence on the operation of the domestic traffic in mainly American-born slaves. In 1787 we find Moses Austin trading in Richmond, Virginia, and advertising in the local press for

> One hundred Negroes, from 20 to 30 years old, for which a good price will be given. They are to be sent out of state, therefore we shall not be particular respecting the character of any of them—Hearty and well made is all that is necessary.

When interviewed in the 1820s, the former slave Betsey Madison reported that in 1792 or 1793 a western planter on a slave-buying trip to Virginia had bought her, separated her from her husband, and removed her and eight other slaves to his plantation in the Natchez (Mississippi) area. About two years later, in 1795, a trader, introducing slaves into Kentucky and probably purchasing in Maryland and Virginia, used the press to announce his intention to "carry on the [slaving] business extensively"; and in 1799 a certain Speers, on a trading trip between Virginia and Georgia, was killed by members of his slave gang. Again for the 1790s, Anita Goodstein found indications of traders operating at Nashville, Tennessee. For 1802 or somewhat earlier, there is evidence that interregional traders regularly operated through the District of Columbia; in January 1802, a grand jury reported as a grievance "the practice of persons coming from distant parts of the United States into this District for the purpose of purchasing slaves." According to the

5. Carl Harrison Brown, "The Reopening of the Foreign Slave Trade in South Carolina, 1803–1807," unpublished M.A. thesis, University of South Carolina, 1968, pp. 2–10; P. S. Brady, "The Slave Trade and Sectionalism in South Carolina, 1787–1808," *Journal of Southern History,* 38 (1972), p. 613; A Vander Horst to Senate, Senate Messages from Governor (3 Dec. 1795, No. 15), Eleventh General Assembly, in Miscellaneous Records of Secretary of State for South Carolina (SCA).

The division of interest between the upcountry and the low country is suggested by the fact that from 1803 to 1807, low-country representatives amassed a 46 to nil vote against reopening the domestic trade, whereas the upcountry accumulated a 36 to 20 total in its favor (Brady, "The Slave Trade," p. 613). The fact that in those years South Carolina, while admitting African importations, still banned domestic importations suggests special anxieties about some aspects of the domestic trade. There seems to have been a fear, especially in the low country, of northern slaves "tainted" with the idea of freedom, and a dread of contagion from Virginia slaves associated with the Gabriel conspiracy of 1800.

jury, the slaves, having been confined in jails until sufficient numbers were collected, were

> then turned out in our streets, . . . loaded with chains as though they had committed some heinous offence. . . . We consider it a grievance [the jury continued] . . . that the interposition of civil authority cannot be had to prevent parents being wrested from their offspring, and children from their parents, without respect to the ties of nature.

In 1803, we find President Thomas Jefferson deciding, as a punishment, to sell one of his slaves into "so distant an exile . . . as to cut him off completely from ever being heard of [again]"; and presumably the vehicle for this exile was to be the interregional trade. And as Frederic Bancroft found when working on his *Slave Trading in the Old South*, by the first years of the nineteenth century the newspapers of Richmond, Virginia, were becoming scattered with the advertisements of interregional traders.[6]

With Charles Ball's *Fifty Years in Chains, or the Life of an American Slave* (first published 1837), we are fortunate in having, for 1805 and indeed for about twenty years earlier, a remarkably detailed record of a slave's experience in the interregional trade.[7] In about 1805, Ball himself was

6. Austin's advertisement is quoted in Robert McColley, *Slavery and Jeffersonian Virginia*, 2nd ed. (Urbana, 1973), pp. 164–65; Betsey Madison's interview is reproduced in John W. Blassingame (ed.), *Slave Testimony: Two Centuries of Letters, Speeches, Interviews and Autobiographies* (Baton Rouge, 1977), pp. 185–88; anonymous slave trader's letter of 24 Jan. 1795, and Charleston (SC) *City Gazette* item of 21 Dec. 1799, both reproduced in Ulrich B. Phillips, J. E. Commons, et al. (eds.), *A Documentary History of American Industrial Society* (11 vols.; Cleveland, 1910–11; New York, 1958), vol. 2, pp. 55–56, 70–71; Anita S. Goodstein, "Black History on the Nashville Frontier, 1780–1810," *Tennessee Historical Quarterly*, 38 (1979), pp. 404–405; the D.C. grand jury's comments are quoted in Frederic Bancroft, *Slave Trading in the Old South* (Baltimore, 1931; New York, 1959), pp. 23–24; Jefferson quoted in Mary Beth Norton, Herbert G. Gutman, and Ira Berlin, "The Afro-American Family in the Age of the Revolution," in Berlin and Hoffman (eds.), *Slavery and Freedom*, p. 185; Bancroft, *Slave Trading*, p. 22. For an even earlier, but probably exceptional, example of interregional trading see Leila Sellers, *Charleston Businessmen on the Eve of the American Revolution* (Chapel Hill, 1934), pp. 97–98. Sellers cites Henry Laurens, the African slave trader based at Charleston, who in 1768 shipped a "parcel" of "country Negroes" from South Carolina to St. Augustine, Florida. According to Sellers, already in the 1760s South Carolina's "country Negroes" (locally born) feared being sold out of state to buyers who valued their knowledge of English and of agricultural and other skills.

7. Charles Ball, *The Narrative of Charles Ball*, ed. Isaac Fisher (New York, 1837), reprinted as *Fifty Years in Chains; or, The Life of An American Slave* (New York, 1858). For a commentary on the narrative see Blassingame (ed.), *Slave Testimony*, esp. pp. xxiii–xxvi.

sold to a trader (the latter formerly having been active in the African trade, but now specializing in the domestic traffic from Maryland to Georgia and South Carolina). Once bought, Ball was added to fifty-one slaves already in the speculator's drove, and was forced to leave his wife and children, the trader volunteering that he "would be able to get another wife in Georgia." It turned out, though, that the speculator, a certain "Colonel" M'Griffin, while travelling South made an extended halt near Columbia, South Carolina, and there sold several of his gang. Ball narrowly escaped sale to a "disgusting and repulsive" individual who offered that, with the African trade open,

> I can . . . by going to Charleston, buy as many Guinea negroes as I please for two hundred dollars each, but as I like this fellow, I will give you four hundred for him.

Ball's fate, in fact, was to fall into the hands of one of the district's substantial planters. Significantly, the fact that the domestic trade was illegal in South Carolina in these years seems to have worried neither trader nor buyers. Indeed, as Ball reported, in the upcountry, short of slaves, the trader was received as a public benefactor.[8]

Long before his own traumatic experiences with M'Griffin, Ball's upbringing had already been bitterly marked by the Georgia traders. In about 1800, when living near Washington, he "frequently saw large numbers of [his] color chained together in long trains, and driven off towards the South." But as early as about 1785 to 1787, when Ball was only five, the interregional trade had devastated his childhood: his mother was sold to a Georgia trader. And because his father protested so strongly over the separation the father too, as punishment, was sold off to another speculator.[9]

Across the two decades from 1787 to 1807 it is clear, therefore, that an organized interregional traffic in American slaves operated. So far, however, it seems possible only to guess at its scale. We have rough estimates of total interregional movements (complicated by the addition of new African arrivals in these years), but for this early period there seems to be no reliable way of distinguishing between the roles of interregional trading and planter migrations. Allan Kulikoff has recently suggested that, before the 1810s at least, planter migrations would very much have predominated. There are, though, certain factors which do suggest the possibility of a substantial interregional

8. Ball, *Fifty Years,* pp. 286, 28–29, 70, 53.
9. Ball, *Fifty Years,* pp. 97–102, 19, 10, 14.

"A Slave-Auction at Richmond, Virginia." From a life study by Eyre Crowe in the *Illustrated London News,* 27 September 1856. Reproduced from D. L. Dumond, *Antislavery: The Crusade for Freedom in America*

trade before 1808. I have already cited evidence from statutes, advertisements, travel accounts, and the like. Besides, there is the persistent natural increase of the old-established slave states; as Pinckney observed, Virginia by 1787 already had "more slaves than she wanted." Added to that is the temptation of greatly higher slave prices in states such as Georgia and Louisiana, compared with Virginia and certain of her near neighbors. But the documentation generated by the domestic traffic of this period was relatively unspectacular compared with the African trade; there is no equivalent to the shipping and port statistics of the latter. Perhaps all we can do for the present is to point to the possibility of a substantial pre-1808 domestic slave traffic. The fact that from 1787 to 1798 only Georgia of the southern states permitted African importations might well have encouraged the domestic trade. Even South Carolina's maverick policy of reopening the African trade from 1803 to 1807 seems not to have greatly affected the numbers for 1787 to 1807 as a whole. African importations, it appears, accounted for rather fewer than half of the 200,000 slaves that were shifted into Georgia and the net importing states.[10]

When we look beyond 1807 and to the 1810s we begin to move to somewhat safer ground. In about 1808, a traveller in Virginia reported that "the Carolina Slave dealers get frequent supplies from this state, particularly from the eastern shore." And in the same year Christian Shultz observed traders with a shipload of blacks on their "slow voyage up river to Natchez." Two years later, William Rochel was advertising in the *Natchez Weekly Chronicle,*

> I have upwards of twenty likely Virginia born slaves now in a flat boat lying in the river at Natchez, for sale cheaper than has been sold here for years.

And, leafing through various Virginia newspapers for 1810, Frederic Bancroft found, for example, that "several regular traders had appeared at Fredericksburg" and, like a certain John Stannard, were announcing "I WILL GIVE CASH for a few LIKELY YOUNG NEGROES." (The significance of cash purchases, as we shall see in a later chapter, was crucial.) In 1812, Hezekiah Niles in his *Weekly Register* (Baltimore) informed his readers that

10. See Kulikoff, "Uprooted Peoples," esp. p. 148. On prices, see Appendix 7 (Figure A7.1), and see also, for example, comments in Paul F. Lachance, "The Politics of Fear: French Louisianians and the Slave Trade, 1786–1809," *Plantation Societies,* 1(1979), esp. pp. 185–86. For statistics on importations from 1787 to 1807, see Appendix 1. On African slave trade prohibitions see, for example, Phillips, *American Negro Slavery,* pp. 132–49.

If there is anything that ought to be supremely hated,—it is the present infamous traffic that is carried on in several of the middle states, and especially Maryland, in negroes, for the Georgia and Louisiana markets. I blush for the honor and art of printing when I see advertisements published in the newspapers openly avowing the trade, and soliciting business, with the indifference of dealers in horses.[11]

Jesse Torrey, from his interviews and investigations into the trade, in 1815 gave a picture of a trading system which had already established long and to him repellent traditions. While visiting the District of Columbia he observed "a procession of men, women, and children, resembling that of a funeral. . . . They were [slaves] bound together in pairs, some with ropes, and some with iron chains," who were being driven by traders to Georgia. He found the trade with Georgia to be so firmly established that "in the middle states, the general title applied to slave traders, indiscriminately, is Georgia-men." And slaves were well versed in the dangers of the trade. "It is," he wrote

a frequent custom in the District of Columbia, Maryland, and Delaware, for masters to endeavor to reform their bad slaves, by terrifying them with threats of selling them for the Georgia market, or 'to Carolina' them; which is often carried into effect.

As to the extent of the District of Columbia's trade, he wrote,

I then supposed the instances of the streets of the city consecrated to freedom, being paraded with people led in captivity, were rare. But I soon ascertained that they were quite frequent, that several hundred people, including not legal slaves only, but many kidnapped freemen and youths bound to service for a term of years . . . are annually collected at Washington (as if it were an emporium of slavery), for transportation to the slave regions.

At about the same time, John Randolph, who had once defended the African trade, bitterly condemned the District of Columbia's involvement in the interregional slaving business. He was "mortified" that slaves were being herded through the capital city "incarcerated and chained down, and thence driven in fetters like beasts," their families rent asunder, all for the gratification of hardhearted masters and traders.[12]

11. Phillips, *Documentary History,* vol. 2, p. 55; Shultz quoted in Joe Gray Taylor, *Negro Slavery in Louisiana* (Baton Rouge, 1963), p. 36; Rochel quoted in Charles S. Sydnor, *Slavery in Mississippi* (New York, 1933), p. 147; Bancroft, *Slave Trading,* p. 24; *Niles' Weekly Register,* 19 July 1812, p. 323.

12. Torrey, *American Slave Trade,* pp. 55–56, 61, 66–67; Randolph quoted in Bancroft, *Slave Trading,* pp. 45–46.

For 1818, the journal of a family of white migrants tells us that, when passing through western Virginia, they "moved forward and fell in with negro traders [and] met several droves of hogs in tolerable roads." But for 1817 to 1820 we have, with the records of F. E. Rives, much more detail on the trade from Virginia (this time to Natchez, Mississippi). With the Rives papers we find contracts between traders, detailed lists of substantial coffles, prices, jail fees, doctors' bills, unsound slaves returned, and profit rates. Manifests of the coastwise trade increase in numbers with, for example, the speculator Abner Robinson of Richmond, from at least 1817, regularly sending large consignments from Richmond to New Orleans. And already, around 1816 to 1818, we find evidence that both South Carolina and Kentucky (still net importers) were developing enclaves of exportation by the interstate trade. In 1816, for example, Edward Stone, buying slaves in the Bluegrass country of Kentucky and trading them to Mississippi and elsewhere in the South, was advertising: "CASH FOR NEGROES! I wish to purchase TWENTY NEGROES, BOYS AND GIRLS from 10 to 25 years of age." And a year or so later Henry Fearon came across fourteen flat boats, loaded with slaves, on their way from Kentucky down the Mississippi. Similarly, from his travels in Kentucky in 1818, Estwick Evans found a thriving export traffic in slaves: "They are a subject of continual speculation and are daily brought . . . from Kentucky and other places to Natchez and the New Orleans market." And for 1818 and 1819 we have valuable letters of the slave traders Allan and Spann, operating between South Carolina and Alabama.[13]

THE ASCENDENCY OF THE TRADE, ABOUT 1820–1860: APPROACHES TO THE PROBLEM OF QUANTIFICATION

When we move ahead to the period from 1820 to 1860 it is possible to offer much more extensive evidence on the scale of trading. For this period, three methods of estimation were used. The first approach concentrated on records relating to the New Orleans trade in the 1840s.

13. "John Owen's Journal of his Removal from Virginia to Alabama in 1818," *Publications of the Southern Historical Association,* 1 (1897), p. 93; Francis Everod Rives Papers (DU); Charles H. Wesley, "Manifests of Slave Shipments Along the Waterways," *Journal of Negro History,* 27 (1942), esp. pp. 160–62; J. Winston Coleman, *Slavery Times in Kentucky* (Chapel Hill, 1940), pp. 144–46; J. Winston Coleman, "Lexington Slave Dealers and their Southern Trade," *The Filson Club Historical Quarterly,* 12 (1938), pp. 1–3; James Spann Papers (SCL).

A second method compared the age structure of the trade against that of planter migration, and concentrated on the 1820s and 1850s—decades for which censuses provide suitable age categories for my analysis.[14] Results from these approaches were then supplemented by a third method—an attempt to catalogue all identifiable slave traders in a sample state (South Carolina) over one of the decades (the 1850s) examined by the age-structure technique. The results of all three methods very strongly indicate, for the years after 1820, the dominance of trading over planter migration.

THE CASE OF THE NEW ORLEANS TRADE

In *Time on the Cross,* Robert Fogel and Stanley Engerman made observations about the sex ratio of the New Orleans trade, and on that basis they developed a general argument that interregional trading was of very minor importance compared with planter migration. A closer examination of the New Orleans record leads, however, to two major conclusions. First, their assumption about the sex ratio of the trade was incorrect for every market except New Orleans. Second, it is clear that as far as the New Orleans coastal route is concerned slave trading was at least three times as important as planter migration.

Let us start by considering Fogel and Engerman's analysis. What they did was to examine documents concerning the coastal trade from the Chesapeake area to New Orleans; there they found a ratio of some sixty males to every forty females. Their assumption was that such ratios were characteristic of the whole domestic trade. Since, using evidence from the census, they quite correctly calculated that the total interregional movement (combining trading and migrations) was only about 51 percent male, it seemed to follow that the trade could have contributed very little to the overall movement of slaves. Indeed, they

14. I shall, for example, trace cohorts which were aged 0–9 years at the start of a decade and 10–19 at its end. The categories used for age enumeration in the censuses for the 1830s and 1840s do not provide a basis for directly tracing such age cohorts from the start of the decade to its end. As valuable work by Zeckhauser and McClelland has shown, it is possible roughly to reconstitute the age categories of the 1830s and 1840s into more usable data (see Peter D. McClelland and Richard J. Zeckhauser, *Demographic Dimensions of the New Republic: American Interregional Migration, Vital Statistics, and Manumissions, 1800–1860* (New York, 1982), pp. 23–25, 27. Indeed, their results for the 1830s and 1840s show essentially similar patterns to those of the 1820s and 1850s. It is considered best for the present study, however, to avoid nonessential "smoothing" and reconstituting of census data, and to concentrate on the more direct evidence of the 1820s and 1850s.

attributed at most 16 percent of all interregional movements to the trade.[15]

This section of Fogel and Engerman's important study had, in fact, dealt with an entirely exceptional branch of the interregional slave traffic. An extensive sampling of speculators' business records (documents specifying the sex of some three thousand slaves, and representing all such records which have been found in research for the present study) reveals the problem with their assumption.[16] This evidence (see Table 2.2) clearly indicates that, in the interregional trade, it was only the New Orleans branch which was sex-selective. All other branches of the domestic trade carried roughly equal numbers of males and females. As we shall see in Chapter 3, the reason for the peculiarity of the New Orleans trade was sugar. Southern Louisiana accounted for the only significant cane sugar production in the South, its labor demands were severe, and its importations were, for the domestic trade, unique. Much more will be said about this market in the next chapter.

The New Orleans coastal manifests also allow us, for this route at least, to make a direct estimate of the relative importance of trading and migration—and it is abundantly clear that the trade was overwhelmingly predominant. When a check is made of the many thousands of slaves carried by this route, it is evident that, although planter migrants did use this route, at least 73 percent of the slaves carried were the property of readily identifiable traders. As Appendix 2 (section 2.2) shows, the detailed sample taken was for thousands of slaves in the 1840s; but checks on sample years in both earlier and later decades produced similar results. At the very least 73 percent, but in

15. See Robert W. Fogel and Stanley L. Engerman, *Time on the Cross: The Economics of American Negro Slavery* (Boston, 1974), vol. 1, pp. 38–58, and vol. 2, pp. 37–53.

16. The following slave traders' papers and accounts (many of which constitute rich sources of information on a whole range of aspects of the trade) were used: the papers of F. E. Rives, O. Fields, J. A. Mitchell, F. L. Whitehead, T. Glen (and also on Glen, the Jarratt-Puryear Papers), all in the Duke University Library; the papers of J. S. Totten, H. Badgett, W. Long, and E. W. Ferguson (all at North Carolina's State Archives); J. W. Pittman Papers (Library of Congress); H. N. Templeman Account Book (New York Public Library); Templeman & Goodwin Account Book and A. & A. T. Walker Account Book (Southern Historical Collection); S. & R. F. Omohundro Slaves Sales Book (Virginia University Library); and the J. R. White Account Book, Chinn Collection (Missouri Historical Society). Also used are the Sales Books (1851–67) of James Tupper, Master in Equity for Charleston District, and the Book of Inventories, Appraisals, and Sales (1850–59) for Charleston District (South Carolina Archives); and for Hughes & Downing see Coleman "Lexington Slave Dealers."

Table 2.2. Sex ratio of the interregional slave trade (excluding Louisiana's sugar area)

Record Type	Name of slave trader	Sex ratio information available for period	Route traded[a]	Numbers of slaves traded (by category): Identifiable males	Identifiable females	Infants (sex not) identified	Other slaves with sex not clearly specified	Percent male (approx.)
P	Badgett, H.	1837–50	N.C.–Ga./Ala.	22	35	1		39
C	Charleston Probate	1850–59	S.C.–LS	104	132	21	144	45
P	Ferguson, E.W.	1855–59	N.C.–LS	14	21		2	40
S	Fields, O.	1822–28	N.C.–S.C.	18	25	6	4	43
S	Glen, T.	1830–36	N.C.–Ala.	217	198	14	31	52
S	Glen, T. (additional)	1824–47	N.C.–Ala.	99	83		15	54
S	Hughes & Downing	1843–44	Kent.–Miss.	7	6			54
P	Long, W.	1836–49	N.C.–Miss.	57	35	5	3	61
S	Mitchell, J. A.	1834–35	Va.–Ala.	28	21		1	57
S	Omohundro, S. & R. F.	1857–62	Va.–LS	150	178	32		46
S	Pittman, J. W.	1835	Va.–LS	3	7			30
S	Rives, F. E.	1817–19	Va.–Miss.	28	25		3	53
C	S.C. Equity	1851–63	S.C.–LS	234	225	11	10	51
S	Templeman, H. N.	1846–47	Va.–LS	40	57	7	3	42
S	Templeman & Goodwin	1849–51	Va.–Ga.	45	48	3	2	48
S	Totten, J. S.	1832–36	N.C.–Ala.	81	87		5	48
S	Walker, A. & A. T.	1851–61	N.C.–Ala.	28	61	16		34
*S	White, J. R.	1846–60	Mo.–LS	217	244	22		47
S	Whitehead, F. L.	1835–36	Va.–Miss.	39	30	4		57
	Totals			1,431	1,518	138	227	49

Sources: Slave traders' papers and accounts used: the papers of F. E. Rives, O. Fields, J. A. Mitchell, F. L. Whitehead, T. Glen (and also on Glen, the Jarratt–Puryear Papers), all DU; the papers of J. S. Totten, H. Badgett, W. Long, and E. W. Ferguson (NCA); J. W. Pittman Papers (LC); H. N. Templeman Account Book (NYPL); Templeman & Goodwin Account Book and A. & A. T. Walker Account Book (SHC); S. & R. F. Omohundro Slaves Sales Book (UVA); and the J. R. White Account Book, Chinn Collection (MHS). Also used are the Sales Books (1851–67) of James Tupper, Master in Equity for Charleston District, and the Book of Inventories, Appraisals, and Sales (1850–59) for Charleston District (SCA), and for Hughes & Downing see Coleman "Lexington Slave Dealers."

Note: In order to achieve estimates of sex ratios, infants of unspecified sex are divided equally between males and females, but the 200 hundred other slaves of unspecified sex are excluded.

[a] LS = Lower South.

C: Purchases from Equity and probate sales by long-distance traders identified in Appendix 4.

P: Information derived from traders' *purchasing* records. The traders concerned were active in the long-distance trade and almost certainly resold these slaves in the Lower South.

S: Information directly derived from traders' records of transportation and sale to the Lower South.

*S: An account book which includes sales (57% of them being males) to Louisiana's thirteen leading sugar parishes ("sugar" sales are excluded from the entry in Table 2.2).

practice probably over 80 percent of slaves shipped to New Orleans in the half century or so before the Civil War arrived there through the trade rather than planter migration. Two further methods show, however, that the dominance of the trade was far from being limited to this route.

THE AGE-STRUCTURE APPROACH, 1820s AND 1850s

The basis of the age-structure method is to establish three elements: the age composition, first, of the domestic slave trade, second, of planter migrations, and third, of the total interregional movement (which combined trading and migration). Broadly, the calculation will aim to demonstrate that the trade was highly age-selective (concentrating mainly on teenagers and young adults), but that planter migrations on average took an entire cross-section of ages from the exporting area's slaves. When I can establish these age contrasts, it will be possible (if I can also establish the age composition of the total movement) to calculate the relative importance of trading and migration in the overall movement.

Let us consider, first of all, the age structure of the trade; here we can draw upon extensive evidence from traders' advertisements, correspondence, and business accounts. Large numbers of traders' advertisements (directly specifying preferred ages) are cited in Appendix 4, and correspondence concerning the ages of slaves traded will be cited in Chapter 3 and elsewhere in this study. Such sources make it abundantly clear that the trade was markedly age-selective, concentrating most heavily on those of about fifteen to twenty-five years of age. Traders' bills of sale and accounts listing slaves traded provide more specific statistics, and an age profile from such sources is provided in Figure 2.1.[17] We can now turn to the age structure of planter migrations.[18]

17. Figure 2.1 describes 614 slaves bought and sold by the traders concerned. A subsample of 384 slaves representing only those known from direct evidence to have been carried to the Lower South and traded there produces an almost identical result to the larger combined buying and selling sample.

18. Two additional points should, however, be noted in connection with the age structure of the trade. It is clear, first, that, because of the sugar crop's special labor demands, the New Orleans branch of the trade was exceptional in a great many respects. That traffic was in fact both more rigorously age-selective than the rest of

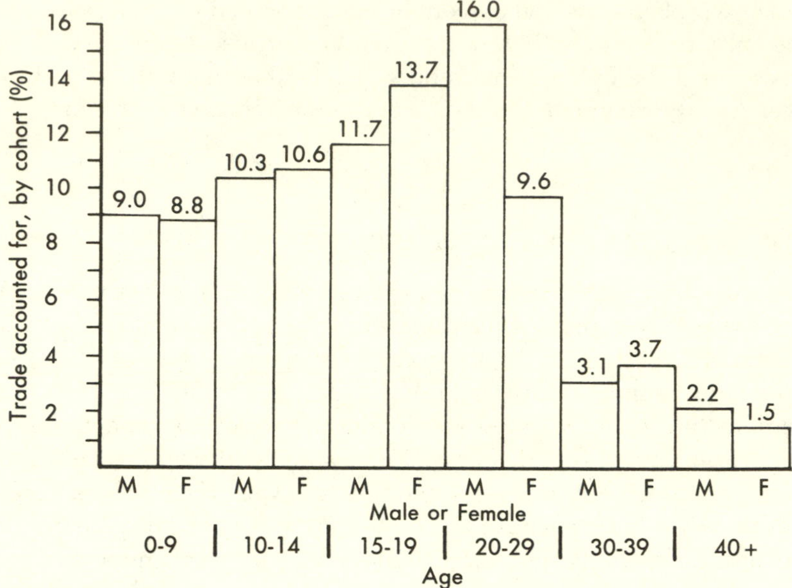

Figure 2.1. Age structure of the interregional slave trade, excluding Louisiana's sugar area, c. 1830–50. Source: collections of bills of sale and age-specific sales lists found in the papers of Templeman & Goodwin, Totten, Long, and Glen (for locations of these papers, see Chapter 2, fn. 16).

---

the trade and, as we have seen, was unique in its male bias. The age structure of the New Orleans trade (based on a sample of some 5,400 slaves shipped by traders identified in Appendix 2, Table A2.1) is indicated in Appendix 3.

Second, although the domestic trade to the South as a whole was markedly age-selective, it did carry some slaves older than thirty, as well as a substantial number of children. In the mainstream trade (excluding Louisiana, that is) about 72 percent were from the key 10–29 age group (compared to only about 43 percent in the population as a whole). But about 18 percent of trading was in slaves aged 0–9 years, and about 11 percent was in those over thirty years of age. Chapter 6 discusses the rationale for selecting slaves according to particular ages (with its implications for family separations) and clear and deliberate patterns emerge in the purchase of those under ten and over thirty. The great majority of those under ten were bought, not as individuals, but as part of mother-with-offspring lots. Those males aged over thirty (and especially from thirty-five to early forties) who were traded seem often to have been skilled or possibly domestics. At least half of the women aged over thirty years were not traded alone, but instead were sold in mother-with-offspring units (usually with an infant who would need close care, and with other older and more valuable children). Even the highly selective New Orleans trade included about 6 percent who were in their thirties and 2–3 percent who were forty years old or a little more.

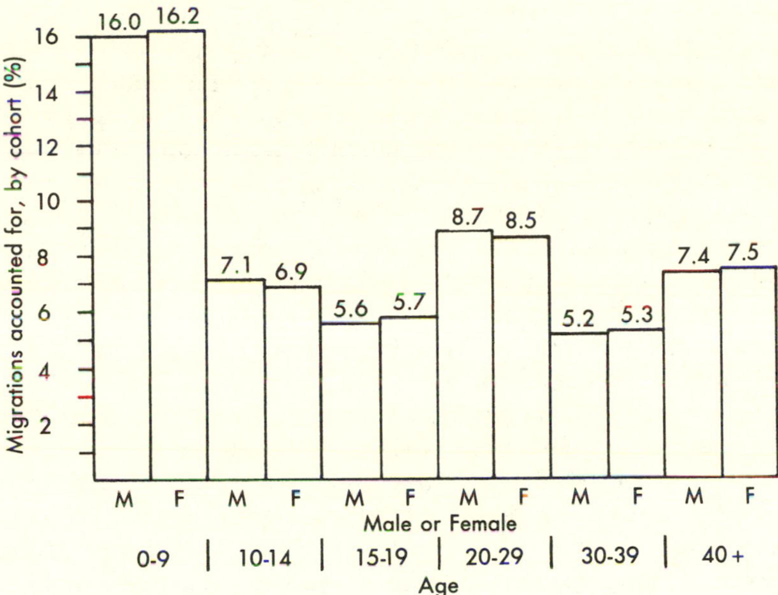

Figure 2.2. Age structure of planter migration, c. 1850. Source: Census data on the structure of the slave population of the exporting states in 1850.

The historical literature on the movement of free populations has repeatedly shown a marked predominance of young-adult males, seeking to make their way in life.[19] Neither in the trade, nor with planter migration, however, were slaves volunteers. Instead, the structure of their population movements followed the dictates of owners. In the trade, movements were highly selective, but in planter migrations they were not; normally, with such migrations, owners simply took whatever slaves they had, although my calculations will allow for some underrepresentation of older slaves in planter migrations. On average, then, the structure of these migrations would have reflected that of the exporting states from which they were drawn (see Figure 2.2, which gives a profile of slaves in the exporting states according to the 1850 census). It is true, as Appendix 2 shows, that a minority of slaveowners introduced a selective element into their migrant group by a policy of

19. For an excellent guide to the literature on migration (and its demographic structure) see Timothy W. Bosworth, "Those Who Moved: Internal Migrants in America Before 1840," unpublished Ph.D. dissertation, University of Wisconsin–Madison, 1980, esp. Chap. 2. See also McClelland and Zeckhauser, *Demographic Dimensions*.

special slave purchases immediately before leaving for the west. Such last-minute purchases are regarded in this study as being part of the trade rather than properly being a part of "planter migrations." (They were based on the same market transactions as the trade, and would have brought about the same sort of family separations.) Our conclusion is, therefore, that planter migrations, just as they were unusual among population movements for their nonselective *sex* structure, were also unusual in their nonselective *age* composition. Much fuller evidence (drawing on travellers' descriptions, migrants' own letters, coastal manifests, and other sources) to establish the nonselective character of planter migrations is given in Appendix 2.

Having considered the structure of planter migrations, we now need to turn to the third and last of our demographic profiles—that of the total interregional movement of slaves. By using the "survival rate" technique we can establish the structure of that movement; and we can then begin to break it down into its trading and planter migration components. The basic assumption on which this device rests is that, across a population generally, those of the same age and sex would, on average, experience the same rate of mortality (and hence the same "survival rates"). Thus, if we find (say for the 1850s) that, in the slave population as a whole, males of a particular age had a 90 percent survival rate, we should expect in that decade the same 90 percent rate for such slaves in both the Upper and Lower South. What we find, in fact, is that in exporting states such as Maryland "survival rates" for key groups (say males aged 10–19 at the 1850 census, and therefore aged 20–29 at the next in 1860) were as low as 60 percent, whereas in an importing state like Texas they could be around 250 percent! From these sharp contrasts in regional "survival rates" we can conclude that heavy interregional importation and exportation must have been taking place, and we can piece together those movements according to age (and sex).

The essential method of calculating the structure of the overall movement now becomes fairly straightforward (Appendix 3 presents evidence on my basic assumptions and detailed calculations). From regional contrasts in age-specific survival rates, we can calculate, for example, the numbers of children, prime adults, and aged slaves exported from the Upper South (or from a particular state). And from this we can estimate (and eventually contrast) the percentage rates at which each age group was exported. To find these rates we need simply compare, for example, the number of prime adults exported over the 1850s with the number of such slaves present in the exporting states at

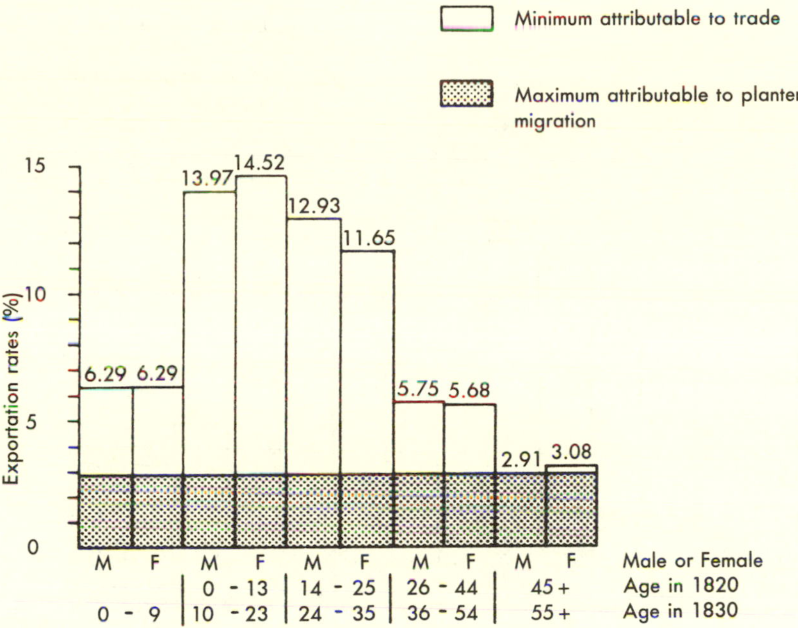

Figure 2.3. The structure of the total interregional slave movement, 1820–29. The maximum share attributable to planter migration is based on the assumption (see Appendix 2) that those migrations were nonselective in age structure. Source: Survival-rate calculations using census data (see Appendix 3).

the start of that decade. The results of such calculations are very striking. Essentially, what they show (see Figures 2.3 and 2.4) is that far higher percentages (and absolute numbers) of the prime-adult population were exported than of children, middle-aged, or older slaves. In the 1820s, for example (see Figure 2.3), the Upper South shed only about 3 percent of its older slaves by the total interregional movement, but it shed some 12–14 percent of the slaves in its prime, young-adult population. Exportation rates, then, provide us with the required age profile of the total interregional movement, and these rates appear in Figures 2.3 and 2.4.

Having established the structure of three key elements—the trade, migration, and the total interregional slave movement—we can now begin to distinguish the relative importance of trading and migration. The key element in disaggregating the total movement into its two components is the fact that planter migrations would have drawn at the same percentage rate (though not, of course, in the same absolute numbers) from all age groups. If in a particular decade planter migra-

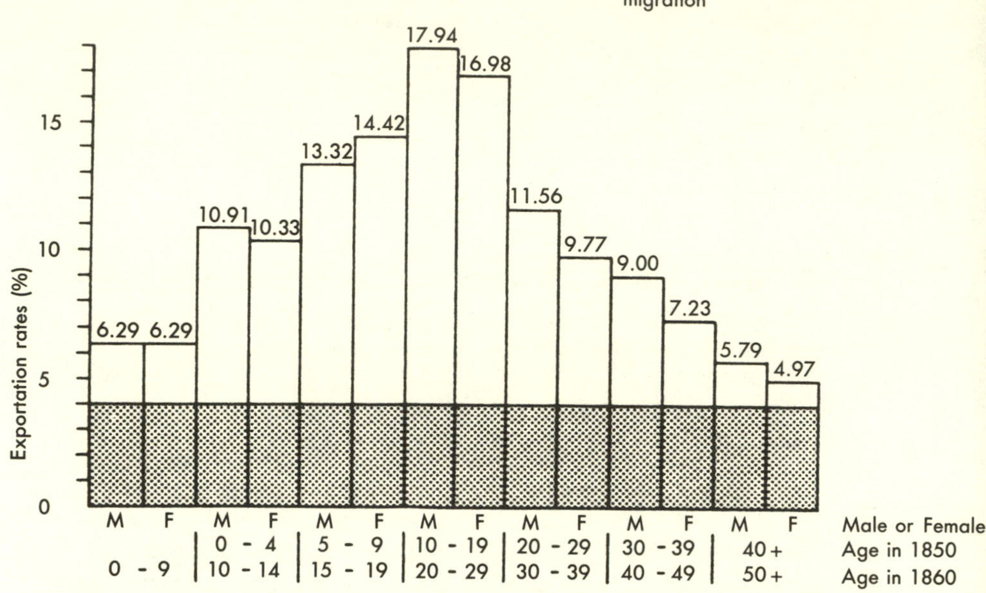

Figure 2.4. The structure of the total interregional slave movement, 1850–59. The maximum share attributable to planter migration is based on the assumption (see Appendix 2) that those migrations were nonselective in age structure. Source: Survival-rate calculations using census data (see Appendix 3).

tion drew, say 3 percent of the exporting area's slaves away to the importing section, it should in doing so have removed slaves at the same 3 percent rate from the child population, prime adults, middle-aged, and older slaves alike. This planter migration rate of 3 percent would have produced the pattern indicated in the shaded area of Figure 2.3. In practice, the situation was dramatically different, as Figures 2.3 and 2.4 show. Exportation rates strikingly reflected, not the unvarying pattern of planter migration, but the age-selective profile of trading.

The age structure of the interregional movement, then, allows us to separate trading from migration. I have calculated that, since planter migration would have drawn at the same percentage rate from all age groups, those migrations would, in the 1820s, have drawn not more than some 47,000 slaves (or 3 percent) from the total of more than 1,600,000 slaves in the exporting states during those years (see Appendix 3). From this, it follows that, with an estimated total of some 150,000 interregional slave movements for that decade, not more than about 30 percent of slave movements in the 1820s could have been produced by migration. The huge 70 percent remainder would have been the result of trading. Similar calculations are possible for the 1850s. In this case, the exportation rate attributable to planter migration would have been a little higher (about 4 percent). Even so, this again suggests that the trade accounted for a substantial majority of that decade's interregional slave movements. Indeed, it seems that in the 1850s, trading represented about 60 to 70 percent of some 300,000 net slave movements from the Upper to the Lower South. Appendix 3 indicates that even if planter migrations had been selective where older slaves were concerned, and had left behind virtually all slaves older than about fifty-five years—which seems unlikely—our calculations would not be significantly affected. We should still find some 60 to 70 percent attributable to the trade.

A CASE STUDY: THE DOMESTIC SLAVE TRADE FROM SOUTH CAROLINA, 1850–1859

A third method of estimation—a statewide case study—further emphasizes the dominance of the trade. As I noted earlier, the state selected was South Carolina, and the decade was the 1850s, one of the periods already studied by the age-structure method. The attempt in this case study was, as far as possible, to reconstruct the pattern of slave trading across a whole state; and the result was a picture of an extremely active export trade in South Carolina slaves.

Let us first put our local study into context. Frederic Bancroft's classic *Slave Trading in the Old South* gave evidence of an active trade at Charleston, South Carolina, but beyond that mentioned only another three possible traders for the entire state in the 1850s.[20] His approach, concentrating on the urban trade of selected states, made it difficult to know what the real quantitative impact of trading was across whole states and for the plantation South generally. The present study differs from Bancroft's in that it goes well beyond urban markets (and Charleston in particular) and looks at the statewide level of trading. By taking South Carolina as my focus I did not select an unusually active slave-exporting state; and in any case my concern was not so much

20. See *Slave Trading*, pp. 165–96, 239–44. Very many of the Charleston enterprises taken by Bancroft to have been trading firms are discounted from the present study on the grounds that they appear to have been general slave auctioneering concerns, rather than undertakings which specialized either heavily or exclusively in the long-distance slave trade.

with the absolute level of exportations as with the ratio of exportations to identifiable trading firms.[21]

Because many potentially valuable sources are not available, this is not by any means a complete census of the South Carolina trade. (In many districts, newspapers, with their traders' advertisements, were destroyed during the Civil War or after, as were many court records. And for the whole state we have only one substantial collection of trader's letters.) Gaps in results—and hence serious undercounting of traders in many areas—were inevitable. What does emerge, however, is clear evidence of a very active slave trade whenever anything like a reasonable core of source material has survived. Where I can supplement these records with slave traders' letters, especially in Sumter district (but also in Charleston district), I have found what must surely have been, compared with planter migration, an overwhelmingly important long-distance trade in slaves.

The results of my survey are summarized in Table 2.3, and Appendix 4, Table A4.2, develops the evidence in much more detail (giving direct extracts from the primary sources used to document each trading firm). Overall ninety-seven "documented" slave-trading firms were found (that is to say, firms where interregional trading in slaves is regarded as having been conclusively proved). In addition, sixteen "probable" or "very probable," and forty-four "possible" firms were identified. Figure 2.5 indicates that areas where very active trading was conclusively documented are spread throughout the state and are not, for example, simply concentrated around the great port of Charleston.

But before analyzing the results in detail, let me first explain the basic method employed. I started with the available newspapers of a particular district, searching for the advertisements of traders who sought to buy slaves for exportation.[22] For most districts these advertisements

22. Typically traders' advertisements began: "CASH FOR NEGROES. The highest cash prices will be given for young and likely Negroes aged between [say] 10 and 25 years. . . ." In fact the advertisements of those who, from independent sources, can conclusively be shown to be traders, allow us confidently to identify traders' advertisements. Such notices normally called for "young and likely slaves" (usually specifying the sort of age range I have indicated above). Further, they asked for substantial numbers of slaves (perhaps twenty-five, fifty, even a hundred or more on occasion), or declared that they would "always be in the market" or would buy "any number of likely Negroes." And they stressed that *cash* would be paid. The contrasts with nontraders were sharp. In the first place, nontraders very rarely needed to advertise to buy slaves (though they would sometimes advertise to sell them). Sales records show, furthermore, that nontraders rarely bought very large numbers of slaves at one time, but when they did so they nearly always bought slave gangs of

Table 2.3. Slave trading firms identified as operating out of South Carolina in the 1850s

District	Annual net outmovement of slaves[a]	"Documented" slave-trading firms	Number of annual outmovements per documented firm (avg. = 67)	Survival of newspapers for evidence	Additional possible/probable firms: Probable or very probable	Possible
Abbeville	293	5	59	Quite good	1	3
Anderson	76	3	25	Extremely poor	0	6
Barnwell	10	0	—	Extremely poor	1	1
Beaufort	654	2	327	Nil	0	0
Charleston	1564	32	49	Good	5	6
Chester	119	2	60	Generally poor	1	0
Chesterfield	41	0	—	Nil	0	0
Colleton	618	0	—	Nil	0	0
Darlington	46	1	46	Generally poor	0	0
Edgefield	357	8	45	Good	1	3
Fairfield	183	1	183	Extremely poor	0	2
Georgetown	395	3	132	Quite good	0	1
Greenville	108	3	36	Generally poor	0	0
Horry	18	0	—	Nil	0	0
Kershaw	356	4	89	Quite good	1	0
Lancaster	48	2	24	Quite good	0	0
Laurens	139	2	70	Generally poor	0	1
Lexington	59	1	59	Extremely poor	0	0
Marion	(60)	1	-60	Quite good	0	0
Marlboro	2	2	1	Nil	0	5
Newberry	176	1	176	Generally poor	1	3
Orangeburg	215	3	71	Extremely poor	0	4
Pickens	31	0	—	Quite good	0	1
Richland	448	7	64	Generally poor	1	1
Spartanburg	150	1	150	Quite good	0	3
Sumter	288	11	26	Good	4	0
Union	181	0	—	Generally poor	0	1
Williamsburg	(22)	1	-22	Extremely poor	0	0
York	(9)	1	-9	Quite good	0	3
Total	6484	97			16	44

Source: The detailed evidence on which this table is based is given in Appendix 4.

Note: Annual net outmovements are based on growth-rate calculations (see Appendix 1). The identification of "documented" trading firms is based on what seems to be conclusive evidence, and that of "probable or very probable" firms is based on strong or quite strong evidence. Those marked as "possible" firms indicate census entries as "trader" or "speculator."

[a] Numbers in parentheses indicate net importations.

mixed ages (rather than buying large numbers of prime young individuals). And typically, as we shall see in Chapter 3 and elsewhere, nontraders (at least those buying on any scale) bought on a credit of many months. Unlike traders, who quickly resold their slaves, they were not in a position to pay cash for large-scale purchases.

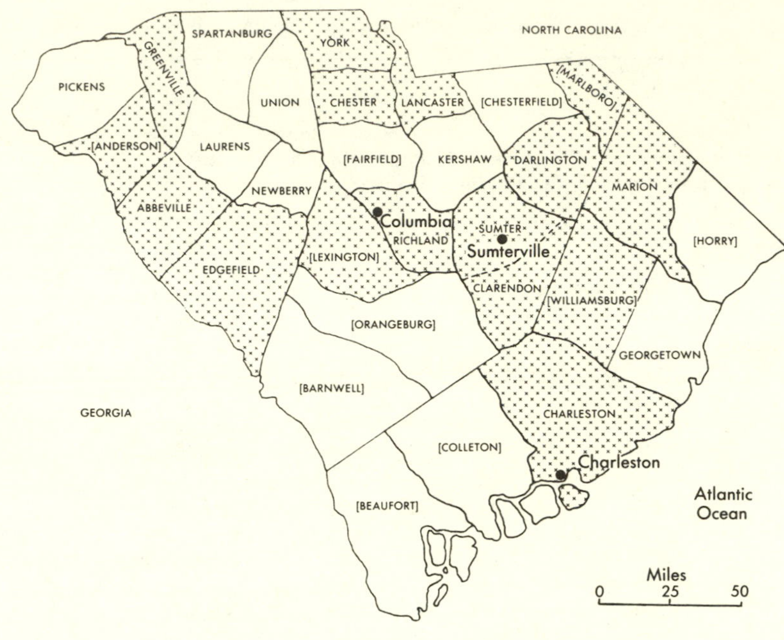

Lower than average number of slave outmovements per "documented" firm
[ ] Survival of local newspapers nil or extremely poor (see Table 2.3)

Figure 2.5. Slave-trading activity in South Carolina districts, 1850–59. Note: in 1855, Clarendon (the southern half of Sumter district) achieved the status of a separate district. Throughout Chapter 2, references to Sumter relate to the entire Sumter-Clarendon area. Source: Files of newspapers held at the South Caroliniana Library, and growth-rate calculations using census data (see Appendix 1).

provide an essential background picture of trading. But even in districts for which abundant newspaper files survive I could not usually hope to identify, by advertisements alone, more than perhaps a third of active trading firms. As the cases of Sumter and Charleston districts clearly show, only a minority of firms actually used newspaper advertisements in their slave-buying operations.[23] Beyond that, for a state-

23. For example, of the eleven trading firms identified as being active in Sumter district in the 1850s, only three seem to have advertised, according to the abundant, surviving newspaper files of that area. One of these, A. J. McElveen, was quite clearly active throughout the period 1853 to 1863, and yet only one or two advertisements by him have been found. Similarly, only about one in five of the thirty-two traders identified as being active in Charleston district in the 1850s were found to have advertised, according to the vast extant records of Charleston newspapers. Ziba Oakes, who, as we shall see, traded on a very large scale, made little if any use of local advertising when buying slaves.

wide study, the value of advertisements as evidence is restricted by the fact that (as Table 2.3 shows) 1850s newspapers simply do not survive (except perhaps the briefest scatter of issues) in eleven of the state's twenty-nine districts.

Newspaper advertisements, then, were only the starting point for my survey. Where local court records survive, searches for evidence of speculation occasionally produced very detailed documentation. Manuscript census returns revealed several firms which had not been picked up from other sources. From this source only those explicitly reported as "slave trader," "Negro trader," or "Negro speculator" were added to the list of "documented" traders.[24]

In addition to "documented" traders (and "possible" traders discussed in note 24), we should note sixteen "probable" or "very probable" slaving firms. Evidence on this group seems to be strong but not necessarily conclusive. The examples of Robert Cook, R. W. Disher,

24. Counting only those explicit descriptions left, however, another fifty to sixty individuals who were reported in the census merely as "trader," "speculator," or "trading." Unless explicit supporting evidence could be found to show that these latter were in fact slave traders (rather than some other sort of trader) they are regarded in this study simply as "possible" rather than "documented" traders—so that Table 2.3 lists forty-four such "possible traders." It is likely, nevertheless, that many of these latter were indeed in the slaving business. "Trader," and perhaps even more so "speculator," tended in the antebellum period to be a shorthand for "slave trader." Numerous "documented" traders (those identified from independent sources) appear in the census merely as "speculator" (see D. N. Boozer, T. B. Adkins, R. H. Sullivan). Indeed, had I relied upon only explicit census reference to "slave trader" (or "Negro speculator," or "Negro trader") in my survey (instead of using other sources such as advertisements and business records), I should have gained conclusive evidence on only eight of the fifty-five "documented" traders whose names have been located in the South Carolina census.

It is possible that the tendency, in the census, not to use explicit terms such as "Negro trader" might reflect a stigma attaching to the trade. The question of stigma will be discussed in Chapter 7. More important, however, seems to be the tendency to use fairly general categories of occupation in the census, together with the fact that many traders had other interests, such as landowning. We find, then, that hugely important traders such as Ziba Oakes and Thomas Gadsden appear as "broker" rather than slave trader, because they sometimes sold on commission and dealt in property other than slaves. In Edgefield county, H. C. Culbreath appears as "farmer," although at that time, as a court case shows, he and J. Crouch were also "partners in the business of buying and selling slaves . . . , Crouch . . . [going] with the negroes to the west." Similarly E. F. and A. G. Teague appeared as "Physician" despite the fact that in the early 1850s they placed advertisements declaring "Negroes for Sale! The subscribers having purchased 15 to 20 likely young negroes for the trade, will offer them on sale day." Appendix Table A4.3 (combined with the detailed evidence given in Appendix Table A4.2) gives many other such examples.

and J. A. Barr will illustrate the kind of evidence found for those in the "probable" or "very probable" category. For the three individuals just mentioned, part of the information comes from a letter written by the trader A. J. McElveen to a fellow speculator. McElveen reported:

> I met Bob Cook here [in Sumter district] the other day . . . . He says he wants to pick up some old negroes. He says he is on his way up country. Mr. Disher came in yesterday and will be here in a day or two. I have just met Mr. Barr from Alabama. He is on his way to Richmond. He tells me prime fellows are worth 1050.

Cook, Disher, and Barr were all, it seems, well known both to McElveen and to Ziba Oakes, his trading partner, and these latter seem to have regarded them as fellow speculators. Moreover, it is clear from other sources (see Appendix 4, Table A4.2) that all three bought slaves extensively during the 1850s, and Cook during the Civil War too. Such individuals are, nevertheless, treated in this survey as "probable" or "very probable" rather than "documented" traders.

Finally, a further largely undocumented group of participants in the trade should, ideally, be added to our survey. These are the planters from the Lower South who visited South Carolina and other exporting states on slave-buying trips. Especially where they bought selectively rather than in families, these too should be regarded as contributing to the trade proper, rather than to planter migrations.[25]

I must stress, then, that my survey provides uneven coverage;

25. The Edward D. Tayloe Papers (UVA) contain discussions of various slave selling arrangements between Virginia and Alabama in the 1830s, and in a letter of 21 Feb. 1839 Henry Tayloe informed his brother that "Some persons [in Alabama] wish to purchase them [slaves] in Virginia from you . . . and bring them out themselves." Sydnor, in *Slavery in Mississippi,* p. 147, wrote that many slaves "came to the state when established Mississippi planters purchased directly from distant markets. Some went in person; others sent special agents to select slaves in Washington, Richmond, and other markets. As much as fifty thousand dollars was sometimes in the hands of one of these masters going in search of more slaves." For an unusual case, a *black* planter adding to his stock, see David O. Whitten, "Slave Buying in 1835 Virginia as Revealed by Letters of a Louisiana Negro Sugar Planter," *Louisiana History,* 11 (1970), pp. 231–44. In the Oakes Papers (BPL) several possible visiting planters are mentioned, as when on 11 November 1854 McElveen reported "A man from Alabama is here [in Sumter district] and wants a blacksmith." And on 2 March 1857 Perry Vogue wrote from Dallas County, Alabama, to inform Oakes that "having some money and wishing to purchase some negroes for my own use and some to sell again" he planned to visit Charleston in April and buy fifteen slaves; see also Elliott to Oakes, 3 Nov. 1856 and Bitting to Oakes, 25 Oct. 1856, Oakes Papers (BPL). See also Kulikoff, "Uprooted Peoples," p. 153.

serious omissions in most areas are inevitable. One major collection of slave trader's papers—the Ziba Oakes papers, some 650 letters, which in the last days of the Civil War were retrieved from a Charleston slave pen—allow us, however, to do much to control for these gaps and to infer a statewide pattern. Special attention will therefore be paid to the areas covered by these records. But let us first consider the overall pattern of results.

If we confine ourselves to the ninety-seven cases marked out as "documented" firms, we find (as Table 2.3 indicates) an average of sixty-seven net outmovements of slaves (by some combination of trading and planter migration) for every "documented" firm. But, from the shortcomings of available documentation on the trade, we know that this ratio must underrepresent the actual number of active traders. Indeed, if we control to some extent for the gaps in availability of newspaper evidence, we find a much lower ratio of annual slave exportations per "documented" firm. When we consider only those districts with "good" or "quite good" surviving records of newspapers (see Table 2.3) the ratio, in fact, falls to fifty annual exportations per "documented" firm.[26] Now, from evidence which will be presented in Chapter 3, it is clear that the annual average of slaves dispatched by a typical long-distance firm would not have been likely to have been fewer than thirty, and was probably more like forty or more. Even though we must set against this the probability that some of the "documented" firms would not have been active for all of the years of the survey, the ratio between exportations and firms already begins to suggest that trading must have accounted for a very large share of the total exodus of slaves.

It is the Oakes Papers, however, which convert my general survey into a realistic indicator of the actual intensity of trading activity. The section of these papers which has been preserved focuses to an important extent on the purchasing activities of Oakes's associate, A. J. McElveen. The latter's principal role was to buy slaves in and around Sumter district and send them on to Charleston, where Oakes would sell them (and many others) to the long-distance trade. Significantly, while abundant local newspaper files identify only three active traders in McElveen's Sumter area, and censuses fail to give conclusive evidence on any, the Oakes-McElveen correspondence positively identifies at least

26. The ratio for the eleven districts with "nil" or "extremely poor" newspaper coverage—in other words, where nothing approaching a representative base of data is available—was, in contrast, just under 1 to 150.

eleven speculators who were active there in the 1850s. Similarly, for Charleston district the evidence of the Oakes letters (and other much smaller manuscript collections) more than doubles the "documented" traders found to have been active, raising the district of Charleston's total to thirty-two "documented" firms. Quite clearly, had the papers of other traders survived for other districts our count of the trade would have risen in dramatic proportion. Moreover, even for Sumter, the Oakes papers, especially since they survive for only July 1853 to May 1857, do not yield a complete listing of traders active in the area over the 1850s as a whole.

With Charleston district, the Oakes evidence means that the ratio of annual exportations to "documented" firms is 49 to 1 (about average for districts with "good" or "quite good" availability of newspapers). Charleston city, as a major entrepôt of the trade, would have been a particularly active center, and, by dealing mainly with the Oakes contacts who crop up in surviving letters, we have surely found only an incomplete sample both of the direct traffic in the very large slave population in Charleston district itself and of the city's entrepôt traffic. It is Sumter district, though, which gives us the best indication of the trade. That district (see Table 2.3) produces a ratio of 26 annual exports per "documented" firm, and the evidence from that area suggests that trading, rather than planter migrations, accounted for the huge preponderance of exportations.

In Sumter district, McElveen's purchases alone would surely have accounted for at least several dozen slaves per year[27]; and for that district we have directly documented at least another ten active traders. Indeed, over the season, while traders came and left with their purchases, McElveen shows that there were often present at the same time eight to ten traders rivalling his own efforts. In November 1856, after many months of very active trading, McElveen reported to Oakes: "I reckon that will be the last of the traders flying round. We had 8 to 10 in Sumter." Two weeks later, however, he wrote that "our country are never clear of buyers. I am certain if I could keep a lot of negroes in

27. From gaps in stories which were being built up by McElveen, it is clear that the 103 surviving McElveen to Oakes letters form only an incomplete record of McElveen's trading activity of the mid-1850s. A substantial gap occurs from April 1855 to July 1856 (perhaps the letters have been destroyed), but McElveen's numerous visits to Oakes also meant that much did not need to be recorded in letters. Nevertheless, surviving letters of 1853 directly document at least twenty-six slaves purchased and traded by McElveen; for 1854, forty-six are directly documented; and substantial trading (including selling trips to the West) continued over the next few years.

Sumter I could sell them well [to the long-distance trade]. We have not been clear of one or more buyers since last July." And in the following month he was still faced with stiff trading competition. "The prices of negroes are such," he wrote, "that [buying for a quick turn-over in the Charleston resale market] I don't see any chance to buy to make a dollar and what I am to do I can't say. The traders West are here buying everything." Competition persisted, and in the following February McElveen reported that, at a Sumter-area sale which he had just attended, "they was some ten western traders here. A good many bought and paid cash."[28]

Trading in Sumter district was, then, clearly a very active and competitive affair. The frequent appearance at a sale of eight to ten rivals to McElveen indicates something of the vigor of the trade, and the presence of such numbers at an individual sale suggests that over a whole season the district would have seen perhaps twenty or so traders actively buying up its slaves. Some of these might well have been merely passing through the area, and have had their main buying area elsewhere, but it seems likely that most would have found it inefficient to spread themselves very thinly over a very wide buying area. The point will be taken up again in Chapter 3, but essentially it appears that most traders found it convenient to concentrate their buying in just one or two main districts (or counties) and their immediate environs.[29] Our upper figure of twenty or so firms active in Sumter over a particular season would then reduce, in effect, to the equivalent of say six or seven firms fully and exclusively committed to Sumter district and buying say thirty to forty slaves each per year.

Such a pattern is very much borne out by manuscript census evidence and by the tone of the McElveen–Oakes letters. Strangely, A. J. McElveen himself has not been located in the census returns for Sumter (perhaps he was in Charleston, or trading in the West), but other traders (L. H. Belser, H. G. Burkett, T. J. Dinkins), with their wives, children and other relatives, do appear. These latter traders were born locally, and the presence of wives and families seems to establish their continuing local commitments—and the likelihood

28. McElveen to Oakes, 4 and 19 November, 2 Dec. 1856, and 2 Feb. 1857, Ziba B. Oakes Papers (BPL).

29. It is clear, for example, that virtually all of McElveen's purchases were in Sumter district, with a supplement coming from the fringes of neighboring districts (Oakes Papers, BPL). Similarly, extensive records on Tyre Glen's purchasing in North Carolina show him buying essentially in two counties, with a few purchases on the fringes of other counties (Glen Papers, DU).

therefore that Sumter was the heart of their slave-buying area. Indeed, Burkett and Belser, at least, frequently crop up in the McElveen–Oakes letters as active buyers. Burkett, of whom McElveen had a very low opinion, at one point entered an arrangement to buy locally with a Louisiana trader; and one of the references to Belser refers to him employing buying agents in Sumter to support his own work. Beyond this, moreover, the tone of the McElveen letters reveals the regular buying activity in Sumter of a series of traders, while others were unknown newcomers. A certain Watson is reported as "a new trader," and Burkett's associate was simply "a Louisiana trader," but others were very well known to McElveen. Manser crops up in several letters and there is some concern for his financial plight; John M. E. Sharp (from neighboring Richland) was clearly a familiar trading visitor, as were Thomas C. and Joseph A. Weatherly (from Marlboro). S. N. Brown (from across the district boundary in Kershaw, and trading to Alabama) was clearly a friend of McElveen who bought very actively in Sumter. Others too—J. K. White, E. C. Briscoe, and J. M. Gilchrist—crop up repeatedly as being active in Sumter and, by the tone of McElveen's letters, were obviously well known to him. Such familiarity must surely indicate, within a broader pattern of trading in Sumter, a network of traders with their principal or at least with substantial speculative interests in the Sumter district.[30]

The Sumter district evidence, then, seems decisively to establish a pattern of slave movements overwhelmingly dominated by speculation rather than planter migration. Significantly, this conclusion was produced from a base (using newspaper and census sources) which initially suggested a below average level of trading activity in the district. (From newspapers and the census, only three "documented" firms were found to account for 288 annual net outmovements of slaves.) Evidence from the Oakes papers transformed this initial finding. The eventual picture of extremely active trading was surely not because there was anything unusual in the intensity of the Sumter trade, but simply because of the windfall of relevant McElveen–Oakes letters.

It is true that McElveen was linked by Oakes to the Charleston market, but the Sumter traffic in general cannot have been unusually strongly linked to that market. The overall pattern of "documented" firms (Figure 2.5) indicates relatively high levels of trading activity in areas which were at opposite ends of the state to Charleston. The

30. See Oakes Papers, throughout (for example, letters of 29 July, 20 Aug. and 16 Sept. 1853).

center of Sumter district (Sumterville) was at least a hundred miles from Charleston city, and was some fifty miles distant from Charleston district's nearest border. There was no reason for the Charleston trade to have spilt over into Sumter any more than it encroached into Colleton, Orangeburg, or Georgetown districts, or, for that matter, into any of the rest of the entire lower half of the state. Indeed, had traders tried to concentrate especially in Sumter or any other buying area, sharp lessons on the relationship of supply and demand to rising prices would surely have quickly changed their minds.[31] As McElveen himself reported, his troubles were not with the Charleston traders, but with the numerous "traders West" (that is those who traded directly with the Lower South). And those "traders West" included not just the anonymous visiting "Louisiana trader," but all or nearly all of the speculators we have encountered in Sumter district. Thus Sumter directly, and the whole network of South Carolina documentation reinterpreted through Sumter's pattern of experience and evidence, seem clearly to establish the very marked predominance of trading over planter migration.

TRENDS IN TRADING AND PLANTER MIGRATION OVER THE ANTEBELLUM PERIOD

I began by suggesting that there is no serious controversy about trends in the total interregional movement of slaves (that is, combining trading and migration). To some extent, in the early years up to about 1807, direct importations from Africa complicate the picture. Broadly, though, there seems to have been from 1790 to 1830 a progressive increase in net slave movements from the Upper to the Lower South, starting with some 40,000 to 50,000 in the 1790s, and rising to some 150,000 by the 1820s. The second half of the antebellum period generally saw a much more extensive movement, with both the 1830s and 1850s exceeding a quarter of a million net movements. Had my calcula-

31. The fact that Sumter was, by South Carolina standards, not an unusually heavily traded area is clearly demonstrated by a comparison of the growth rates of slave populations for that district and the state as a whole. For the 1850s, the growth rate of the South Carolina slave population was 4.5 percent; that of Sumter was higher at 9.5 percent. Both, as one would expect from exporting areas, were well below the 1850s average for the slave population of the entire South (23.4 percent). Because Sumter exported less intensively (per head of its slave population) than did South Carolina as a whole, its growth rate was, however, less dramatically low than in the state in general.

tions made greater allowance for subregions within states (rather than generally taking whole states as net importing or net exporting blocs), even higher totals would have been indicated. As we shall see later in this study, fluctuations in slave movements in practice reflected the state of the economy; periods of high interregional movement tended to coincide with buoyant staple prices and high demand for slaves in the importing states.

The real problem has been to separate the interregional movement into its component parts—trading and planter migration. For the period following 1820, there is detailed supporting evidence for concluding that the trade was dominant, but for earlier years (especially up to about 1807) only tentative suggestions are made. Even for that early period, though, the likelihood is that trading was of major importance. Against this latter view of the early years, three main objections might be advanced: the idea that African importations took care of the bulk of the West's demand for slave purchases; the notion that in new western land there would inevitably have been an early phase of settlement based simply on planter migrations (not interregional trading); and the view that there would have been a substantial lag before the trade became sufficiently organized to supply a new region.[32] It seems clear, however (see discussion of Table 2.1 in Appendix 1), that even before 1810 there were marked interregional slave movements in excess of any impact from new African arrivals. And, further, since the interregional trade was generally based *not* upon sophisticated urban markets, but upon roving speculators who toured villages and the countryside in pursuit of clients, the slave traffic seems to have been flexible enough quickly to have followed up expanding settlement areas. There is also reason to question the remaining proposition that the early phase would "naturally" have been dominated by planter migrations.

Work on the early phase of establishing the slaveholding system in new western areas has been rather sketchy, but a series of general studies suggests that large-scale planter migration was very far from being the dominant pattern of early development. It seems probable that small early slaveholdings could well, within a year or two of first settlement, have been supplemented by purchases, so that the lag before the trade made inroads in a new area could have been very slight. Ulrich B. Phillips suggested that larger planters were generally slow to migrate, while "the smaller planters and farmers with lighter

32. For detailed suggestions on these points, see Kulikoff, "Uprooted Peoples," pp. 145–56.

stake in their homes . . . , with lighter impedimenta for the journey, with less to lose by misadventure . . . responded more readily to the enticements [of migration]." Similarly Rosser H. Taylor considered that it was the small slaveowners who were particularly attracted to the West, and, he wrote, "in the early stages of the movement of North Carolina folk to the Southwest, the small farmers and slaveowners predominated." In the same vein, Avery Craven wrote that "as nearly as can be determined, the great majority of planters in any given 'black belt' were self-made men who achieved their planter status in a single lifetime." And, he continued, "it appears that a majority developed on the spot or came from older western [not eastern] regions and did not migrate with plantations full-blown from the Atlantic seaboard." Everett Dick's conclusion was similar. It seemed to him

> that the majority of planters who carried with them the plantation system came from the piedmont [not the seaboard] and brought few slaves. Their broad acres and the large numbers of slaves were gained in the deep South.[33]

The pattern, no doubt, was not strictly one of "self-made men," but rather one in which nonslaveholders and small slaveholders rapidly expanded their initial property ownership or slaveholding by prospering in the southwest. Occasionally, we find migrants' letters which more or less directly document this sort of pattern. One such is from a settled planter in Georgia who wrote back to a friend who was planning to migrate from South Carolina:

> You must not be low spirited or despair. Think of me, I moved in wretched health with only money enough to buy necessaries the first years, without any money to buy land with, and I am now tolerably settled, my land paid for, and own 23 negroes more than I brought to the country.

If we apply our survival-rate method of analysis to each state, we find, too, that even in their early stage of development nearly all southwestern states showed a highly age-selective pattern of slave importa-

33. Phillips, *American Negro Slavery,* p. 174; Rosser H. Taylor, *Slaveholding in North Carolina: An Economic View* (Chapel Hill, 1926), pp. 57–58; Avery Craven, "The Turner Theories and the South," *Journal of Southern History,* 5 (1939), p. 311; Everett Dick, *The Dixie Frontier: A Social History of the Southern Frontier from the First Transmontane Beginnings to the Civil War* (New York, 1948), pp. 53–54. See also Charles D. Lowery, "The Great Migration to the Mississippi Territory, 1798–1819," *Journal of Mississippi History,* 30 (1968), pp. 190–91.

tions. Such a pattern, of course, is very much consistent with the early supplementing of labor by the slave trade.[34]

On the early trade, before about 1810, we have, then, certain direct evidence of trading and, less directly, the probability that early migrants would quickly have looked to supplement their labor forces. Since the scale of the overall slave movement with which we are dealing in these early years was not vast, it is possible that even a rather loosely organized trade could have taken a large percentage share. For a slightly later period, the 1810s, a recent study has allotted the trade about a one-third share of interregional movements.[35] From the admittedly incomplete evidence which we have, it seems in fact not unreasonable to take this one-third share as a *lower* bound (with an upper bound being perhaps 50 percent or so), and to apply this sort of estimate not just to the 1810s but for the period from 1790 to 1820 generally.

When we move forward to the years from 1820 to 1860, we have much fuller evidence, and our age-structure approach suggests (both for the 1820s and 1850s) a share of at least some 60–70 percent for the trade. The fact that the 1820s was a period of relatively moderate economic performance and the 1850s, in contrast, one of generally rapid advance, helps to suggest that from 1820 to 1860 as a whole the trade would have accounted for a fairly similar substantial majority of slave movements. For the 1850s, the detailed South Carolina evidence supports this conclusion and, across half a century, evidence from the New Orleans route is fully consistent with this conclusion. The Civil War period is not of great importance for this study, but it is perhaps worth noting that the war did not altogether halt the trade. Prices and orientations of markets were distorted, but, as several manuscript collections indicate, some sort of interregional trade persisted.[36]

Later chapters of this study will say a good deal about the signifi-

34. Munnerlyn to Shackelford, James Shackelford letter (SHC). The survival-rate calculations here considered are especially those for the 1820s, and they show for almost all importing states, including pioneering areas such as Mississippi and Arkansas, highly age-selective importations. The possible exception to this pattern is Alabama. See detailed evidence in Appendix 8.

35. See Kulikoff, "Uprooted Peoples," pp. 151–52.

36. See letters on Virginia-Alabama trade (1861–1863) in Lucy Chase Papers (AAS); and see Hector Davis & Co. Day Book, 1860–1864 (NYPL); Badgett Papers (NCA); Omohundro Slave Sales Book 1857–1862 (UVA). For a discussion of the trade in this period, see Bell I. Wiley, *Southern Negroes, 1861–1865* (New York, 1938), pp. 85–98.

cance of the trade for masters as well as for slaves. One or two comments on general tendencies might, however, be useful at this stage. Our evidence suggests that the chances of a slave from the Upper South falling into the hands of traders were quite high. It seems that, from 1820 to 1860, teenagers from this area would have faced rather more than a 10 percent chance of being traded, and those in their twenties perhaps an 8–10 percent chance. By their thirties, the danger of falling into the grasp of interregional speculators would have eased to about 5 percent; and for older slaves the danger would have been dramatically reduced to perhaps 2 percent or less. For slave children living in the Upper South in 1820, the cumulative chance of being "sold South" by 1860 might have been something like 30 percent.[37]

37. In general terms, the procedure employed in calculating the chance of being sold was firstly to note the decennial rate of slave exportation (combining planter migration and the trade) for the Upper South. This rate in the 1820s was about 9 percent, in the 1830s about 17 percent, in the 1840s about 10 percent, and in the 1850s about 9 to 10 percent. Since the 1850s exportation rate of 9–10 percent was similar to (in fact, a little *below*) the average for 1820 to 1860, the detailed (age and sex) exportation rates of the 1850s are taken as having been fairly typical of (or a little below) those for similar age and sex groups during the three previous decades. The detailed cohort-exportation statistics of the 1850s are therefore used to calculate the accumulated chances of an Upper South slave aged 0–9 in 1820 being traded over the next four decades. Such calculations suggest that up to 12–15 percent of the exporting area's slave population who were under ten years old in 1820 would by 1860 have *migrated* with their owners to the Lower South, and at least a further 29–32 percent would by 1860 have been *traded*.

More specifically, calculations of the chance of involvement in migration and the trade were as follows. Firstly, by attributing a 4 percent decennial exportation rate to planter migration in the 1850s, we see that slaves in the Upper South had a 96 percent chance of *not* taking part in an interregional planter migration. Over the four decades from 1820 to 1860, Upper South slaves would therefore have had a $(0.96)^4$ = 84.9 percent chance of *not* taking part in a planter migration, or a 15.1 percent chance of taking part in such a migration. Further, when I combined statistics for males and females of the same age group (see transfer totals in Appendix 3, Table 3.2, line 6, as percentages of line 1 of that table) and scaled down cohort-transfer rates to take account of a 4 percent-migration transfer rate, I found that the 0–9/10–19, 10–19/20–29, 20–29/30–39, and 30–39/40–49 cohorts had chances of *not* being traded during a given decade that were, respectively, 91.85, 86.58, 93.32, and 95.9 percent. Upper south slaves aged 0–9 in 1820 would therefore, from the four decades which followed, have had a $0.9185 \times 0.8658 \times 0.9332 \times 0.9590$ = a 71.17 percent chance of *not* being traded; or would have had a 28.83 percent chance of *being traded*. If I had (perhaps more accurately) attributed a 3 percent rather than a 4 percent transfer rate to migration, the chance, over the forty-year period concerned, of being traded would have risen to about 32 percent and that of being transferred by

These observations about chances of being traded relate, in fact, to *cycles* in the risk of forcible family separations. Several broad patterns begin to emerge. In importing areas, slaves locally born would, as plantations were being built up, have been at relatively less risk of sale and forcible separation than were slaves in the Upper South. But the slave owners of the importing states were in their way (through importing broken families) as involved in forcible separations as were the sellers of the Upper South.[38] As far as slaves were concerned, the chances of a first marriage being forcibly broken by sale were high in the Upper South (and were higher than for those born in the importing states). In the Upper South, however, as slaves moved out of the principal slave-trading years their chances of stable unions increased greatly. But against this, in the cycles of separation, was the increasing chance that their growing children would be sold away from them. Later in this study we shall return to discuss these issues in detail—indeed, they seem to be at the very center of slave-master relationships. But let us first try to develop a picture of the trading system in which masters speculated and slaves found themselves ensnared.

---

planter migration would have fallen to about 11.5 percent.

38. For comments on cycles of separation, see also Herbert G. Gutman, *The Black Family in Slavery and Freedom, 1750–1925* (New York and Oxford, 1976), pp. 129–38.

3

Slave Buying in the Upper South

In some ways the trade and its buying phase looked at first sight haphazard, even in a sense amateurish. We know, for example, that part-timers were involved in speculation; a good many doubled as planters or farmers, and some even appeared in the census as shopkeepers and the like. But the trade was dominated by hard-headed businessmen, seriously dedicated to the pursuit of profit; their trafficking, inevitably, was geared toward a series of well-established tendencies and practices. This chapter will examine the essential tendencies in the marshalling of slaves for sale to the Lower South; the next chapter, by investigating practices adopted in the selling states of the Lower South, will complete our overview of the trade's essential framework.

There were, as we shall see, very good reasons why the vital areas in which traders made slave purchases were in the countryside and not just in a few large towns. There were, too, powerful reasons for buying on cash and not credit terms—and for purchasing, in the main, directly from slaveholders, and not from public auction sales. Again, there were, as we shall see, very special circumstances relating to the New Orleans market (and in turn relating to Louisiana's sugar crop) which caused that slaving center to develop highly specialized links with a network of urban markets in the Upper South. The unique New Orleans traffic would lead directly to very unusual demographic patterns, profiles far more closely resembling those of the West Indies, Cuba, and Brazil than those usually found in North America. And the availability, among Lower South planters generally, of funds and credit at the time their crops came to market meant, too, that trading would very much be geared toward a seasonal pattern. There were, in addition, good reasons why, in transporting their slaves out of the Upper South, speculators normally used overland "coffles" (droves of slaves, mostly chained or roped together) rather than the coastal shipping facilities which became

"Slave coffle crossing the Rapidan." Reproduced from D. L. Dumond, *Antislavery: The Crusade for Freedom in America*

well known from the New Orleans route. Let us begin to examine these characteristic tendencies of the speculating business.

THE GRASS ROOTS OF THE TRADE

Traders, as evidence in the previous chapter has suggested, tended, in their buying, to be semi-itinerant and to rove over one or two counties (and perhaps the fringes of others). They might have a base at a particular town or village and might attend the public auctions at local county-towns, but usually they directly sought out their clients in the country districts. This practice, no doubt, stemmed from the advantages of developing local knowledge and of offering sellers the least troublesome and hazardous way of disposing of their slaves. We have already seen something of the almost daily wanderings of McElveen in Sumter district and its environs. Similarly, for a small patch of territory in the hills of the North Carolina-Virginia border, the Tyre Glen Papers provide a jigsaw of evidence on local purchasing itineraries. Traders' slave-purchasing advertisements, too, sometimes directly point to the roving nature of buying in the exporting states. One such advertisement, that of Clinkscales and Boozer, announced that "young and likely negroes between the ages of 12 and 25" were sought, and informed the public that

> Those having such property to sell, will find it in their interests to bring them to us, or drop a line to us and we will come and see them. One of us can always be found at home, prepared to pay the highest prices for such negroes as suit us, in cash.

And, similarly, the trader A. J. Hydrick advertised that

> Persons having . . . [suitable Negroes] and desiring to dispose of them, by addressing a line, at 'Poplar P.O., Orangeburg District,' may do so to advantage. Such persons will please state the age, quality and price of the negroes, and if the stipulated figures are not above the market CASH VALUE, I will in a short time after the receipt of their letter give them a call.[1]

The narrative of John Brown, a former slave, includes a brief description of his purchase by a roving trader, the latter just completing a gang to be taken South. "One day," Brown wrote,

> a negro speculator named Starling Finney arrived at James Davis's [Brown's master's] place. He left his drove on the highway, in the charge of one of his companions, and made his way up to our plantation, prospecting for negroes. It happened that James Davis had none that suited Finney, but being in want of

1. Tyre Glen Papers (DU); advertisements in *Laurensville Herald* (S.C.),15 May 1858 and *Sumter Watchman* (S.C.), 18 Mar. 1857.

money, as he was building a new house, and Finney being anxious for a deal, my master called me up and offered to sell me. I was then about or nearly ten years of age, and after some chaffering about terms, Finney agreed to purchase me by the pound!

After being weighed in a makeshift balance, the lad was marched off to the main road and was chained with other slaves who "had been purchased in different places, and were for the most part strangers to one another and to the negroes in the coffle."[2]

Buying "by the pound," it should be added, was quite common among roving traders (and with those based at urban slave depots). We find, for example, the speculator Tyre Glen instructing his brother that

If you can buy young fellows at 700 that is as likely as Aaron Shope, Nelson Hutton or Nathan Williams . . . I would be willing and glad to get them or if the fellows is very likely 750 can be stood, for likely field girls 500–550 or if they are very likely 600, for plough boys 5 or 6 dollars per pound. If the boy is very likely and weys 60 or 90 or 100 — 7 may be gone. If you can get Ned's boy at 7 per pound take him.

A. J. McElveen repeatedly referred to the weighing of purchases he had made, and reported in precise terms the weights of slaves purchased. Indeed, he seems to have considered himself something of an expert on slave weights, so that on one occasion he reported that he had not weighed a particular purchase but added, with a certain professional pride, that he was "pretty good at guessing." It was, in fact, very common for children, whose work output would closely relate to their stage of physical development, to be bought by the pound or to be bought according to height. The specialist circulars and price lists of the trade routinely classified children by height or weight (more so than by age), and traders in describing any purchase often gave a note of height and weight.[3]

Roving speculators were, of course, keenly interested in the state of competition in their localities, and letters between trading associates quite often touch on the matter of tactics to employ in working their areas.[4] One such speculator was A. W. Lewis, who, after concentrating

2. L. A Chamerovzow (ed.), *Slave Life in Georgia: A Narrative of the Life, Sufferings, and Escape of John Brown, a Fugitive Slave, Now in England* (London, 1855), pp. 13–16.

3. Glen to Glen, 9 Jan. 1836, Glen Papers (DU); McElveen to Oakes, 2 Aug. 1856, etc., Oakes Papers (BPL). More is said about trade circulars later in this chapter; Chapter 6 (in dealing with the separation of children from parents) says more on the use of weighing and measuring.

4. In very many cases (Appendix 4, in documenting the South Carolina trade,

his purchasing in the countryside around Raleigh, North Carolina, decided to try his luck at Nashville, a North Carolina village some forty miles distant. "I have tuck up a stand at Nashville" he wrote to his trading associate, and will see

> if I cant make sum trade out her[e]. There is negrows a bout her for sal and one very likely feller witch can be had for a fa[i]r price. He is No. one [first class] in any market. There is sum others bin offerd to me. I want you to come down in a few days and see me that I can give you all the hang of the trade. I have got where I have not got so much imposement in the trade of Negrows . . . [and] I flatter myself to say I think I have got a fust rate plas to do sum trading this season. The market about Raleigh is sode up with too miny Traders and they are too damn smart to make any money.

When attending public auctions, rival traders would sometimes come to arrangements so as to avoid bidding up prices and, instead, would make joint purchases, as J. J. Toler and certain fellow speculators did in a Sussex County, Virginia, sale in 1859. At the same sale, however, a second group, traders normally based at Petersburg (in a neighboring county), failed to cooperate and in so doing incurred Toler's displeasure. "I want to keep a good look out beyond Petersburg," Toler told his partner,

> and if there is any sales we will both attend them and we will help them along and give them [the trading rivals] a good time and then they wont be so fond of going over your way so much.[5]

Another trader, Tyre Glen, also wrote of trading compromises, and at one point expounded on the general principles of trading in his own little patch of territory on the North Carolina–Virginia border. He wrote that his friend Puryear, in order to discourage an influx of trading competition,

> Advises me to put fellows that is tip top to 550 [dollars] which I shall not do untill I hear from you again . . . , and for the following reasons. Thar is at this time very little competition. I can close several trades at the prices of last summer say 350 to 375 [for women?], 450 to 500 or the extreme 525 [for men?]. . . . [He] thinks that I ought to put Negroes up $50, purchase all I can, send the negroes to you, . . . and continue in the market myself to keep out

---

ner, or perhaps with more than one partner. Indeed, it was often convenient for one partner to specialize in buying and for another to concentrate his main efforts on selling in the importing states.

5. Lewis to Boyd, 28 May 1848, Archibald H. Boyd Papers (DU); Toler to Ferguson, 4 and 11 Mar. 1859, Ferguson Papers (NCA).

other purchasers, as he thinks . . . that this is the cheapest market in the United States and that other purchasers would flock in here in my absence.

Glen's conclusion, however, was to stick to the simple approach. "I dont intend to run the price mutch until they make a run on me," he wrote.[6]

"NOTHING DOES AS WELL AS THE CASH"

In making up purchases for trading, court sales (auctions by county sheriffs, probate authorities, and the like) were indirectly of great importance for speculators who toured the countryside and villages of the exporting states in search of slaves. Such sales offered intelligence on trends in slave prices, meeting places both for trading colleagues and for traders and members of the public who were interested in contacting slave buyers; and, from time to time, of course, suitable supplies of slaves. It was probably Darlington district's monthly court sale that A. J. McElveen, seeking to contact slave sellers, had in mind when he advertised in the *Darlington Southerner*:

The subscriber wishes to purchase 50 young and likely negroes for which the highest cash prices will be paid. Any person having slaves they would like to dispose of will do well to apply at once. *I will be at the Darlington auction on Monday next.* A. J. McElveen, Sumter, S.C. [emphasis added].[7]

Evidence in Chapter 5 will, however, indicate that judicial sales accounted for only a few percent of traders' purchases. And there were very sound reasons for this pattern. Traders preferred to buy slaves singly (rather than buying the families and mixed age groups often offered at judicial sales). Further, they were interested in *cash* purchases, and not in the terms of extended credit which usually obtained at judicial auctions.

The trader's great preference for cash purchases arose essentially because of a desire to avoid expensive interest payments. And since traders (unlike the public at large) purchased with a view to a very quick resale, they were, almost uniquely, in a position to undertake large-scale purchases for cash. To do this they needed in turn, to sell in the Lower South for cash or at least "good cashable paper," and their clients (since the latter bought only on a small scale) could, as we shall see, generally command sufficient funds (perhaps with the aid of

6. Glen to Jarratt, 29 Dec. 1833, Jarratt-Puryear Papers (DU).
7. *Darlington Southerner* (SC), 13 Mar. 1863.

factors or banks). In haggling over prices in the Upper South, the trader's offers of immediate cash also, in a land of credit and promises based on future crops, gave him a special cutting edge.[8]

The special attractions of cash crop up in numerous letters. In one, C. C. Cooper informed Ziba Oakes that the terms of a certain sale had been fixed at twelve months' credit, but "had the money to have been paid on delivery of the property they would have sold 20 percent lower." Cooper added that "should any cash sales take place I will keep you informed." A letter from A. J. McElveen to Oakes similarly emphasized the importance of cash purchases. McElveen reported that he would be "at another sale on Wednesday. I suppose I will have some chance as the sale will be for cash—that is unless the creditors [who would not need to make payment] come in competition." The speculator E. W. Ferguson, in instructions to a buying agent, called upon him to "get the lowest cash price"; and the trader Samuel Logan informed his partner that with available funds "we can make some purchases upon a short credit, but," he added, fully imbibing the traditions of the trade, "you know nothing does as well as the cash."[9]

Fully aware of its powerful attraction to the slave-selling public, the traders usually emphasized immediate cash payment in slave-purchasing advertisements. Thus we find that about 75 percent of all traders advertising in South Carolina newspapers of the 1850s specifically announced that payment would be in cash. The remaining 25 percent or so declared, of course, that generous prices would be paid—and no doubt followed a payment policy similar to the rest of their colleagues. Available collections of bills of sale made out by traders again tell the same story of a massive preponderance of cash purchases.[10]

Extensive cash purchases by traders came, no doubt, partly through "ploughing back" profits, but would have been made possible to a

8. On the importance of credit arrangements in the antebellum South, and on the general shortage of hard cash, see L. C. Gray, *History of Agriculture in the Southern United States to 1860* (Washington, 1933), vol. 2, pp. 711–15; and see M. B. Hammond, *The Cotton Industry: An Essay in American Economic History*, pp. 107–12, in Publications of the American Economic Association, New Series, vol. 1 (New York, 1897; 1966).

9. Cooper to Oakes, 12 Nov. 1853, and McElveen to Oakes, 5 Mar. 1855, Oakes Papers (BPL); Ferguson, undated note, Ferguson Papers (NCA); Logan to Meek, 8 Mar. 1835, Negro Collection (AU).

10. Only a handful of the more than 800 traders' purchases recorded in the surviving Glen, Pascal & Raux, Badgett, Ferguson, Robards, and Long bills of sale seem to have been other than for cash, and the few exceptions seem to have concerned a credit of six months or less.

great extent by loans from banks and other sources. Such loans, however, were short-term, the trader aiming to send back funds immediately on sale of his stock of slaves. In the flush times of the middle 1830s, when a feverish interest in "Negro speculation" held sway, we find Allan Gunn (of the firm Gunn & Totten) reporting from Yanceyville, North Carolina: "Negro fellows are a selling here for $600 and every man that can get credit in the bank and his situation will let him leave home is a negro trader." At about the same time, J. J. Gurney, a Quaker reformer, reported an assurance he had received that

> Two-thirds of the funds of the Bank of North Carolina were invested in loans to slave merchants; and that no less than a million dollars had been expended the year before [that is, in about 1836], in the single county of Caswell for the purchase of Negroes on speculation.

Gurney being a critic of slavery, we might expect him to have exaggerated the sordid profiteering in slaves, but no less an authority than the president of the Union Bank of Tennessee gave unwitting support to such a claim. Early in 1837, as the forces of the Panic were mounting, the president, John M. Bass, wrote of his plans to put his financial house in order. "It has been," he commented,

> a subject of complaint against the Union Bank that too large amounts of its accommodations have been extended to Negro traders and others to the exclusion of the Planter and Merchant — It is the intention of the Board at least not to merit this imputation in the future.

The need for reform clearly pointed to former links with traders, and it is likely that as business confidence revived so loans to traders again expanded.[11]

As the papers of Joseph Meek and his associates show, private capitalists, too, lent support to the trade. A letter to Meek from his partner Samuel Logan referred to the possibilities of such loans, and informed Meek:

> I have been promised from $500 to $1000 by Lewis Smith for the last 4 or 5 weeks [but] he has not let me have it yet . . . . John M. Prescott will not yet promise me, only in this way, that if he can get in money more than he needs he will during the summer let me have some.

11. Gunn to Totten, 14 Jan. 1835, Totten Papers (NCA); Gurney, quoted in G. G. Johnson, *Ante-Bellum North Carolina* (Chapel Hill, 1937), pp. 473–74; Bass to Cooper, 1 Feb. 1837, papers in private possession (quoted in C. C. Mooney, *Slavery in Tennessee* [Bloomington, 1957], p. 44).

Some months later, in May 1836, Logan wrote of his plans for borrowing on a far larger scale. Logan wrote that (by a scheme which would involve the traders foregoing interest on "acceptances" received in payment for slaves) a certain Colonel White was prepared to "raise cash that would suit us, from fifty thousand to $100,000." Loans from both banks and private investors are documented in the A. & A. T. Walker slave-trading accounts, in the Badgett papers, and in other slave-trading papers.[12]

CHARLESTON'S TRADING NETWORK

I have not so far placed great emphasis on urban centers, and, given the percentage of the trade they accounted for, this lack of emphasis on towns and cities is appropriate. There was in the Upper South, nevertheless, a group of very substantial urban centers of speculation, and I shall turn first of all to the network which reached out from Charleston, South Carolina. In Chapter 2, I documented thirty-two trading firms known to have been active in and around Charleston city during the 1850s. Many more must have gone undocumented in my study, and in addition there were numerous auctioneers and agents (a prominent example being Alonzo J. White, whose detailed account book survives) who dealt in slaves purely or essentially on a commission basis and who, therefore, do not rank in our count of traders proper. For our present purposes, however, we shall confine our investigations of Charleston's trading patterns to insights provided by the Ziba Oakes papers.[13]

Oakes, as we have seen, was a resident trader (or, as he called it, "broker") at Charleston. Through various agents as well as personally, he bought very extensively and, from his Charleston depot, resold to long-distance traders (as well as to some members of the public at large). Many traders bought from Oakes simply as a result of visiting his slave pen and selecting suitable "stock," but others also entered into more deliberate arrangements with him, one such being Robert S. Adams of the Mississippi firm of Adams & Wicks. In July 1853, Adams, then visiting North Carolina for the purpose of buying slaves, wrote to Oakes to ask whether he had bought any slaves for him,

12. Logan to Meek, 8 Mar. 1835, 4 May 1836, Negro Collection (AU); entry on page 29 (1857) in A. & A. T. Walker Account Book, 1851–1861 (SHC); contracts of 24 June 1843 and 15 July 1846, Badgett Family Papers (NCA).

13. On Charleston's trade see also Bancroft, *Slave Trading*, pp. 165–96. White's account book is preserved at the South Carolina Historical Society.

and if so how many. State what time you can have them in Wilmington [North Carolina, and] if you think you could put them in [the] charge of a captain and send them . . . . I have bought about 80 in Richmond and Baltimore and am now getting them together . . . . I have bought at high prices and hope that you have done better.

Oakes did indeed make purchases for his Mississippi-based client, and a few months later Adams wrote appreciatively to him that "should we buy next summer we will probably request you to buy for us again. We have done well with your purchases this year." Another satisfied trade customer in September 1856, on setting out to Alabama with a coffle of slaves, informed Oakes that "the Negroes I bought of you are all doing well." He added, "I have an arrangement with my bankers to send you $10,000 the first of December to invest in negroes."[14]

Oakes's trading arrangements, in fact, extended to most of the slave-importing areas of the South. With John S. Montmollin, a Georgia dealer, there was an arrangement to supply "a few young Negroes the season through." Rees W. Porter of Nashville, in the "mixed" state of Tennessee, bought regularly from Oakes, and in 1856 suggested a special trading connection which would concentrate on rather young slaves (between nine and fourteen years), and on women with infants. Oakes was active in the Florida market too, and in 1854 one Bryant recommended to him a man well qualified

to be connected with you [Oakes] in sales of negroes in Florida, in accordance with the plan you proposed. It is Mr. John D. McKinley, tax assessor and collector in our county — he is well acquainted with the whole district and suited to your business. He can if you desire [Bryant added] give a bond for $5000 for the faithful discharge of his duties.[15]

And beyond that, Oakes clearly had important links with the Louisiana market. Indeed, he seems to have had strong associations with those interested both in the cotton area and the sugar section of that state. Thus in 1856 James H. Bryan wrote to him from New Orleans saying:

I am now a citizen of this place, and am in the trade as I was at Charleston, and would be happy to do some business with you in that way, between the two places . . . . No doubt in January, February and March there will be a great demand for negroes, and as I have a plantation up in that section of the country

14. Adams to Oakes, 22 July 1853, 4 Jan. 1854; Weatherly to Oakes, 6 Sept. 1856, Oakes Papers (BPL).

15. Montmollin to Oakes, 20 Sept. 1856, 31 Jan. 1857; Porter to Oakes, 21 Oct. 1856; Bryant to Oakes, 6 Nov. 1854, Oakes Papers (BPL).

[in north-western Louisiana] and a general acquaintance with the country people it gives me a great advantage in selling negroes as planters come down to the city.

And a year later, one of Oakes's associates wrote to inform him:

I have had an understanding with the gentleman whose card I enclose to this effect that he will make sales . . . [for a fee of] 3 percent. . . .

This Mr. Vignie is a French creole, a gentleman of good standing that will readily command the entire confidence of the french sugar planters, and will no doubt be able to command from $100 to $200 higher than sales reach by trade generally. . . . [And, he continued] Mr. Vignie says that he will be able to make sales of 500 negroes to good advantage in January, February, and March.

The arrangement, it seems, was a particularly "choice one." N. Vignie was "universally known to old residents" and commanded the confidence of "french creole capitalists," who would be "more ready to discount" his promissory notes than those of others. His father had for many years been a leading banker and commanded the entire "respect and confidence of the wealthy portion of the community."[16]

THE REGIME OF THE RICHMOND MARKET

Charleston, as we have seen, but even more so Richmond and the Chesapeake ports, had important links with the New Orleans market. But before exploring Richmond's special links with New Orleans and the Louisiana sugar districts, let us first sketch something of the essential routine of slave handling at Richmond. The function of the Richmond slave market, like that of Charleston, was to a great extent to supply, not locally based traders, but those normally based in the importing states. Many of these latter found it convenient to visit the leading marts of the Upper South and there, in return for the convenience of making quick purchases from abundant, readily available stocks, they would pay enhanced prices. By contrast, most of Virginia's own traders, like those of South Carolina, would prefer to seek out their own purchases in their local villages and countryside.

As a slave collecting and reselling center, Richmond supported numbers of speculators like Silas and R. F. Omohundro, who bought in the countryside around Richmond and then from their city depot sold to long-distance traders. Similarly, there were large numbers of traders

16. Bryan to Oakes, 12 Dec. 1856, Oakes Papers (BPL); Ellis to Oakes, Miscellaneous Manuscripts (NYHS). Bancroft, *Slave Trading*, pp. 337–38, confirms Vignie's distinguished status.

Betts & Gregory,
AUCTIONEERS,
Franklin Street,
RICHMOND, VA.

Richmond, July 20th 1860

Dear Sir:

We beg leave to give you the state of our Negro Market, and quote them as follows:

Extra Men,	$1550	to	$1625
No. 1 do.	$1450.	to	$1550
Second rate or Ordinary do.	$1100	to	$1200
Extra Girls,	$1375	to	$1450
No. 1 do.	$1300.	to	$1350
Second rate or Ordinary do.	$900	to	$1100
Boys 4 feet high,	$575	to	$675
Boys 4 feet 3 inches high,	$695	to	$775
Boys 4 feet 6 inches high,	$850	to	$950.
Boys 4 feet 9 inches high,	$1000	to	$1150
Boys 5 feet high,	$1150	to	$1275

Girls of same height of boys about the same prices.

Young woman and first child $1250 to $1400. Good negroes are selling readily at the above figures, but inferior ones are rather dull. — Now is the time to ~~bring~~ buy good ones & bring them in. Hoping to see you soon, with a good lot

We are
Very Respy.
Betts & Gregory.

Price circular of Betts & Gregory, Richmond auctioneers who supplied the interregional slave trade. Reproduced from the original in the D. M. Pulliam papers, Perkins Library, Duke University, Durham, North Carolina

like J. J. Toler who purchased in the counties near Richmond but, not having depots of their own, sold through city auctioneering firms. Several such auctioneering firms flourished at Richmond, as at Charleston and elsewhere—their business being essentially, for a commission of some 2 or 3 percent, to act as middlemen between the local traders (and public) and the long-distance trade. At Richmond in the

ESTATE SALE!

BY ORDER OF EXECUTOR.

By LOUIS D. DeSAUSSURE.

January

On Wednesday, 19th Inst.

AT 11 O'CLOCK, A. M. WILL BE SOLD IN

CHARLESTON, SO. CAROLINA,

AT

MESSRS. RYAN & SON'S MART,

IN CHALMERS STREET,

By order of the Executor of the late Mr. and Mrs. WM. BARNWELL,

A PRIME GANG OF

67 NEGROES,

Accustomed to the Culture of Sea Island Cotton and Provisions,

IN BEAUFORT DISTRICT. Amongst whom are several

HOUSE SERVANTS.

CONDITIONS:—One-third Cash; balance by Bond, bearing interest from day of sale, payable in two equal Annual Instalments, to be secured by a Mortgage of the Negroes, and approved Personal Security. Purchasors to pay for papers.

Announcement of large probate sale [January 1859?] to be conducted by Louis D. DeSaussure, Charleston, S.C. The terms of the sale (extended credit) did not suit slave traders. Reproduced by permission from the collections of The South Carolina Historical Society (Hutson-Lee Collection).

$1200

TO

1250 DOLLARS!

FOR NEGROES!!

THE undersigned wishes to purchase a large lot of NEGROES for the New Orleans market. I will pay $1200 to $1250 for No. 1 young men, and $850 to $1000 for No. 1 young women. In fact I will pay more for likely

NEGROES,

Than any other trader in Kentucky. My office is adjoining the Broadway Hotel, on Broadway, Lexington, Ky., where I or my Agent can always be found.

WM. F. TALBOTT.

LEXINGTON, JULY 2, 1853.

Advertisement of Kentucky slave trader buying for the New Orleans market. From J. Winston Coleman, Jr., *Slavery Times in Kentucky* (copyright 1940, 1968). Reproduced courtesy of The University of North Carolina Press.

1840s, the most prominent of this class of auctioneering house were the firms of Hodges, Ray & Pulliam; R. H. Dickinson & Bro.; and Sidnum Grady. By the next decade some reorganization had taken place; the firms of Dickinson, Hill & Co.; Pulliam & Betts; and Hector Davis & Co. were dominant.[17]

Major auctioneering firms of the sort just mentioned commanded considerable respect in the trade, and their circulars, by which they regularly informed suppliers about market trends, were widely regarded as yardsticks for the business of slave speculation. Somewhat typical of such market guides was a Dickinson, Hill & Co. circular which, on 20 December 1858, announced:

Dear Sir. The demand brisk for likely Negroes

Extra No. 1 men	$1500
No. 1 "	$14–1475
Extra No. 1 fieldgirls	$13–1350
No. 1 "	$12–1275
Likely ploughboys 17 and 18	$12–1350
" " 15 and 16	$1050–1175
" " 12 to 14	$ 850–1050
Likely girls 14 and 15	$1000–1150
" " 12 and 13	$ 850–1000
Girls 10 and 11	$ 700–825
No. 1 woman and child	$1250–1350

Families rather dull and hard to sell.
Yours respectfully, Dickinson, Hill & Company.

Auctioneers specializing in the trade could, it seems, often be attentive to the wishes of their supplying clients and would hold slaves until they could be sold to advantage. Thus Joseph Donovan, on sending a slave to Dickinson, Hill & Co., wrote that "if he is not in good condition, or the market is depressed, keep him until you think all things favorable. Exercise your own judgement in the matter." Some clients attached more or less strict conditions to the auctioning of slaves. One such client was John Shelton who, with some preference for his slave not to be sold out of state, wrote:

If you can dispose of him in Richmond or in such a way that he will not leave the state, for what you consider his value or near it, I would be glad — I presume

17. See S. & R. F. Omohundro Slave Sales Book, 1857 to 1862 (UVA), and Omohundro to Jordan, 12 Dec. 1853, John A. Jordan Papers (DU); and see Richmond auctioneers' circulars quoted in Appendix 6.

Slave house of J. W. Neal & Company, whose main office was near the Centre Market, Washington, D.C. From the holding "pen" of the slave house slaves were driven into areas further south in coffles. Reproduced from D. L. Dumond, *Anti-slavery: The Crusade for Freedom in America*

you have applications sometimes for servants of particular descriptions — but I had rather you should not make much delay in the sale.[18]

As well as straining for the best prices, advising clients, and following special instructions, the major auctioneers offered a further brutal convenience to slaveowners—that of "nigger jails." But apart from auction houses, there were also specialists in these jails and in "negro accommodation"—individuals, that is, like Bob Lumpkin who would house and "fix up" slaves prior to sale. From a visiting northerner, Otis Bigelow, we have a description of the Lumpkin jail in the 1850s. The "barracoon," he wrote, was centered upon a large court.

On one side of the court [was] . . . a large open tank for washing. . . . Opposite was a long, two-story brick house, the lower part fitted up for men and the second story for women. The place, in fact, was a kind of hotel or boardinghouse for negro traders and their slaves. I was invited to dine at a large table with perhaps twenty traders, who gave me almost no attention,

18. Dickinson circular, Joseph Dickinson Papers (DU); Donovan to Dickinson, 14 July 1860, Richard H. Dickinson Papers (CHS); Skelton to Dickinson, Feb. 1846, Chase Papers (AAS).

Price, Birch & Company slave pen, c. 1865. Reproduced from original at the National Archives, Washington, D.C.

and there was little conversation. They were probably strangers to one another.[19]

Although, as we have noted, the trade as a whole was dominated not by urban centers but by the rural grassroots, the traffic at Richmond was clearly a very extensive one. In August 1856, for example, one trader "was told by good authority, that there was [at that time] $2 million in Richmond to buy Negroes"; and when the editor of the *Warrenton Whig* visited Richmond early in 1857 he was told by Dickinson, Hill & Co. that the gross value of that firm's slave sales during the previous year had "reached the enormous sum of two million" dollars. The editor concluded that "the entire sales of other houses of a similar kind in Richmond would make the amount go over four million, and still the business is increasing." A series of letters from the trader J. J. Toler gives further indications of the scale of the traffic which the major Richmond auctioneering houses handled. On 21 December 1858, for example, Toler wrote that during the previous day Pulliam & Betts had offered forty slaves for sale and Hector Davis seventy, and added that

19. Bigelow manuscript quoted in Bancraft, *Slave Trading*, pp. 100–103.

Interior of slave pen, Alexandria, Virginia, c. 1865. Reproduced from A. S. Link et al., *The American People: A History,* vol. I

"Mr. Hill says he will have today 125 to sell, so you may judge there is a great many selling." A few days later, Toler wrote "the three [principal auctioneering] houses are selling 100 to 125 negroes a day. I think I haven't seen as many selling for years." And some weeks later, on 15 February, there was still, he reported, "a rite smart of buyers coming in." An account book for 1846–49 records that in those years—not, as we shall see, outstandingly active ones for the trade—the single firm of R. H. Dickinson & Bro. sold about two thousand slaves per year, with the overwhelming majority going to traders.[20]

SUPPLYING THE SUGAR DISTRICTS OF LOUISIANA: PECULIARITIES OF DEMAND AND DEMOGRAPHY

In the previous chapter, we noted something of the peculiarities of the New Orleans market, with its exceptionally heavy demand for males and, in particular, for sturdy adult males. This pattern of demand, stemming from the proximity of New Orleans to southern Louisiana's sugar-producing region, meant that the supplying of slaves for the

20. McElveen to Oakes, 2 Aug. 1856, Oakes Papers (BPL); *Whig,* quoted in Bancroft, *Slave Trading,* p. 116; letters of Toler to Ferguson, Ferguson Papers (NCA); R. H. Dickinson & Bro., Slave Dealers' Account Book, 1846–1849 (AAS).

"Crescent City" became a business of unusual complexity and sophistication. In fact, the highly selective pattern of demand from the sugar areas (and therefore New Orleans) lent itself unusually well to purchasing at major urban slave-collecting centers. There (by the agency of resident "brokers," petty traders, and commission agents) slaves were assembled in sufficiently large numbers to allow traders to draw off specialist lots suited to the New Orleans trade. This meant, therefore, that several cities in Missouri, Tennessee, and Kentucky which enjoyed relatively easy river communications with New Orleans developed an important role in this traffic. But probably even more important in the New Orleans trade were the Chesapeake ports of Baltimore, Alexandria, Norfolk, and above all Richmond—ports which formed a major slave-collecting complex.

The Chesapeake–New Orleans trade has, in the historical literature on the slaving business, gained a position of special prominence. Relatively easy coastwise shipping links explain the development of the route. The historical prominence of this traffic—exaggerated in relation to the grassroots of the trade—stemmed, no doubt, from its visibility. Tours by antebellum travellers routinely took in New Orleans and the Chesapeake cities, and written reports of such travels were very widely available. Behind the traffic itself, of course, lay the exceptionally heavy demands of the sugar crop. Sugar called, in the season, for frantic cutting, stripping, hauling, and boiling of cane, and this involved long hours of work, including much night work. And it demanded, too, much exhausting work in such tasks as ditching and draining, digging out old cane, chopping and hauling wood for the sugar house. For all of this, strength was needed, and adult, especially adult male, labor. U. B. Phillips made the same point when he wrote:

> All of the characteristic work in the sugar plantation routine called mainly for able-bodied laborers. Children were less used than in tobacco and cotton production, and the men and women, like the mules, tended to be of sturdier physique. This was a result partly of selection, partly of the vigorous exertion required.[21]

Advertisements placed by a class of speculators who supplied the New Orleans market often referred, directly or indirectly, to the specialized nature of that market. In 1859 and 1860 for example, Webb, Merrill & Co., and Lyles & Hitchings were advertising in Nashville, Tennessee, that they "would at all times purchase NEGROES suited to

21. Phillips, *American Negro Slavery,* p. 245. On the labor regime of sugar planting, see also Gray, *History of Agriculture,* vol. 2, pp. 739–51.

the New Orleans market." At the same time, N. B. Forrest's advertisement in Charleston ran: "500 NEGROES WANTED. I WILL PAY MORE THAN ANY OTHER PERSON, FOR No. 1 NEGROES, suited to the New Orleans market." In the 1830s, Lewis Thomas's advertisement announced: "I will give the highest price for likely young negroes, say from 10–25 years of age. Fellows will be preferred with proper certificate for the New Orleans market." In contrast, the advertisements of speculators who supplied other areas, since they sought routine types of purchases, almost never specified the particular market for which they bought.[22]

The specialist nature of the New Orleans trade was indicated, too, in the circulars periodically sent out by these Richmond auctioneering firms which specialized in selling to the long-distance trade. One such firm, Betts & Gregory, in a circular of September 1860, suggested the special quality of the New Orleans market by informing their suppliers:

> We would say our negro market continues dull except for first rate negroes. There are several persons here now making up lots for the New Orleans market and if you have any on hand now is the time to bring them in.

A Pulliam & Slade report of 1850 ran:

> This will inform you negroes are selling a *shade* better than when you were here [at Richmond]. Boys and girls are selling here — the demand for men has increased. Good shipping men [for the coastal trade to New Orleans] are in demand. Murphy has arrived. Hagen is buying also Davis. [All three bought for the New Orleans market.][23]

References to field girls suitable for the New Orleans market implied that they too were to be those particularly capable of hard physical work. A Pulliam & Davis circular of 1854 began:

> This is to inform you negroes are selling as follows . . . No. 1 young men 18–22 years mostly in demand also girls 16–20 years heavy set and very smart, suitable for shipping purposes.

And the special quality of the New Orleans market was again made apparent when Thomas A. Clark replied to an R. H. Dickinson circular.

22. For the advertisements, see Bancroft, *Slave Trading,* p. 249; *Charleston Courier,* Jan.-Mar. 1860; and Taylor, *Slaveholding in North Carolina,* p. 61.

23. Betts & Gregory circular, D. M. Pulliam Papers (DU); Pulliam & Slade circular of 30 Oct. 1850, Harris–Brady Papers (UVA).

Clark reported that he had purchased two women, both with young children, but added:

I am sorry that I have not got any good negroes on hand that will suit the New Orleans market. . . . Likely young men such as I think would suit the New Orleans market are very hard to find and also stout young women.

Letters of Phillip Thomas, a trader well established in the overland traffic to Mobile, give some indication of the special place which New Orleans occupied in the interregional trade and in the Richmond buying market in particular. Thomas advised that, in making end-of-season purchases at Richmond, his trading partner should "hold off until 1st March, then the New Orleans Traders will be out of the market. . . . Compared with the New Orleans Traders," he reminded his colleague, we are "only a small drop in the bucket."[24]

Some speculators in the Chesapeake area were involved, regularly and extensively, both in providing the Richmond market with slaves for the general export trade and in themselves directly shipping some of their best slaves to New Orleans. In February 1850, for example, B. M. Campbell (a member of a prominent Baltimore firm) wrote to a Richmond auctioneer to indicate that he was "making up a shipping lot" for New Orleans. And at the same time he informed the auctioneer:

I send you a good lot of Negroes which I have bought myself this week. None of my buyers got in this week . . . or I would have sent you a larger lot. . . . I want all the negroes sold. I think from the present disposition to sell that I can give you a lot every week.

Thomas Williams adopted similar practices, buying in the Baltimore and Washington areas, shipping directly to New Orleans (as manifests of the coastal trade show), but also supplying large numbers of slaves for the Richmond resale market. In June 1847, for example, Williams wrote from Washington to inform the auctioneer R. H. Dickinson: "I have six agents out in the country buying so you may look for negroes from me pretty often." Two weeks later, he informed Dickinson that

If your market [at Richmond] will justify it I will send some 40 to 60 or perhaps 75 Negroes between now and July 15. I am determined to buy 150 from now to 1st September.[25]

24. Harris-Brady Papers (UVA); Clark to Dickinson, 10 Feb. 1846, Lucy Chase Papers (AAS); Thomas to Finney, Jan. 1860, W. A. J. Finney Papers (DU).

25. Campbell to Dickinson, 9 Feb. 1850, Dickinson Papers (CHS); Williams to Dickinson, 9 and 28 June 1847, Chase Papers (AAS).

The business of supplying the New Orleans trade was, then, a specialist affair, often involving the major urban entrepôts of the Upper South. In turn, the selectivity of the importations, concentrating as it did on prime adult males, had profound effects upon the demography of slavery in Louisiana's sugar districts. Indeed, as I have already briefly noted, the natural increase rate of slaves in Louisiana's sugar region reflected much more closely the disastrous experience so often found among slaves in the West Indies and much of Latin America than it did the typical North American slave experience. A detailed examination of the evidence on natural increase among the slaves of Louisiana lies beyond this study, but a brief outline of its essentials emphasizes the peculiarities of the New Orleans trade.

New Orleans, in sharp contrast to the rest of the domestic slave trade outside of Louisiana, imported about 60 percent male slaves. If we look more closely, we find that the New Orleans sex ratio actually hides some of the peculiarity of the sugar district. When we look specifically at slaves imported by the domestic trade into the sugar region, we find actually that some 68 percent were male (whereas Louisiana's cotton districts imported only 50 percent male).[26] New Orleans, serving wide areas of the state, reflected the combined influences of cotton and sugar. We find, too, that the sugar districts were alone in showing low natural increase among slaves. In the 1850s, the crude growth rate of the slave population in the thirteen sugar-dominated parishes of Louisiana was only 18.3 percent. This figure included additions to the area's population from all sources—and clearly there were large-scale importations. The significant point, however, is that at 18.3 percent—with all of the importations included—the growth rate of the area's population was still well below the 23.4 percent average from natural increase alone in the South as a whole. When we subtract importations, we in fact find a natural growth rate for the sugar region of not more than 6 or 7 percent (and probably it was substantially below even that low figure).[27]

26. What is meant here by "the sugar region" is the thirteen Louisiana parishes which ranked highest in sugar and molasses production per head of the slave population. These parishes in 1849–50 produced less than 1 percent of Louisiana' cotton, but yielded almost 80 percent of her sugar. The thirteen parishes were Ascension, Assumption, Baton Rouge West, Iberville, Lafourche, Plaquemines, St. Bernard, St. Charles, St. James, St. John Baptist, St. Mary, Terrebonne, and Jefferson. On importations, see note 27.

27. The scale of the sugar area's importations can be estimated by at least two approaches. First, if we look at *survival* rates instead of the growth rates just mentioned, we can gain some valuable indications. Survival-rate calculations for indi-

Such evidence provides clues to the general problem of slave natural increase—to the debate, that is, as to why natural increase was so dramatically higher in North America than elsewhere in the Americas. Louisiana provides a test case within North America and yields evidence to support those (like Barry Higman) who have, directly or indirectly, suggested that the key to the contrast was the insignificance of sugar in North America (outside of Louisiana) and its great importance elsewhere in the Americas.[28] The work regime of the sugar crop seems to have produced low birth rates (linked to the scarcity of potential child-bearing women), low fertility among women present (probably linked in part to overwork during pregnancy and in the period of infant rearing), and high mortality among adult workers.

---

vidual age and sex cohorts (as used in Chapter 2, and Appendix 3) actually show that survival rates in the sugar area (for the1850s cohorts 5–9/15–19; 10–19/20–29; 20–29/30–39; and 30–39/40–49) greatly exceeded the South's typical survival rates. This suggests net importations of at least 8,000–9,000 slaves (about 68 percent of them being male). If we subtract importations of this order from the sugar area's population of 1860, we find that between 1850 and that date the area's slave population can, through *natural* increase, only have grown at most by 6 or 7 percent, vastly below the South's 23.4 percent average for that decade. It is very probable, in fact, that (because of the effects of high mortality on the statistics) importations have been underestimated, pointing to an even lower rate of natural increase than the 6 or 7 percent just mentioned.

Another source confirms that the sugar area's population was artificially expanded by heavy importation. Coastal manifests give only a very incomplete record of total importations (partly because many manifests have been lost, and partly because the overland route was probably at least as important as the coastal route in Louisiana's overall importations). Nevertheless, a sample of surviving manifests for the1850s (based on the years 1850 and 1851, when a combined total of 2,657 slaves are listed) directly suggests 13,285 importations over the decade (imports were, in fact, possibly made at a greater rate as the decade progressed). Since the sex ratio of the major portion which was accounted for by traders was about 66 percent (typical of the demands of the sugar area) it appears that a large share of these slaves would have gone to the sugar parishes. Again, then, evidence points to heavy importation but very low growth by means of *natural* increase. The fertility ratio of the area was also extremely low by national standards, and by those of the importing area too. In 1860, for example, the census shows that the ratio between slave children 0–9 years and slave women of 15–49 years was, in the southern states as a whole, 1,320 children per 1,000 women. In the importing states, taken as a region, it was significantly lower at 1,104 per 1,000; but in the Louisiana sugar parishes it stood at the exceptionally low level of 922 per 1,000.

28. Barry W. Higman, *Slave Population and Economy in Jamaica, 1807–1834* (Cambridge, England, 1976), esp. Chapter 6; and *Slave Populations of the British Caribbean, 1807–1834* (Baltimore, 1984), esp. Chapter 9.

Demographic peculiarities, too, would have affected marriage markets and family patterns.[29]

THE MOMENTUM OF THE TRADING SEASON

The business of slave purchasing in the Upper South—a business which was particularly active in the summer and autumn months—reached its culmination when, mainly from about October or November onwards, slaves were started on the journey south. Trading was indeed a seasonal affair, and the primary spur to its seasonality came from the marketing, in the autumn and winter months, of the Lower South's staple crops, when planters in the importing states could most readily command funds for purchasing slaves. About this time, too, they assessed their labor requirements and made out their plans for the next crop year.

Traders' letters repeatedly point to the seasonal character of the trade, and it appears that in the New Orleans market the active period of slave selling ran from January until about the end of March. Thus in December 1856 the trader James H. Bryan, reviewing the prospects for the New Orleans season, wrote that "no doubt in January, February and March there will be a great demand for negroes." Similarly Vignie, the New Orleans auctioneer, when looking to the prospects for the 1858 season, was confident of being able "to make sales of 500 negroes to good advantage in January, February, and March." The first picking of the cotton crop was typically made several weeks earlier than sugar cane cutting began, so that away from the New Orleans market the Lower South's slave-trading season tended to open in December rather than in January. This was reflected in a letter of September 1844 which informed the trader William Long that in Alabama

> This is the dullest season for the negro market, the winter and early spring is the best time to sell. . . . I think cotton will hardly bear quite as good a price as last season and that in consequence negroes will be some lower. . . . It will depend a great deal on the numbers in the market, negroes will be in great demand here in the early part of spring from December till April.[30]

29. A forthcoming article will expand greatly on this analysis of Louisiana data and the connection between sugar and demography—and upon the implications of this connection for slave regimes across the Americas.

30. Bryan to Oakes, 12 Dec. 1856, Oakes Papers (BPL); Ellis to Oakes, 6 Oct. 1857, William D. Ellis letter (NYHS); Woolf to Long, 19 Sept. 1844, Long Papers (NCA). On the seasonal character of the trade, see also Laurence J. Kotlikoff, "The Structure of Slave Prices in New Orleans, 1804–1862," *Economic Inquiry,* 17 (1979), pp. 503–504.

At the same Alabama market in the 1858–59 season, the trader Jack Finney appears to have begun his sales in December, and in mid-January 1859 his partner wrote from North Carolina: "I am well pleased at your sales and think as the trade has opened brisker there it will remain good until 1st April." Quite often traders sent out more than one consignment of slaves during a particular season, but, with the "closing out" of the Lower South season in prospect, slave exportation from the Upper South, and indeed slave buying in that area, fell away by late January. In a letter of 1 February 1860, Zack Finney reflected upon his partner Jack Finney's proposal to send out a further slave coffle at that advanced stage in the season. "I have been thinking seriously," he wrote,

> and taking into consideration the slight differences in price here [in Alabama] and in the Richmond market, the expenses, the risk and the shortness of time we have to sell in, together with the fact that we would have to come in competition with the closing out of all the stock now upon the market and to come here, I think it will be prudent to abandon the project [of an end of season trip]. . . . I am anxious to get money out of the trade as anyone and need it as much but I am rather afraid to risk it further this season.[31]

"SOUL DRIVING" AND THE JOURNEY SOUTH

The active period of dispatching slaves to the Lower South followed, then, the hunches of the speculators and the broad impulses of the trading season. For the journey southward, grassroots traders, working from the countryside of the Upper South, usually found it most convenient to send their slaves on foot in overland "coffles," and indeed such droves probably dominated the trade from urban centers too. In the Louisiana traffic and in some other cases, though, coastal shipping or river routes were used, and in later years traders, where convenient lines were established, exploited the new technology of the railway.

A history of Rowan County, North Carolina, published in 1881, provides one of the few available accounts by a white observer of the departure of a coffle destined for the Lower South. The author, the Reverend Jethro Rumple, drawing upon his recollections of slavery times, wrote that before their departure, troublesome slaves were carefully secured in a "barracoon" or jail, while the other slaves were less closely confined. Then, Rumple continued,

31. Thomas to Finney, 12 Jan. 1859, and Finney to Finney, 1 Feb. 1860, W. A. J. Finney Papers (DU).

on the day of the departure for the West the trader would have a grand jollification. A band or at least a drum and fife would be called into requisition, and perhaps a little rum be judiciously distributed to heighten the spirits of his sable property, and the neighbors would gather in to see the departure. First of all one or two closely covered wagons would file out of the 'barraccon', containing the rebellious and unwilling, in handcuffs and chains. After them the rest dressed in comfortable attire, perhaps dancing and laughing, as if they were going on a holiday excursion. At the edge of the town . . . the pageant faded away, and the curious crowd who had come to witness the scene returned to their homes.

After some months had passed by, the trader's wagons returned

loaded with luxuries for his family. In boxes and bundles, in kegs and caskets, there were silks and laces, watches and jewelry, ribbons and feathers, candies and tropical fruits, wines and cordials, for family use and luxurious indulgence, all the profits of an accursed traffic in human flesh and blood, human tears and helpless anguish and oppression.[32]

Rumple's account was not completely complacent, but contemporary black sources provide fuller insights into the mood of the coffle slaves and into their "jollifications." Sella Martin, in 1867, recalled his experience and that of his mother as a trader, or "soul driver," sent out his gang on the journey from North Carolina to Georgia. "Next morning," he recalled,

we started with this negro trader upon that dreaded and despairing journey to the cotton fields of Georgia. Mother has often told me of the heart-breaking scene. A long row of men chained two-and-two together, called a 'coffle', and numbering about thirty persons, was the first to march forth from the 'pen'; then came the quiet slaves—that is, those who were tame in spirit and degraded, then came the unmarried women, or those without children; after these came the children who were able to walk; and following them came mothers with their infants and young children in their arms.

The slaves quite often sang, but in many cases it was at the dictate of the trader who, no doubt, found it convenient to reinforce among white observers the myth that blacks were a carefree people. And as Sella Martin recalled, part of this plan was, as far as possible, to separate the coffle gang from making contact with fellow slaves. He explained that,

32. Jethro Rumple, *A History of Rowan County, North Carolina, Containing Sketches of Prominent Families and Distinguished Men, with an Appendix* (Salisbury, N.C., 1881), pp. 323–24.

When the order was given to march, it was always on such occasions accompanied by the command, which the slaves were made to understand before they left the 'pen', to 'strike up lively', which means they must begin a song.

Oh! what heartbreaks there are in these rude and simple songs! The purpose of the trader in having them sung is to prevent the crowd of negroes who usually gather on such occasions, any expression of sorrow for those who are being torn away from them.

In 1826, the Reverend J. H. Dickey came upon a coffle led by two slave musicians, and similarly, in the 1840s, the British visitor G. W. Featherstonehaugh encountered a coffle, as he thought, "happily" singing "Old Virginia Never Tire." Such coffle songs, however, as Sella Martin's evidence suggests, far from being carefree, were more likely to be produced under threat, and even then to be "farewell dirges" and songs of communal dignity.[33]

In another ex-slave's narrative, Charles Ball recalled his feelings of anguish, despair, and resignation as he was taken south by the trader "Colonel" M'Griffin. Ball remembered that, in this coffle of over fifty slaves, the women

were tied together with a rope, about the size of a bed cord, which was tied like a halter round the neck of each; but the men . . . were very differently caparisoned. A strong iron collar was closely fitted by means of a padlock round each of our necks. A chain of iron about a hundred feet long was passed through the hasp of each padlock, except at the two ends, where the hasps of the padlocks passed through a link of the chain. In addition to this, we were handcuffed in pairs. . . .

The poor man to whom I was ironed, wept like an infant when the blacksmith, with his heavy hammer, fastened the ends of the bolts that kept the staples from slipping from our arms.

For his own part, Ball added, "I felt indifferent to my fate. It appeared to me that the worst that could come had come and that no change of fortune could harm me." The trek from Maryland as far as South Carolina took some four weeks, with the slaves at night sleeping in "those miserable public houses . . . called *ordinaries*." On nearing his southern market, the "Colonel" began gradually to adjust his slaves to the idea of being resold, and on their first morning in South Carolina he

33. Sella Martin's narrative in Blassingame (ed.), *Slave Testimony,* pp. 702–35 (quotation pp. 702–4); J. H. Dickey, cited in Coleman, *Slavery Times in Kentucky,* p. 145; G. W. Featherstonehaugh, *Excursion Through the Slave States* . . . (New York, 1844), p. 36. On protest through song, Lawrence W. Levine's *Black Culture and Black Consciousness: Afro-American Folk Thought from Slavery to Freedom* (New York, 1977), provides magnificent evidence and comment.

"Hail Columbia! Happy Land!!!"

AUTHENTIC ACCOUNTS OF UNITED STATES' SLAVERY.

" A good tree cannot bring forth evil fruit, neither can a corrupt tree brin orth good fruit. Wherefore by their fruits ye shall know them."

Slave coffle, satire. Reproduced from D. L. Dumond, *Antislavery: The Crusade for Freedom in America*

lavished upon them a special meal "to welcome" them to that state. Ball recorded that he

> then addressed us all, and told us we might now give up all hope of ever returning to the place of our nativity; as it would be impossible for us to pass through the states of North Carolina and Virginia without being taken up and sent back. He further advised us to make ourselves contented; as he would take us to Georgia, a far better country than any we had seen; and where we would be able to live in great abundance.

Some days later as the slaves approached Columbia, the capital of South Carolina, M'Griffin removed the chains which had bound his male slaves, and from that time began in earnest to make his "stock" ready for the South Carolina and Georgia markets.[34]

34. Ball, *Fifty Years*, pp. 29–37.

Another former slave, Catherine Beale, recalled her coffle journey from Richmond to Macon, Georgia. She reported that

> There was some big ol' gypsy wagons an' some er the Niggers that was too little to walk, rode in the wagons but most of us walked behin' . . . and late in the even's we stretched the tents and cooked supper and spread out blankets an' slept. Then after breakfas', bout sunup we start travelin' again.

From a very different perspective, that of the "soul driver" himself, the William Long Papers provide a detailed description of a coffle which set out from North Carolina to Mississippi in December 1845. The coffle was supervised by Thomas Burton, who was assisted by J. D. Long, teenage son of trader William Long. On December 15, Burton informed William Long that

> We have got along very well. So far all well and able to eat a good allowance, with the exception of colds. J. D. Long and myself has very severe colds. We are worse off than any of the negroes. . . . We have travelled 20 miles per day since we left you. We are now 150 miles from home. We have had a severe time for travelling today . . . [it] has been raining and freesing all day but slow and we have drove some 22 or 3 miles.

Later that month, Burton wrote:

> When I left my camp I travelled all day yesterday and arrived at my old friend John Gobers in Franklin County, Georgia, last night and this morning it was raining very hard and has continued all day so far as I thought it was . . . best for me to remain all day as it has rained all the time and would be very unpleasant travelling. My friend Gober finds me a good comfortable house for the negroes and myself and wood also free of charge.

In the same letter, with the coffle some "525 or 50 miles from home," Burton reported that, apart from one slave who had been attended by a doctor, the gang was in good health "with the exception of light colds, and there is no end hardly to their eating."[35]

By night the coffle rested, sometimes in tents, sometimes in accommodation provided by Burton's acquaintances, and sometimes perhaps at the same sort of "ordinary" of which Ball wrote. On 29 December, Burton, writing from Coweta County, Georgia, reported:

> I now take up my seat to write you a few lines. We are all well as common. We are getting clear of our colds. We now have fine weather for travelling though

35. Catherine Beale's narrative in Blassingame (ed.), *Slave Testimony,* pp. 572–80 (quotation p. 575); Burton to Long, 15 Dec. and late Dec. [date unclear] 1845, Long Papers (NCA).

the roads are rough and hard frozen every morning. We will get in Alabama on Wednesday next to Jesse Gunns. . . . I have travelled from 20 to 32 miles per day when I could travel.

It appears that on nearing Alabama, Burton, with his thoughts on giving his slaves a "good and orderly" appearance, unshackled most of those who had been chained; and at that time, in late December, the trader was well pleased with his gang. He wrote that,

Old Harry is the sprightliest boy in the company and has taken the road every morning and goes ahead until night and has quit complaining alltogether. They are all as hearty a set of negroes as I ever saw in my life. It seems they never know when they get enough to eat.

In early January some sales were made at Tuscaloosa, Alabama, and shortly afterwards Burton passed into Mississippi where, without any show of resistance from the authorities, he happily flouted that state's ban upon slave-trade importations.[36]

The Jarratt–Glen slave-trading papers, too, give glimpses of the character of slave coffles. In November 1832, for example, Glen writing from his home base in Huntsville, North Carolina, informed his partner:

Carson [an assistant] and myself expect to start the last of next week. We expect to purchase a few more and will have when we start about 40. One only under the size of the boy I bought of Walker. We have a few likely girls and a choice lot of boys and fellows. 8 or 10 boys of 13 to 17 and as many 17 to 22 or 3 and some 24 or 5. No old property yet nor no very small boys. The littlest weighs 68 pounds and the smallest girl 100. We expect to start with about 8 fellows chained all of which is very likely. We have five of them in Goal.

Glen's wife was not always prepared to be left behind on such expeditions, and on 3 March 1834, rather late in the season, they both set out from North Carolina with a gang of slaves which was

well assorted and generally likely. He [Glen] has about 16 fellows, seven boys, the balance women and girls, except one child. . . . He has 12 fellows in the chain all of which jumping Jinny [Glen's wife] drives before her. She carries up the rear armed and equipped in a style which reduces it to a certainty that if life lasts you will see her in Montgomery — Glen has employed Baldy Kerr to go with him, with [Glen having] the privilege of dismissing him at any time.[37]

36. Burton to Long, 29 Dec. 1845. On Burton's evading of the law, see Chapter 4.

37. Glen to Jarratt, 2 Nov. 1832, Isaac Jarratt Papers (SHC); Puryear to Jarratt, 3 Mar. 1834, Jarratt–Puryear Papers (DU).

Some observers reported huge coffles. The traveller G. W. Featherstonehaugh, for example, observed, on its way through Virginia and on to the sugar areas of Louisiana, a massive drove of 300 slaves, led by 200 men who were bound together in chains. Ethan Andrews, too, on visiting Franklin & Armfield's slave pen at Alexandria, D.C., was informed that the firm sent out very large coffles of some 150 slaves. From traders' slave-purchasing advertisements, account books, and correspondence it appears, though, that coffles were usually of much more modest size, ranging commonly from about thirty to forty slaves. And as records already cited suggest, on days when travel was possible, coffles generally progressed at something over twenty miles per day. Ethan Andrews was informed that twenty-five miles per day was the usual rate of progress. Travelling at something like that rate, a Cochran & James coffle took forty-four days in journeying from Richmond to Natchez; while James A. Mitchell's coffle on its "wet and muddy journey" from Pittsylvania County, Virginia, to Natchez "was just 7 weeks on the road"; and Thomas Burton's slave gang, in the winter of 1845–46, took about a month in their trek from Yanceyville, North Carolina, to Hinds County, Mississippi.[38]

Although it seems clear that coffles were, for the trade, by far the most important means of transportation, speculators also moved slaves by rail. As the Ferguson and the Oakes papers show, traders active in the business of supplying the Richmond and Charleston market often found it convenient to send slave purchases down to those cities "on the cars," and to have their partners collect the slaves at the railhead. The railways were, however, also used for much longer journeys. In 1857, for example, Jeremiah Smith sent out many of his slaves, bound for New Orleans, on the South Carolina Railroad, and two years later the same trader sent his slaves by the Jackson and New Orleans railroad. Lyman Abbott, a northern visitor to the South, found in 1856 that "every train going south has slaves on board. . . . , twenty or more, and [has] a 'nigger car', which is generally also the smokers' car, and sometimes the baggage car." An article published in the *Petersburg Express* and reproduced in the Austin, Texas, *State Gazette* of

38. Featherstonehaugh, *Excursion through the Slave States,* pp. 36–37; Ethan A. Andrews, *Slavery and the Domestic Slave Trade in the United States* . . . (Boston, 1836), p. 130; Cochran & James coffle noted in Bancroft, *Slave Trading,* p. 289n; Mitchell to Mitchell, Dec. 1834, Reid Papers (UVA); Burton to Long, 15 Dec. 1845, 8 Jan. 1846, Long Papers (NCA). For slave traders' advertisements see Appendix 4, and for traders' accounts see Table 7.1 (Bolton & Dickens's entry and certain J. R. White entries in that table refer to multiple consignments).

Slave coffle moving toward newly settled areas of the West. From William Loren Katz, *The Black West*. Reproduced from the original in William Loren Katz's private collection, New York City

12 February 1859 pointed to the scale of the movement by rail. It reported:

SLAVE EXODUS — an almost endless outgoing to slaves from Virginia to the South has continued for more than two weeks past. On Tuesday morning the car allotted to servants on the Richmond and Petersburg Railroad was filled to such an extent that one of the spring bars over the track broke down, without, however, producing any harm.[39]

In a little less technical way the *Boston Whig*, in 1848, described the scene at a Washington, D.C., railway depot where slaves bound for the Georgia market were being made ready for departure:

An Affecting Scene — Last eve as I passed the railroad depot, I saw quite a large number of colored people gathered round one of the cars. . . . I found in the car towards which they were so eagerly gazing fifty colored people some of whom were nearly as white as myself. A majority of them were the number who attempted to gain their liberty last week. . . . The men on the train were ironed together. [At the end of the car] . . . stood two ruffianly looking personages, with large canes in their hands and if their countenances were an indication of their hearts, they were the personification of hardened villainy itself. In the middle of the car stood the notorious slave dealer of Baltimore, [Hope H.] Slatter, who I learn is a member of the Methodist Church "in good and regular standing".

The journey by rail offered certain advantages, especially in encouraging quick "turnover" and delivery of "stock" in good condition. In October 1856, for example, it took A. J. McElveen and his gang of slaves only thirty-six hours to travel by rail from Bamberg, South Carolina, to Montgomery, Alabama; and in 1859 it took the trader Phillip Thomas fifty-five hours to travel by rail from Montgomery to Richmond.[40]

Numerous references to shipping slaves by river (in this case down the Mississippi, from St. Louis to New Orleans) appear in the narratives of William Wells Brown, a slave hired as an assistant to a trader named Walker. As the boat stopped at various points on its voyages down the river, the slaves gained some opportunity for exercise but usually it seems that they were kept in "a large room on the lower deck . . . , men and women promiscuously — all chained two and two." In the 1840s, the speculators Hughes & Downing conducted a similar traffic from Kentucky, down the Ohio and Mississippi rivers, to

39. Ferguson Papers (NCA) and Oakes Papers (BPL), throughout; Smith to Oakes, 17 Feb. 1859, Oakes Papers (BPL); Thomas to Finney, 11 Nov. 1859, W. A. J. Finney Papers (DU); Abbott, also *State Gazette*, quoted in Bancroft, *Slave Trading*, p. 290.

40. *Boston Whig*, 22 April 1848; McElveen to Oakes, 13 and 15 Oct. 1856, Oakes Papers (BPL) and Thomas to Finney 8 Nov. 1859, W. A. J. Finney Papers (DU). On the comparative expenses of different modes of transporting slaves see T. H. Wells, "Moving a Plantation to Louisiana," *Louisiana Studies*, 6 (1967), pp. 279–99.

Natchez. On those trips, according to S. W. Tod, one of the firm's agents, "the negroes were all put on deck of the steamboat. . . . They were chained together two by two until we got to the mouth of the Ohio River, when [no doubt to allow exercise and to improve morale] they were unchained." Some firms employed a combination of various modes of transport, one such firm being Myers & Belser, which in 1849 took slaves by rail from Columbia, South Carolina, apparently as far as Montgomery, Alabama, and then by river and sea to New Orleans.[41]

The Chesapeake to New Orleans coastal routes, by far the most important sea routes in the trade, were systematically organized, with several specially fitted-out slaving ships regularly in service during the season. In the 1830s, Franklin & Armfield, who also traded very extensively in their own right, offered facilities to others, mainly traders, who sought to ship slaves from Alexandria, Virginia, to New Orleans. Their advertisement of 1 September 1834 announced:

> Alexandria and New Orleans Packets: Brig Tribune, Captain Smith, and Brig Uncas, Captain Boush, will resume their regular trips on the 20th of October: one will leave this port every thirty days throughout the shipping season. They are vessels of the first class, commanded by experienced officers, and will at all times go up the Mississippi by steam, and every exertion used to promote the interests of shippers and comfort of passengers. Apply to the Captain on board, or to Franklin & Armfield. Alexandria. September 1.

Another Franklin & Armfield advertisement, probably of the following year, referred, in addition to the brigs *Uncas* and *Tribune,* to the brig *Isaac Franklin;* and announced that one or other vessel "will continue to leave this port [Alexandria] on the 1st and 15th of each month throughout the shipping season." The advertisement added that "servants that are intended to be shipped, will at any time be received for safekeeping at a fee of 25c per day."[42]

On such vessels, according to the evidence of Joshua Leavitt, an antislavery clergyman, accommodation was not dissimilar to that of the Atlantic slave trade's "Middle Passage." Leavitt's letter of 23 January

41. W. W. Brown, *The Narrative of William W. Brown: A Fugitive Slave* (Boston, 1847; Reading, Mass., 1969), pp. 14–26; Tod quoted in Coleman, "Lexington Slave Dealers," p. 7; Sumter district Equity Court (S.C.), *Belser* v. *Myers et al.,* 1852, Bill 180 in new series (SCA).

42. Advertisement of 1 Sept. 1834 quoted in William Jay, *Slavery in America or an Inquiry into the Character and Tendency of the American Colonization and American Anti-Slavery Societies* (London, 1835), p. 149; advertisement quoted in William Jay, *A View of the Action of the Federal Government in behalf of Slavery* (New York, 1839), p. 86.

1834 reported that the captain of Franklin & Armfield's *Tribune* "very obligingly" took him to all parts of the vessel.

> The hold was appropriated to the slaves, and is divided into two apartments. The after-hold will carry about eighty women, and the other about one hundred men. On either side [of the hold] were two platforms running the whole length; one raised a few inches, and the other half way up the deck. They were about five or six feet deep. On these the slaves lie, as close as they can be stowed.

Normally, it seems, the slaves were allowed exercise for a good part of their voyage. Nathan Ross, an exslave, left the following description of his experience and that of his fellow slaves during their voyage from Richmond to New Orleans in about 1846:

> [The trader] brought 'bout 50 or 60 all de way by boat to New O'leens. We drifted down de Jeems to Po'tsm'oth an' den we was put on de New O'leens ship. Dere was 30 or 40 uthahs owned by tradahs. On board de ship we was treated well; had plenty to eat. We was allowed to walk on deck. We was not in de hol' cep'n at night er when it sto'med. At New O'leans we was taken to a tradah's office.

When slaves became rebellious the closest of confinement was of course possible, and in January 1830 Niles's *Register* reported:

> The schooner *Lafayette*, with a cargo of slaves from Norfolk, Virginia, for New Orleans, narrowly escaped being captured by them on the voyage. They were subdued after considerable difficulty, and twenty-five of them were bolted down to the deck, until the arrival of the vessel at New Orleans.[43]

As Leavitt's and Ross's evidence suggests, the size of coastal shipments were often very considerable. Indeed, the ship's manifests—documents required by law in the coastwise movements of slaves—indicate that the average size of consignments sent by individual traders was not less than about 20 slaves (and composite cargoes of whole ships quite often totalled 100 or 150 slaves). Those manifests show, too, that the normal shipping time from the Chesapeake ports was twenty to twenty-five days. The facilities of this well-organized shipping system would have afforded traders special advantages, allowing them to dispatch and receive slaves while themselves continuing in the business of slave buying or selling.

43. Leavitt, quoted in Jay, *Slavery in America*, pp. 149–50; recollections of Ross, recorded in Bancroft, *Slave Trading*, p. 279n; *Register*, 9 Jan. 1830.

Slaves who were "sold south," and especially those trekking hundreds of miles in chains, must of course have suffered great physical hardships, although such stresses and indeed the dangers to health could not compare with those of the Atlantic "Middle Passage." Distances were shorter and slaves confronted no fundamentally new disease environment, so that death while in the hands of even the most brutal of domestic slave traders seems to have been very rare.[44] But, of course the real evils of the domestic trade lay, not with physical experiences, but with the deeply racist white assumptions on which the traffic was built, and with the emotional sufferings of slaves callously separated from parents, offspring, siblings, and other members of their community. These issues, ultimately the most important for this study, will be the focus of the chapters in Part 2. Before directly addressing these questions, however, the remaining chapter in this section will try to complete the outline of the slave trade's organization.

44. As well as traders' letters, which very rarely mention loss of slaves through death, speculators' account books and ships' manifests (listing slaves both at outset from the exporting states and at arrival in the Lower South) testify to the low mortality in the trade (see Appendix 7, note 4).

4

The "Fatigues and Troubles" of the Selling Season

VIEWED from the appallingly restricted perspective of the trader, the selling business in the Lower South often seemed to be full of burdens and anxieties, but the speculator's concern was, of course, for his own hardships and prospects and not for those of his slaves. With the most absolute of racist credentials, traders could write, as far as their slaves were concerned, only of "hearty appetitites," of "good" and "bad niggers," of getting slaves to "talk up right" and "look lively," but slave selling, for the traders themselves, was presented as a business heavy with "fatigues and troubles." One potential problem came with the prohibitions which states sometimes imposed against the trade, but in practice such restrictions were generally very lightly regarded within the slavemongering fraternity. Far more serious concerns of the speculator were, simply, catching market trends, "getting top prices" (and for cash or "reliable" paper), and supporting long periods of travel and, perhaps, isolation. The trader's mental world merged into the wider world of profound racism across the white South as a whole, though the perspectives of the professional speculator were in some ways more open and straightforward. To traders and their friends at home, their business seemed demanding, sometimes even heroic. And, it was quite overtly commercial—indeed, traders often saw themselves as at the cutting edge of enterprise and self-improvement.

QUESTIONS OF "SELF-DENIAL," ECONOMICS, AND SECURITY

In Chapter 2, I have already briefly considered certain early prohibitions against the trade and noted that, although there was in some cases a strand of Quaker and humanitarian influence, those restrictions stemmed essentially from very practical considerations. The significant pressures were fears that unruly slaves might be brought in from particular areas (the middle and northern states, in this case), the need to forgo importations which could not be afforded, and clashes of sectional interest within states. If we now move to consider, in a little more detail, the later period (from 1820 or so), we find that the Quaker and humanitarian factor barely, if at all, comes into view; but otherwise the same sorts of considerations as in the early years persist. Periods of opposition to the trade were unusual and stemmed, not from any moral outrage, but instead from considerations of economics, security, and local self-interest.

In fact, after about 1820, prohibitions fall into two main categories. First, two "mixed" states, Georgia and Tennessee (states which contained substantial areas of both net importation and net exportation of slaves), officially banned the trade until the 1850s. Secondly, three very heavy importers of slaves (Alabama, Mississippi, and Louisiana) introduced much briefer bans. In the two "mixed states," prohibitions came essentially from intrastate sectional tensions. Old-established areas already had all the slaves they needed, feared further importations, and had the political power to legislate prohibitions. But sections within these states which "needed" slaves paid little or no attention to their legislative impositions.[1] In the much briefer prohibitions of Alabama, Mississippi, and Louisiana, temporary economic panics (and to some extent concern over slave insurrections) explain the resort to legislation.[2]

1. Georgia's ban had been introduced in1817 and was officially in force for most of the period until 1855; Tennessee's ban ran from 1827 to 1853. On political representation in Tennessee and Georgia see C. S. Sydnor, *The Development of Southern Sectionalism, 1819–1848* ([Baton Rouge], 1948), pp. 45–47 (Vol. 5 in W. H. Stephenson and E. M. Coulter [eds.], *A History of the South* [Baton Rouge]: Louisiana State University Press and Littlefield Fund, 1948–]).

2. For much of the period from 1820 to 1860 Delaware, Maryland, and Virginia—always at the core of the net-exporting section—operated bans against *importation* from other states. The bans had little practical effect and seem to have been reflections of long-standing worries over the possible introduction of "troublesome" blacks from further north. As well as the bans discussed in this chapter, there were also numerous restrictions which did not concern the interregional trade generally but which related only to the importation of convicted criminal slaves. Planter migrations, as distinct from the trade, were never or almost never prohibited, although such migrations had in certain cases to be registered with state authorities. For the dates of the various prohibitions, see the statutes of the various states, partial digests of which appear in J. C. Hurd, *The Law of Freedom and Bondage in the United States* (Boston, 1858–62; New York, 1968); Collins, *The Domestic Slave Trade,* pp.

Evidence on attitudes in Georgia, one of the "mixed states," comes from the fears expressed in a local newspaper of 1821. In December of that year, the *Milledgeville Journal*, a publication from and reflecting the interest of the state's net-exporting section, urged that pressure to legalize the trade should be resisted. The *Journal* declared:

Everyone knows that the speculators would constantly introduce into the state the dregs of the colored population of the states to the north of us; . . . and the jails of North and South Carolina, Maryland, and Virginia would be disgorged upon this deluded state.

Such fears of unruly slaves proved a persistent theme, but economic factors were of great importance too. In 1849, Judge Floyd, representing Bibb County (in the net-exporting section) drew attention to the frequent violation of Georgia's prohibition law. Significantly, he lamented that the large influx of slaves from Virginia and elsewhere had undermined slave prices in Georgia's exporting counties and had, by increasing the production of cotton, depressed the market price of that Georgia staple. In 1855, Judge H. L. Benning of the Georgia Supreme Court, in attempting to explain his state's prohibitions, mentioned both economic and noneconomic factors. "The main reason for the enactment [of prohibitions]," Benning argued

was, I think, a fear that this traffic, if permitted, would in the end, empty the more northerly of the slave states of their slaves, and thus convert those states from friends and allies into enemies and assailants. The chief reason was, I think, not at all to promote abolition in this State, but to prevent abolition in other States. Another reason was, no doubt, a disposition to keep the proportion of the free population to the slave from being materially changed. And avarice probably had some degree of influence—the avarice of slaveholders already in the state, the value of whose slaves would be diminished as the supply from abroad should be increased.[3]

Alabama, Louisiana, and Mississippi were great importers of slaves and were surely among the states least likely to be suspected of moral

---

109–39; Coleman, *Slavery Times in Kentucky*, pp. 149, 155, 159; R. B. Flanders, *Plantation Slavery in Georgia* (Chapel Hill, 1933), pp. 183–85; J. B. Sellers, *Slavery in Alabama* (Tuscaloosa, 1950), pp. 179–94; and Kenneth M. Stampp, *The Peculiar Institution: Slavery in the Antebellum South* (New York, 1956), p. 253.

3. *Milledgeville Journal* quoted in Phillips et al. (eds.), *Documentary History*, vol. 2, pp. 67–70; Floyd and Benning cited in Flanders, *Plantation Slavery in Georgia*, pp. 184, 253. Comparison of the growth rates of the local slave population with that of the South as a whole establishes that the counties concerned were indeed net exporters at the times indicated.

opposition to the trade. And yet all three enacted prohibitions—Alabama from 1827 until June 1829, and again for much of 1832; Louisiana from June 1826 to 1828 and again from late 1831 until 1834; and Mississippi from mid-1837 until early 1846. The explanation, as I have noted, lay not in moral considerations, but in questions of security and, especially, economics.

Bans in Alabama and Louisiana were almost contemporaneous and seem (as indeed does the Mississippi ban) to have stemmed essentially from the same economic motive: relieving the heavy exportations of funds which were occasioned by slave purchasing from the trade and which became undesirable during economic crises. Those first Alabama and Louisiana bans, introduced in 1827 and mid-1826, respectively, followed periods of massive slave importation and were rooted in the economic depression which set in during 1826. The revival of the Alabama and Louisiana bans in 1832 and late 1831, respectively, owed a good deal to alarm at Nat Turner's slave revolt of 1831 in Virginia. Indeed, immediately after the Turner revolt, a special session of the Louisiana assembly was called and was warned by the state governor, Dupré, of the dangers posed by importing slaves who might be infected by the insurrectionary virus. But Governor Dupré was also very much concerned with economic factors, and earlier in 1831 had already warned the legislature of the alarming drain upon funds which slave importations imposed upon the state. Louisiana, he had told the assembly, annually purchased slaves "to the amount of $2½ million, principally from the states of Maryland and Virginia."[4] It was this drain on funds which the Virginia–New Orleans trader Paul Pascal considered to have been behind Louisiana's 1831 prohibition. In November 1831 he informed his partner:

> Quand je vous ais écrie dachette des negres est les [sic] envoyer les plus tôt possible on ne pouver sutendre aucune lois aussi injuste que celle que la législature a passer. Ils lont fait qu'a leur avantage et pour chasser de leur etat les persons qu'il suppose qui emporte beaucoup de leur argent.[5]

4. On Louisiana's legislation of 1826 and 1831 see Taylor, *Negro Slavery in Louisiana*, pp. 39, 41–44; on the financial drain see Gov. Dupré, cited in Wendell H. Stephenson, *Isaac Franklin: Slave Trader and Planter of the Old South* (Baton Rouge, 1938), p. 74n. It is perhaps worth noting, too, that by the mid-1840s, with Alabama becoming increasingly a "mixed" state, influential men from net-exporting areas within that state were calling for further bans on slave trade importations and were using much the same sort of arguments voiced by members of net-exporting counties in the "mixed" state of Georgia. On the (unsuccessful) pressure for late antebellum bans in Alabama, see Sellers, *Slavery in Alabama*, pp. 178–91.

5. Pascal to Raux, 21 Nov. 1832, Pascal Papers (HLH): "When I wrote to you to buy

Factors similar to those at work in Alabama and Louisiana in the early 1830s seem to have been responsible for the inclusion in the Mississippi constitution, drawn up in 1832, of a provision to prohibit importations by the domestic trade. Given the booming prosperity of the mid-1830s, no legislation was passed to bring this constitutional provision into force. Mississippians imported slaves at a massive rate during the early and mid-1830s, doubling the state's slave population. In the financial panic of 1837, therefore, the Mississippi state government banned further importations and, drawing conveniently (but with very dubious justification) on the constitutional provision of 1832, declared that all of the state's importations since May 1833 had also been illegal. With this, Mississippians (though they would face difficulties with the U.S. Supreme Court) repudiated their slave-trading debts, declaring that all notes arising from slave-trade purchases of 1833–37 were void.[6]

A "FREE COUNTRY" FOR SLAVE TRADING

Prohibitions carried few terrors for the trader. Bans that stemmed from short-term panics over economics or security were either quickly repealed or soon, as demand revived, massively evaded. And in the principal "mixed states," evasion was a way of life; the old-established sections of these states had the political weight to pass laws against the trade but were completely lacking in the means of enforcing such laws in areas where they were unpopular.

The Louisiana ban of 1831–34 was, perhaps, sufficiently short-lived to have had some effect, although the pressure against prohibition was at the same time restricted by a falling off in demand for slaves. Letters of Pascal & Raux, a firm operating between Virginia and New Orleans, give indications of traders' reactions and tactics. The fact that their buying area centered on Southampton County, Virginia, the very county in which the Turner rebellion had occurred, presented no great problem—misleading documentation for purchases could easily be devised. There was, however, still the basic problem of how to bring

---

negroes and send them as soon as possible, one could not have suspected any law as unjust as that which the legislature has passed. They have only done it to benefit themselves and to drive away from their state people who they think carry off a great deal of their money."

6. On the severe impact of the Panic and depression in Mississippi, see Phillips, *American Negro Slavery,* p. 372, and R. C. McGrane, *The Panic of 1837* (Chicago, 1924), pp. 115–17. On Mississippi's policy of 1837, and on clashes with the Supreme Court of the United States, see Sydnor, *Slavery in Mississippi,* pp. 164–71.

slaves in undetected. In December 1831, when the ban had been in force for a month, Pascal reported that he had not yet thought out a smuggling scheme: "Je n'ais pas encore découvert le mistère pour l'introduction des esclaves en contrebande." He added, though, that demand for slaves was still slack and that slaves already in New Orleans were not selling.[7]

By February 1832, Pascal seemed to have solved the contraband mystery, adopting a practice of importing slaves who, rather than being the object of general speculation, were *supposed* to be imported to meet the orders of specific Louisiana residents. As the legislature moved to close such loopholes, Pascal looked to prospects in the nearby Mississippi market. There, too, a temporary downturn in economic activity had depressed demand. He consoled himself, however, that the cholera epidemic would soon come to his rescue: "restocking" would soon be essential after heavy losses through mortality.[8]

In the early 1830s, Mississippi, caught by the Nat Turner scare, passed laws designed to prevent the importation of slaves who might be of dangerous character. But as the advice of one of Pascal's associates, Bacon Tait, shows, the legislation put little strain on the ingenuity of the trader. Tait, writing from Richmond, acknowledged that the certificates of good character which Mississippi required for imported slaves,

> like all other on the subject, is more trouble than profit but for the sake of safety I would advise friend Pascal to go provided with . . . [one]. He may not have to use it at all, but the laws of Mississippi demand it and to prevent the possibility of a difficulty I would advise them to take one along — you can put as many negroes as you please in *one certificate.*
>
> The usual way as I understand of obtaining these certificates is to get two freeholders to go along and look at your negroes. You then tell them the name of each negro—the freeholders then say that they know the negroes and give the certificates accordingly.

The text of certificates, to quote the specimen offered by Tait, was to run:

> We the undersigned citizens of the county and state aforesaid do hereby certify that we know the following described slave of this county lately purchased and owned by Paul Pascal and Bernhard Raux, viz a male named John, 5 feet 6 inches black color about 20 years old . . . etc and further do testify that the above named and described slaves have not been guilty of or convicted of

7. Pascal to Raux, 29 Oct., 24 Dec. 1831, Pascal Papers (HLH).
8. Pascal to Raux, 9 and 21 Feb., 14 Sept. 1832, Pascal Papers (HLH).

murder, burglary or arson or any felony within our knowledge and belief within the county and state aforesaid. . . .

The clerk of the county court then confirmed that the two witnesses were "respectable freeholders of the county," affixed a seal, and the ruse was tidily completed.[9]

Many traders at first reacted cautiously to Mississippi's direct prohibition on slave-trade importations between 1837 and 1846. Thus, in order to sell to Mississippi customers but at the same time to avoid the possible legal consequences, the trader Newton Boley set up just outside Mississippi's jurisdiction. Boley's advertisement in the *Mississippi Free Trader and Natchez Gazette* (20 December 1838) announced: "NEGROES FOR SALE. The subscriber has for sale at Vidalia, La., opposite Natchez, between 70 and 80 Negroes." A similar practice was followed by the trader Rice C. Ballard who,

during the spring of 1840, stated to witness that he felt somewhat uneasy about the decision of the Supreme Court of Mississippi and proposed to . . . arrange [the sale of slaves] by passing the bill of sale in Louisiana.

And S. A. Heydenfeldt observed that many traders adopted the practice of bringing slaves into Mississippi, working them on local plantations for a year, and then (the slaves having fulfilled residence qualifications) selling them and restocking with newly imported slaves.[10]

J. R. Long, however, had never been impressed by the Mississippi ban and as early as May 1838 was urging his North Carolina trading colleague William Long to "bring all [the slaves] you can get and I can sell them. The laws can take no hold on me." Perhaps William Long was at first more cautious than was J. R. Long, but in the early 1840s demand increased, and, apparently like many other traders, he paid less and less attention to legal restrictions on the Mississippi trade. On 19 January 1846, Thomas Burton, one of William Long's trading associates, wrote from Mississippi:

As for the stop law the voice of Mississippi is for repeal and there is no doubt it will be [repealed]. . . . There is no presumable danger in bringing negroes here. There is some [negroes] in Vicksburg and . . . at Clinton.

A few days later Burton wrote from Monroe County, Mississippi:

9. Tait to N. Courier, 4 Oct. 1832, Pascal Papers (HLH).

10. Boley advertisement quoted in Bancroft, *Slave Trading,* p. 274n; testimony of J. M. Pelton on Ballard, 11 Oct. 1841, Quitman Family Papers (SHC); Heydenfeldt cited in Sellers, *Slavery in Alabama,* p. 185.

William and Samuel Harper . . . are here at Wallington with a lot of negroes. They are doing nothing as well as myself. This county are full of negroes, they are at every village in the county.

And from Burton's letter of 20 February 1846 it appears that the Mississippi trade had also been quite active in the winter of 1844–45. His letter, from Jasper County, Mississippi, reported that slaves were

selling slow in consequence of the quantity in this county. There is double the quantity here that there were last winter and what is selling are for better prices.[11]

Tennessee's geographical location was such that many traders who drove and shipped slaves to Lower South markets found it convenient to pass through that state or to travel by the Mississippi River (which formed its western boundary); because the right of transit through Tennessee could not constitutionally be denied to traders, the influx of slaves was considerable.[12] In all states, the trader's right of transit must very seriously have hampered any attempts to restrict the trade, but in Tennessee this right permitted the development of Memphis, on the Mississippi River, as a major trading center. Leading trading firms, no doubt under the pretense that they sold exclusively to traders and planters who would carry the slaves to more southerly states, established themselves at Memphis, and in that city's newspapers they openly advertised that they kept on hand a constant supply of Virginia and other out-of-state slaves.[13] Memphis, well situated as an important entrepôt for the lower-Mississippi trade, was also ideally positioned for playing its part in subverting the ban which, from 1827–55, Tennessee officially imposed upon trade importations.

In Georgia (which like Tennessee was a leading "mixed" state) evasion of prohibitions was a long-standing tradition, and that evasion took several forms. One important device was for traders to take slaves to a point just outside Georgia, there to make sales to Georgia residents. In another, traders directly introduced slaves into Georgia, but trader and buyer then withdrew a short distance beyond Georgia territory to sign the official deed of sale. And by still another device slaves were taken into Georgia and were sold, not as the property of the trader, but supposedly as the long-standing property of some

11. Long to Long, 22 May 1838; Burton to Long, 19 and 24 Jan., 20 Feb. 1846, Long Papers (NCA).

12. For comments on this constitutional position see Phillips, *American Negro Slavery,* p. 203, and Bancroft, *Slave Trading,* p. 273.

13. For such advertisements, relating to the 1830s, '40s, and early '50s, see Mooney, *Slavery in Tennessee,* pp. 46–52, and Bancroft, *Slave Trading,* pp. 258, 274.

Georgia resident. In some cases, however, pseudolegal forms seem to have been dispensed with, so that smuggling was quite open.

Hamburg—a small town on the South Carolina side of the Savannah River, linked to Georgia by a railway bridge—was ideally situated for the first type of evasion. In the early 1830s one of the traders active at Hamburg was Joseph Wood who, according to his advertisement, was "a gentleman dealing in slaves." He had "on hand a likely parcel of Virginia Negroes" and, at his Hamburg depot, was receiving "new supplies every 15 days." Similarly in September 1838 Benjamin Davis advertised that he had just arrived in Hamburg from Petersburg, Virginia, and had 120 slaves for sale to planters and traders; and in November 1840 a certain T. Goldsmith, based at Hamburg, advertised in a local paper and in Georgia's *Augusta Constitution* that he had a stock of Virginia Negroes for sale. Passing through Hamburg in 1839, the British visitor J. S. Buckingham observed that Hamburg had two depots to which Virginia slaves were brought for trading purposes, and from which they were carried forward to Georgia and the Southwest.[14]

Charleston, too, was an extrepôt for the Georgia trade, and in 1847 petitioners to the South Carolina Senate complained that since Georgia had prohibited the introduction of slaves for speculation,

> This state [South Carolina] and the city of Charleston in particular, have become a common place of meeting between the slave dealer from places north of us, and the purchaser south-west of us — that the motive of the slave dealer is not only to approach as near as he can to his buyer, but to remove the slave as far from his old range, and from notorious bad characters as possible. That while on sale here many vicious slaves are palmed upon careless and confiding citizens among us, and their mixture with our own has a sensible influence upon the docility and usefulness of our own slaves.

In 1856, the Charleston City Council made similar reference to the Georgia prohibition, whose effect had been "to make Charleston a mart for the sale of slaves drawn from states lying to the north of us." The Council considered, though, that a substantial city tax imposed on this aspect of the trade was lessening the nuisance created by these traders.[15]

14. Wood advertisement quoted in Jay, *A View,* p. 78; Davies quoted in Rev. William Goodell, *The American Slave Code in Theory and Practice; Its Distinctive Features Shown by its Statutes, Judicial Decisions, and Illustrative Facts* (London, 1853), p. 40; *Edgefield Advertiser* (S.C.), 26 Nov. 1840; James S. Buckingham, *The Slave States of America* (London, 1842), vol. 1, p. 170.

15. Petition to Senate of South Carolina by certain citizens, 1847, in Slavery: Loose Legislative Papers, Box 4 (SCA); Proceedings of Charleston City Council, reported in *Charleston Courier,* 10 Jan. 1856.

An example of a Georgia-based firm well situated to use the device of contracting sales just beyond the Georgia boundary was the Savannah firm of Wylly & Montmollin. Their trade notice ran:

Beaufort district, South Carolina, March 1853. Having opened in the Union Ferry Road (Dr. Scriven's) *opposite Savannah, Georgia* . . . a Slave Depot for the purpose of buying and selling Negroes and Real Estates, [we] would inform the public generally that . . . [we] have constantly at said depot, Negroes of all descriptions for sale, and at the same time are prepared to purchase, for highest cash prices, Negroes, either singly, in families, or gangs, having numerous orders to fill. We will also buy and sell on Commission, and having a similar establishment at Savannah, will afford our friends many advantages [emphasis added].

Another Savannah firm following this practice was that of Wright & Company. In January 1854, Wright wrote to the Charleston dealer, Ziba B. Oakes:

I will take the woman and try to sell her for you. It is against the law to sell negroes into the state but as we are on the boundary line I can take her across the River and make titles.

Nine months later, Wright urged Oakes to keep him informed as to the Charleston market and to send him some slaves as, he wrote, "I intend to cross the river [into South Carolina] to make titles from another stall this season — it being done here frequently." And according to the editor of the Savannah *Republican*, Georgia's prohibition was

constantly evaded by corrupt speculators, and hundreds of negroes are annually introduced and sold. It is a practice among these speculators, after having agreed with their several purchasers upon the price to be paid, to take the Rail-road or stage out of Georgia to the nearest point in Alabama or South Carolina, and there make out and sign their bills of sale. . . . All this is a corrupt violation of the law.[16]

The Anderson district, South Carolina, firm of Seaborn, Cobb, and Daniels had very long connections with the Georgia market, and seems to have used the device of drawing up sale contracts as if the slaves concerned had been the long-standing property of some Georgia resident. A letter from a certain Thomas Harrison shows that, at least as early as 1837, Seaborn and his colleagues were trading in Georgia, and many years later, in the winter of 1852–53, the young

16. Printed trade notice with, on reverse, letter from Wylly & Montmollin to Oakes, 7 July 1853; Wright to Oakes, 24 Jan., 10 Oct. 1854, Oakes Papers (BPL); Savannah *Republican* quoted in Stampp, *Peculiar Institution,* p. 256.

Jesse Cobb, newly recruited into the family business, purchased slaves who "were to be taken to Georgia and title made there by somebody." After purchasing his slaves, "Jesse Cobb went with the Negroes . . . [to Georgia]," where E. M. Cobb and George Seaborn already had "15 or 20 Negroes" for sale. A court case establishes that as late as 1859 the Cobbs "had a depot for slaves, in Carnesville, Georgia, kept by one Reynolds." During the Georgia prohibition on the trade, it was perhaps this Reynolds who had arranged for doctoring the titles to the slaves traded.[17]

It is not clear whether, in trading in Georgia in the 1840s, the North Carolina firm of Badgett & Glass made any pretense of conforming to legal enactments. Certainly, they were far from being short of competition in their section of the Georgia market. In November 1847, J. and J. D. Glass reported from Georgia on that season's illicit trip:

> We are too late this season. We don't know where to go to sell. All trade seems to have stop[ped] in a measure. . . . Alford is here and only sold one girl . . . Bracken is here. He has sold some 10 or 12 negroes all before we came.

Two months later, J. D. Glass reported from Covington, Georgia, that he still had fourteen Negroes unsold; but added that he had decided against moving to a different part of the state since, he said,"I have seen several traders and our prices is better then they are." And in December 1849 Henry Badgett wrote from Putnam County, Georgia, to his wife and children:

> We are doing a very fair business in the way of selling [having sold 21 at good prices] . . . so you can see that we shall make a very good trip if [unless] we have bad luck.

Badgett, who was well accustomed to the illegal trade, was able to ease any doubts which his wife might have had about the safety of his work by adding: "The law prohibiting the selling of slaves is now repealed so that we are in a free country running no risk of being troubled about selling."[18]

17. Harrison to Harrison, 6 Mar. 1837, James Thomas Harrison Papers (SHC); testimonies of S. Reid, J. Pike, and S. D. Berry, Anderson district Equity Court (SC), *Campbell et al.* v. *Cobb et al.*, 1854, Bill 202 (SCA); South Carolina *Reports, Fountain* v. *Bryce,* 12 Rich, Eq. 234.

18. Glass to Badgett, 25 Nov. 1847 and 12 Jan. 1848; Badgett to Badgett, 19 Dec. 1849, Badgett Papers (NCA).

"THE TRADER IS OFTEN MIGRATORY WITH HIS SLAVES"

Just as roving rural traders were overwhelmingly predominant in the Upper South, so, in that vast army of speculators which moved each season upon the Lower South, the rural, not the urban, operators formed the great bulk of the foot-soldiers. Obediah Fields was just one from this army of slavers. In the 1820s his selling area was the countryside and village markets in and around Greenville district (in the quite thinly settled South Carolina upcountry). Dr. Thomas C. Weatherly was another such trader, and during a selling trip of 1856 a fellow speculator reported from Hayneville, Alabama: "Dr. Weatherly is here. He lives in his tents. He told me he sold ten negroes last week at fair prices. [As a means of finding customers] he is following the counties round attending the courts." A certain Warner was another speculator who concentrated on rural markets, and in 1846 Peter Stokes, himself trading at the Alabama village of Gainesville, informed a friend that "Warner got here a few days ago with 13. He made no stop at this place but went on into the hills."[19]

Some impression of the scale of the trade in the countryside of Alabama and Mississippi is given by letters which the speculator T. W. Burton wrote in the first months of 1846. From Lowndes County, Mississippi, he reported that "There is a vast quantity of negroes in the Market and traders are holding them high"; and in neighboring Monroe County he found that traders were offering slaves "at every village in the county" and the area was "full of Negroes." Having moved to Alabama, he found that "there is negroes [offered by traders] all through the state." In his practice of moving from county to county to make sales, Burton was not at all unusual. As Chief Justice Chilton of Alabama explained when he reviewed the difficulties involved in imposing taxes upon the great numbers of speculators, "A slave merchant or trader may engage in this business without being located in any particular county. He is often migratory with his slaves," selling in several different counties.[20]

Traders of the migratory type sometimes, as we saw in the case of Dr. Weatherly, accommodated their slaves in tents. Some, like Starling Finney, used local plantations as their base. In a narrative of his

19. Fields to Fields, 29 Nov. 1822, etc., Obediah Fields Papers (DU); McElveen to Oakes, 21 Oct. 1856, Oakes Papers (BPL); Stokes to Hatchett, 11 Mar. 1846, William Haney Hatchett Papers (DU).

20. Burton to Long,16 and 24 Jan., 9 Mar. 1846, Long Papers (NCA); Chilton, quoted in Sellers, *Slavery in Alabama*, pp. 154–55.

experiences under slavery, John Brown, one of the many slaves taken by Finney from Virginia to Georgia, recalled that after the long trek from Virginia

> At last we stopped at one Ben Tarver's place in Jones County, Georgia. This man was a Methodist Minister, and had a cotton plantation and a good many slaves. During the time I staid there, which was two weeks, Finney used to take out his slaves every day, to try to sell them, bringing those back whom he failed to dispose of. Those who did not go out with Finney, for the market, were made to work in Tarver's cotton fields.

Having disposed of most of his slaves in private sales, Finney then, with the season coming to a close, sold his remaining slaves at an auction in Milledgeville. The writer Daniel Hundley, no friend of what he saw as the trader's "Yankie" commercialism, gave this sketch of the migratory speculator at work in the Lower South:

> At every village of importance he sojorns a day or two, each day ranging his 'gang' in a line on the most business [busy?] street; and whenever a customer makes his appearance, the oily speculator button-holes him immediately and begins to descant in the most high falutin fashion upon the virtuous lot of darkies he has for sale. Mrs. Stowe's Uncle Tom was not a circumstance to any of the dozen he points to. So honest! so truthful! so dear to the hearts of their former masters and mistresses![21]

Apart from the sort of markets to which we have just been referring, the Lower South, of course, possessed several major *urban* markets, and of these latter markets New Orleans was surely the most important. In a letter of January 1834, written, that is, at the very start of the New Orleans slaving season, a trading contact informed the North Carolina speculator, Isaac Jarratt: "I cannot say as to the number of negroes in the [New Orleans] market [at present] though am of the opinion there is 12–1500 and upwards, and small lots constantly coming in." And in February 1842, after several weeks of that season's trade had already been completed, the Baton Rouge *Gazette* reported that at that time there were some one thousand slaves for sale at New Orleans.[22]

Over the full New Orleans season, stretching from early January until the end of March, the accumulated total of sales would, no doubt,

21. Chamerovzow, *Narrative of . . . John Brown*, pp. 19–20; Daniel R. Hundley, *Social Relations in Our Southern States* (New York, 1860), pp. 141–42.

22. Jarvis to Jarratt, 16 Jan. 1834, Jarratt-Puryear Papers (DU); *Gazette*, cited in Taylor, *Slavery in Louisiana*, p. 53.

have been considerably higher than the number of slaves reported as being in the market at any one time. Manifests of the coastal slave movement provide further information on the extent of the New Orleans trade, and in the 1840s, for example, they directly document an annual average of over one thousand slaves sent to New Orleans traders. The 1840s by no means constituted an exceptionally active trading decade, and the manifest collections are very far from being complete. Furthermore, apart from the coastal route, many slaves would have been carried to New Orleans via overland routes and the Ohio and Mississippi rivers. Indeed, there were sometimes as many as 3,000 slaves held at New Orleans by traders. In late December 1859 (on the eve of the 1859–60 trading season) the trader Phillip Thomas reported that at New Orleans "I find about 3,000 negroes in the market and none selling." A week or two later, however, the trade would no doubt have opened.[23]

After New Orleans, Natchez was one of the most important of the urban markets in the importing states. In the 1832–33 season some Louisiana speculators were diverted to Natchez because of Louisiana's prohibition on the trade. In December 1832, very early in the trading year, the trader Paul Pascal estimated that the season's sales at Natchez had already amounted to "apeupres [about] 1000 negres." Two years later, after Louisiana's slave-trade restrictions were lifted, the trader James A. Mitchell wrote from Natchez on 10 December 1834: "There is not many at this place for sale. Not more than between 2 and 300." Over a full trading season, however, the Natchez traffic was often very extensive. In 1902, General William T. Martin, who fifty or so years earlier had been a Natchez lawyer specializing in breach of warranty cases which arose out of the slave trade, told the historian Frederic Bancroft:

> In some years there were three or four thousand slaves here [at Natchez]. I think that I have seen as many as 600 or 800 in the market at one time. There were usually four or five large traders at Natchez every winter. Each had from fifty to several hundred negroes, and most of them received fresh lots during the season. They brought their large gangs late in the fall and sold them out by May.[24]

23. Thomas to Finney, 26 Dec. 1859, Finney Papers (DU). On numbers of slaves recorded in manifests for the 1840s see Appendix 2, Table A2.1, and on the incompleteness of available manifest collections see Wesley, "Manifests of Slave Shipments," pp. 155–74. On the scale of trading in the 1840s compared with that from 1820 to1860 generally, see Table 2.1.

24. Pascal to Raux, 19 Dec. 1832, Pascal Papers (HLH); Mitchell to Mitchell, 10

The urban slave markets of Alabama, though less important than New Orleans and perhaps Natchez, also handled a substantial traffic. At about the same time as Phillip Thomas reported that the New Orleans market was stocked with about three thousand slaves, he estimated, in December 1859, that there were four hundred slaves for sale at Mobile; and in mid-January of that year Thomas reported that stocks at the Mobile market would be supplemented with "several large lots . . . next week." John C. Calhoun, Thomas's assistant, considered that Montgomery was a far better market than Mobile. In January 1859, he wrote of Mobile:

> This market is as I expected to find it and as I have often told you — dull as hell and every man for his self. This is no place for outside traders. There are not near as many negroes sold here as in Montgomery and not for as good prices as in the Montgomery market.

The evidence of Frederic Bancroft's survey of slave traders' advertisements in Mobile and Montgomery newspapers suggests that, in the 1850s at least, the Montgomery market was indeed a good deal more important than that of Mobile. For the 1850s, Bancroft found almost no evidence that long-distance traders had been active at Mobile, but found that each season numerous traders advertised in Montgomery newspapers.[25]

THE DAILY PROCEEDINGS OF THE SLAVE PENS

The various urban markets would each have been supplied with slave pens suited to the trader's needs; the advertisement for C. F. Hatcher's pen in Gravier Street, New Orleans, was fairly typical of the very numerous newspaper announcements relating to such jails: "Notice to Traders and Slaveholders," the advertisement declared,

> Having built a large and commodious showroom, and otherwise improved my old stand, I am now prepared to accommodate over 200 Negroes for sale.
>
> The owners can have comfortable rooms and board in the same premises at reasonable terms.

Indeed, at about the time Hatcher's advertisement appeared, the neighborhood around New Orleans's Gravier, Baronne, and Moureau streets

---

Dec. 1834, Richard R. Reid Papers (UVA); Martin, quoted in Bancroft, *Slave Trading*, pp. 304–305.

25. Thomas to Finney, 31 Dec. 1859, 14 Jan. 1860, and Calhoun to Finney, 12 Jan. 1860, Finney Papers (DU); Bancroft, *Slave Trading*, pp. 294–300.

was dominated by traders' pens and offices: in 1854, there were no fewer than seven slave dealers in a single block on Gravier, while on a single square on Moreau Street there was a row of eleven particularly commodious slave pens.[26]

The narrative of John Brown, a fugitive slave whom we have already encountered, provides an account of slave experiences and traders' practices in the slave pens of the Lower South. Having first been traded from Virginia to Georgia, Brown eventually came into the possession of the trader Freeman (very probably Theophilus Freeman, a trader noted in Appendix 2 of the present study) and was held at Freeman's New Orleans pen. "I may as well describe here the order of the daily proceedings," Brown wrote,

> as during the whole time I remained in the pen, they were, one day with the other, pretty much the same. . . .
>
> As may be imagined, the slaves are bought from all parts, are of all sorts, sizes, and ages, and arrive at various states of fatigue and condition; but they soon improve in their looks, as they are regularly fed and have plenty to eat. As soon as we were roused in the morning, there was a general washing, and combing, and shaving, pulling out of grey hairs, and dying the hair of those who were too grey to be plucked without making them bald. When this was over — and it was no light business — we used to breakfast, getting bread and bacon, and coffee, of which a sufficiency was given us, that we might plump up and become sleek. Bob [a "mulatto" assistant of the trader] would then proceed to instruct us on how to show ourselves off, and afterwards form us into companies, according to size; those who were nearly the same height and make being put into seperate lots; the men, the women, and the children of both sexes, being divided off alike. In consequence of this arrangement, the various members of a family were of necessity separated, and would often see the last of each other in that dreadful showroom.

Brown then went on to describe the routine of exercising, "looking spry," and being sold: "The buying," he wrote,

> commenced at about ten in the morning, and lasted till one, during which time we were obliged to be sitting about in our respective companies ready for inspection. At one we used to go to dinner, our usual food being a repetition of the morning meal, varied with vegetables, and a little fruit sometimes. After dinner we were compelled to walk, and dance, and kick about in the yard, for exercise; and Bob, who had a fiddle, used to play up jigs for us to dance to. If we did not dance to his fiddle, we used to have to do so to his whip, so no wonder

26. Hatcher advertisement in *Charleston Mercury,* 2 Jan. 1860. On New Orleans pens generally, see R. C. Wade, *Slavery in the Cities: The South, 1820–1860* (New York, 1964), pp. 187–206, esp. p. 199.

we used our legs handsomely, though the music was none of the best. When our exercises were over, we used to be "sized out" again, ready for the afternoon sale, which commenced at three, and ended at six. This over, we had tea, and were then free to do what we liked in the pen, until Bob rang us off to bed at ten.[27]

By coincidence, a second slave narrative relating to the Freeman pen survives; it records the experiences of Solomon Northup, who was traded from Virginia in the 1840s. After describing the "sizing out" process in a similar way to Brown, Northup again emphasized the trader's keen interest in having his slaves "look smart." On the day after he had arrived at the pen, as Northup's narrative records:

customers called to examine Freeman's 'new lot'. The latter gentleman was very loquacious, dwelling at much length upon our several good points and qualities. He would make us hold up our heads, walk briskly back and forth, while customers would feel of our hands and arms and bodies, turn us about, ask us what we could do, make us open our mouths and show our teeth. . . . Sometimes a man or woman was taken back to the small house in the yard, stripped and inspected more minutely. Scars upon a slave's back were considered evidence of a rebellious or unruly spirit, and hurt his sale.

Another exslave described similar scenes at the Memphis pen of the trader (and later Confederate cavalry general) Nathan Bedford Forrest. When the slaves were lined up for inspection at the pen, the witness reported,

buyers would stand by and inspect us as we went by, stop us and examine us. Our teeth, and limbs and [sic] a Doctor generally if there were sick negroes. They always my mother said (who explained much of this to me when I grew older) looked to see if there were any scars on our body from a whip as it indicated as they said a "bad nigger."

J. H. Ingraham, a white visitor to a Natchez pen, again described a similar spectacle, and commented in particular on the careful dressing of the slaves. Each man, he wrote,

was dressed in the usual uniform of slaves when in the market, consisting of a fashionably shaped, black fur hat, roundabout and trousers of coarse corduroy velvet, precisely such as are worn by Irish laborers, when they first 'come over the water'; good vests, strong shoes, and white cotton shirts completed their equipment. . . . Opposite to the line of males was . . . a line of females, extending along the left side of the court. They were . . . dressed in neat calico

27. Chamerovzow, *Narrative of . . . John Brown,* pp. 112–13.

frocks, white aprons and caps, and fancy kerchiefs, tied . . . around their heads.[28]

The narrative of another exslave, William Wells Brown, provides further detail on the business of preparing slaves for sale. Brown was obliged for some time to serve as an assistant to a trader named Walker, and recalled one lot of slaves shipped by Walker down the Mississippi River. "There was in this lot," Brown wrote,

> a number of old men and women some of them with grey locks. . . . [and] on my way down [river] . . . I had to prepare the old slaves for market. I was ordered to have the old men's whiskers shaved off, and the grey hairs plucked out where they were not too numerous, in which case we had a preparation of blacking to color it, and with a blacking brush we put it on. This was new business to me, and was performed in a room where the passengers could not see us. These slaves were also taught how old they were by Mr. Walker, and often after going through the blacking process they would look ten or fifteen years younger; and I am sure that some of those who purchased slaves of Mr. Walker were dreadfully cheated, especially in the ages of the slaves which they bought.

The practice of "feeding slaves up" so that they would be in good condition for sale obviously recommended itself to traders. Among many traders' letters that refer to holding sales over until the slaves were in good condition is one in which A. J. McElveen wrote to his associate Ziba Oakes: "I suppose it will be some time before he [the slave Joe] will be fit for sale as he needs feeding up."[29]

If slaves were to be disposed of at good prices, it was important that they not only "looked spry" but that they "talked up right." As the fugitive slave John Brown explained,

> A man or woman may be well made, and physically faultless in every respect, yet their value be impaired by a sour look, or a dull, vacant stare, or a general dullness of demeanor. For this reason the poor wretches who are about to be sold, are instructed to look "spry and smart", to hold themselves well up, and put on a smiling, cheerful countenance. They are also told to speak up for, and recommend themselves; to conceal any defects they may have, and especially

28. Solomon Northup, *Twelve Years a Slave: Narrative of Solomon Northup, a Citizen of New York, Kidnapped in Washington City in 1841, and Rescued in 1853 from a Cotton Plantation Near the Red River, in Louisiana* (Auburn, 1853), pp. 78–80; Horatio J. Eden, pp. 631–32 in Blassingame (ed.), *Slave Testimony;* J. H. Ingraham, *The South-West, by a Yankee* (New York, 1835), pp. 192–97.

29. Brown, *Narrative of William W. Brown,* p. 16; McElveen to Oakes, 8 Sept. 1856, Oakes Papers (BPL).

not to tell their [true] age whether [when] they are getting past the active period of life.

Sometimes "bad talking" by slaves does not seem to have been deliberate; in one letter the trader A. J. McElveen wrote of a slave, Henry, who was sixteen years old, "likely, had good sense, fine teeth, but talks badly. He talks well to negroes, but can't speak well to white persons." In other cases, however, "bad talking" was a deliberate ploy which the slave used to try to frustrate his sale. Thus McElveen complained that

James is cutting up his contrariness. I could sell him like hot cakes if he would talk right. You may blame me but the fact is, and Dr. Weatherly will tell the same, the boy is trying to make himself *unsound*. He says he wore a trust [sic] in Charleston. I think it would be well to see his former master and know the facts and write me to Montgomery. I will be there next week.[30]

The mood of the narratives makes it clear that punishment and threats were the key to the trader's regime, and there is no reason to question that these indeed constituted the basic groundrule of the trading system. Such tactics, nevertheless, were sometimes supplemented by somewhat more subtle devices. Traders, as Charles Ball showed, might try to encourage their slaves by claiming that they had been brought to "the finest country in the world." They might promise too that, if a slave cooperated, he would be sold to a kind master; and sometimes those promises were backed up by small rewards. Thus a memorandum of the North Carolina speculator Obediah Fields records:

It was understood that I should give the negroes a present if they would try to get homes and not do anything against the interest of their sales, and to Isaac I gave $3; to Dick $2; to Fan $1; to Isabel $2; Dick and Isaac a hat each at 1 = $2.

A similar system of rewards was followed by E. Lockett, a New Orleans trader. The slave John Brown recorded, however, that "every day there was flogging going on" at the New Orleans pen which he was forced to visit. According to Brown, it was

a rule amongst "nigger traders," not to flog with any instrument that will cut the skin, because this would depreciate the value of the "property" therefore the punishment is inflicted with what is called a "flopping paddle". The flop is of leather, about a foot-and-a-half long, and as broad as the palm of one hand; perhaps a little broader; the handle is of wood, and about two feet long. . . .

30. Chamerovzow, *Narrative of . . . John Brown*, pp. 115–16; McElveen to Oakes, 10 May 1854 and 21 Oct. 1856, Oakes Papers (BPL).

"Flopping" was inflicted for many offences, especially the unpardonable one of "not speaking up and looking bright and smart" when the buyers were choosing.[31]

By a range of stratagems, then, the trader could expect, sooner or later, to gain the compliance of his slaves. Sometimes, indeed, it fell to one of the slaves to extract for the trader the cooperation of the slaves generally. One such trader's assistant was the "mulatto" Bob, who worked at Freeman's New Orleans pen; another was William Wells Brown who, as we have seen, for some time acted as assistant to a speculator named Walker. The "mulatto" Bob's attitude toward his work is not revealed, but there can be no doubt that William Wells Brown was aware of the tragic situation in which he was placed. An important part of Brown's task was to see that the slaves, when offered for sale, looked bright, smart, and cheerful. "Before the slaves were exhibited for sale," he wrote

they were dressed and drawn out into the yard. Some were set to dancing, some to jumping, some to singing, and some to playing cards. This was done to make them appear cheerful and happy. My business was to see that they were placed in those situations before the arrival of the purchasers, and I have often set them to dancing when their cheeks were wet with tears.[32]

TERMS OF SALE

It is clear from correspondence, narratives of exslaves, reports of visitors to slave pens, and advertisements, that traders almost always disposed of their "stock," not at auction, but by private negotiations with individual clients. In a minority of cases, especially perhaps where special skills were claimed for the individuals in question, slaves were lent out for trial periods prior to a final sale. Josiah Brown of New Orleans was one client who took advantage of the trial system; before buying the slave Sandy, he put him "with a good carpenter for a few days" to see what he was worth. The speculator Phillip Thomas reported that he had "got Henry out on trial at 1200": after the trial period the slave was sold, apparently to the same customer, for $1150. N. C. Trowbridge, trading in Georgia in 1850, wrote about one of his slaves: "The girl Ann I let a gentleman in Burk Co. take for a day or

31. Charles Ball, *Fifty Years in Chains,* pp. 36–37, 92; memorandum of 11 Feb. 1828, Field Papers (DU); Lockett to Dickinson, 13 Feb. 1846, Chase Papers (AAS); and Chamerovzow, *Narrative of . . . John Brown,* pp. 114–15.

32. Brown, *Narrative of William W. Brown,* pp. 17–18.

two and he will give 800 if she pleases his wife"; similarly the trader A. Gunn reported, in 1833, that he had a seamstress out on trial.[33] With field hands, trial periods seem to have been very uncommon, but guarantees of good health were often given.[34]

The numerous traders' accounts and correspondence collections used in this study suggest that, in a particular season, a speculator would have sold only a small number of slaves (between one and four) to an individual client.[35] Such transactions would have been to suit specific customer requirements (for a couple of field hands, "a good breeding wench," a seamstress, and so on). For these purchases, customers could perhaps sometimes command cash—but on many other occasions, and for purchases on a larger scale, clients would probably have had to raise loans or have their "paper" or "acceptances" guaranteed by a creditworthy firm or individual.[36] It was essential to comply with the speculator's very strong preference for payment in cash or its near equivalent. In their turn, the traders' preferences were founded on very sound business principles. They would have found it difficult to establish the creditworthiness of large numbers of individual clients; but, as we know, even more important was the fact that

33. Brown to Oakes, 24 Nov. 1853, Oakes Papers (BPL); Thomas to Finney, 12 Jan. 1860, Finney Papers (DU); Trowbridge to Dickinson, 6 Apr. 1860, Dickinson Papers (CHS); Gunn to Totten, 23 Nov. 1833, Totten Papers (NCA).

34. On guarantees of health, see Chapter 7. Sometimes, as well as directly selling, traders (particularly between themselves) swapped slaves. Thus, the trader Peter Stokes wrote "Nathan and Betsy I swopped for a girl and got $90 to boot, and [I] got scared about her title and sent [her] to New Orleans" (Stokes to Hatchett, 8 Feb. 1846, Hatchett Papers [DU]). In 1850, N. C. Trowbridge informed his trade associate: "I exchanged your boy Patrick today and got a No. one boy 18 and 50 dolls. A fust rate swop." Quite numerous references to swapping occur in the business accounts of Obediah Fields and of other traders (see Trowbridge to Dickinson, 4 Mar. 1850, Dickinson Papers [CHS]; Fields Papers, throughout [DU]).

35. Stephenson, in *Isaac Franklin,* pp. 86–93, analyzed the records of Franklin & Armfield's sales in the Lower South and found that, for a given consignment, 84 percent of purchasers bought not more than three or four slaves. He also found, however, that 2 percent of purchasers bought as many as twenty to thirty slaves. In the records used for the present study, purchasers of large numbers seem to have been significantly rarer than in Stephenson's sample.

36. Factorage firms, handling planters' crops, generally considered financial assistance to planters to be an integral part of their business. Thus, at about the time when crops began to come on to the market, they were often prepared to support slave purchasing. On the importance of loans in the business activities of factors, see R. E. Roeder, "Merchants in Ante-Bellum New Orleans," *Explorations in Entrepreneurial History,* 10 (1958), pp. 113–22. See also Gray, *History of Agriculture,* vol. 2, p. 713.

they wanted to be able to repay their own bank loans and to turn over their capital quickly for maximum profits.[37]

For the reasons outlined, wariness over sales on extended personal credit is a recurring theme in the correspondence of traders. The comment of S. A. Browning, who was active in rural Louisiana and Mississippi, was typical of many trader's reports on sales conditions in the Lower South: "I could have sold all the property by taking say one half cash," he wrote, but "that wont suit as you know so I have to hold on." James A. Mitchell, in much the same vein, wrote from Mississippi: "There appears a good demand for them [slaves] but I cant get no money. They all want [to buy] on credit and that dont suit me for I want cash." And similarly, W. S. Belser, frustrated by his inability quickly to effect satisfactory sales, reported that Montgomery, Alabama,

> is a poor market for negroes unless you can sell on twelve months time and in that case fellows would command $1100, but in my opinion there is no small amount of swindlers located here and [the] least a man has to do with them the better.

Perhaps the frustration proved too much: a court case suggests that Belser eventually ran off with his remaining slaves and the receipts so far gained, and quietly swindled his trading partners back in South Carolina.[38]

On terms of sale, several traders' account books give quite detailed evidence. Thus, W. H. Stephenson, after examining the available sales records of Franklin & Armfield, traders active in both the New Orleans and Natchez markets, reported that 69 percent of that firm's sales were wholly cash transactions. An examination of the Pascal & Raux records for 1832 to 1834 (sales being made mainly at Natchez), shows that about 50 percent of sales were for cash, about 35 percent were for credit not exceeding six months (mostly, in fact, 60 days credit, with a 50 percent deposit), and the remaining 15 percent or so were on credit not exceeding twelve months. References to discounting "notes" suggest that many of the firm's "payments on time" would have taken the form of

37. "Good paper" used in payment to traders often took the form of "acceptances" which were endorsed by a bank or acceptance house. The acceptances generally realized their full face value after sixty or ninety days, but were negotiable and, at a discount, were convertible into cash before maturity.

38. Browning to Boyd, 24 Mar. 1849, Boyd Papers (DU); Mitchell to Mitchell, 10 Dec. 1834, Reid Papers (UVA); Belser to Belser, 2 Nov. [1849], letter given in evidence at Sumter district Equity Court (SC), *Belser* v. *Belser*, 1852, Bill 180 in new series (SCA).

"acceptances." J. R. White's account book (covering some one thousand slaves sold in the New Orleans market) similarly suggests that most sales were for cash or "good acceptances." And in his survey of several thousand bills of sale reflecting the New Orleans trade, Kotlikoff found 74 percent of sales to be for cash.[39]

ALARMS AND PROFITS

Although, as we shall see, the trade usually returned substantial profits, trading confidence was occasionally disturbed by major crises in American economic or political life.[40] One such disturbance attended the financial panic which hit America in April 1837 and which caused the prices of agricultural staples, slaves, and other property to plummet. The Panic of 1837 meant that for several years the planter's ability to pay for new slaves and his confidence in making new purchases were considerably weakened. And while the panic resulted in a marked slackening in the pace of the trade overall, in Mississippi (where, as we have seen, debts to out-of-state traders were repudiated), the speculator's problems were especially severe. Mississippi's repudiation obviously had no effect on already completed cash sales, but it is likely, nevertheless, to have affected a good many sales since acceptances and other debts owed to traders would probably not have been honored.

Not surprisingly, the Civil War and the severe sectional tensions which immediately preceded it had a markedly depressing effect on the trade in slaves. In November 1859, as the sectional crisis mounted, the speculator Phillip Thomas could still feel defiantly confident about the prospects for the trade. He wrote from Virginia that there was a

> good deal of talk about Harper's Ferry . . . [but] nobody cares a damn if the Union is dissolved. Everybody nearly wants to volunteer to go to fight, but no serious danger is apprehended. I have tendered the Governor the services of my company and so has all the volunteer companies. . . . Tell the Southern people not to fear old Virginia any more . . . Virginia can whip the whole North

39. Stephenson, *Isaac Franklin*, p. 86; Pascal & Raux sales accounts, covering Nov. 1832 to Oct. 1834, and involving 118 slaves, Pascal Papers (HLH); J. R. White, Account Book, Chinn Collection (MHS); Kotlikoff, "The Structure of Slave Prices," p. 504. Traders' newspaper advertisements concerning the sale of slaves show a similar stress upon cash and "good cashable paper." See, for example Bancroft, *Slave Trading*, illustration facing p. 316.

40. On profits, see Appendix 7.

herself. . . . Negroes have fallen some in Richmond [as a result of Harper's Ferry] but it is only momentarily, say about $100.

By 3 December, however, Thomas was far more anxious, and wrote:

Jack, I look upon it as quite a critical time to be engaged in the Negro trade. Brown no doubt was hung yestidy but the others will not be till 16th, then I believe the whole thing will die away . . . but I am firmly of the opinion that times are growing worse and worse as fast as the moments flee and the sooner we get out of it the better . . . or at least say if our present lot was sold we then could wait till it became more settled. I do not mean to sell any how but I do mean that I would actually take $25 net profit on the head if I could not do better.[41]

As Appendix 6 shows, a recovery in slave prices took place in January 1860 and was maintained until the autumn, when a sharp decline began. On 9 November, a Betts & Gregory trade circular informed speculators: "The election excitement is very intense and doubtless is the cause of the extreme flatness and inactivity of the present and past state of the market. There has been nothing doing for the past 2 or 3 weeks." By 28 December, the Richmond dealers Dickinson & Hill were profoundly pessimistic about the trade, and advised that as a result of "political derangements" and the excessive economic "speculations and extravagancies of the last three years . . . we think for some years to come negroes will not command over $1000 for best men and $800 for best women." Such figures represented a decline of some $500 compared with quotations for mid-1860.[42]

Major economic panics and extreme sectional tensions represented, of course, highly exceptional problems. A little more common were the problems and, indeed, the speculative opportunities brought by disease epidemics. In December 1848, S. A. Browning, trading at Millikin's Bend, Louisiana, reported that as a result of a cholera epidemic planters were not prepared to risk slave purchases. "I could sell if it was not for the excitement about the colria [cholera]. I hope it will blow over soon. If it does not the consequences may be bad." But at the start of the following season he was able to report that, as a result of the cholera epidemic, "the planters has lost a great many negroes and have to replace them"—a good trading season was therefore anticipated.[43]

41. Thomas to Finney, 26 Nov., 3 Dec. 1859, Finney Papers (DU).

42. Betts & Gregory circular, Finney Papers (DU); Dickinson & Hill circular, Dickinson and Washington Papers (DU). For Civil War slave prices, both in inflated Confederate currency and in real value, see Wiley, *Southern Negroes*, pp. 85–98.

43. Browning to Boyd, 26 Dec. 1848, 22 Aug. 1849, Boyd Papers (DU). Comments

Disease epidemics, apart from disturbing demand for slaves, sometimes depleted the trader's stock. It appears, for example, that at Natchez in 1833 Isaac Franklin "lost a great many with cholera" and "has buried 18 at one time." At times of epidemics traders, in fact, would quite often take refuge by insuring or perhaps by vaccinating the slaves they had purchased. Thus, in January 1859, Phillip Thomas wrote to his trading partner that "It is very sickly here [at Richmond] among negroes. One or two dies everyday. I am having all I buy insured." And a few days later he expanded upon his anxieties. "Jack," he wrote,

> I have had all my brains at work now for a week thinking whether to buy any more or not. You know we have money enough to buy a good lot but I tell you that you cannot conceive the amount of sickness here unless you were present. . . . They die daily and I suppose there are at least 60 or 100 sick at this time. Some has actually died on the cars going South. Five or six has died out of Lumpkin's jail, and the worst of it is they die in some 24 hours of being taken. One of our children is very sick this morning. I have sent for the Doctor, but all the grown ones I have had insured as soon as I bought them.

Again in November of that year Thomas talked of insuring his slaves—at "20 or 30 dollars per head." In February 1854, A. J. McElveen was anxious about a smallpox outbreak at Charleston, and urged his partner to "be sure to send to the Rail Road" for a group of slaves being sent—"also please have my negroes vaccinated on arrival" in the city. Too much should not be made of losses through epidemics, however, because (as we have seen in an earlier chapter) in most seasons traders could confidently expect that few if any of their purchases would die before being resold.[44]

Usually the problems of the trader were far less spectacular than epidemics or financial panics. The perennial concerns were the frustrations of delay and competition, problems of getting slaves to "talk up right," and guessing when the season would begin to "close out." By studying market trends and by considering the development of the season, traders had to determine whether to sell quickly at unspec-

---

on the opportunities created by epidemics also occur in Pascal to Raux, 14 Sept. 1832, Pascal Papers (HLH); and Watkins to Watkins, 14 July 1833, Palmore Family Papers (UVA).

44. Thomas to Finney, 24 and 30 Jan., 26 Nov. 1859, Finney Papers (DU); and McElveen to Oakes, 6 and 7 Feb. 1854, Oakes Papers (BPL). For a general discussion of slave insurance, mainly concerning hired, industrial, and specially skilled slaves, see Todd L. Savitt, "Slave Life Insurance in Virginia and North Carolina," *Journal of Southern History*, 43 (1977), pp. 583–600.

tacular prices—or to hold out for top prices and risk being caught by the downturn which quite suddenly set in as the season drew to a close. In fact, the profit margins of the trade (as we shall see) fluctuated considerably from period to period, so that, at times of relatively tight profit margins, the trader had particular reason carefully, and often anxiously, to appraise the state of the market.

The uncertainties and frustrations of the business of slave selling in the Lower South frequently drew comments from traders, and, in their correspondence at least, the speculators' "sacrifices" in the West sometimes reached lofty proportions. During the 1845–46 season, for example, T. W. Burton found the Alabama market "glutted" with traders' gangs, and as a result he found "negroes a perfect dead drag." In March 1846, with ten slaves still on hand, he was "anxious to get home and . . . sick and tired of trading especially in such times as the present." The trade, he reminded a colleague, demanded much "time, patience, and energy." J. K. White wrote in similar terms: "You both know," he lamented, "it requires a man of a great deal of patience to deal in negro property." And J. W. Nelson, on proposing a trading partnership, wrote: "I am willing to undertake any part of the business except the selling part, as I have a perfect aversion to that." If one were to believe the eulogy that Samuel Logan (for the most part a sleeping partner) proffered his colleague after a successful selling mission, the trader would rise almost to heroic stature! "You certainly have made money on our drove beyond all expectations," he wrote.

> I am very much gratified at your success and feel indebted to you more than will ever be in power to pay. I know but little, but I can well imagine the fatigues, troubles and anxieties you have to go through: if I could, it seems to me that I would not undergo what you do for any consideration. However, nature has so formed us that we can become accustomed to anything.

Such insensitivity, self-congratulation, and deeply racist complacency could hardly be exceeded but, as Part Two of this study will argue, they were routinely equalled by the slaveholding community at large.[45]

45. Burton to Long, 27 Feb., 15 Mar. 1846, 1 Mar. 1845, Long Papers (NCA); White to Oakes and McElveen, 23 Jan. 1855, Oakes Papers (BPL); Nelson to Totten, letter of March 1846, Totten Papers (NCA); Logan to Meek, 6 Nov. 1835, Negro Collection (AU).

Part Two

Slave Trading and the Values of Masters and Slaves

5

Planter Speculation and the Myth of the Reluctant Master

I HAVE so far concentrated on the extent and structure of the trade and on the operations of the agents in the process of speculation, the specialist long-distance traders. Part Two of this study will be concerned with broader issues. It will focus not just on traders, but on the masters who supplied and bought from those agents, on the slaves themselves, and indeed on the essential character of relationships between slaves and masters.

At the core of the paternalist thesis in proslavery propaganda before the Civil War were always the interlinked claims that masters were emotionally attached to their slaves, encouraged the institution of the family among them, and sold slaves (especially to traders) only in the most extreme of circumstances. Such "necessities" might be the indebtedness or death of an owner (and the need to pay creditors or divide estates), or the "need to discipline troublesome slaves." From the outset, however, fundamental problems arise with this line of argument. Given the massive scale of trading which we have observed, we would have to portray southern slavery as a system in chronic disorder, with special "emergencies" and "necessities" spilling out from every farm and village. In reality, the great traffic in slaves stemmed, not from special emergencies, but instead from the fundamental racist insensitivity of most masters, and from their receptiveness to the temptation of making extra profits through sales.

Let us start by trying to set the scale of the slave traffic into the context of individual masters and slaves. Many slaveholders in the South held only one or two slaves, so that, whatever their inclinations, such masters could only occasionally have dealt with the trader. The average slaveholder in the exporting states would, however, at any one time have owned about nine slaves; thus (making approximate allowance for births and deaths) he would have owned about seventeen different individuals over a given decade.[1] Because about 6 percent or more of all Upper South slaves were traded away each decade (see Chapter 2), even the average slaveholder (with a fairly small number of slaves, and many of them either too old or too young to be well suited for the trade) must, typically, have sold to the trader about once in every ten or twelve years. Furthermore, since the average Upper South slave lived on a holding of about forty slaves, the owner of the typical slave in that region would, on average, have sold a slave to the trader about once every three years.[2]

In a vital sense, however, the situation for the slave was even more threatening than these initial figures suggest. As we know, it was principally teenagers and young adults who were the victims of the trade. In practice, then, masters can be seen as waiting for numbers of their slaves to reach these most valuable years and then selling them off. For slaves, therefore, the risk of being sold rose dramatically in this period of their lives, and in looking at masters the real judgment to be made should perhaps concern the rate at which they sold off those slaves who were of most interest to the trader. As we saw in an earlier chapter, the cumulative chance of an Upper South slave being traded away was, over the first forty years or so of his life, as high as about 30 percent. Moreover, there was also a very high rate of *local* sales, at least as high and probably higher than the per capita rate of interregional sales of Upper South slaves. A proportion of these local sales, too, would have been speculative, not involuntary, on the part of the owner.

The patterns of probability and sales just described, from the outset,

1. The census shows that in the South as a whole the mean number of slaves per owner in 1850 was 10.1, but it also reveals a slightly lower figure of about nine for the exporting states. See U.S. Bureau of the Census, *Agriculture in the United States in 1860* (Washington, D.C., 1864), p. 248 (1850) and p. 247 (1860). My calculation allows for the typical holding of nine slaves at the start of the decade and expands it by a 25 percent natural increase (excess of births over deaths) during the decade. Slaves owned at the end of the decade are added to those owned at its start, even if they would have died by its ending.

2. It is often assumed that the typical slave lived on a unit smaller than this, but Daniel Scott Smith, in "Averages for Units and Averages for Individuals within Units: A Note," *Journal of Family History,* 4 (1979), pp. 84–86, seems decisively to have demonstrated the pattern of slaveholdings. He demonstrates that in the South in 1850 "while as many owners had fewer than five slaves as those who owned five or more, the average slave was the property of a master who owned more than forty [in fact owned 40.9] slaves" (p. 86).

make the paternalist thesis of "necessary" sales dubious in the extreme. As we shall see in more detail in Chapter 7, the proslavery school paraded a varied and ingenious array of scapegoats and special circumstances to account for the traffic in slaves. These scapegoats and rationalizations give us important insights into the minds of the slaveholders but reveal little about the actual traffic in slaves. For all slaves growing up in the selling states, the threat of being traded away was very real—indeed, was a fundamental fact of life. From the scale of trading by typical masters, we must judge that they were very likely indeed to involve themselves in slavemongering. The very size of the trade, as I have already noted, makes the dominance of involuntary sales extremely unlikely. But, by using traders' records in conjunction with other sources, we can go further. Several layers of evidence in these sources point to the conclusion that tempting speculative opportunities, not "necessities" and "emergencies," were the overwhelmingly important forces acting upon those who supplied the trader with his abundant stock.

THE TEMPTATION TO SELL

If traders' purchases had come about essentially through the deaths of owners or through public sales for debt, this would surely have been directly reflected in traders' purchasing records. Available bills of sale recording traders' purchases show, however (see Table 5.1), that only about 4 or 5 percent seem to have come from all such sales in combination. In the huge remainder of cases (except for a few sales by trustees), the owner of the slaves (rather than some public official) directly sold to the trader.[3] Slave traders' correspondence collections, by repeatedly referring to private purchases from slaveowners, and by only very occasional references to purchases at judicial sales, support this result. Detailed evidence on judicial sales in Charleston district, South Carolina, also points emphatically to the same conclusion. Although in

3. It is possible that a very slight undercount of purchases from judicial sales occurs in this sample because a few (but less than 1 percent) were bought from other identifiable traders who might in turn have bought from judicial sales. This small exception apart, the count of purchases from judicial sources seems complete since, in signing bills of sale, sheriffs, masters in equity (selling property as a result of certain legal disputes), and administrators and executors of estates can be expected to have indicated the official capacity in which they acted. Any failures to do so would very probably have meant that the bill of sale concerned was not legally binding, and such bills of sale would surely not have been accepted by purchasers.

Table 5.1. Slave traders' sources of purchase as indicated in collections of bills of sale

Trader	Total number of slaves	Source of purchase indicated in bill of sale: Slave owner	Trustee of owner	Probate sale	Sheriff's sale	Master in Equity sale	Recorded as being from judicial sales (%)
Badgett	58	56			2		3.4
Ferguson	35	28		4		3	20.0
Glen	214	201	9	3	1		1.9
Long	100	90		3	5	2	10.0
Pascal & Raux	146	139	1	6			4.1
Robards	71	71					0.0
Total	624	585	10	16	8	5	4.6

Sources: For locations of the manuscript collections concerned, see list of primary sources. These six sets of traders' papers were the only collections located which included substantial files of bills of sale.

absolute numbers the large trading fraternity, in combination, bought many slaves at those sales, purchasing from all sources was so very extensive that individual traders like Ziba Oakes can have bought only a very few percent of their total purchases there. This finding is, moreover, not particularly surprising: as we know, traders sought slaves of selected ages and had a very strong preference for cash purchases. The mixed lots available at judicial sales and the long credit which usually operated there were not well suited to the traders' purposes.[4]

There are also many larger reasons why this result (at least where debt sales are concerned) is unsurprising. The latest and, it seems, decisive round of enquiry into crop production under slavery demonstrates that slave agriculture in both the importing and exporting states was highly profitable.[5] If so, public debtors' sales should not have been numerous enough to account for a major part of the extensive traffic in slaves. Favorable profit ratios in slave agriculture further suggest that the trader

4. On Charleston's sales, see "The Local Market in Slaves," later; for evidence on the prevalence of mixed lots at judicial sales see Chapter 6, and on long credit at such sales see Chapters 2 and 6 (esp. note 5).

5. Fogel and Engerman, for example, concluded that the average annual rate of return for slaveholders was "about 10% on the market price of their bondsmen. Rates of return were approximately the same for investment in males and females. They were also approximately the same across geographical regions" (*Time on the Cross*, Vol. 1, p. 70). Talk of such rates of profit is no longer controversial—see, for example, Paul A. David, Herbert H. Gutman, et al., *Reckoning with Slavery: A Critical Study in the Quantitative History of American Negro Slavery* (New York, 1976)—and Fogel and Engerman assigned, in the Upper South's profits, only a very minor role to returns from slave sales. (Although generally agreeing with Fogel and Engerman about high profit levels, some historians have doubted whether efficiency rather than, for example, monopoly market positions produced slavery's profits.)

would normally have bought from viable ongoing slaveholdings, not from slaveholders selling off to avoid public bankruptcy.[6] Indeed, an intensive study of the trader Tyre Glen's records shows that the overwhelming majority of his purchases at least were from ongoing slaveholdings.[7]

We can go further than this, however, and advance a general rule that the periods of heaviest sales to the trader were precisely those during which, from crop production alone, the Upper South sellers were already enjoying particular success and prosperity. Sales to the trader came, therefore, as very attractive bonuses, rather than as economic necessities. This general rule can be tested against two levels of evidence—first, broad trends in price levels for staples and in trading activity, and, second, detailed data for South Carolina.

I have already shown that the trade dominated interregional movements of slaves both in years of booming prosperity and in periods of more modest advance, and that interregional movement (and hence the trade) was especially vigorous in the 1830s and 1850s. These were predominantly periods of particular prosperity for the Upper South's staples (see Figure 5.1).[8] At this general level, then, the rule holds

6. This contrasts with Fogel and Engerman's claim that sales from ongoing plantations were rare (*Time on the Cross,* vol. 1, p. 54).

7. All of the speculator Glen's bills of sale dating from 1830 to 1837 and headed "Stokes County, North Carolina," or describing the seller as being resident in that county, were examined, and wherever possible the names of the sellers were traced in the county's tax lists. Those records indicate the number of taxable slaves (that is, slaves aged from fifteen to fifty years) owned by each person taxed; of the twenty-eight slave sellers traced at least twenty were the owners of ongoing slaveholdings, and in the year following their documented slave sale still owned taxable slaves. In seven of the eight cases which cannot be shown to have been from ongoing slaveholdings, the owners, immediately before the sale, owned not more than one taxable slave. The twenty-eight slave sellers traced represent a 25 percent sample of extant Glen bills of sale from 1830 to 1837; they suggest that, at the very least, 70 percent of Glen's purchases were from ongoing plantations. (A further eight Stokes County sellers were not traced, mainly because signatures on bills of sales were unclear, or because bills of sale indicated only the seller's surname, whereas tax lists gave more than one resident of that description.) Tyre Glen Papers (DU), and Stokes County List of Taxables, 1830–1837 (NCA).

8. The cotton boom was a major part of the expansion of slavery in the 1830s, but tobacco (the other key staple for much of the slave-exporting area) was also booming. In those hectic years, a contributor to the *Farmers' Register,* in 1836, declared: "Within the last two years, there are men actually attempting, and do really think, that they are going to become rich, immensely rich, from making tobacco who scarcely know a tobacco plant from a mullein plant. . . . It is really amusing to see and to hear such characters speak of what, they say, they can afford to give for rented land, and hired negroes, to make this precious and all-valuable plant. . . .

Whilst I am constrained to ridicule the promiscuous and indiscriminate cultiva-

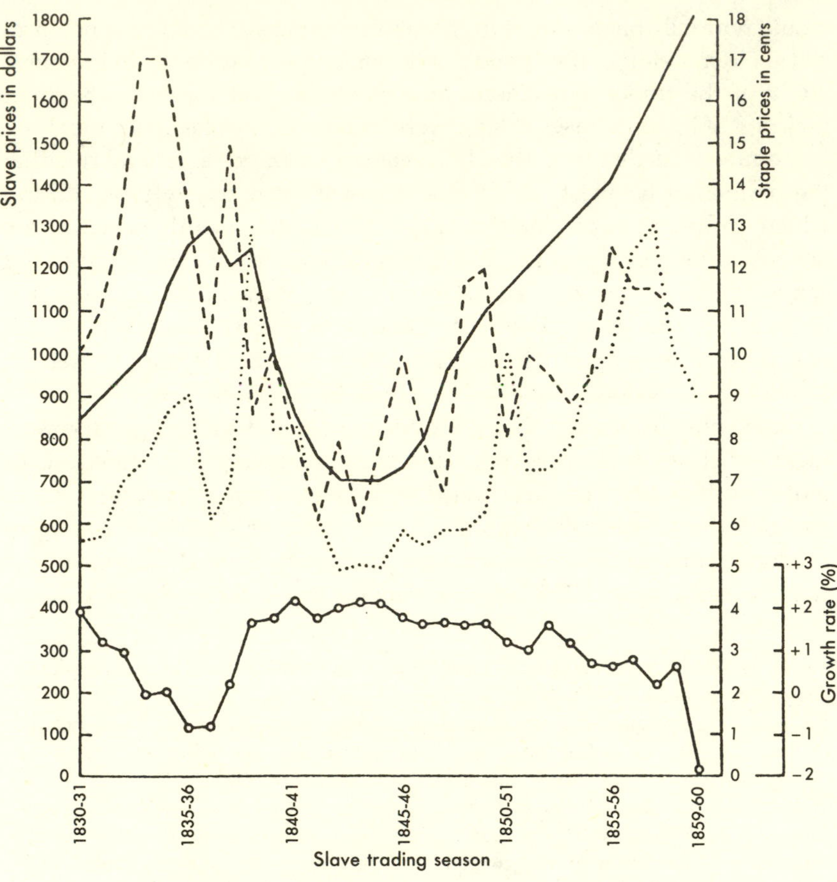

Figure 5.1. Correlation between rate of slave exportation and slave and staple prices. Sources: Cotton, tobacco, and slave prices are from U. B. Phillips, *Life and Labor in the Old South* (Boston, 1929 and 1951), p. 177. Annual growth rates for South Carolina's slave population are calculated from data in South Carolina's *Reports and Resolutions* (SCA). On these rates, see also note 9 in Chapter 5.

---

tion of tobacco, I am fully sensible that there are many, very many planters, getting rich from its cultivation." And Lewis C. Gray, in his standard work on antebellum agriculture, wrote that the 1850s were years not only of very profitable cotton planting but also of massive expansion in tobacco planting, when tobacco growers enjoyed "exceptional prosperity." (*Farmers' Register* [Virginia], vol. 3, p. 711, quoted in Gray, *History of Agriculture*, vol. 2, p. 768; Gray quotation, p. 769).

good. The trade rose with the booming prosperity of the early and mid-1830s, was less active in the generally slower economic activity of the 1840s, and surged forward in the boom of the 1850s. Figure 5.1, however, provides much more accurate data. For South Carolina, a key exporting state, it provides not just general population totals, but a year-by-year profile in the growth rate of the slave population.[9] With these data, the lower the population growth rate, the higher the exportation of slaves. High exportation periods fit very neatly and consistently with years of high and especially profitable staple prices. Slave prices generally responded to staple prices, and in years of growing agricultural prosperity South Carolinians tended to cash in on the extra-buoyant demand for slaves.

Overall, then, the evidence of bills of sale and of exportation rates, together with the general evidence of slavery's profitability, point to the conclusion that the great majority of sales to the trader were not involuntary or reluctant. Essentially, the Upper South seems to have been releasing slaves who were "surplus," in the narrow sense that their work would yield even higher profits in the importing than in the exporting states. When slave price trends were favorable (times when profits from the Upper South's crop production would also have been building up), typical Upper South slaveholders seem to have found it more attractive to sell surplus slaves in return for dramatic profits than to accept a more gradual access of profits by using those slaves to expand crop production at home.[10]

9. Slave population statistics are found in the exhibits of evidence on taxation which the South Carolina Comptroller General presented each September. These exhibits, published in South Carolina's *Reports and Resolutions* (SCA) appear to give a very reliable guide to trends in the state's slave population. Possibly because of a little tax evasion, they consistently produce totals 20,000 or so lower than do the U.S. census figures, but the trend is similar to that of the census, and there seems to be no reason to suggest that any changing fashion in evasion could produce the remarkable year-by-year patterns seen in Figure 5.1. Slave population totals were, in the *Reports* and federal census respectively, (for 1830) 285,430 and 314,401; (for 1840) 303,392 and 327,038; (for 1850) 364,485 and 384,984; (for 1860) 385,689 and 402,406.

South Carolina differed from most other major exporting states in being a cotton rather than a tobacco producer, but Appendix 5, Table A5.2, suggests that its slave growth rates were essentially typical of the principal exporting states.

10. Some slaveholders might, it is true, have sold not for their own direct benefit but perhaps to finance gifts to friends or children. Even here, self-advancement for the owner and his primary group of contacts would have been the ruling influence.

No doubt individual cases of relative poverty or of mismanagement of resources, amid the general prosperity, induced some to sell slaves. William Wright, a Savannah slave dealer, found one "poor" client who aroused his compassion, though his tender feelings seem not to have spilled over to the benefit of the slaves concerned. In sending a slave woman and child to Oakes, he wrote:

> I wish you to do the best you can with them for they belong to a very poor family here who have but little to support them. I think they might bring [$]1200. They are sound and all right.

The dealer's tenderness for his white clients, however, led him to give the further advice that "The woman has been doing pretty much as she pleased and no doubt you will have to whip her to make talk right." Generally, though, clients do not seem to have been in economic circumstances that traders would have considered "difficult." The lack of desperation among sellers is suggested, for example, by the speculator McElveen, who reported a very nice bargain, but added, "I can't buy negroes as low as them without I meet men in a great strain for money." Thus both patterns of private slave purchase and the general context of planter profitability suggest that sales to the trader came essentially, not from distressful emergencies and necessities, but from the temptations of attractive speculative opportunities.[11]

THE LOCAL MARKET IN SLAVES

It is probable that many local sales of slaves were, like the interregional sales, also speculative in character. Such local sales would sometimes have been directly transacted between private individuals, but on many occasions auctioneers and commission agents would have been involved, and on some occasions resident urban dealers (like Ziba Oakes at Charleston) would have resold slaves within the local market. Certainly, the Oakes papers contain scattered letters from local residents who wanted to buy "a woman and child," a "seamstress," a "boy" of a specified age, or who complained that a recent purchase from his depot was unsound, or requested information on the local background of a slave who, after purchase, had run away.[12] Advertise-

11. Wright to Oakes, 28 Mar. 1857, and McElveen to Oakes, 1 Dec. 1854, Oakes Papers (BPL).

12. See, for example, letters in the Oakes Papers (BPL) dated 30 Nov. 1854, 22 Dec. 1854, 4 Oct.1856, 1 Dec.1856, 12 Dec. 1856, 7 Mar. 1857, 31 Jan. 1857, and 16 May 1857.

Table 5.2. Slaves sold in Charleston district judicial sales, 1850–59

Type of sale	No. slaves sold	Bought by identifiable traders (%)
Probate	4,193	9.6
Master in Equity	2,134	17.5
Sheriff	427	8.0
Total	6,754	12.0

Sources: Charleston District Court of Ordinary: Inventories, Appraisals, and Sales (3 ms. vols., 1850–59, SCA); Charleston District Court of Chancery and Equity: Sales Book of James Tupper, Master in Equity (1 ms. vol., 1851, SCA); ms. sales books of H. Skinner (1848–52) and J. C. Rhame (1852–56), sheriffs of Sumter district, S.C. (SCSO). For an explanation of the assumptions underlying these estimates, see Chapter 5, note 14.

ments in local newspapers give indications of great numbers of both judicial and nonjudicial local sales. Individual court sales, often of whole estates, could involve anything from one or two slaves to a hundred or more, but so too could noncourt sales. Noncourt sales, of all sizes, seem to have occurred sometimes simply to raise money, but also, for example, when an older planter decided to sell up and retire, or when an heir to an estate, perhaps living far away, decided against taking up new planting duties.[13]

It is somewhat easier to quantify the local level of court sales than to count local noncourt sales. Both, although with important variations in the level of incidence, would have brought divisions of families and arbitrary upheavals (see Chapter 6). Charleston district, South Carolina, provides a convenient basis for attempting a count of such sales. As Table 5.2 indicates, the combined total of these Charleston district sales was (in the 1850s) about 6,750 slaves; identifiable traders picked up about 12 percent.[14] By assuming that per capita rates of planter

13. For correspondence on a substantial noncourt local sale (of fifty-nine slaves), see letters of James H. Hammond to W. R. Hodgson, 16 Nov. 1846, 24 Jan. 1847, James H. Hammond Papers (DU). For numerous large noncourt local sales, see Alonzo J. White List Book of Negroes for Sale (SCHS).

14. The records used—bound volumes compiled by clerks of the relevant courts—are considered fully representative of sales during the period covered. For both probate sales (1850–59) and sales by James Tupper, Master of Equity (Oct. 1851 to Dec. 1859) records were continuous; the Tupper results were slightly expanded to take account of the whole decade. Charleston district, representing the First Circuit of the South Carolina Court, was in the 1850s concurrently served by *two* masters in equity; both, as a result of court cases, held regular sales of slaves and of other property. I assumed that Tupper and his colleague accounted for equal numbers of sales. Charleston district records of sheriff's sales do not survive for the 1850s; the estimate

mortality (and therefore probate sales) and of sales for debt and other judicial purposes were similar across the South, one can arrive at broad estimates of judicial sales, without insisting on a high degree of accuracy.[15] Charleston district represented about 10 percent of the state's slave population; I suggest, therefore, that in the 1850s South Carolina saw about 67,500 slaves sold at judicial sales. Making allowance for purchases by identifiable traders (12 percent) and for unidentified traders and out-of-state purchasers (probably at most another 8 percent), one can conclude, very approximately, that private local residents may have bought some 54,000 slaves at the state's judicial sales; thus in this sample decade South Carolina's judicial sales to local private individuals were about 30 percent greater than purchases (from all sources) by traders in that state.[16]

Combining, then, local and interregional sales statistics, it seems likely that slaves in South Carolina and across the exporting states generally in the 1850s had at least about a 14 percent chance of being sold through the interregional trade or through local judicial sales.[17] If we allow for nonjudicial local sales the figure would rise, probably to 17 percent or a little higher.[18] Over a lifetime, then, the cumulative

---

was based on the records (and population size) of Sumter district, S.C.

15. Charleston District was mainly rural, but about one third of its slaves lived within Charleston city. The mortality rate for city-based slaveowners (and hence the rate of probate sales) might have been slightly higher than for rural owners, and perhaps urban factors slightly increased economic risks (and hence court sales for debt). These possible biases are, however, not likely to be of an order which would have made this district greatly different from the general pattern.

16. An allowance of 8 percent for unidentified traders and out-of-state purchasers is probably too generous. If so, the effect will be to undercount sales to local nontraders and thereby to undercount local sales in general. The 30 percent figure attributes 39,000 slaves, or 60 percent of the decade's interregional movement from South Carolina (see Table 2.1), to the trade.

17. These estimates are based on exportation and trading rates calculated in Chapter 2.

18. The ratio of court to noncourt local sales is hard to determine with confidence, but newspaper advertisements give valuable clues. The very large number of South Carolina newspapers consulted for the 1850s (see Chapter 2) suggest that about 30 percent of slaves advertised principally for the local market were offered at noncourt sales and the rest at court sales. Some notes of explanation should be added. In South Carolina at this time traders would only very rarely have advertised to sell slaves; their advertisements were to buy slaves. Some of the slaves advertised in the sample with which we are concerned would have been picked up by traders rather than by locals, but the terms of sale and the types of slave offered suggest that this would have been a small percentage. Traders, then, do not seem greatly to complicate the data. It seems likely that the advertisements would have been a very reliable guide to

chances of being sold would have been high in all regions, and in the exporting states it would have been quite rare to have survived into middle age without being sold locally or interregionally.

THE QUESTION OF "SLAVE BREEDING"

There is a long tradition, stemming especially from abolitionist polemics, that the speculative system of the Upper South was carried to its ultimate obscenity: slave breeding. Abolitionists frequently claimed that in the exporting states agriculture was exhausted, and that those states survived economically only through a deliberate system of breeding slaves for sale to the Lower South. In the 1830s, Robert Finley of the American Colonization Society wrote a brief summary of this claim:

> In Virginia and other grain growing states, blacks do not support themselves, and the only profit these markets derive from them is, repulsive as the idea may justly seem, breeding them, like other live stock for the more southern states.

And in 1841 the American Anti-Slavery Society outlined its view of the Upper South slaveholder. Typically, it was suggested, he

> selects his "breeders," he encourages licentiousness, he rewards amalgamation, he punishes sterility, he cooly calculates upon the profits of fecundity,

---

court sales. Master of Equity and sheriffs' sales were conducted directly by the public officials concerned and the nature of these sales was clearly advertised; probate sales were conducted by auctioneers and dealers and not by public officials but the consistent practice seems to have been to advertise them specifically as "estate sales." The class of sales most likely to have been undercounted by a survey of advertisements is that of local noncourt sales, some of which were probably conducted between neighbors without making use of newspaper advertisements. To allow for this, the share of noncourt local sales compared to local court sales is raised to 40 percent.

One source suggests, at first sight, that this might be a gross underestimate of local noncourt sales. In a sample of some 5,400 slaves for whom 1850s bills of sale were filed with South Carolina authorities, noncourt sales seem actually to have comprised 75 percent of these overwhelmingly local sales (Bills of Sale, Miscellaneous Records of the Secretary of State's Office, Misc. R., 1847–1862, vols. 6D 149 onwards, SCA). It is clear, however, that these publicly filed sales represent only a tiny fraction of the 1850s sales actually completed in South Carolina, and they seem to represent a skewed sample. An unusually high proportion were complicated transactions (involving several parties, trustees, gifts), and perhaps with these there was a particular concern to have the transactions clearly established with the state officials. Perhaps with court sales, which would already have had some official documentation, there was relatively less concern to have bills of sale publicly filed.

takes vengeance for miscarriages and holds mothers accountable for the continued life and health of their offspring. On the head of the new born child he sets its future price. He trains it in premeditated ignorance, he feeds it for the same purpose for which he feeds his swine—for the shambles. From the day of its birth he contemplates the hour he shall separate it from the mother who bore it . . . and when that hour comes . . . no entreaties or tears can surprise him into pity. The mother's frenzied cry, the boy's mute look of despair, move him not. He tears them asunder, handcuffs the victim, and consigns him to the *soul driver.*

And, the Society continued, the master habitually imposes his brutal lust upon his slave woman, for his licentiousness

is both a passion and a [business] pursuit. . . . especially since the mixed blood demands a considerably higher price than the pure black.[19]

The abolitionists were not usually specific about the way that this "breeding system" worked, but sometimes their claims have been interpreted in terms of a widespread system of "stud farms" employing a few selected prime males and perhaps a considerable number of "breeding" females. Understood in this sense, the breeding thesis does not seem credible. Had such a system operated widely, a viable slave family and community would surely have been impossible, and yet studies from the 1960s onward have developed impressive evidence of such social institutions.[20] Certainly, masters may very often have forced the pairing of individual slaves, have sexually abused female slaves, and have entertained an almost universal enthusiasm for vigorous natural increase (and hence capital growth) among their slaves. Speculators, as with animals, referred to their slave gangs as so many "head" of Negroes, and closely inspected every detail of their physical makeup. In a sense, the Upper South was like a stock-rearing system, in that a proportion of the natural increase of its slaves was regularly sold off. But these sold off were not infants, nor were they the product of an extensive system of deliberately organized stud farms. Moreover, slaves took a far more positive role in developing their family and community lives than a system of "stud farms" would allow.

Before we can properly dismiss notions of slave breeding, though, we should look more closely at the key claims involved: that the Upper

19. R. S. Finley, quoted in [T. D. Weld (ed.)], *American Slavery As It Is: Testimony of a Thousand Witnesses* (New York, 1839), pp. 182–83; American Anti-Slavery Society, *Slavery and the Internal Slave Trade,* pp. 25, 42, 31. On "slave breeding" see also, for example, *Slavery As It Is,* pp. 15–16, 39, 85, 184–87; Philo Tower, *Slavery Unmasked,* pp. 54–56; and Dumond, *Antislavery,* pp. 68–70, 324.

20. On these issues, see Chapters 6 and 8, below.

South (more than the Lower South) deliberately concentrated on breeding, and that this process involved stud farms. The principal support by historians for these kinds of hypotheses has come from articles of 1958 by Conrad and Meyer and 1975 by Richard Sutch. In Conrad and Meyer's article two main lines of argument were advanced: first, that there were, in the Upper South, remarkably high fertility ratios (suggesting, they argued, successful "breeding") and, second, that in those states the price of female slaves (potential breeders) was especially high. Sutch added to these the observations that, among exported slaves from the Upper South, males were 7 percent more numerous than females (suggesting, he maintained, a desire to retain "breeding" females). Further, he argued from census evidence that a number of probable cases of breeding farms had been located.[21]

Other historians have cited the testimony of exslaves who, when interviewed in the 1930s, reported their own experience of "breeding farms." Thus Elige Davison, who some seventy years earlier had been a slave in Virginia, told his interviewer:

> I been marry once 'fore freedom, with home weddin'. Massa, he bring some more women to see me. He wouldn't let me have jus' one woman. I have 'bout fifteen and I don't know how many children. Some over a hunerd, I's sho'.

And when aged over ninety years, Jeptha Choice, born in Texas in 1835, told his interviewer that his master in slavery times had been

> mighty careful about raisin' healthy nigger families and used us strong, healthy young bucks to stand the healthy nigger gals. When I was young they took care not to strain me and I was as handsome as a speckled pup and was in demand for breedin'. Later on we niggers was 'lowed to marry and master and missus would fix the nigger and gal up and have the doin's [wedding celebrations] in the big house.[22]

21. See A. H. Conrad and J. R. Meyer, "The Economics of Slavery in the Ante-Bellum South," *Journal of Political Economy,* 66 (1958), pp. 95–122; Richard Sutch, "The Breeding of Slaves for Sale and the Westward Expansion of Slavery, 1850–1860," in S. L. Engerman and E. D. Genovese (eds.), *Race and Slavery in the Western Hemisphere: Quantitative Studies* (Princeton, 1975), pp. 173–210. One of the more influential studies to accept the slave-breeding hypothesis has been Gunnar Myrdal, *An American Dilemma: The Negro Problem and Modern Democracy* (New York, 1944,1964), vol. 1, pp. 121–22. See also Dumond, *Antislavery,* pp. 68–70 for support of this hypothesis. D. Lowenthal and C. G. Clarke discussed and rejected the notion of slave breeding on the West Indian island of Barbuda in "Slave Breeding in Barbuda: The Past of a Negro Myth," in V. Ruben and A. Tuden (eds.), *Comparative Perspectives of Slavery in New World Societies,* (New York, 1977), pp. 510–35.

22. Davison and Choice exslave narratives recorded by the Federal Writers Project

None of the evidence from Conrad and Meyer, Sutch, or the slave narratives seems, however, to establish the existence of a widespread system of stud farms or a regional specialization in breeding. The high fertility ratio of the exporting states is in fact explained, not by a regional promotion of fertility, but rather by the impact of the interregional trade (and in particular by the system of selling teenagers and young adults at a far more intensive rate than young children). Similarly, the male bias in the trade is explained, not by any Upper South concern to retain a surplus of female slaves, but by the special demand for males in the sugar area of Louisiana. The evidence for a relatively smaller proportionate gap between female and male prices in the Upper South as against the Lower South turns out to be very sketchy, with no reliable sample of data. Sutch's ingenious work, from the Parker-Gallman data base of census evidence, also seems ultimately to be unconvincing. From a sample of 2,600 slaveholdings, he identified 47 "possible breeding farms," where there were disproportionately high numbers of women and children in relation to men. Using such a large sample it was not, however, especially surprising to find a number of unusual demographic combinations. Such mixes can be explained simply by other factors than deliberate slave breeding—the residence of some husbands on neighboring plantations, or the inclusion in the small slaveholdings concerned of several female domestics. Again, no decisive regional concentration was shown, since twenty out of the forty-seven possible cases of breeding were actually in the *importing* states. Moreover, the suspected breeding units actually showed *below* average fertility ratios.[23] The evidence in the slave narratives might sometimes have represented boastful exaggerations of former youthful days, and, significantly, narrative reports of something like breeding farms seem to be very rare. Not only that, when they do occur (as in the case of Jeptha Choice, born in Texas) they are not confined (just as Sutch's possible farms were not) to the so-called breeding states.

---

and cited in George P. Rawick, *From Sundown to Sunup: The Making of the Black Community* (Westport, Conn., 1977), p. 88, introductory volume to G. P. Rawick (ed.), *The American Slave: A Compositive Autobiography.*

23. In his forty-seven farms, the average ratio of slave children (0–14 years) to slave women (15–44 years) was 2,055 per thousand. In the southern slave population as a whole, the ratio, according to the 1850 census, was 2,267 children per thousand. The Parker-Gallman data (from the 1860 manuscript census) is described, for example, in Robert E. Gallman, "Self-Sufficiency in the Cotton Economy of the Ante-Bellum South," *Agricultural History,* 44 (1970), pp. 5–23.

There is a wider and more basic set of reasons that a broad system of stud farms and regional specialization in breeding seem untenable hypotheses. The abolitionists seem, all along, to have exaggerated the economic difficulties of the exporting states. Agricultural production there does seem to have yielded healthy profits, so that economic survival was not usually based essentially on the selling of slaves (this point is taken further in a later section of this chapter). It is also abundantly clear that the interregional trade did not want substantial numbers of very young children (except in units of mother and offspring). The age structure of the trade means, therefore, that any slave-breeding farms would have had to wait at least eight to ten years for their human "crop" to become readily saleable. Such a time lag would surely have had few parallels in antebellum enterprise. And in the meantime the agricultural unit (dominated by women and children) would have been impossibly inefficient. What the trade did demand was teenagers and young adults, not isolated infants. Moreover, as we have seen, when young infants were bought they were accompanied by their mothers—a circumstance which would have cut short any specialist breeding plans. Had stud farms been at all common they would surely have been mentioned in traders' correspondence, but this source, too, fails to provide support for the stud farm thesis. No mention of breeding farms has been found in the many hundreds of traders' letters consulted.

THE BREEDING THESIS AND LIGHT-SKINNED SLAVES

Abolitionists also claimed that light-skinned blacks commanded particularly high prices, so that the sexual abuse of female slaves by masters and overseers was "both a passion and a [business] pursuit." It seems undeniable that very many cases of such abuse occurred, but the claim concerning light-skinned slaves was correct only for a minority of cases. Certainly, J. A. Bitting, writing to the trader Tyre Glen, considered that "black negroes were more desirable and saleable and freer from disease" than "yellow" slaves. The slave dealer Silas Omohundro, in a report on the Richmond market, quoted prices for "second class and yellow women" and, although he quoted no price for black females, his market report suggests a price differential between black and "mulatto" or "light mulatto" women. And this impression is reinforced by trade reports such as that of Hector Davis, which, in January 1860, quoted Richmond prices for "best young men" and "best *black* girls." The report ran:

Our Negro market is very brisk indeed at this time. In fact good young men are as high or higher than I ever saw them. Best young men 19–24 years bring 1550–1650. Best black girls 16–20 1450–1475. If you can bring any good negroes I would advise you to do so.[24]

What did operate, though, was a market in so-called "fancy girls"—usually light-skinned black women, commanding extremely high prices. Thus, while the prices of light-skinned blacks were generally below those of darker skin, light-skinned "fancy women" proved to be the great exception. In the 1830s Ethan Andrews, collecting information on the slave trade in the southern states reported:

A gentleman who has conversed much with slave traders tells me that, though mulattos are not so much valued for field hands, they are purchased for domestics, and the females to be sold for prostitutes.

And typical of many traders was R. M. Owings, who told a Charleston slave supplier that he was "at all times" interested in buying "all likely and handsome fancy girls . . . if they can be got at reasonable prices." Correspondence relating to the Richmond market quite frequently refers to the sale of "fancies," usually described as "bright" or "brown skinned girls" and selling some 30 percent and often more above the price of "No.1" field girls of the same age.[25]

One instance which, in some ways, with its remarkably callous attitude to offspring, fits the abolitionist theory of "passion and business" was that of the slaveholder Ephraim Christopher. The judge in a South Carolina court case of 1854—partly, no doubt, because it blurred the notion of "white supremacy"—deplored the octogenarian Christopher's "depraved appetite for the society of the wench [Maria]." And

24. Bitting to Glen, 5 Nov. 1857, Glen Papers (DU); Omohundro to Jordan, 12 Dec. 1853, John A. Jordan Papers (DU); Hector Davis report, 31 Jan. 1860, Richard R. Reid Collection (UVA).

25. Andrews, *Slavery and the Domestic Slave Trade,* p. 166; Owings to Oakes, 24 Dec. 1856, Oakes Papers (BPL). On "fancies" see also Scruggs to Oakes, 20 July 1854, and Otey to Oakes, 20 Mar. 1857, Oakes Papers (BPL). On "fancies" in the Richmond market see Thomas to Finney, 26 July, 22 Oct., and 24 Dec. 1859, Finney Papers (DU); Toler to Ferguson, 15 and 26 Feb. 1859, Ferguson Papers (NCA); and S. & R. F. Omohundro Slave Sales Book (UVA). On "whole baracoons of beautiful slave women . . . kept in any quantity to let to gentlemen for sleeping companions," see Philo Tower, *Slavery Unmasked,* pp. 16–27. In examining New Orleans records, Laurence J. Kotlikoff's valuable study of slave prices found, on average, a premium placed on light-skinned women, with certain anomalies ("Structure of Slave Prices," esp. pp. 515–17). The distinction between field hands and "fancies" in this major urban market might well explain these anomalies.

the court heard evidence that Christopher, at the time of the hearing, was

> living in the same house with the slave Maria [a woman of 37 years], and living with her as his mistress. Her 13 children were all mulattos and supposed to be the children of the complainant. He had been selling one [of the children] almost every year. John Bates senior had purchased four or five of them at the several times when each one of them was about 9 or 10 years, at about $225. . . . The Rev. David Blythe had purchased one of them, and Mr. Cox had likewise purchased one.

The libidinous old slave seller no doubt gained great profit from his dazzling abuse of parenthood, but probably did not gain the spectacular prices of the similarly corrupt market in "fancies."[26]

AN ALMOST UNIVERSAL ENTHUSIASM FOR NATURAL INCREASE FROM "SLAVE PROPERTY"

The observations made so far should not be seen as denying the possibility of a few isolated cases of breeding units, and certainly not of denying slaveholders' very keen interest in natural increase among their slaves. References to enthusiasm for natural increase crop up everywhere in the selling states (but probably just as much in the buying region). An Upper South planter, J. H. Hammond, for example, lamented his lack of success with slave increase. He wrote:

> I have taken more pains to raise young negroes and nurse all than to do anything else. It has been p[reying?] on my mind and I have read, consulted with everyone and spared no exertion—but all in vain. The hand of fate appears to interpose and forbid prosperity to me.

Ziba Oakes often got letters from local clients like the following, asking,

> If Clarissa advertised by you [as] cook and washer is not sold, please inform me by return of her age, color, etc., if a breeding woman, if she has had children or miscarried, and her cash price.

Of another slave, Oakes was asked, "What are the qualifications, character, general appearance of the girl and how many children has she had and what is the lowest price will buy her." The trader Thomas Burton did not mince words in reporting that one of the women he had

26. Greenville District Equity Court (SC), *Christopher* v. *Bates*, 1854, Bill 208 (SCA).

bought had borne a child. He reported that the slave "Barbra" had had a son.

> As regards the cost about this matter it will be triffling. I had no physician with her at all. I had an old negro woman that lives in this place. . . . Thats $100 to your stock[!]

Sometimes, however, the auctioneer Alonzo J. White of Charleston noted problems associated with childbearing. In a sale of T. P. Alston's large gang of slaves he noted numerous slaves "half threated," "three-quarters threated," or afflicted with fallen womb; and listed Binah, age 40, "full hand weakly from breeding fast," Mary, 35, "has bred fast," Silvey, 36, "weakly from fast breeding." Clearly, there was great interest in gynecological conditions and in breeding histories and potential.[27]

That the Lower as well as the Upper South was interested in high natural increase is suggested, for example, by the sex and age structure of the interregional trade. As we have seen, all areas except the sugar region of Louisiana imported equal numbers of males and females. In itself, this suggest a desire for increase. But the ages of the slaves imported give further evidence (see Figure 2.1). With males, the Lower South preferred to import those who were at or near the peak of their physical fitness (especially aged, say eighteen to twenty-four years) and who were able to promise a long career of strenuous labor. The preference in importing females was for those who were rather younger (from early teens to about nineteen or twenty). Such females, as Chapter 6 will emphasize, were already likely to be very effective workers, but had the (presumably decisive) advantage that they were at or near the start of their childbearing years. Trade circulars and traders' correspondence give further evidence that slaveholder interest in natural increase was not especially concentrated in one region. As circulars relating to the Richmond market indicate (see Chapter 3), "woman with first child" was a staple in the export trade, suggesting that, in the importing region as elsewhere, a premium was placed on proven early fertility. Similarly, traders' letters show quite frequent Lower South enquiries about "breeding women"; for example, a client in the buying states enquired from Oakes the prices of "well trained cotton hands, . . . boys from16 to 20 . . . and men from 20 to 35 . . . and young women and breeding women with children."[28]

27. Hammond Diary, 5 Nov. 1841, James H. Hammond Papers (SCL); Sumter to Oakes, 26 Feb. 1853, Wright to Oakes, 29 Nov. 1856, Oakes Papers (BPL); Burton to Long, 13 Feb. 1845, Long Papers (NCA); Alonzo J. White, List Book (SCHS).

28. Cannon to Oakes, 1 Mar. 1857, Oakes Papers (BPL).

In some cases the buying of slaves seems to hint strongly at the forced pairing of the new purchases. A suspicion of this sort arises, for example, when we find the slaveholder G. B. Wallace asking a neighbor to "please be so good as to look out for me a breeding woman under 20 years of age—also a young active man."[29] The probability is, however, that, rather than being hopelessly wrecked by the slave-breeding strategies of masters, the marriage market of slaves was largely run by the slaves themselves. Given the many small slaveholdings within which mates were not available for all adult slaves, and where masters were not prepared to buy mates, it is likely that the slaves themselves had a major role in finding off-plantation partners. Similarly, it is probable that on larger slaveholdings, with a fuller internal marriage market, masters usually found it convenient to leave the slaves to choose their own partners. Such situations would be very far from representing stud farms. Birth rates were high (so too were infant mortality rates), but such high birth rates were almost inevitable in a situation where sex ratios were usually balanced, contraceptive knowledge unscientific in the extreme, and long periods of saving to set up home were not necessary or possible before marriage. Although the sexual abuse of slaves by whites may have been very direct in a numerous minority of cases, the most important disruption of family life among slaves came not with "slave breeding" but, as we shall see, with the forcible separation of a high proportion of families.[30]

PROFITS, MOTIVATION, AND RESPONSIBILITY

The slaveholders of the Upper South were not, then, reluctant sellers to the trader, and the slaveowners of the Lower South must have bought with enthusiasm. The vast majority of Upper South sales were not involuntary debt or probate sales, but private transactions directly undertaken between owner and trader. Sales were most numerous, too, in exactly those periods when returns from agriculture were especially favorable and there was least economic necessity to sell. It might help to put these sales into closer perspective if we now attempt to set their cash value against the value of staple-crop production in the exporting area. The calculations outlined below are approximate but suggest, for the 1830s onward at least, that sales to traders tended to bring to the sellers gross receipts equivalent to about 15 or 20 percent of

29. Wallace to Grinnan, 18 Apr. 1855, Grinnan Family Papers (UVA).

30. For a much fuller discussion of fertility see especially Richard H. Steckel, *The Economics of U.S. Slave and Southern White Fertility* (New York, 1981).

their gross receipts from staple crops. When we consider the evidence which seems firmly to have established the general profitability of antebellum crop production by slaves in all regions, the receipts from the sale of slaves seem to represent very substantial windfall profits—not incomes which were absolutely necessary for the economic survival of slavery in the exporting states.

Calculations of the slaveowner's receipts from the sale of slaves are presented in some detail in Appendix 5, and here I shall simply note the basic procedures involved and the results produced. In order to make these calculations, I needed information on several factors: slave prices according to age, sex, and date; the composition and volume of the trade; and the volume and value of staple-crop production in the region. We already have detailed evidence on the scale of the trade and on slave prices, and data on staple prices are quite readily available. The remaining evidence—statistics on staple crop production—is available in federal censuses for the crop years 1839–40, 1849–50, and 1859–60, and my calculations focused on those three sample years.

The results of my calculations are summarized in Table 5.3; they are based on attributing 60 percent of interregional slave movements to the trade, and estimating values for tobacco, rice, sea-island cotton, and short-fiber cotton. As Table 5.3 suggests, the sale of slaves to the trade appears in 1839–40 to have been equivalent in value to about 20 percent of the value of staple-crop production in the region, and the percentages for 1849–50 and 1859–60 seem to have been, respectively, about 16 and 15 percent. Of course, had we included the value of livestock production and food crops generally, the relative value of slave sales would have been much lower.

What significance should we attach to these results? Firstly, of course, they are approximations, are for sample years only, and do not deal with the experiences of individual owners and slaves. In one sense—but that not the most important, if we are to consider attitudes and relationships between masters and slaves—we could say that such sales were merely part of the inevitable expansion of the frontier or even of the world-economic system. After all, Europe and New England's demand for cotton was the great spur to much of the expansion of American slavery, and cotton in turn yielded those cheap consumer goods which were so important for industrial takeoff in many newly industrializing areas. Planters were caught up in a wider economic system.[31] Some, like U. B. Phillips (who would have had little enthusi-

31. In talking of something like a world-economic system, I have particularly in

Table 5.3. Value of sales to the trader compared with value of staple-crop production in the principal exporting states

Year	Value of staple crops ($ million)	Value received from sale of slaves to trader ($ million)	Value of slave sales as % of value of staple crops
1839–40	$31.82	$6.24	19.6
1849–50	$29.98	$4.84	16.1
1859–60	$60.32	$9.26	15.4

Sources: Values for staple crops are derived from Gray, *History of Agriculture*, vol. 2, pp. 765, 1031; and A. H. Cole, *Wholesale Commodity Prices in the United States, 1700–1861* (Cambridge, Mass., 1938). Basic evidence on slave prices is derived from a manuscript price scale in the Richard R. Reid Papers (UVA). Details on slave prices appear below in Appendices 5 and 6.

Note: The "principal exporting states" are here defined as Delaware, Kentucky, Maryland, the Carolinas, Virginia, and the District of Columbia.

asm for notions of a "world-capitalist system" or for talk of relationships between "core" and "periphery") might set the seller's role in another context. In Phillips's view, slaveholders were acting in the best interests of their slaves when they found ways of moving them from the "wornout" lands of the exporting states to the "richer opportunities" of the importing region. Population growth and pressure on resources, he suggested, were eased by westward expansion. Phillips, the classic spokesman for the old-style paternalist concept of slavery, would, of course, have seen planter migration and not the trade as the key to expansion. He would also have attributed trading, to a great extent, to "economic hardships" bearing upon masters.[32]

We could, then, from more than one ideological position dilute the slaveholder's personal responsibility for the selling of slaves and see him as part of a wider system. Phillips's formulation goes against evidence on the trade which we have already presented, and his approach cannot be accepted. But a world-system analysis, a very different sort of concept, can be of great interest in pointing to long-run economic and social tendencies. In considering day-to-day attitudes of masters, however, such broad approaches can form only

---

mind work by Immanuel Wallerstein and by Genovese and Fox-Genovese. See, for example, I. Wallerstein, "American Slavery and the Capitalist World-Economy," in his *The Capitalist World Economy* (Cambridge, U.K., 1979), pp. 202–21; E. D. Genovese, *The World the Slaveholders Made* (New York, 1969), esp. Part 1; Elizabeth Fox-Genovese and E. D. Genovese, *Fruits of Merchant Capital: Slavery and Bourgeois Property in the Rise and Expansion of Capitalism* (Oxford, 1983).

32. See Phillips, *American Negro Slavery*, pp. 203, 401; Phillips, *Life and Labor in the Old South* (Boston 1929, 1951), pp. 215–16.

part of the process of establishing the context within which individual attitudes were formed and decisions made. Long-term tendencies helped to set up circumstances of special advantage which planters, individually and collectively, would find ways of legitimizing for their own benefit and security. Slaveowners, after all, were at least as free as any other individuals to decide what values they would develop within their own economic system.

My present concern is with the attitudes of antebellum planters toward their slaves: were those attitudes essentially humane and paternalist or speculative and profit-maximizing? The circumstances in which planters sold slaves—when they were not under severe economic pressure, and when sales merely formed substantial supplements to already viable incomes—strongly indicate speculation. An even closer test, though, is the *manner* in which they sold their slaves, whether separately or in families. As the next chapter will demonstrate, the tendency was overwhelmingly toward breaking up families for speculative profit. Economic self-interest combined with profound racism to make this practice possible. Later chapters suggest that the racism of most masters was so profound that they saw black families as ephemeral concerns and blacks' emotions and thoughts as infantile or even bestial, and thus found it easy to regard themselves as paternalists. Their "paternalism," however, was essentially that of white-supremacists who easily convinced themselves that the white presence alongside blacks would be civilizing and beneficial to the latter, regardless of the form that presence took.

6

Family Separations and the Lives of Slaves and Masters

FROM the outset, this study has emphasized that any broad theory of master–slave relationships in antebellum America must either take careful account of family separations or rest upon treacherous foundations. For such relationships, it surely mattered crucially whether the forcible separation of families was kept to a minimum by a protective white community or, at the other end of the spectrum, was the ready resort of a society ruled by crude, uncomplicated impulses of economic self-interest. The evidence of the trade strongly suggests that we should not simply take some compromise middle position along the spectrum of possible interpretations. Instead, it indicates, for the substantial majority of slaveholders, an easy resort to self-interest, sale, and separation.

It is certainly important, particularly for the slave experience, to examine changes over time and according to place. Indeed, we should consider separations as a cycle of experiences bearing upon slaves in different ways over the period of their lives. With masters, we shall need to consider variations relating to the number of slaves held (and, in later chapters, according to a range of owners' attitudes). But the fundamentally important feature of the trade was that, each decade, it carried hundreds of thousands of slaves, mostly children and slaves of marriageable age, and yet virtually no child was traded with its father, nor wife sold with her husband. There were, as we shall see, "sound" trading and slaveholding reasons for this remarkable process of destruction, which left slaves and the slave community the awful task of repairing and restarting lives—a task made possible by the nature of the cycle of separations. At the same time, these processes of wilful destruction by owners and creative repair by victims would have daily yielded the slaves material with which to judge their masters.

EVIDENCE FOR THE STUDY OF FAMILY SEPARATIONS

There are still few quantitative studies of separations; the 1974 study by Robert Fogel and Stanley Engerman is, like all their work, interesting and challenging. Their data base was an extensive collection of New Orleans bills of sale; their method was to make a count of marriage separations (based on bills of sale showing mothers sold with offspring but without husbands), and to supplement it by a count of child separations (records showing a child sold without either parent). From these investigations they concluded that rather few forcible separations occurred. I have shown, however, that the New Orleans trade was atypical, carrying exceptionally low proportions both of children and of women, so that, even with the method which Fogel and Engerman adopted, data on markets other than that of New Orleans might yield very different results. Furthermore, the use of mother-and-offspring lots does not reveal, for *any* market, the full extent of the forcible separation of spouses. Many women sold without husbands and (for reason of infertility, child mortality, or child sale) without children might also have been parted from their husbands by the trade. Many of the vast numbers of "single" men who dominated the New Orleans trade might also have been separated from spouses.[1] It is possible,

1. By their count of mother-and-offspring lots, Fogel and Engerman concluded that at most 13 percent of interregional sales brought marriage separations. Because they considered the extent of the interregional trade to be very small indeed (far less important than planter migrations), they suggested that the total interregional movement destroyed only 2 percent of marriages involved in that process. They estimated, too, that only about 9 percent of New Orleans sales were of children aged under thirteen years and suggested that, instead of being separated from their families by the trade, they could very well already have been orphans before being sold. As for the separation of spouses, they argued that it was by no means clear that the "destabilizing effects of the westward migration on marriages was significantly greater among blacks than it was among whites." (*Time on the Cross,* vol. 1, pp. 49–52; vol. 2, pp. 48–51.)

As I noted earlier, however, the trade generally sold virtually no slaves in husband-and-wife units. The New Orleans trade was dominated (some 50 percent) by men of marriageable age sold alone; how many were husbands forcibly separated from wives? When we add to this Fogel and Engerman's children sold separately, and mothers and offspring sold without fathers, a hugely different view of the New Orleans market from that given in *Time on the Cross* becomes possible and, indeed, very probable.

furthermore, to refine and extend the categories to be employed in searching bills of sale and other documents for indications of forcible separation.[2]

Apart from records of the New Orleans trade, two other types of primary sources, marriage certificates and slave narratives, have been emphasized in recent work on separations. Both sets of sources, in different ways, focus on the perspectives of slaves. At the ending of the Civil War, former slaves recorded marriage certificates with army and Freedman's Bureau officials. These documents registered both new marriages and unions dating back far into slavery, and they frequently reported the forcible separation of previous partnerships by masters. In his very detailed work on the Mississippi certificates (concerning almost 9,000 slaves), Herbert Gutman found that about 17 percent of all registrants of new or continuing marriages reported that a previous union had been forcibly broken by a master during slavery. With slaves fifty years and over, who would have had a fuller and more representative exposure to the long-run risk of separation, the reported rate of forcible separations rose to 23 percent.[3] The narratives of exslaves comprise vast and varied sources of evidence on family life and often strongly emphasize the bitter experience of separation.[4]

2. Laurence Kotlikoff examined the same sample of New Orleans records as Fogel and Engerman, but concluded that most of the 77 percent of slaves who were sold there without relatives would in fact have had living relatives and therefore would have suffered family separations (Kotlikoff, "Structure of Slave Prices," pp. 512–15). Donald Sweig emphasizes the possibility of separation where women of marriageable age were sold in that market without offspring or husband ("Reassessing the Human Dimension of the Inter-State Trade," *Prologue*, 12 [1980], pp. 11–12, 17; "Northern Virginia Slavery: A Statistical and Demographic Investigation," unpublished Ph.D. dissertation, William and Mary College, 1982, pp. 211–57). Sweig deemphasizes the separation of children from parents.

3. Gutman, *Black Family*, pp. 144–52. A few years earlier, John Blassingame, in *The Slave Community: Plantation Life in the Antebellum South* (New York, 1972), pp. 89–92, made a less detailed but important pioneering study of these and similar records, and found an even higher rate of forcible separations (27–39 percent overall, depending on locality). On differences between Gutman and Blassingame's results, see Gutman, *Black Family*, p. 569n, and Blassingame, pp. 148–49 in Al-Tony Gilmore (ed.), *Revisiting Blassingame's 'The Slave Community': The Scholars Respond* (Westport, Conn., 1978).

4. Stephen C. Crawford, "Quantified Memory: A Study of the WPA and Fisk University Slave Narrative Collections," unpublished Ph.D. thesis, University of Chicago (1980), has produced very detailed statistical evidence from these records (some is cited later). Paul D. Escott, *Slavery Remembered: A Record of Twentieth-Century Slave Narratives* (Chapel Hill, 1979), provides a valuable overview. Apart from these twentieth-century interviews with former slaves, a great many other pub-

Especially for details on particular points, this chapter will draw upon the studies mentioned, but this analysis of separations is based essentially on a different set of records: slave traders' lists, letters, bills of sale, circulars, and accounts. These records allow a broad-based study of separations across the South; because they are derived from traders, they are least likely to exaggerate separations or their psychological effects. Evidence in Chapter 2 allows us to set this material into the context of trading, and therefore permits conclusions about the scale and broad significance of interregional separations.

RATIONALES FOR SEPARATING OR NOT SEPARATING FAMILIES: TRADING AND LOCAL SALES

As far as family separations were concerned, slave selling tended to fall into a series of significant patterns, those of the interregional trade contrasting with some found in local sales. In both local and interregional sales, the predominant forces were the demands of the market and the self-interest of slaveowners; but the interregional trade concentrated on the recruitment of selected slaves of the highest labor efficiency and potential, and that selectivity tended persistently to destroy slave marriages and families. With local sales (especially of substantial gangs that included significant numbers who were of very limited immediate labor value), there was a strong tendency to sell in lots of mixed ages; the effects were to keep quite a high proportion of families together, but also to allow the disposal of individuals who otherwise would have been difficult to sell.

The selective demand of the interregional trade produced a series of key trading categories: young slaves of eight or ten years of age to midteens, mothers with offspring, young females in early womanhood, and prime adult males. These categories quickly translated themselves into a traffic in fragmented families. Such forcible wrecking of families, it might be argued, would have been bad for plantation morale and ultimately uneconomic. The adverse effect on morale is undeniable; but the system of antebellum slavery seems in the great preponderance of cases to have operated, not on a "human relations" philosophy of management, but on the cruder principles of some raw version of "scientific management." Efficient labor units, coupled with a mix of sanctions skewed toward the sharply negative, seem usually to have been the central concepts in the slaveholding system.

---

lished narratives (usually much earlier) also provide very valuable insights into separations and the family life of slaves.

A comparison of sets of records for Charleston district, South Carolina, and Boone County, Missouri, shows something of the main approaches to slave selling within the local market. In all local markets the overwhelming tendency was to sell, not for cash, but for long credit (most often a down payment of about one third, and the balance with interest over one, two, or three years).[5] Extensive Charleston auction records show techniques used in selling large gangs, which were sold mainly in family-based lots of mixed ages. The Missouri data, in contrast, record the sale of small slave units in which, apparently, very high rates of family separations were involved. In both of these seemingly different cases, the logic of the market prevailed.

The Charleston records concern some 3,000 slaves listed in the Hutson–Lee Collection of slave sale handbills and Alonzo J. White's List Book of Negroes for Sale, as well as some 4,000 slaves sold in Charleston district probate sales of the 1850s.[6] The Hutson–Lee and White records were almost exclusively of large gangs, ranging from 40 to 100 slaves, whereas the probate records contained many such gangs as well as slaves sold in smaller lots. With the large sales in these record groups, the very strong tendency was to offer slaves in family lots of mixed ages, set at a "round" or average price per head. The object was not simple altruism, though in individual cases that might have played a role. With large gangs, selling in the round was a virtual necessity: as part of a "family" lot, old, very young, feeble, and other less attractive slaves could be disposed of advantageously. Offered singly, many such slaves would have had a very slow sale indeed. Auctioneers could offer the inducement that the slaves were local, well settled and adjusted; but as James H. Hammond noted to a neighboring planter, "in buying gangs one is obliged to take pensioners and invalids and many others that do not suit."[7] In such sales, some separations would certainly have occurred; 10–15 percent of the Hutson–Lee and White slaves were sold in mother-and-offspring lots (without a father) where the youngest child was under four years of age. But the combined Hutson–Lee and

5. Of 800 slaves listed in James Tupper's Master of Equity Sales Book (SCA) for 1851 to 1859, only 14 percent were sold for cash, 26 percent for half cash and the balance paid in twelve months, and the rest (60 percent) were sold on a credit of two to three years. The credit of the purchasers was secured by personal endorsements by two or three local citizens and by mortgages on the slaves concerned. The same pattern was found overwhelmingly, both in small and large local sales, in advertisements across South Carolina and other states checked.

6. The Hutson–Lee and White records are at SCHS, and the probate records are at SCA.

7. Hammond to W. R. Hodgson, 16 Nov. 1846, James H. Hammond Letters (DU).

White sample shows that 45 percent were bid off in complete father-mother-and-offspring units, sometimes with other relatives added to these groupings. In this sample the average size of the holding being sold was 60 slaves, but a similar result was found in a subsample of 350 slaves held in middling-sized gangs which averaged 20 slaves (with 10 to 30 in each unit). Only about 2 percent of slaves in either the main or the subsample were, it seems, children under fifteen years sold without either parent.

Evidence published by James W. McGettigan for Boone County, Missouri, provides a dramatic contrast. As was almost certainly the case with the Charleston records, the purchasers here were overwhelmingly local.[8] But Boone County was an area of small slaveholders (average size of holding about five or six in the 1850s), and estate and other sales showed much evidence of family separations. McGettigan reported a persistent pattern: the only family units regularly left intact were mothers and very young offspring (under about five or six years of age). From his sample of 1,078 slaves, 322 (30 percent) were children under fifteen who were sold without either parent. As he pointed out, the selling of slave children singly was not simply because the ownership of some families had already been divided by cross-plantation arrangements before the sale in question. Instead, persistently, where a slaveholding comprised a mother, her infants, and certain of her older offspring of about six years and upwards, the owner was likely to sell each of the older children in separate lots. As McGettigan noted, "the evidence appears conclusive that the majority of Boone County slaveowners had little concern for the breakup of slave families. Economic and legal forces usually prevailed over any humanitarian forces in the county [p. 295]." With noncourt sales economic self-interest prevailed, and at court sales this was reinforced by the legal duty of the auctioneer to gain the highest possible price.[9]

To some extent, the Boone County results might be explained by the

8. James W. McGettigan, "Boone County Slaves: Sales, Estate Divisions, and Families, 1829–1865," *Missouri Historical Review,* 72 (1978), pp. 192–97, 281–95. McGettigan's sample was of about 1,100 slaves sold in Boone County, mainly at probate sales, from 1820 to 1864. He checked each purchaser against Boone County census lists, the county's Probate Court Index, and the subscriber lists for the local *Missouri Statesman,* and found 98 percent to be locals. Sample checks on South Carolina probate records produced similar results (but buyers are not indicated for the Hutson-Lee and White records).

9. See also C. L. Mohr, "Slavery in Oglethorpe County, Georgia, 1773–1865," *Phylon,* 33 (1972), p. 12; E. W. Phifer, "Slavery in Microcosm: Burke County, North Carolina," *Journal of Southern History,* 28 (1962), pp. 89–90.

possibility that, in a county of small slaveholding units, there might not have been sufficient demand for buying more than one or two slaves at one time. But this is at best a partial explanation. What was more important, it seems, was the type of slave group to be disposed of at a sale. The large South Carolina gangs, with many "quarter hands" and nonworkers, were suited to selling "in the round," but other slaves in the same area might be sold to greater advantage if divided. Thus we find a handbill of the Charleston auctioneer Richard Clagett offering for sale:

> A valuable Negro woman, accustomed to all kinds of house work. Is a good plain cook, an excellent dairy maid, washes and irons. She has four children, one a girl 13 years of age, another 7, a boy about 5, and an infant 11 months old. Two of the children will be sold with the mother, the others separately if it best suits the purchaser.[10]

The point here, as with many small lots which appeared in Charleston probate sales, was that the older children were sufficiently marketable to be offered singly and at the same time there would be no damaging effect on the sale of the remaining slaves. Market forces, rather than sentiment for family, were apparently always likely to predominate with slaveowners.

Local sales, then, produced a mixed picture. The typical 1850s southern slave (as Chapter 5 showed) lived on a holding of just over forty slaves, so that for most the chance of separation at local sales was more likely to approach the pattern suggested in the Hutson–Lee and White sample and subsample than the Boone County pattern. Buyers at these sales were local (98 percent in the Boone County case were from within that county), so that often the separate sale of family members locally would still allow family life to continue in an amended form. But even local sales could sometimes impose so much physical distance between family members that in practice it brought an end to family life. And this destruction could occur not just with the initial division of families, but also in cases where previously viable cross-plantation families were rendered nonviable by a further sale.

Local sales, clearly, posed serious hazards for the slave family; they reflect very badly on the priorities which slaveholders put on the slave's family sentiments as opposed to the master's convenience and economic self-interest. Nevertheless, such sales were in general not so systematically oriented toward separation as was the interregional

10. Clagett handbill, 5 March 1833, Richard Clagett Papers (SCL).

trade; later evidence will suggest indeed, that the greatest fear among slaves was long-distance sale by the trade. Later in this chapter, in a calculation of total family separations (combining local and long-distance), the weighting given for local separations will be a very tentative estimate of that proportion of separations from local sales which in effective made family contact impossible.

The selling pattern just described meant that very often sales geared to the local market were not of prime interest to the slave trader. As Chapter 3 showed, the trader had a very strong preference for buying on cash terms, but local court sales and many noncourt sales were on long credit. Further, the mixed lots offered at many local sales did not suit him. Buying in such circumstances would have yielded too many young children, unsound, weak, or aging slaves. With married slaves, the price which owners set for one partner (considering health, physique, demeanor, whip marks), might seem to the trader excessive, whereas he might happily buy the other partner. Moreover, slave husbands, as we shall see, were often six to ten (sometimes more) years older than their wives; this produced many cases where the speculators found a slave wife a far more attractive trading prospect than her spouse. The disadvantages of buying "family" slaves were quite often reflected in traders' letters, as, for example, when the firm of Cox & Pickard wrote from Savannah, Georgia, apparently after attending court sales.

> I want to buy 10 or 12 Negroes. I am not particular about the kind so [long as] they are young and likely from 14–23. There appears to be a good many negroes here but mostly all in families.

Similarly, in 1855 the trader A. J. McElveen reported that he had been attending court sales in his area but had not bought because the conditions of sale (long credit) did not suit, and neither did the fact that the slaves were to be bid off in lots of mixed ages. He wrote:

> If I cannot buy in the country at prices to suit what will I do. . . . I reckon [that at a recent court sale of a gang of 98 slaves] the negroes sold for 50 to 1500. Young women sold as high as 1200, but few likely fellows single. The most of fellows was in families.[11]

The trader was not being shunned by zealous guardians of the slave family, but simply encountered at these sales a set of practices which were designed to serve the interests of masters and which could sometimes coincide with the well-being of the slaves.

11. Pickard & Cox to Oakes, 7 Jan. 1857, and McElveen to Oakes, 5 Mar. 1855, Oakes Papers (BPL).

WHY SEPARATE FAMILIES IN THE INTERREGIONAL TRADE?

The interregional trade, as we know, was highly selective, and a particularly revealing guide to the categories of slaves in greatest demand comes from the circulars of those major Richmond auction houses (like Betts & Gregory, or Dickinson, Hill & Co.) which specialized in supplying that traffic. These firms were discussed in Chapter 3, where several of their circulars are reproduced (Appendix 6 summarizes many more). Such circulars point to the special categories noted earlier in this chapter. Young slaves from eight or (more usually) ten to about fifteen years are regularly quoted as a staple of the trade. With these slaves, description was sometimes explicitly by age, but was often by height (and sometimes by weight). Thus references often start with "boys 4 feet high" and move up to "boys 5 feet high." Circulars often indicated (as with the Betts & Gregory examples): "Girls of same height as boys, about the same price." Another leading staple comprised "girls 16–22 years"; and a further routinely quoted category was "woman and first child." The "market leaders" were "No.1 men 20 to 25 years of age." Very frequently, special supplementary notes emphasized the importance of bringing in "good quality" and "likely" Negroes, and occasionally a reminder was given that "scrubs" (poor stock) sold badly. Circulars, then, emphasized the dominant staples of the trade and the essential pattern of demand. They usually added, following the listing of key staples, that "other Negroes sell in the usual proportions." We know, from evidence on the age structure of the trade (Chapter 2) that selected "other Negroes" (older than the key age categories cited in circulars) made up some 15 percent of the trade, but older slaves, like younger ones, usually seem to have been carefully and not randomly chosen. The categories of the trade were almost custom-built to maximize forcible separations. A statistical examination of traders' buying and selling records (broadly in line with these staple categories) will allow us to estimate the scale of those separations, but let us first give a little fuller consideration to the significance of the staple patterns in the trade.

We should note, first, that the traffic in young slaves was no casual affair, no mere picking up of makeweight slaves. The vast majority of slaves traded and aged eight to fourteen or fifteen years were purchased alone, and were bought as very deliberately considered acquisitions. Such slaves made up 25 percent of the interregional trade as a whole. They were in demand especially because they were young slaves, full of potential, who were entering or had recently entered their period of very effective work output.[12] Sometimes, perhaps when adults were in short supply through heavy trading, speculators placed special emphasis on the traffic in young slaves. Rees W. Porter of Nashville, Tennessee, wrote to Ziba Oakes of Charleston:

> I am of the opinion that money could be made between your city and this . . . if a man could buy small negroes say girls from 9–14 and ploughboys and women with one or two children, young women. . . . Brown and Bulger . . . are sending me negroes of that description and I suppose doing well.[13]

Inevitably, the large-scale trade in young slaves of this type brought a high rate of forcible separations.[14]

Among slaves in the twelve- to fifteen-year-old category, females were especially in demand, outnumbering males by three to two. There were good reasons for this bias, relating once again to the crucial tests of selection for the trade: net earnings capacity and potential. Females tended to mature more quickly than males and were on average taller than males in the years thirteen to fifteen.[15] There is evidence suggesting that they made significantly more effective workers in cotton picking than males aged thirteen to fifteen or sixteen, and possibly more effective workers at younger ages too.[16] Moreover, girls were in great demand

12. On the very active and effective working of slaves in this age group, see Jacob Metzer, "Rational Management, Modern Business Practices, and Economics of Scale in Ante-Bellum Southern Plantations," *Explorations in Economic History,* 12 (1975), esp. pp. 135–36. See also Fogel and Engerman, *Time on the Cross,* vol. 1, pp. 73–77.

13. Porter to Oakes, 21 Oct. 1856, Oakes Papers (BPL).

14. Children under eight years of age were very rarely sold separately in the interregional traffic; their level of independence and work output did not yet justify it. Louisiana (in 1829) passed legislation banning the sale away from their mothers of children under ten years of age (but made no other restrictions on trading separations). The Louisiana law, however, would have had very little practical effect on interregional selling at least, especially since New Orleans imported a peculiarly low proportion of children. On this legislation see Collins, *Domestic Slave Trade,* p. 127, and Taylor, *Slavery in Louisiana,* pp. 40–41. On Louisiana's *Code Noir* (and a rejection of the idea that French and Spanish influence made the conditions of slaves and their families better in Louisiana than elsewhere in the United States), see D. C. Rankin, "The Tannenbaum Thesis Reconsidered: Slavery and Race Relations in Ante-Bellum Louisiana," *Southern Studies,* 18 (1979), pp. 5–31.

15. Richard H. Steckel, "Slave Height Profiles from Coastwise Manifests," *Explorations in Economic History,* 16 (1979), p. 368.

16. On the greater efficiency of females in cotton picking at these ages, see Metzer, "Rational Management," p. 136. Fogel and Engerman (in *Time on the Cross,* vol. 1, pp. 74–77, 82) point to higher earnings for female slaves up to age eighteen than for male slaves, even excluding any returns from child bearing. Kotlikoff ("Structure of Slave Prices," pp. 509–11) suggests that until about age twenty-three the prices of females were actually higher than those of males. Most indicators suggest, however,

as domestics, and traders received many enquiries like the following, addressed to E. H. Stokes, a Virginia-based speculator:

> I am anxious to buy a small healthy negro girl—ten or twelve years old. . . . I will take her on trial of a few weeks—please let me hear from you as soon as possible—I would like a dark mulatto—describing the girl and stating the price—Address Mrs. B. L. Blenkenship. . . .

The preference for a "mulatto" (and other details) suggests that a house servant was required, but numerous Ziba Oakes letters clearly specify orders for girls as domestics.[17] Overall, the acquisition of girls usually meant, then, the recruitment of effective workers, and with the older ones there was the bonus of gaining potential childbearers for the quite near future.

The rationale for selecting, as a key staple of the trade, "woman with first child" (that is, young women with proven fertility) seems to be clear.[18] At the same time, the immediate potential for Upper South families is equally apparent. Again, demand for young women of about sixteen to twenty-two years and men in their late teens and early twenties made good economic sense: purchasers gained women of childbearing age, with good work potential, and prime male workers at or approaching the peak of their powers. Because the typical slave woman, as we shall later see, would have been married by about age nineteen and most males by about age twenty-four, buying policy again had the effect of striking hard against Upper South marriages. Middle-aged slaves were generally far less saleable than prime young slaves, but slaves of thirty years and older did make up some 10–11 percent of the trade, and those over thirty-five perhaps 4–5 percent (see Figure 2.1). Thomas Otey of Richmond included a rather cautious reference to such slaves when he wrote to Ziba Oakes:

---

that long-run earnings potential meant that teenage males *were* more expensive (if sometimes only slightly) than teenage females. True, some Richmond circulars (see Appendix 6) give similar prices for boys and girls aged ten to fifteen years, but usually males are quoted at significantly higher prices. The Reid price scale (also Appendix 6) gives a clear indication of higher male prices. Betts & Gregory circulars regularly indicate that boys and girls of the same *height* commanded the same prices, suggesting that girls aged thirteen to sixteen (being taller than males of those ages) might have been, at a given age, more expensive than boys.

17. Blenkenship to Stokes, 29 Mar. 1863, Chase Papers (AAS). On the high rate of employment of slave girls as domestics, see Crawford, "Quantified Memory," pp. 52–53.

18. Traders and clients quite frequently referred to "breeding women," as when W. H. Cannon enquired the price of "young women and breeding women with children." See Cannon to Oakes, 1 Mar. 1857, Oakes Papers (BPL).

> Negroes are very high [but] women and children are not so high as they have been nor middle aged [slaves]. . . . If you think you could sell some women and children and middle aged I can buy some.

Those males of thirty years and over who were selected by traders were, as I noted in Chapter 3, quite likely to have special skills, while the women were very likely to be part of a mother-and-offspring group (usually including an infant needing nursing care and valuable older children).[19]

The balance in the sex ratio of the mainstream (non-Louisiana) trade tended, then, to conceal certain trading preferences according to age, sex, and slave type, and these did much to encourage separations. Owners, in separating families, sometimes did so for purposes of "discipline," out of spite, or for other immediate reasons. But they, too, responded to the preferences of the trade—that is, to that rationale of economic calculations which potentially and actually had vicious effect upon the integrity of huge numbers of family relations. The efficient relocation of labor by masters and their trading go-betweens left the slave family to recover as best it could from its traumas.

The letters of traders make ugly reading and clearly reflect the rationale of selectivity and separation. Preserving the slave family, certainly it if looked as though that course might involve any financial cost, almost never comes through as a concern for sellers, traders, or buyers. The most one finds, and that only very rarely indeed, is a reference like the following: "The owner says that George has a wife and that he would not disturb him without he was getting more than he was worth." Even this letter suggests a curiously flexible set of values: the higher the price offered, the less worthy a slave family. In part, perhaps, the almost total lack of reference to any owner's reluctance to sell separately might be because traders came to know who would and who would not divide families—and therefore whom to avoid. But the trade was so very extensive that, as we shall see, a very large proportion of owners must have been willing sellers and separators. Instead of owners' unease about selling separately, what we get in traders' letters are quite numerous instructions from clients that particular slaves were to be "sold off" (that is, sold out of state, far from relatives and friends). We get, too, repeated references to bloodhounds being sent after slaves who had been alerted to impending separations; and indications of the need to "paddle" (beat, but without scarring) those

19. Otey to Oakes, 23 July 1853, Oakes Papers (BPL). For details on older slaves in the trade, see Chapter 2.

unwilling to leave their families. And for traders, as long as Lower South demand permitted, the urge was, as an agent told Ziba Oakes, to "buy all you can that is likely [as] active persons . . . [are always] coming in and buying everything [they can]."[20]

With traders, attitudes to the black family were rarely sentimental. One trader, T. W.. Burton, expressed scant sympathy for two members of his coffle who had "taken up with each other as man and wife, though when I have an opportunity of selling either of them they go certain." Burton was as good as his word on this occasion, and soon had the pair sold off to different masters. The attitude of the speculator who bought Charles Ball was that he should not be allowed a last meeting with his wife and children, but that he "would be able to get another wife in Georgia." The trader J. W. Pittman took no more serious a view of slave emotions and family ties, and considered himself particularly unlucky not to be able to prise a mother away from her child. "I did intend to leave Nancy's child," he lamented, "but she made such a damned fuss I had to let her take it. I could of got $50," he added, if the child had been sold separately. Ziba Oakes, frequently encountered in this study, seems to have taken a somewhat softer line than his colleague J. A. Weatherly, and led the latter to worry that

> As to your own views about Mary [a slave sent to Oakes for sale], I think as I always have thought that about such things you are too sensitive. Another cause of uneasiness with you and to your business seems to me to be too great a desire to please negroes. By allowing them to visit their friends in your office, you give them trouble, and also [give] annoyance to purchasers.

In practice, however, both Weatherly and Oakes got on with the business of selling slaves and destroying families. Oakes's traffic, indeed, was probably much more extensive than that of his colleague, and his respect for slave families and the humanity of blacks no more real. Weatherly's use of language, downgrading family relationships into "friendships," was significant, and echoed the widespread and fundamental white view that slave emotions were merely passing fancies, and families no more than loose associations.[21]

20. Browden to Suttle, 20 Jan. 1838, David S. Reid Papers (DU); McElveen to Oakes, 16 Sept. 1856, Oakes Papers (BPL). As well as the Oakes Papers, the Finney Papers (DU) and the Chase Papers (AAS) (the latter mainly comprising letters to major Richmond auctioneers) are particularly revealing on the attitudes of traders' clients.

21. Burton to Long, 20 Feb., 24 Mar. 1845, Long Papers (NCA); Ball, *Fifty Years*, p. 29; Pittman to Williamson, 20 May 1835, John W. Pittman Papers (LC); Weatherly to Oakes, 7 Aug. 1856, Oakes Papers (BPL).

Whether an owner of a family sold one spouse away from another or a child away from its parents could depend on many factors. The trader might, because of price, age, fitness, attitude, prefer one family member to another. An owner might find it more convenient to sell off one slave rather than another. Such considerations come through repeatedly in letters to Ziba Oakes. In February 1854, for example, McElveen reported to Oakes that he had purchased several slaves but "I could not send them . . . on account of trying to buy the woman's husband, and I wished to see if the fellow came according to promise." Ultimately, the deal was not made, and husband and wife were separated. In July 1853, McElveen recorded that he was sending a girl bought from a Darlington district planter, and he added "I hope I can get her brother at 700, weighs 100 lbs. His master asks me 750." The owner's decision as to whether or not to separate the siblings from each other hung on the outcome of haggling over fifty dollars, and, whatever the outcome, one or both siblings, it seems, were to be separated from the parents who had brought them up. Sometimes owners left the matter of carving up families simply to the professional calculations of dealers. One such was a planter from Hickory Fork, Virginia, who informed the auctioneers Dickinson & Co.:

> I sent up yesterday by my brother in law . . . 31 negroes for you to do your best with. . . . Divide the children and manage matters as you think best . . . fix them up as well as you can before sale.[22]

TRADERS' RECORDS AND FAMILY SEPARATIONS: FORCIBLE SEPARATION IN THE INTERREGIONAL TRADE

When I undertook a quantitative estimate of the scale of separations in the interregional trade, the results were consistent with the rationale of separations just outlined, and with the narrative evidence from traders' correspondence. I started with a very broad sample of speculators' bills of sale and accounts, gaining from these preliminary indications of *marriage* separations caused by trading. Having done this, I used a smaller sample of records (those giving details of ages for substantial numbers of slaves traded) to gain a much fuller view of the separation both of spouses and of children from parents. No claim for accuracy to within a few percent is made, but the consistent character of results covering several decades and many markets leads to confidence that

22. McElveen to Oakes, 6 and 7 Feb. 1854, 29 July 1853, Oakes Papers (BPL); Catteu to Dickinson, 1 Aug. 1848, Chase Papers (AAS).

the broad pattern of separations has been established. That pattern, as I shall show in detail later, suggests that just over half of all slaves who fell into the hands of the trader would either have been forcible separated from a spouse or have been children who were forcibly separated from one or both of their parents.[23]

We can conveniently begin a detailed analysis of separations with the broad sample of traders' bills of sale and accounts (see Table 6.1 for a summary). The sampling method here was simply to take all available traders' buying and selling records (excluding sales to the exceptional Louisiana market) and to observe the units in which slaves were traded.[24] The contrast with the slave population in general, where the vast majority of slaves, it now appears, were born into viable two-parent families, is striking in the extreme.[25] Some 50 percent or more of the trade were of marriageable age, and yet units of husband with wife

23. A preliminary and less detailed version of these results appeared in Tadman, "Slave Trading and the Mentalities of Masters and Slaves in Ante-Bellum America," in Léonie Archer (ed.), *Slavery and Other Forms of Unfree Labour* (London, 1988), pp. 188–205.

24. Most record groups used in Table 6.1 (and all in Tables 6.2 and 6.3) itemized slaves against individual sellers to or buyers from the trader, so that the task of identifying the units in which slaves were traded was usually straightforward. Such units were normally either individual slaves (one individual per bill of sale or buying client), or groups specifically described as being mother with offspring (e.g., "Rebecca 29 years, and her children Ned aged 5, Ben aged 2, and Alice aged 5 weeks"). Occasionally, a client sold a trader a group of slaves which was not a simple mother-with-offspring unit, but here, when ages were given, those ages in all except an insignificant number of cases made it clear that husbands with wives could not be involved. Such groups might, for example, be a batch of four slaves: "Ben aged 16, Agg aged 10, Jesse 8, and Judy 9." A very small number of ambiguous cases (groups of slaves not described as mother-and-offspring units, but without age details) occur in the Badgett, Pittman, and Ferguson papers. Detailed results in Table 6.2 (where all ages are identifiable) are so similar to those in Table 6.1 that it is very unlikely that Table 6.1 underrepresents husband-and-wife units of sale or purchase. One or two ambiguous cases occur in the Glen (i) records (Table 6.1); but even including ambiguous cases, possible husband-and-wife units rise from 4.3 to only 6.8 percent of slaves in the entire slave subset.

25. Crawford, "Quantified Memory," pp. 177, 184, indicates that, despite the early loss of some parents through death or sale, 80 percent of slaves aged up to four years lived in viable two-parent families (that is, where something like regular meetings between spouses were allowed), while almost all of the rest lived with their mothers. Over the years of the child's growing up, the proportion living in two-parent families would be substantially reduced by sale, mortality, and migration, but at age nineteen, 50 percent still lived in such families. Gutman, *Black Family,* pp. 9–11, 47, 156, 160, 180, emphasizes the overwhelming tendency of slaves (where allowed) to live in two-parent families, and he provides detailed statistics. See also Fogel and Engerman, *Time on the Cross,* vol. 1, pp. 138–42.

Table 6.1. Percentage of trade accounted for by mother-and-offspring lots, as against husband-and-wife lots (with or without offspring)

Record type: trader's buying or selling records	Slave trader	No. of slaves	Husband and wife (with or without offspring)	Mother-and-offspring units (no husband)		
				Mothers	Offspring	Mothers + offspring
Buying	Badgett	58	0.0	13.8	15.5	29.3
	Ferguson	37	0.0	8.1	8.1	16.2
	Glen (i)[a]	351	4.3–6.8	6.4	16.2	22.6
	Long	70	0.0	4.3	7.1	11.4
Selling	Fields	53	3.8	13.2	13.2	26.4
	Glen (ii)	[186]	[2.7]	[7.9]	[18.4]	[26.3]
	Hughes & Downing	13	0.0	0.0	0.0	0.0
	Pittman	10	0.0	0.0	0.0	0.0
	Rives	56	3.6	3.8	3.8	7.6
	Templeman, H. N.	107	0.0	5.6	6.5	12.1
	Templeman & Goodwin	40	0.0	15.0	17.5	32.5
	Totten	173	8.7	7.5	11.0	18.5
	Walker	105	0.0	13.3	19.0	32.3
Bought and sold	Omohundro	360	2.2	5.3	8.9	14.2
Specialist auctioneers	Dickinson & Bro.	6,889	1.7	7.7	12.9	20.6
Slave total and averages		8,322	2.0	7.6	12.7	20.3

Note: The Dickinson records are included here but not in Table 6.2, since in minor part they concern local and not just interregional sales. The J. R. White records (principally concerned with Louisiana), and the J. A. Mitchell and F. L. Whitehead data (lists of slaves, with no basis for identifying ages or relationships) are omitted. The Glen, Long, Totten, and Templeman & Goodwin records which provide age-specific data are used; the simple lists of slave names available for certain trading trips are omitted. The large contribution from Dickinson & Bro. (major Richmond auctioneers specializing in supplying the trade) does not introduce any likelihood of bias to overall results, because data for the other thirteen firms combined produced results very similar to those for Dickinson.

[a] Slaves in Glen (i) appear in purchasing records, but not necessarily in sales records. Slaves in Glen (ii) often appear in purchasing records, but also specifically appear in Lower South sales. Since differences between samples (i) and (ii) are slight, the larger sample (i) is used in contributing toward the overall total and averages in this table; sample (ii) is omitted from these figures.

Table 6.2. Slaves traded, according to key units of buying and selling

Buying or Selling	Slave trader	No. of slaves	Mother-and-offspring units				Children sold without either parent, by age						Adults sold without spouse or offspring, by age							
			Mothers (a)		Children (b)		0–7 (c)		8–11 (d)		12–14 incl. (e)		Females 15–19 (f)		Females 20+ (g)		Males 20–24 (h)		Males 25+ (i)	
			No.	%	No.	%	No.	%	No.	%	No.	%	No.	%	No.	%	No.	%	No.	%
Buying	Glen (i)	351	24	6	61	16	5	1	32	9	50	14	32	9	22	6	31	9	29	8
	Long	70	3	4	5	7	7	10	3	4	8	11	8	11	6	9	10	14	10	14
Selling	Glen (ii)	186	15	8	35	18	3	2	19	10	24	13	17	9	15	8	20	11	15	8
	Totten	173	13	8	19	11	0	0	11	6	28	16	23	13	15	9	21	12	11	6
	Templeman & Goodwin	40	6	15	7	18	0	0	2	5	6	15	10	25	0	0	5	13	2	5
Slave total, and averages according to type of unit		634	7%		14%		2%		8%		15%		12%		7%		11%		8%	

Notes: This is a subsample of Table 6.1. The Glen (i) and (ii) samples are constructed in the same way. The bills of sale used for the Glen (i) and (ii) samples also included 25 and 4 slaves, respectively, who were not described by age (and not referred to as mother, infant, or child), and in calculating the percentages relating to mother-and-offspring units (but not otherwise) these slaves are included. The procedure avoids any overcount of mother-and-offspring slaves in the Glen samples.

Table 6.3. Proportion of slave traffic experiencing major family separations as a result of being traded (N = 634)

	Mother-and-offspring units		Children sold without either parent, by age			Adults sold without spouse or offspring, by age				Cumulative
	Mothers	Children	0–7	8–11	12–14 incl.	Females 15–19	Females 20+	Males 20–24	Males 25+	%
	(a)	(b)	(c)	(d)	(e)	(f)	(g)	(h)	(i)	(j)
1. Percentage of trade	7	14	2	8	15	12	7	11	8	84
2. Family separations as a % of total trade	5	10	2	7	14	2	3	3	5	51

Note: Separations by death and voluntary separations can be roughly estimated as follows:

Mother-and-offspring units

Mothers in these units were typically in their late twenties or early thirties. Since the average age at first marriage is taken to be nineteen for women and twenty-four for men, these mothers would on average have been married ten years before being traded. Given the ages of their husbands and applying age-specific survival rates (Chapter 2), these husbands would, since marrying, have had about a 75–80 percent survival rate. Some 20–25 percent of the mother-and-offspring units, therefore, had probably lost husbands through death. Gutman (*Black Family,* p. 147, Table 21) found that slaves at these ages were about six to eight times more likely to be separated by death than by the slave's own choice. Thus voluntary separations and separations by death together accounted for about 28 percent, or a little less, of all marriages in this group of women.

Children without either parent

Available evidence suggests (see p. 151 n.27) that less than 1 percent of children under age thirteen or fourteen would have lost both parents through death. An appropriate scaling is applied to account for such orphans.

Adults sold without spouse or offspring

Percentages in row 1 are (in row 2) scaled down to account for mortality (based on age-specific mortality rates of spouses) and (as in [ii]) for voluntary separations.

(including any offspring) made up only about 2 percent—in other words, complete nuclear families were almost totally absent. Table 6.1 does, however, show a good deal of evidence of broken families. Twenty percent of the sample was made up of mother-and-offspring units, sold without a father.[26] Even if we allow that some marriages were broken voluntarily and some ended by the husband's death, we are still left with the conclusion (see Table 6.3) that nearly three-quarters of these mother-and-offspring groups had been forcibly sepa-

26. Kotlikoff, studying New Orleans records ("The Structure of Slave Prices," pp. 512–13) found a similar pattern. In his sample of 5,785 slaves sold, there were only 18 instances of husband-and-wife units and 22 of husband, wife, and offspring sold together. Twenty-three percent of his sample did involve some sort of family relationship, the vast majority being instances of mothers sold with offspring (but without husbands). Apart from these units, he found twelve instances of siblings sold together and two cases of grandmothers sold with granddaughters.

rated by the trade from spouses and from the fathers of the children. The conclusion that these fragmented families were the product primarily of selective purchasing is further supported by the fact that the trade carried no equivalent groups of fathers with offspring (but without mothers). Those few two-parent families actually bought by the trader were not usually separated by him in a later sale—a fact which suggests that these particular families might have had some special value when sold as a unit; perhaps the adults were valued house servants whose work was interlinked.

Table 6.2, based on collections of bills of sale and virtually continuous runs of trading accounts, shows similar results for mother-and-offspring units, but because we can now look at several key, age-specific categories of trading, these records allow us to suggest the scale of family separations. Firstly, with age-specific data we are able to make an approximate count of slave children sold away from their parents. Some children sold without parents would have been orphans even before falling into the hands of the trader, but statistics suggest that not more than about 1 percent of children under thirteen or fourteen years would have lost both parents through death.[27] Even after scaling down to allow for orphans, we find, therefore, (see Tables 6.2 and 6.3) that probably some 2 percent of the trade was made up of children aged 0–7 years, forcibly separated from parents, 7 percent by separations of 8–11-year-olds, and 14 percent by 12–14-year-olds who were sold away from parents. The pattern fits with what we have seen earlier: little demand for those under eight years, but, as work capacity increased with maturity, a very significant upward trend in trading.

By using the age-specific data, we can also go beyond the evidence of mother-and-offspring units in searching for indications of the destruction of marriages by masters. In this we can, first, take account of women sold without children who might have been traded from husbands and, secondly, consider the likely rate of selling husbands away from wives (see columns f–i in Tables 6.2 and 6.3). To do this we need to know the typical ages by which slaves would have entered into marriage and have been at risk of forcible separation. I assume that the

27. James Trussell and Richard H. Steckel, "The Age of Slaves at Menarche and Their First Birth," *Journal of Interdisciplinary History,* 8 (1978), p. 478n, calculate that less than 1 percent of slaves aged under thirteen would have lost both parents through death. For a similar result, see also Richard Sutch, "The Treatment Received by American Negro Slaves: A Critical Review of Evidence Presented in *Time on the Cross,*" *Explorations in Economic History,* 13 (1975), pp. 409–10. See also Crawford, "Quantified Memory," p. 149.

average age at first marriage for slave women was nineteen years and for slave men was twenty-four years.[28] Evidence on the ages by which slave women had borne their first child gave a guide to the likely proportions of women married by particular ages.[29] Even allowing, conservatively, for the possibility that unmarried women were more likely to be traded than married women (but this goes against all the evidence of trading records), perhaps 20 percent of women aged fifteen to nineteen who were traded were married, and at least 60 percent of those over twenty. This age distribution for females suggests that, in the trade, some 30 percent of males aged twenty to twenty-four would have been married, and some 70 percent of males aged twenty-five years and older (including slaves up to their early forties).[30]

28. From his sample of ex-slave narratives, Escott (*Slavery Remembered,* pp. 53–54) inferred ages of 17.6 years and 22.4 years for women and men respectively. Fogel and Engerman (*Time on the Cross,* vol. 2, p. 115) gave estimates of 20 and 24 years for women and men, respectively. My estimates are, therefore, close to those of Fogel and Engerman. They are also broadly in line with the average age gap between spouses (about five or six years) suggested in Gutman, *Black Family,* pp. 146–48, and *Slavery and the Numbers Game: A Critique of Time on the Cross* (Urbana, 1975), pp. 153–57, and with Richard Steckel's suggested average age gap of 4.2 years ("Slave Marriage and Family," *Journal of Family History,* 5 [1980], p. 417.).

29. Trussell and Steckel's sample of some 600 plantations seems very clearly to establish that the average age of antebellum slave women at birth of first child was 20.6 years ("Age of Slaves at Menarche," esp. p. 491, Table 5). More specifically, they found that the proportions of women *without* children were, according to successive age groups: women 15–19 years, 78 percent without children; 20–24 years, 35 percent; 25–29 years, 22 percent; 30–34 years, 18 percent; and 35–39, 14 percent. Since slaves were very often married well before the birth of their first child (Gutman, *Black Family,* pp. 149, 570n), such data suggest an average age at marriage in the late teens. This is further supported by Gutman's evidence on marriage separations (*Black Family,* p. 147, Table 21): by age 20–29, 38 percent of female slaves in Gutman's sample (exslaves registering new or continuing marriages in 1864–65) had been separated from a previous marriage (22 percent by death, 12 percent by force, and 4 percent voluntarily). Given the typical mortality rates of their husband's age group (some 25 percent per decade for males in the late twenties to early thirties), this points to almost a 100 percent marriage rate for slave women by their mid-twenties.

30. When calculating the rates of sale of husbands away from wives, we have estimates by Escott and by Fogel and Engerman for ages of men at marriage, as well as data on the age gap between spouses. Gutman (*Black Family,* p. 147, Table 21) states that among male slaves aged 20–29 (and, like the women, likely to have been evenly distributed over that age range) 22 percent had already been separated from a wife (8 percent by death, 10 percent by force, and the rest mostly voluntarily). This rate of loss by mortality (using the decennial mortality rates of around 13 percent for females in their late teens and early twenties) suggests that the substantial majority

This age-specific information allows us to scale the gross percentages in Table 6.3 (row 1, columns f–i) to allow for the likely percentage married, the loss of spouse through death (using age-specific survival rates described in Chapter 2), and voluntary separations. The results (Table 6.3, row 2), increase by a further 13 percentage points the proportion of slaves traded who experienced major forcible separations of family. Among the women sold without spouse or offspring, many might not have produced their first surviving child by the time of sale, but some would also, by their sale, have been separated from children.[31] Fathers, too, would have left children behind after being sold south.

Later in this chapter, I shall begin to consider the significance for blacks and whites both of slave sales and forcible separations, but let us for the moment simply take stock of the general pattern which emerges from our statistics. For most of the antebellum period the interregional trade seems, each decade, to have removed some 10 percent or more of slaves from the Upper to the Lower South. Just over 50 percent of these slaves, by being traded, would have experienced major family separations (young children and those in their early teens separated from parents, or husband divided from wife). And, as Gutman noted, the sale and separation of each individual slave would have had a "geometric effect"—parents, siblings, spouses, and other relatives who were left behind all feeling the impact of the separation.[32]

The separations in virtually every case came not when the trader divided up any family lots in his possession, but when those who sold to him themselves directly broke up families by supplying him. This pattern is clearly illustrated in the Tyre Glen records, but is equally marked in our trade sample as a whole. All groups bought by Glen and specifically listed by him as husband and wife units (with or without children)

---

of male slaves aged 20–29 (average age 25) were married by age 25. Gutman's Table 2.1 also suggests this sort of conclusion. Women in their teens (15–19), who were much more likely to be married than men of that age, already reported forcible separations from husbands, but the small sample of male teenagers did not. By age 20–29, however, men seem almost as likely as women to have been married: 10 percent reported forcible separations and, at 12 percent, the rate was not much higher for women.

31. Gutman, in studying marriage registers, found exactly the same rate of forcible separations from husbands for those women with children and for those without (Gutman, *Black Family,* p. 149). That pattern is similar to the one suggested by comparing Table 6.3, row 2, column a with columns f and g.

32. Gutman, *Black Family,* pp. 146–48.

were kept together when he resold them.[33] Again, Glen bought large numbers of mother-with-child units, and almost never separated them at resale (except perhaps sometimes splitting off older children). Occasionally, though, traders mentioned that siblings were among those young slaves and teenagers bought without parents. Such slaves, having no special economic value as a unit, were usually divided at resale.[34] When Professor Ethan Andrews visited the Alexandria, D.C., slave pen of the prominent trading firm Franklin & Armfield, Armfield told him that "in selling his slaves he [the trader] never separates families, but in purchasing them he is often compelled to do so."[35] Making a major exception for the trader's separation of siblings, there is probably a large measure of truth in what Andrews was told. The patterns of buying and selling, however, reflected no greater respect for slave families among traders than among their clients. They were, instead, simply a reflection of the conveniences and market realities in the business of selling people.

PLANTER MIGRATIONS AND THE FORCIBLE SEPARATION OF BLACK FAMILIES

For whites, and for some slaves too, the moving of a whole plantation labor force to new lands in the Lower South could be a great adventure. But such migrations could also spell danger or ruin for many slave families. Sometimes the threat came through the planter's buying of extra slaves, though perhaps more usually it came through failure to purchase the close relatives of the black migrants. Just before Leonard Covington, in 1809, sent his slaves from Maryland to a new plantation in Mississippi, he had prepared for the undertaking by the selective purchase of additional young and vigorous slaves. Those purchases

33. Only "possible" husband-and-wife units (those not actually described as husband-and-wife units, but where the ages of those who were jointly purchased made such a relationship possible) were separated in resale. This accounts for differences between Glen (i) and Glen (ii) entries in Table 6.1.

34. Much more commonly than specific references to siblings, one finds references indicating that a seller provided the trader with a group of young slaves (sold without a mother) who might have been siblings. Such "possible" sibling groups were almost always resold separately. In a coffle taken south in the 1833–34 season, Glen took Beck (aged 15), Tom (13), Ike (11), Zilph (9), and Ellick (7). All had been bought from the same owner, but were divided among at least four purchasers at resale. Such patterns appeared in most Glen coffles. In 1831, for example, Laury (15) and Jack (11) were bought and sold in this way, as were Pompey (22) and Sam (15), Nepton (13) and Malinda (9), and Julius (19) and Lavinia (14). See Glen Papers (DU).

35. Andrews, *Slavery and the Domestic Slave Trade,* p. 147.

had, no doubt, broken up families. A similar preparatory buying campaign preceded the migration, in January 1835, of James R. Polk's slaves from Tennessee to Mississippi. On 10 October 1834, Polk's overseer for the new plantation expressed satisfaction that his employer had bought five new Negroes, but reported problems in his own attempt to buy a blacksmith (who had run away). In letters of 4 and 10 October, the overseer (Ephraim Beanland) was, however, able to write that

Silamin claim hear . . . and I bought A negro boy from him for $600 the boy is 22 years olde and I told hi[m] that I would give $5 hundred dollars for the Boyes wife and two children. . . . I told him if I liked hear [her] I would give it. Rite to me and let me know what to do.

As so often seems to have happened, the business of striking the right bargain was the question at issue, and against that consideration the integrity of the family took the lowest of priorities. Later in the month, Beanland reported problems in securing certain purchases, and added "so I thinke that we had beter go to negro tradinge." A few months after the migrants had set out, Polk was still looking to buy selected blacks, again apparently with no notion that buying in families should be a significant consideration. A friend, G. T. Greenfield, wrote from Washington, D.C., of his promise to try to buy for Polk

a couple of negro men, or a man and a boy, or a woman and a man. I have not yet purchased any male negroes. . . . There are a great many traders here, and men and boys are very scarce at any price. Should I succeed in getting all the negroes I want, you can have your choice of two, and *if you are supplied* before I get out, it will make no difference with me, as I wish to settle a plantation [as Polk was doing] in Mississippi.[36]

With planter migration, the threat to slave families probably came more commonly, not from special purchasing campaigns, but rather from circumstances in which the ownership of family members in the old states had been spread across neighboring plantations. Betsy Crissman was one of thousands of slaves to suffer from such ownership arrangements. In an interview made in 1866, she testified: "I was married in East Tennessee, and lived with my husband six years. Then his master took him to Alabama, and I never saw him anymore." Henry Stevenson recorded a similar story:

36. Polk correspondence of 4, 10, 26 Oct. 1834 and 29 Mar. 1835, reproduced in John S. Bassett, *The Southern Overseer as Revealed in His Letters* (Northampton, Mass., 1925) pp. 77–86. On Polk, Covington, and other such migrants, see Appendix 2.

My first wife was Amanda; she belonged to a neighbor named John Connelly. My missus moved to a place near Lebanon, in Boone County, Mo., and I went with her. That parted me from my wife and little son. I never saw them afterward.

Similarly, Lewis Hayden wrote of the loss of his father, when "my father's owner moved off and took my father with him, which broke up the [family]".[37]

Something of the excitement which whites (and perhaps some slaves who were not losing close relatives) felt when migrating comes over in records of the Brownrigg migration from North Carolina to Mississippi in 1838. Sarah Sparkman, with three white males, led the migration of ninety-one slaves, her brother (who was ill) following on some months later. Shortly after setting out Sarah wrote back to her brother:

The Negroes are all in high spirits, they run and play like children along the road. It is remarked by everyone that they have never seen so many without being chained. . . . 91 Negroes and only 4 whites we are stared at such a caravan. . . . Imagine you see me writing in the middle of the tent with my writing desk and my lantern on it.

The great majority of slaves in this large migration very probably did not have spouses or children owned by other masters or mistresses than the Brownriggs, and this, aided perhaps by patronizing assumptions on the part of the whites, probably accounted for their reported good humor. But the migration did bring personal disaster to a minority with close relatives on neighboring plantations. Thus in September 1835, shortly before the migrants set out, the slave Phebe Brownrigg wrote to her daughter:

My dear daughter — I have for some time had hope of seeing you once more in this world, but now that hope is gone forever. I expect to start next month for . . . the Mississippi river. . . . My dear daughter Amy, if we never meet in this world, I hope we shall meet in heaven where we shall part no more. . . . Let us pray for each other, and try to hold out faithful to the end.

The following February, another migration brought a further crushing blow to Emily, the daughter. Emily wrote to her mother:

In my last letter to you I felt happy to tell you about my wedding — but [now] . . . my husband is torn from me, and carried away by his master. . . .

37. The testimony of Crissman, Stevenson, and Hayden is from Blassingame, *Slave Testimony,* pp. 468, 530, 695. On separations arising out of planter migrations, see also Gutman, *Slavery and the Numbers Game,* pp. 104–7; and see the American Anti-Slavery Society's *Slavery and the Internal Slave Trade,* pp. 69–71.

> Although [the latter] was offered $800 for him that we might not be parted, he refused it. . . . He said he would 'get his own price for him' so in a few short months we had to part.[38]

Emily was particularly unfortunate to have her husband taken from her by one migration and her mother by the great Brownrigg exodus. Clearly, however, the Brownrigg migration brought other separations. A letter sent home by a white emigrant included a note that "George Rumbo [one of the Brownrigg slaves] says please buy his boy off B. White, and King [another slave] says give his love to his father." A second letter included notes from slaves to the effect that

> Dick says he sends his love to his wife and children and wishes you to buy them if possible. Jacob says he wishes his wife to come to Mississippi if you can purchase her. Arthur says tell Amy he is very well and his children also.

Another note reported:

> This is from Harry Frod [sic] to his wife Rose Small. I have kept very well since we parted and I hope you have also. Do go to see master John and get him to send me word how you all are for there is no other chance of hearing from you. Your affectionate husband Harry.[39]

The per capita rate of major family separations would have been higher, no doubt, when very small slaveholding units were involved (and where cross-plantation marriages were therefore likely to be especially common). We know, however, that most slaves did not live on very small slaveholdings; and the fact that cross-plantation marriages formed only a quite small minority of all marriages will be discussed later. Nevertheless, planter migrations would have caused many families to be broken, and in such cases the safety valve for owners was often the notion of "trying to buy the wife" or other relative who would otherwise be left behind. As we know, the owner of Emily Brownrigg's husband wanted to "get his own price for him" and would not sell for $800. No letters have been found to establish whether or not George Rumbo's boy, Jacob's wife, or Dick's wife and child were bought by the Brownriggs. The mere gesture of promising to try to buy rela-

38. Sarah to her brother, General R. T. Brownrigg, 20 Oct. 1835, Brownrigg Family Papers (SHC). Slave letters appeared in *Human Rights*, 1 (1836), p. 2, and are reproduced in Blassingame, *Slave Testimony*, pp. 22–23. The proportions of off-plantation as against on-plantation marriages are discussed later, and such marriages are defined in note 44.

39. Sparkman to Brownrigg, and Hoskins to Brownrigg, both 6 Nov. 1835, and Sparkman to Brownrigg, 4 Nov. 1835, Brownrigg Family Papers (SHC).

tives in order to reunite families would in many cases be enough to persuade a migrant that the best chance of seeing a spouse or child again was to cooperate and to work well on the new plantation.

Where white emigrants were at all serious about reuniting families, the matter of dollars and morality then arose. The exslave Sarah Fitzpatrick reported one such "matter of conscience." She related that

> Ma' mamma's Mistus got mar'ied to a white man in Alabama . . . an' when she come down here she brung all o' her "Nigger" property wid her. Dat wuz ma' mama an' her six chillun. Dey tried to buy her husban' f'om de white man what owned 'im, but he wouldn't sell so she had to come on widdout 'im.[40]

It is not revealed whether the planter concerned would not sell at any price, would not sell at the bidder's price, or even whether the promise of bidding was really any more than an invention to dull the impact of separation and to shift the blame to a safer and more distant quarter. Certainly, in such cases as Sarah Fitzpatrick's, the white community failed to rally to the rescue of black families. In instances of this sort, white priorities ranked either the convenience of keeping the services of a valuable slave or the inconvenience of settling at an unattractive price higher than the moral worth of slave families. Evidence on the fate of families in sales does indeed suggest that white migrants and the slaveholding class generally set a low priority on the slave family.

In some cases, contempt for black families was not blurred by pretences. James Curry, for example, wrote that his mother

> was separated from her husband by the removal of his master to the south. The separation of the slaves in this way is little thought of. A few masters regard their union as sacred, but where one does a hundred care nothing about it.

Whites, he added, would look after their own families but, unless it suited them, wanted to know nothing of "a nigger's wife" or family. Where slave migrants were likely to be particularly unhappy about their forced exodus to the west, they were probably given little notice of their trip and then closely supervised during its progress. James Polk quite clearly anticipated tension with his slave migrants, and wrote to his wife: "The negroes have no idea that they are going to be sent to the South, and I do not wish them to know it, and therefore it would be best to say nothing about it at home, for it might be carried back to them." When coming upon a caravan of some twenty-five slaves migrating with their owner, the British traveller Basil Hall observed

40. Fitzpatrick's narrative in Blassingame, *Slave Testimony,* p. 639 (and see, also, for example, Lorenzo Ivy, pp. 736–37).

what at first seemed to be the curious sight of two men in the slave gang "apparently hand in hand, pacing along very sociably." The two, it turned out, were chained and bolted together, the explanation being that

> One of them . . . was married, but his wife belonged to a neighboring planter, not to his master. When the general move was made the proprietor of the female not choosing to part with her, she was necessarily left behind. The wretched husband was therefore shackled to a young unmarried man who having no such tie to draw him back might be more safely trusted on the journey.[41]

SPECULATING WITH FAMILIES: OWNERS, SALES, AND SEPARATIONS

When Upper South slaveholders caught "Alabama fever" or some other strain of the urge to move west, slaves, then, often had reason for unease. For a significant minority of the blacks drawn into these migrations, the uprooting meant loss of immediate kin.[42] Even the apparently contented Brownrigg migrants probably had anxieties about what their trip might bring. Certainly, on arriving at their new plantation they became "thunderstruck" that their master had not yet set out to join them "and think now that they are to be sold."[43] My principal concern, though, is not so much with planter migrations as with that much more extensive westward movement, the slave trade, and with the owners who supplied that traffic and the slaves who were its victims. We know both the approximate scale of that trade and the very high proportions of broken families in it—families whose separations were caused primarily by the act of sale. The pattern of slaveholding will reveal, furthermore, that the great majority of separations came about, not by the complexities of cross-plantation marriages, but by the direct breakup of families whose members had lived on the same plantation.

Although the typical slaveholder owned (in the 1850s) only some ten slaves, the typical slave lived on a unit of some forty slaves—a circum-

41. Curry's narrative in Blassingame, *Slave Testimony,* p. 129; Polk's letter in Bassett, *The Overseer,* p. 78; and see Hall, *Travels in North America,* vol. 3, pp. 128–29.

42. An indication of the relative dangers posed by sale and planter migration is provided by Escott, who found a ratio of eleven family separations caused by sales for every one caused by planter migration (*Slavery Remembered,* Table 1.6, p. 48). (His "sales" category would have included local as well as interregional sales).

43. Brownrigg to Brownrigg, 20 Dec. 1835, Brownrigg Papers (SHC).

stance which made it possible for on-plantation marriages greatly to predominate over off-plantation unions between slaves. Evidence for this predominance is, however, much more direct than this. Escott, in his survey of the Fisk and W.P.A. narratives, found that on-plantation marriages outnumbered off-plantation unions by about three to one.[44] Crawford's result, using the same sources, was consistent with Escott's. He found that for every slave child (aged up to eight years) who was part of an off-plantation marriage, there were four or five who lived with their parents in an on-plantation union. It is significant, too, that the samples which Escott and Crawford used were not skewed toward areas of unusually large plantations, but were broadly representative of the South as a whole (with, if anything, a slight Upper South bias). There seem to be no grounds at all to doubt the representativeness of the results from the narratives. The exslaves had no reason to overemphasize on-plantation unions, and, indeed, what an individual reported about these and off-plantation unions fitted very well with the size of holding on which the respondent had lived.[45] Both Escott and Crawford emphasized the emotional strength of both off-plantation and on-plantation marriages, but in practice the former were less secure—such unions depended upon the whims and fortunes of not just one but two masters.[46] But so large an interregional trade could not have been mostly supplied by slaves from off-plantation unions, and

44. See Chapter 5, note 2, for size of slave units. Escott's finding was that only 27.5 percent of marriages were off-plantation, or "abroad" as it was often called (*Slavery Remembered,* pp. 50–51). In this study, I use the term "on-plantation marriage" to refer to a situation where spouses were owned by the same master or mistress and lived together on the same holding (plantation, farm, or other dwelling). "Off-plantation marriage" refers to unions which linked those who lived on different holdings, but where the spouses lived near enough to each other to make visiting possible.

45. On holdings of 1–5 slaves, only 16 percent of slave children lived with their parents in on-plantation marriages; on units of 6–15 slaves the proportion increased to 28 percent, and on units of 16–49 slaves, to 59 percent. With slave children aged 0–3 years, Crawford found that 66 percent lived with their parents in on-plantation unions; 14–18 percent were part of off-plantation marriages; 15–18 percent were with their mother in broken marriages; and 1 percent lived without their parents. At ages 4–7, sales and other factors meant that the percentages were, respectively, 56, 11–16, 19–24, and 6; a further 2 percent by then lived (probably as domestics) in their master's house (Crawford,"Quantified Memory," p. 187, Table 58, and pp. 155, 177–79, Table 54).

46. On the strength of off-plantation unions, maintained by regular visiting wherever possible, see Crawford, "Quantified Memory," pp. 151–54 and Escott, *Slavery Remembered,* pp. 50–52.

with most forcible marriage breakups, the owner was unable to scapegoat some "uncooperative neighbor." The separation was unmistakably attributable to the seller—a fact of profound significance for master–slave relationships.

In the context of the dynamic frontier environment of the developing South, it has sometimes been suggested that the family disruptions of slaves might not have been greatly more severe than those of whites who moved west or children sent from poor white families to become apprentices or servants. Such notions should be given little weight and do not begin to take account of the extremities of suffering inflicted upon black families. The exodus of slaves was forced, long-distance, and permanent. It had nothing to do with moving west so as to make one's fortune. There was, with whites, nothing remotely equivalent to the forcible breakup of marriages. Young white servants and apprentices might feel great isolation, but contact with families was generally possible. In contrast, slave children sold away to the west almost certainly faced the prospect, forever, of a total loss of contact with and support from their old family. And the extensive literature on white migration across the South shows, too, a very strong tendency to move, not alone, but with family and friends. Whites in the South, like free migrants in so many other places, tended quickly to build up clusters of kin and contacts in the new land, a process which did much to recreate the mutual aid and informal welfare systems of the old country. As Frank Owsley wrote:

> The method of migration and settlement in the South was fairly uniform during the pioneer period. Friends and relatives living in the same neighboring communities formed one or more parties and moved out together, and when they had reached the new promised land they constituted a new community. . . . [L]ater comers would often be relatives of those who had come first, or friends of their relatives. . . . Thus the early communities of the newer states and territories were essentially transplanted organisms rather than synthetic bodies.[47]

47. Frank L. Owsley, "The Pattern of Migration and Settlement on the Southern Frontier," *Journal of Southern History,* 11 (1945), pp. 147–76. The same sort of pattern is reported in Dick, *The Dixie Frontier,* pp. 53–62. It is emphasized again in Bosworth's "Those Who Moved," a thesis which traces from geneological magazines the careers of 684 southern migrants (see esp. pp. 228, 272, 297). But the pattern of group migrations and the continual renewal of links between old and recreated communities occurs again and again in the literature of the white movement to the Southwest. See, for example, advice from old to new migrants and evidence for

Nor did slaveholders manage to be completely unaware of the huge contrast between the processes of black and white migrations westward and, in particular the mental agonies which family separations brought to slaves. At the same time, deep-rooted racism generally allowed masters to see such "upsets" among their slaves as temporary, quick to flare and die away, or otherwise unimportant. Again and again, then, one finds sellers and traders resorting to strategies to break the initial impact of sale. Sometimes the tactics were simply force and bullying, but an other occasions they were a little more elaborate. A common ploy was simply secrecy and a sudden strike by the owner. The slave Reuben Madison suffered one such sudden disaster when his wife and child were sold away "with so much secrecy, that he had no opportunity even to bid her a last farewell." Another slave, Charity Bowery, vividly remembered being called away on an errand by her mistress, and on her return found her daughter weeping by the side of the mistress, who was counting dollar bills. It was "Broder's money," the little slave told her mother—the mistress had sold her brother away while the mother had been distracted by an errand. And the southern lady drawled out, "Yes . . . [and] I got a great price for him." Henry Stewart's mother came upon a similar ploy when, as her master was in the process of counting through his money, he sent for her son while bidding the mother go off on some errand. The latter, rightly, became suspicious that her son was to be sold and hid the boy in the woods.[48]

Another slave put on her best clothes and joyfully accompanied her master, who had told her that her free papers were at last to be

---

clustering in recreated (though often more thinly spread) communities in the Shackelford Letter and T. C. Hanson, Miscellaneous Letters, Addition (SHC), and also in both the Covington and Lides papers (discussed in Appendix 2). See also, for example, John Q. Anderson, "The Narrative of John Hutchins," *Journal of Mississippi History*, 20 (1958), pp. 1–29 (esp. pp. 2–3); Timothy Horton Ball, *A Glance into the Great South-East, or Clarke County, Alabama, and its Surroundings from 1540 to 1877* (Chicago, 1882), esp. p. 207; Louise F. Hays, *History of Macon County, Georgia* (Augusta, 1933), esp. pp. 110–53; Rev. J. D. Anthony, *Life and Times of Rev. J. D. Anthony: An Autobiography with a Few Original Sermons* (Atlanta, 1896) p. 14; W. O. Lynch, "The Westward Flow of Southern Colonists before 1861," *Journal of Southern History*, 9 (1943), pp. 303–28; Wells, "Moving a Plantation to Louisiana," pp. 279–82; Bayrd Still, "The Westward Migration of a Planter Pioneer in 1796," *William and Mary Quarterly*, 21 (1941), pp. 318–43; and Rachel Klein, "The Rise of Planters in the South Carolina Back Country, 1767–1808," Ph.D. dissertation, Yale, 1979, pp. 34–35.

48. Madison, Bowery, and Stewart narratives, in Blassingame, *Slave Testimony*, pp. 185, 264–65, 415.

completed if she went with him. The paper signed by the master was, however, a bill of sale: the result was delivery to a trader and separation from her family. Another seller was more open, but still made excuses. As Catherine Beale well remembered,

> Miss Kate took me and my sister out on the back steps and tol' us we would have to be sold. She said she hated it because she had to sell us and take us away from our mother and family but there wasn't any money an' they had to have some from some place and they had decided to sell us [to a trader in Richmond].

Another slave, unmanageable after his wife had been sold from him, was secretly sold to a speculator; but the problem of his collection remained. The stratagem attempted was to inform the slave that he was suspected of stealing a pig from a neighbor. Although his own master was confident of his innocence, it would clear matters up if he went with certain white men to visit the neighbor. The slave, full of suspicion, ran off before the posse of speculators returned. Such stratagems, and sometimes escapes, must have been part and parcel of the routine of speculation, particularly at those times when traders began to collect up for their coffles those slaves whom, instead of securing in jails and barracoons, they had temporarily left with former owners.[49]

WITH AGONY IN THEIR HEARTS: SLAVES AND FORCIBLE SEPARATIONS

The fear of being torn from the closest of kin, the agonies of separation, and the long-run reaction to that experience never ceased to echo and re-echo through the slave states. Here was the inescapable context of slave life in the antebellum period, and the key to so much of the relationship between slaves and masters in the Old South. And yet there were, in a sense, certain limits to the impact of separations. Had the massive numbers of separations which have been established been turned exclusively against one relationship—that between spouses or that between parents and offspring—or, again, had the overall scale of separations, high as it was, been dramatically higher, then the sense of family and the hope of family life could hardly have survived. There was, however, amid all of the cruel dangers to family unity, room to cling together as spouses, to strive to protect children, and to hope that

49. Northup, *Narrative,* pp. 50–53, 81–82, 84–88; Beale narrative in Blassingame, *Slave Testimony,* pp. 574–75; Ball, *Fifty Years,* pp. 12–14. On "collecting in," see for example receipt from Lewis Wood, 15 May 1835, Totten Papers (NCA); and Haynes to Meek, 29 July 1836, Negro Collection (AU).

families would survive or that family members could become grounded in material with which to live through their hardships. In practice, families passed through cycles of danger, sometimes severely threatening, sometimes less pressing. The resilience of families in the trials of slavery—a resilience increasingly well documented in the scholarly literature—brought comforts and mutual support.[50] At the same time, the vigorous sense of family meant deep-seated resentments against forcible separations—and such reactions carried through into a broad perspective on slavery.

Fear of being sold away from kin is, indeed, a constantly recurring theme in slave autobiographies and in so many other records of slavery. In the early years of the nineteenth century it was, as Jesse Torrey reported, already a routine device of social control to threaten slaves, for any misdemeanor, that they would be sold to the "Georgia-men," who would take them forever from their kin. Some years later, a slave told his interviewer,

> The trader was all around, the slave-pen at hand, and we did not know what time any of us might be in it. Then there were the rice-swamps, and the sugar and cotton plantations; we had had them held before us as terrors, by our masters and mistresses, all our lives. We knew about them all; and when a friend was carried off, why, it was the same as death, for we could not write or hear, and never expected to see them again.

Madison Jefferson bitterly recalled the time when his sister was sold

50. The literature on the slave family has moved quite decisively beyond the "mark of oppression" school of the 1950s and early 1960s, which had maintained that, because of the severities of slavery, the slave family was almost always weak and disorientated. There have been disagreements as to the extent to which masters threatened the family, but since the 1960s very solid evidence of basic family strength has come from many sources. Fogel and Engerman, for example, have emphasized the dominance of nuclear families and the significance of child-spacing patterns (see *Time on the Cross,* vol. 1, pp. 127–44). Gutman's extremely important work has produced crucial evidence on such issues as slave naming practices and the strength of kin, exogamous marriage patterns, length of marriage, the very high rate of black marriage registration in the decades after slavery, and the vital supporting role of fictive kin (*Black Family*). Although some of his evidence (on naming practices, for example) related to unusually large slaveholdings, much of it (on length of marriage and rates of marriage, for example) was drawn from a cross-sample of slaves and exslaves from all types of holdings. Many other studies, including Crawford's "Quantified Memory" and Steckel's *Economics of Fertility,* confirm the resilience of the slave family. Studies of slave culture, for example, Lawrence Levine's rich and significant *Black Culture and Black Consciousness,* have added greatly to our knowledge of the family and its context.

away. The grief of the whole family was intense but, he explained, it had to be concealed from their oppressors who, "if they caught them crying, would tell them that they would give them something to cry for." The fear of separation constantly hung over families, he went on, and slaves "have a dread constantly on our minds . . . for we don't know how long master may keep us, nor into whose hands we may fall." The evidence of the slaves Tabb Gross and Lewis Smith fitted the recurring pattern, and their interviewer reported:

> The continual dread of this separation of husband and wife, parents and children, by sale . . . is inseparable from the state of slavery. . . . The slave may forget his hunger, bad food, hard work, lashes, but he finds no relief from the ever-threatening evil of separation.[51]

White observers, making a tour of the South, quite often commented on slave sales—their descriptions usually being of the highly visible public auctions which were held at court houses and at other prominent locations. Their recorded impressions seem usually to have been dependent upon the basic nature of the proslavery or antislavery philosophy which they had brought with them to the South.[52] A northerner, J. H. Ingraham, came with the view that, though freedom and time might change things, life for slaves was "a mere animal existence, passed in physical exertion or enjoyment." It was not surprising, therefore, that, when observing private sales at a trader's pen in the Lower South, he reported that the male slaves took little interest in their fate, while "the women were constantly laughing and chattering with each other in suppressed voices, and appeared to take, generally a livelier interest in the transactions." Having already been brought to the Lower South, such slaves, however, would usually have already gone through the initial crisis of separation, and would, in what liveliness they mustered, generally have been responding to the threats

51. Torrey, *American Slave Trade,* p. 61, and narratives of Hayden, Jefferson, Gross, and Smith in Blassingame, *Slave Testimony,* pp. 695–97, 217–19, 347. See also similar narratives in Blassingame, pp. 13–14, 46–47, 54–56, 87, 117–19, 137–38, 251–52, 277–78.

52. For detailed contemporary accounts of slave auctions see, for example, Mortimer Thompson [American Anti-Slavery Society], *Great Auction of Slaves at Savannah, Georgia, March 2nd and 3rd 1859* (New York, 1859), and N. S. Dodge, *A Charleston Vendue of 1842* (n.p., n.d.). Both of these antislavery accounts concede that at the major probate sales concerned, father, mother, and young offspring were usually sold together as family units, but maintained that where separations did occur they were very deeply felt. See also, for example, Basil Hall, *Travels in North America in the Years 1827 and 1828* (2nd ed., Edinburgh, 1830), pp. 34, 144–45, 194.

and coaching of the speculator. John Brown, as a victim of the trade, gave a very different perspective than that of Ingraham. The exslave wrote:

> I do not think that anyone could describe the scene that takes place. . . . The companies, regularly 'sized out', are forced to stand up, as the buyers come up to them, and to straighten up as stiffly as they can. When spoken to, they must reply quickly, with a smile on their lips, though agony is in their heart, and a tear trembling in their eye. They must answer every question, and do as they are bid, to show themselves off; dance, jump, walk, leap, squat, tumble and twist about, that the buyer may see they have no stiff joints, or other physical defect.

But sometimes he added, the trader's threats were of no avail and a "perfect Bedlam of despair" broke out.[53]

The narratives of exslaves shout out with bitterness and grief at the betrayal of their hopes through family separations. Moses Grandy, devastated at seeing his wife, from a neighboring plantation, carried off by a trader, tried to speak to her. The speculator, however, brandishing a pistol, refused all conversation except at a distance. "My heart," Grandy lamented, "was so full that I could say very little. . . . I have never seen or heard from her from that day to this. I loved her as I love my life." Charles Ball's mother, on seeing her son sold away from her, had to be lashed "with heavy blows about the shoulders" but still protested with all of her powers. Mary Ovington, sold as a child from her family, had had no effective way of protesting, but told her interviewer

> De hardes part ob dose days was being sold. It done seem as tho yer couldn't to bear it. When I was sold away by de speculators it seem like I griebe ter death. I had a good mudder and sisters and brudders, but one mornin' dey took me off an' I never see'd one of 'em again.

Indeed, almost every slave autobiography told of betrayal and separation by force.[54]

When directly asked by one critic of slavery how slaves reacted to separation, the speculator John Armfield gave the rather bland reply

53. Ingraham, *The South-West, by a Yankee,* pp. 120–27; Chamerovzow (ed.), *Narrative of . . . John Brown,* p. 117.

54. Moses Grandy, *Narrative of the Life of Moses Grandy, Late a Slave in the United States of America* (Boston, 1844), p. 11; Ball, *Fifty Years,* p. 11; Ovington narrative in Blassingame, *Slave Testimony,* p. 536. For similar narratives describing deep distress at sale or the prospect of sale, see *Slave Testimony,* pp. 95–97, 108–9, 114, 160, 166–71, 215–16, 263, 286–87, 332, 339, 373, 403–404, 456, 504, 548–49, 593, 597–98, 616, 708, 738–39.

that "sometimes they don't mind it a great deal; at other times they take on right smart, for a long time." Presumably the sort of assumptions behind this were that black emotions were often fleeting, sometimes overpassionate, and in any case mattered little when set against the "needs" and priorities of the white world. Such notions, discussed more fully later in this study, seem indeed to have been core components of southern racism and of the rationalization of antebellum slavery. Unwittingly, however, slave traders, in their correspondence, provide records of slave reactions to separation which are much less bland than Armfield's brief comment. Constantly, traders wrote that slaves would have to be threatened, chained, secured in jail, beaten, and guarded because of their reaction to sale and separation. The speculator C. Haynes of Abingdon, Virginia, wrote for example of several slaves who had "run off." As he told his partner: "They made a battle when we attempted to take them. One of Col. Smith's was with them and fought with sticks and butcher's knives." Thomas Williams, a Washington speculator, sold a woman and children away from her husband, and noted to R. H. Dickinson, the Richmond auctioneer: "She is qualified certain, first rate washer and ironer and cook and I warrant her to be such and a good paddling will make her bring a good price." Another trader sent a man, wife, and child, apparently intending Dickinson to sell them separately; he noted that the man was "a damned rascal" and wanted him ironed. He added, in the professional chatter of the slave dealer, that he wanted Dickinson quickly to sell all of his purchases still left at the auctioneer's depot—"Get rid of all those blame subjects that are on hand; Isbell with the rest when it can be done to advantage—and paddle all the crazy ones until their senses are right."[55]

Another Dickinson letter revealed the success of a mother in returning to her family. Alex Fitzhugh wrote to Dickinson:

> I fear you cannot sell Lucy, in her low spirited situation for more than four hundred and twenty five dollars, which sum I am not disposed to take. Therefore if you cannot get four hundred and fifty dollars twenty four hours after the receipt of this be so kind as to send her [back]. . . . Tell her to bring her child's clothes.
>
> I feel grateful to you . . . believing you have used your best exertions to sell her but her hysterical, low spirited situation thwarted your best intentions. . . . Assure her I will keep her myself or sell her [locally] in Falmo.

Another client, as a middleman explained, required Dickinson to

55. Andrews, *Slavery and the Domestic Slave Trade,* pp. 137–38, 148; Haynes to Meek, 26 Oct. 1836, Negro Collection (AU); Williams to Dickinson, 28 June 1847, Campbell to Dickinson, 5 Aug. 1848, Chase Papers (AAS).

sell Susan the first opportunity whatever you can get for her [. A]s she is making so many complaints and says she is not sound he [the seller] is not willing to warrant her soundness . . . but [said the agent] I believe it is all pretentions and false representations she is making with the hope of returning to King George [district, whence her present owner had bought her] to live with her husband which she will never do.[56]

The papers of the Charleston dealer Ziba Oakes, like those of Dickinson of Richmond, repeatedly show the problems of selling separated slaves. A letter of January 1854, for example, concerned a slave who was sent to Oakes after already frustrating the efforts of a Savannah dealer to sell her. The owner, A. G. Porter, explained that she had been sent for sale because "she displeased me in disobeying my orders and in her conduct in keeping things from me respecting her children." Porter felt that there was "no doubt she will try every way that she can invent . . . so I may take her back home." Nevertheless, Oakes was instructed to ignore the slave's complaints, and was told to gain her cooperation by the threat that if she did not alter her conduct she would be sent "further from home where she can never hear from any of her people again." A few days later, Oakes's associate McElveen bought a slave woman and reported: "The woman will complain but she is unwilling to leave [her husband]. I think she will need correcting. I could not buy her husband." In very exceptional cases, a slave might be able to make a more or less direct record of the agony felt at separation; one such was Fatima, whose husband had been sent to Oakes and awaited sale at his depot. The slaveowner asked that, "as his so called wife wishes to send some message," the following farewell be passed on:

Howdy and goodbye, for I never expect to see you again. Try to do the best you can, and if you have a good master behave properly to him, and try to think about your master in Heaven. If I had known you were going to be sold I would have been better satisfied, but I am very much distressed now at being separated from you. Remember me and I will think of you. Write to me after you are settled. Your wife Fatima. [written in her master's hand]

The letter was restrained, and no doubt necessarily so, when passed via messengers who thought so little of slave "wives" and "husbands."[57]

From traders' files, we could find a great many more examples, not perhaps of letters like Fatima's, but of the agony of separation. Ulti-

56. Fitzhugh to Dickinson, 24 Feb. 1846, Tiffy to Dickinson, 7 Feb. 1847, Chase Papers (AAS).

57. Porter to Oakes, 17 and 26 Jan. 1854, McElveen to Oakes, 7 Feb. 1854, Fatima [by her master, Edwards] to Oakes, 14 April 1857, Oakes Papers (BPL).

mately more important, however, than individual examples is the context of forced separation—the very vigorous sense of family that has been documented for the slave communities of the southern states. Inevitably, that context ensured that separations left profound and permanent imprints on the lives of slaves and upon the whole character of their interactions with their masters and mistresses.

CYCLES OF SEPARATION

In the concluding chapter, I shall say a good deal more about the significance of sales for relationships between slaves and their owners, but for the moment let us examine the slave family and the impact of forcible separations upon it. Speculators' assaults upon the family reached deep into the lives of antebellum slaves, and, since each destructive foray was unpredictable, the dread of separation was unending. Separations, nevertheless, did not occur entirely at random: risks were higher in some areas than others, and they fluctuated as a slave's life passed through successive phases. Indeed, there were certain "cycles of separation" which help both to describe patterns of risk and to explain the ability of the slave community to live through such extreme stress. In describing and interpreting these broad cycles, I shall concentrate first upon the exporting states and upon the individuals within a family.

Because families begin with a union between spouses, let us start by considering the extent to which the marriages of Upper South slaves were at risk from sales to the trader. The extent of the trade—each decade carrying away from the Upper South perhaps 10–15 percent of all young-adult slaves, almost all sold with no accompanying spouse—itself suggests a very real risk of separation. And wherever slaves and exslaves were able to give evidence on their experiences, stories of separation were almost certain to be a major theme. We can go further than this, however, and suggest, at least in general proportions, the likely level of risk that a marriage would be terminated as a result of trading. When we weigh the impact of the trade against other factors (especially the importance of mortality) in ending marriages, it seems that about one in five of the first marriages of Upper South slaves would have been broken by the trade.[58] An indication of the cumulative

58. Appendix 8 gives detailed calculations on the likely proportions of marriages broken by the trade, local sales, the nonmarket activities of owners, and mortality. The data seem to give a fairly reliable ranking of the various causes which terminated marriages, but (especially because mortality data for specific ages are not entirely trustworthy) close precision is not claimed.

Table 6.4. Cumulative proportions of Upper South slaves with first marriages broken by the trade: Mid and late antebellum period

Approximate ages of partners (yrs)	% in each age group
Male 24 Female 19	6.6
Male 34 Female 29	15.5
Male 44 Female 39	19.1
Male 54 Female 49	20.1

Note: This table uses data on the structure of the trade (see traders' papers used for Table 6.2), the volume of the trade (Chapter 2), and age-specific survival rates (Chapter 2). I first made separate estimates (for various ages) of the risk of husbands, then of wives, being traded away from a partner. Results for males and females were then combined so as to indicate the probability of marriage terminations. Data were selected for males who were approximately five years older than females because this seems to have been the typical age gap between slave spouses.

destructive effect of the trade upon marriages is given in Table 6.4; Appendix 8 provides much fuller evidence and comments upon the likely level of reliability of the data.

In order to gain a more complete view of the forcible separation of Upper South marriages, we should consider certain additional factors. As we know from evidence earlier in this chapter, local sales tended to be much less destructive of families than did interregional trading. Local sales, added to the trade, might then have raised the proportion of the region's marriages forcibly broken to something like one in four. Beyond that, certain nonmarket transactions—planter migrations, gifts of slaves (often between relatives), and estate divisions between beneficiaries—would have caused additional disruption. The evidence of slave narratives, though, is that sales (combined local and long-distance) caused almost four times as many separations as did all of these nonmarket factors taken together.[59] Overall, then, forcible separations

59. For evidence from the narratives, see Escott, *Slavery Remembered,* p. 48, Table 2.6. The heavy emphasis on sale rather than nonmarket transactions also agrees with the recurring emphasis of full-length slave autobiographies. On gifts and estate divisions, see also Crawford "Quantified Memory," p. 177; Gutman, *Numbers Game,* pp. 132–37; Gutman, *Black Family,* pp. 128–29, 135, 138. Nonmarket transactions are likely to have been less age-selective than sales, so that some of the separa-

probably destroyed about one in three of all first marriages between Upper South slaves. Against this, as we noted earlier, only a tiny percentage—perhaps 4 percent—would have been voluntarily broken by the slaves themselves. The proportions just outlined—not reliable to within a few percent, but probably broadly representative—suggest, then, that the risk of the forcible termination of a first marriage was very real indeed. But against this, the substantial majority of Upper South marriages would seem to have run their natural course, and would have been ended only by the death of a spouse.

In these initial comments on trading and members of the family group, we can now turn to the experience of Upper South children. As we know, speculators had very little interest in children under about eight years (unless they were part of mother-and-offspring lots). It is likely, then, that only a fraction of 1 percent of Upper South slaves aged seven and younger were traded without either parent. Again, we know that the risk of being sold away from parents increased with age, and it seems that about 5 percent of the region's slaves aged eight to eleven, inclusive, would, rather consistently from 1810 or 1820 to the Civil War, have been separated from parents and sold separately to the trader. From those aged twelve to fourteen, inclusive, something like a further 16 percent would have been sold from parents (see Appendix 8, section 8.1). Children, however, suffered separation not just when they were sold away without parents, but when they were traded away from their fathers in mother-and-offspring lots, and also when parents themselves were sold away. These additional sales raised to perhaps something like one in three the proportion of Upper South children aged fourteen and under who were separated from one or both parents by the trade.[60] Local sales and nonmarket transactions might have raised

---

tions brought by nonmarket factors might have involved older slaves and second marriages.

60. Calculations for parents traded from offspring are based on estimates (given later) of marriages broken by trading, an allowance being made for marriages which would still have been childless. The overall patterns of estimated separations between offspring and parents fit quite closely with those of Crawford in "Quantified Memory" (pp. 174–75, 163, 184). As he pointed out, his data on this issue were based on a far smaller sample than for most of his other results (only 109 slaves reported the specific ages at which they were traded from parents). The available testimony suggested to Crawford that children aged up to nine years had about a 5–7 percent chance of being sold from their parents, and that by ages ten to sixteen the cumulative risk rose to between 20 and 28 percent. In addition, Crawford found that between 8 and 23 percent of children lost one parent or both through the sale of the parents themselves. The evidence which he reported combined local and long-distance sales and was for a general southern sample (rather than being for the

the proportion to almost one in two. Again, then, the risk of separation from parents was very real indeed; parents with several children would surely have found one or more sold away, if the children survived to their early teens; and siblings would have faced a similar risk of separation from a brother or sister. Against all of this we shall, nevertheless, have to consider the probability that the vast majority of children lived with their parents for at least ten years, and a majority for some years longer. Such a circumstance, together with the threat of separation, would surely have built very deep-rooted ties between parents and children.

Having said something of the hazards of sale and their immediate connection with individual members of Upper South families, I can now begin more fully to set these separations into their context. As I noted earlier, certain cycles of separation operated. Herbert Gutman pointed to one major cycle: the regime of "destruction, construction, and dispersal" relating to the career of a typical successful slaveowner.[61] A consideration of two further patterns—which we might call a lifetime cycle and a regional cycle—will also help to establish the significance of separations resulting from the trade. Let me start by summarizing the important pattern which Gutman described. With detailed evidence from the careers of owners like John Cowper Cohoon of Virginia, he plotted a common pattern which slaveholders tended to create. Their careers in slaveowning might begin with "destruction"—that is, in order to create substantial holdings, Cohoon and other rising planters began by selective purchases. Their purchases were not of settled families, but of mother-and-offspring lots, "likely" children, prime field hands, and the like. Instead of any genuine sponsorship of the slave family, they served their own interests, destroying one generation of families by their purchases, and then preaching the values of family stability to their unfortunate recruits. The second phase, the "construction" stage, would see an owner keeping possession of his growing slave gang, encouraging natural increase, generally welcoming family ties, and selling off slaves only exceptionally (perhaps as punishment for infringements of his code). In this phase the "sponsorship" of families suited his interests. The desire to progress from farmer to planter was dominant. Aspiring planters, so recently the destroyers of families, could now indulge more lavishly in the comfort-

---

Upper South specifically). As we noted earlier, he also found that despite sale and other factors, by age nineteen some 50 percent still lived with their parents.

61. Gutman, *Black Family*, pp. 129–38.

able rhetoric of family and paternalism. Their circumstances and strategy made it convenient for them not to break up the families developing within their force of slaves. A third phase, however, again worked toward a new set of conveniences for the owner and his white family. When well established and perhaps advanced in years, our planter "arrivé" might well make gifts of slaves to daughters "needing" servants or sons starting out as the new generation of planter aspirants. And finally, with the planter's death, estate divisions might threaten to unravel the stable complex of family ties which had developed within the slave force.

Gutman's synoptic theory provides invaluable insights into the plantation syndrome and the slave experience. His theory fits neatly with the whole body of evidence which the records of the slave trade reveals. Consistently the slave family, in the priorities of owners, comes a very distant second to their own convenience. Despite that ordering of priorities, however, the slave family and slave community could achieve great richness, strength, and resilience. The "construction" phase would allow increasing "kinship imbeddedness"—a growth of family connections linking high proportions of a large slave gang, and yet maintaining a framework of exogamy.[62] And as Gutman pointed out, the "dispersal" phase of the plantation syndrome, while it brought anguish and tragedy in many cases, also tended to spread and deepen family and community links across quite wide local areas. Local sales and marriages off-plantation indirectly, and quite independently of any intention among owners, could extend slave contacts and widen the perspective in which they viewed their circumstances.

In this analysis of the family experience we should now consider two patterns mentioned earlier: the lifetime and regional cycles of separation. These interconnected with Gutman's three-stage cycle, and though hinged upon the systematic destructiveness of masters' self-interested strategies, failed to crush the slave family. But they did bring slaves the bitter experiences and materials with which to generalize about their plight and to see through their condition of bondage.

The lifetime cycle of separations for Upper South slaves in this period, as evidence in this chapter has already suggested, began in the great majority of cases with at least eight or ten years spent with parents (or with one parent if father or mother had died). Thus when

62. On "kinship imbeddedness" see Charles Wetherell, "Slave Kinship: A Case Study of the South Carolina Good Hope Plantation, 1835–1856," *Journal of Family History*, 6 (1981), pp. 294–308.

sale from parents or sale of a parent did occur, there would usually have been ample time for the deepest of attachments to develop, and for the most bitter of anguish to be felt during and long after parting. Most children did not lose their parents through sale, but the risk was real enough.

Later in life, when slaves married, most would *not* be separated by sale, but again, the risk was so dramatically high as to form a constant preoccupation, especially for those of ages such as to make them likely recruits for the trade. Evidence in Appendix 8 (especially Table A8.4) supports the view that slave marriages would normally (that is, when not prematurely ended by the master) have lasted at least twenty years, and a quarter of them thirty years of more.[63] But, as noted earlier, the trade would probably have prematurely broken about 20 percent of Upper South marriages. Even with slaves in their early twenties, trading would have broken about 7 percent of the region's marriages; and for those in their early thirties it seems that it would have broken about one in six (see Table 6.4).

So, among Upper South slaves, the marriage institution as a normal expectation and right of life could flourish; but, at the same time, forced separations were sufficiently widespread for deep distrust of those who

63. Fogel and Engerman, using Evans's survivor table, estimated that the typical duration of a slave marriage broken only by death was twenty-four years (*Time on the Cross*, vol. 2, p. 115). It is possible that Evans's table exaggerated the life expectation of adult slaves somewhat, and those of children more markedly. See Robert Evans, Jr., "The Economics of American Negro Slavery, 1830–1860," pp. 185–256 and especially p. 212, in Universities–National Bureau Committee for Economic Research (ed.), *Aspects of American Labor Economics* (Princeton, 1962); and see Edward Meeker, "Mortality Trends of Southern Blacks, 1850–1910: Some Preliminary Findings," *Explorations in Economic History*, 13 (1976), pp. 13–42. The general conclusion about duration of marriage seems, however, to be valid. Table A8.4 in Appendix 8 suggests that, unless prematurely broken by masters, 41 percent of marriages would still have been intact for males aged fifty-four and their spouses five years younger. This would have been twenty years after the typical slave had married, and perhaps fifteen years after the proportion ever married among these slaves had reached over 90 percent. Given that a very large percentage of slaves would have married before ages nineteen and twenty-four (for females and males, respectively), a "typical" marriage duration of twenty years or so seems very probable. On long marriages, see also Gutman, *Black Family*, esp. pp. 150–51. A marriage of twenty years would compare very closely with marriages in preindustrial (eighteenth- and nineteenth-century) Europe, but because of lower mortality among American whites would fall perhaps some ten years below that of antebellum whites. See Peter Laslett, *Family Life and Illicit Love in Earlier Generations* (Cambridge, England, 1977) p. 184; Laslett, "Philippe Ariès and 'La Famille'," *Encounter*, 45 (1976), pp. 80–83; Robert V. Wells, "Demographic Change and the Life Cycle of American Families," *Journal of Interdisciplinary History*, 2 (1971), pp. 273–82.

wrecked marriages—the masters—to be endemic. With increasing years, slaves reached a phase of life where marriages came less under threat because the spouses became less saleable, but the offspring of those unions would increasingly be of interest to the traders. Even those who were widowed at an early age, in circumstances of high slave mortality, could still strive to hold on to children and other kin. The lifetime cycle of separations, however, moved inevitably into a phase when one or more offspring were likely to be seized and traded away.[64]

Because slave lifespans were typically about thirty to forty years after age twenty, life for the great majority of slaves would usually have been dominated by childhood, child-rearing, and what Peter Laslett, in another context, called "the intense complex of emotional relationships" represented by the family.[65] For slaves, then, the lifetime cycle of separations combined very real dangers of major family disaster with, at every phase, realistic hopes of preserving family relationships and values. Such a mix of hope and anxiety seems to have been exactly calculated to preserve in the slave community at large both a deep sense of family and an equally keen distrust of the master and of the system which put families under such agonizing stress.

So far, we have concentrated upon the lifetime cycle of Upper South slaves, but that pattern merged with a regional cycle of separations. In some ways, it was the Upper South family which was most affected by the trade. For those born within the importing states the danger of forced separation was relatively low, perhaps only about one third of the level of risk faced by Upper South slaves.[66] As a consequence, slaves born in the importing region could expect longer marriages and fewer forced interruptions to their child-rearing. But against this there

64. In some white societies, poor families sometimes found it necessary to send children away from home, usually to be kept elsewhere as servants. Richard Wall's study, "The Age at Leaving Home," *Journal of Family History,* 3 (1978), pp. 181–202, found significant local variations, but generally he found this practice to be exceptional in preindustrial and modern Europe. When free parents, however reluctantly, sent their own children from home the situation was significantly different from that of slaves. With the separation of slave families through sale, the perception of the slaves would be that outsiders (slaveowners) were directly to blame, and an equally direct alienation from those outsiders was likely to result. But free whites who sent their children from home would have participated in the decision, and a particular outsider would not usually be identifiable as the cause of the separation.

65. On life expectation, see Evans, "Economics of American Slavery," p. 212, and Meeker, "Mortality Trends," p. 38. For Laslett's statement, see his "Philippe Ariès and 'La Famille'," p. 83.

66. See earlier discussion of effects of trading compared with local sales and nonmarket transactions.

were crucially important countercurrents. Old-established importing areas, over time, gradually developed enclaves (and in the cases of Georgia, Alabama, and Missouri by the 1850s, vast sections) of net exportation with all of its attendant increases in alarm and danger. Perhaps of even greater importance was the impact of newly imported slaves and the values carried with them. As Appendix 8 (Tables A8.5 and A8.6) shows for the 1820s and 1850s, a single decade's importations by the interregional trade might increase the slave population of an importing state by 30—even 50–100—percent. The regional cycle meant that heavy importers of slaves were (on a per capita basis, taking imports and local-born together) often even more dramatically influenced by marriage and family separations caused by the trade than were the exporting states. Vast proportions of Lower South slaves would have had the bitter experience of losing a first spouse through trade or of being traded as children from their parents.

Our understanding of the regional cycle can be enhanced by comparing data on Upper South slaves (from Table 6.4) with evidence which Herbert Gutman collected on the Mississippi slaves who, at the time of the Civil War, officially recorded their marriages.[67] First, let us compare the impact of the interregional trade on Upper South slaves and that of all forcible marriage separations (including those from local sales) on slaves living in Mississippi (whether imported or locally born). Males born in the Upper South would by age twenty-four have faced about a 7 percent chance of a marriage being broken by the trade (see Table 6.4). A male slave of that age who lived in Mississippi would have had about a 10 percent chance. For males who reached their thirties and forties, the cumulative chance of suffering a forcible marriage separation would have been about 24 percent among those living in Mississippi; again, this was several percentage points higher than for the typical male of that age who had been born in the Upper South. Among slave women living in Mississippi, rates of forcible marriage separation were again slightly higher (by around 1–3 percent, it seems) than was generally the case for women who had been born in the Upper South. When Upper South statistics are made fully comparable to those for Mississippi by adding marriage separations arising out of local sales and nonmarket transactions, the overall rates for the two areas, for about the 1840s and 1850s at least, become very similar.

67. Gutman, *Black Family,* Table 21, p. 147. It is not clear what proportion of the marriages were being newly entered into and what proportion had in practice already existed for some years before registration. The significant thing for the present purpose is that each registrant gave details of any previous marriage which had been broken.

Rates of forcible marriage separation in the importing states were not always similar to those of the Upper South, but varied according to the per capita level of importation or exportation. As Tables A8.5 and A8.6 show (Appendix 8), several states, in the decade or so before the Civil War, were more intensive importers than Mississippi; they would have experienced higher per capita rates of forcible marriage separation among their overall slave population. There were, however, still processes which allowed family traditions to recover.

The remarriage rate among Mississippi slaves was high. About 45–55 percent of those Mississippi slaves who were aged thirty and over when they registered a marriage with the Union Army clergy reported that a previous marriage had been terminated: rather more than half of those marriages had been broken by a master, and nearly all of the remainder had been ended by bereavement. Remarriage seems to have been common for women up to about age thirty; for men it continued at a significant rate into the mid-forties.[68] With remarriage, family life could gradually be rebuilt, while children who had been sold from parents and brought to Mississippi and other Lower South states would usually themselves marry and start families. These new Lower South families would be far less at risk of forced separation than had been the families of the Upper South, though local sales and estate divisions would scatter some of their members within the new Lower South locality and, as a side-effect, would tend to spread common ideas, experiences, and contacts. Inevitably, however, those who had been sold from the Upper South and suffered the bitter experiences of separation from brother, sister, parent, or spouse would pass on to their

68. There seems to be no reason why the marriage certificates should greatly misrepresent the percentage of Mississippi slaves, according to age, who experienced forced separation. But after a certain age slaves would have been unlikely to remarry, so that those older than that age would likely have been recording continuing rather than new marriages. Younger slaves, in contrast, would have been registering a mixture of new and old marriages. Thus the typical mortality rates of the slave population which was older than the key remarriage cutoff date are not reflected in the certificates. (Separations which occurred through force after the key age would also be omitted, but for older slaves mortality ended far more marriages than did force.) Of female registrants in their thirties, 53 percent reported that a previous marriage had been terminated at some unspecified time in the past; but for women in their forties or even their fifties the cumulative termination rate was only 1 percent higher. This suggests that after about age thirty, very few women were remarrying. Among males in their thirties, 44 percent reported that a previous marriage had ended; for males in their forties the figure was 54 percent, and for those over fifty years it was 58 percent. This suggests that some males remarried up to about their mid-forties—a finding that fits with earlier evidence about the age gap between spouses.

new families their knowledge of what masters did to slaves; and all around them, newly arrived victims of the trade would press home those stories of sorrow and betrayal.

The statistics in Chapter 6 have assumed that the trade accounted for about 60 percent of interregional movements. This assumption seems to be well founded (see Chapter 2), but the general patterns and cycles of separation would not have changed dramatically if the percentage were lower. A trade accounting for only 45 or 50 percent of movements, say, would still have broken about one in six Upper South marriages, and the impact upon the population and attitudes of slaves in the importing area would surely have been essentially similar to that outlined here. Some changes did occur over time; the period before 1810 was perhaps less profoundly marked by trading and separation. The evidence for those early years is much less solid than for later, but even in the first years of the antebellum period fear of "Georgia-men" and of separation was, it seems, well established among slaves.

In Chapter 8, more will be said about the attitudes of slaves toward masters and toward slavery. Before that, however, Chapter 7 examines the place of the trader in the social order of the South, to form a fuller basis for commenting upon slaveholders' attitudes toward speculation, families, slaves, and slavery.

7

The Question of Status: Traders in White Society and Southern Mythology

AT the level of grand theory and sectional politics, the South had, with the trader, a problem of some delicacy. Inevitably, in northern minds the speculator was associated with the separation of families and with hard commercial exploitation—so that, whatever grass-roots opinions and practices were, it was difficult to give him a free run within the official theory of southern life. The official defense of slavery and much of the private rationalizing were essentially paternalistic, resting on notions that slavery benefitted the enslaved as well as the masters. In official theory, safety nets were available to protect slaves from virtually every conceivable abuse of arbitrary power, the white community supposedly rallying in almost every case to keep wouldbe slave exploiters in line and to maintain southern standards. Potentially, the link between paternalism and the supposed encouragement of stable institutions among blacks meant that, for the individual slaveholder and in sectional polemics, there existed a permanent tension over family separations (and the trader) as against wider southern values. This awkwardness led, in public print and more privately, to quite frequent southern condemnations of the trader. None of this should lead us to conclude, either that traders were usually social outcasts, or that a permanent crisis of conscience on separation ran through the South. In practice, the nature of racism in the South seems largely to have preempted both of these outcomes.

Southern paternalism rested on profound racism, and racism, in turn, meant that whites should always judge what was best for blacks. It meant, too, that black families were not to be taken by owners as serious equivalents to those of whites. Blacks were seen as permanent children, or worse. They might have sometimes "excitable" attachments to family, but essentially such feelings were seen as short-lived.[1] Whites "knew" that their general scheme of slaveholding and "race control" should not be broken by anxiety over "temporarily unsettling" and "discomforting" slaves. Owners could decide which traders and "brokers" to deal with, and the owners, too, could best order and determine the priorities of their plantation and its "people." In debate and less formal discussion, they would routinely observe that separations were not common and that the trader was not central to slavery. And from their perspective, such propositions need not trouble the conscience, because—so ran the argument—separations were not the purpose of slavery. Instead, its great goal was race control and the safe and fruitful employment of "less advanced" peoples. Racism was, of course, the heart of slavery, and, doubling as paternalism, could in the minds of its devotees cope with any inconsistency which the abolitionists could bring before them. In practice, then, "paternalism" was almost infinitely permissive toward speculation, while yielding for propaganda and internal purposes a convoluted literature and mythology on the role of the trader himself.

UNCLE ROBIN AND UNCLE TOM

A sample of southern propaganda on the trade appears in that series of some fifteen or twenty proslavery novels which were speedily published in response to Harriet Beecher Stowe's *Uncle Tom's Cabin* (1852). In Stowe's own novel, the trade and family separation had been a crucial linking theme, so that those replying critically to her work faced the problem of whether or not to address the awkward matter of speculation. Most "replies" chose to avoid the trade, but in the several which gave it some consideration we find a considerable parade of improbable scapegoats.[2] When the trader appeared in Randolph's *The Cabin and the Parlor* (1852) it was because "Messrs. Skin and Flint, factors and merchants of *New York*" [emphasis added] had, by charging excessive commissions and interest, forced their southern client, Mr. Courtney, to make a sale of his slaves. The feelings of southern commu-

1. For a fuller discussion of proslavery views on the black family, see Chapter 8.
2. For a discussion of many of the "replies," see J. B. Tandy, "Pro-Slavery Propaganda in American Fiction of the Fifties," *South Atlantic Quarterly*, 21 (1922), pp. 41–51, 170–79.

nities on such occasions were, however represented as having been such that

> The slaves . . . were all purchased to remain in the district. Even among those planters who showed little concern for the ruined Courtneys there was a sentiment of honour on this point. . . . A trader who had made his appearance was hustled away rather rudely by one or two present, so that, after making a few ineffectual bids, he thought it prudent to retire.[3]

Again in J. W. Page's novel entitled, with consummate awkwardness, *Uncle Robin in his Cabin and Tom Without One in Boston,* it was northern interference which threatened to bring disaster to the slave. Incited by visiting abolitionists, two bondsmen were persuaded to run away to the North and, in order to gain provisions for their journey, stole hams from a meathouse. As luck would have it, though, the theft was from an unreformed New Englander who, still with all of his "prejudices," had recently settled in the South. In a desperate bid to frustrate this "evil" northerner's desire to have the slaves hung for theft, the gentle owner of the runaways hit upon the idea of selling them away to a trader. The latter, a certain Mr. Bosher, was not at all surprised to find that the slaves had "brought trouble upon themselves" by planning to run away. "Our trade," he explained to the good-hearted master,

> would be completely broken up . . . if t'want for runaway negroes; and I think sir, we have to thank the abolitionists for that; they entice them off, and we grab them flying. I know a *yankee* trader who gets whole lots that way. [emphasis added]

The plot of Page's novel suggested, too, that unlike their truly southern counterparts, northern-born slaveholders, interested only in brutal profit, frequently sold slaves without regard to their ties of family. Indeed, these Yankee planters were represented as providing the trader with the greater part of his stock. Moreover, according to Page, the traders themselves, more often than not, turned out to be Yankees![4]

From Mrs. Eastman's *Aunt Phillis's Cabin* (1852), it appeared that sales which resulted in family separation were "the worst feature of slavery, . . . but were very uncommon." Nevertheless, "outside interference," that enduring southern scapegoat, could occasionally disturb the gentle routine of the plantation. Such an instance occurred in Mrs. East-

3. J. T. Randolph, *The Cabin and the Parlor; or, Slaves and Masters* (Philadelphia, 1852), pp. 31, 42.

4. J. W. Page, *Uncle Robin in his Cabin and Tom Without One in Boston* (Richmond, 1853), pp. 21–53, 230–36.

man's book when scheming, opinionated "Abolitioners" bullied a group of slaves into running away. "The Abolitioners, sir, . . . they wouldn't let the poor devils rest until they 'duced them to go off," a slave explained. Most of the fugitives, however, were captured and one was sold to a trader—because "our servants say they wants no runaways to live 'long o' them." Happily, though, with another runaway a kindly and forgiving southerner stepped in, rescued her from the trader and restored her to her family. Again a last-minute rescue occurred in Reverend Baynard R. Hall's *Frank Freeman's Barber Shop* (1852). Mistakenly believing Frank to have been involved in a massacre of whites, the local community—until the truth was dramatically revealed—had thought it best to allow him to be "sold South." With Thomas Bangs Thorpe's *The Master's House,* (1854), slavery was seen to have had isolated cases of abuse, but these were attributed to Major Dixon, the slave trader, and Mr. Toadvine, the overseer—a nasty, evil, and universally detested pair who delighted in the brutal treatment of slaves.[5]

Northerners and other outsiders could, then, sometimes read about the "outcast" trader in proslavery novels, and travellers to the South often heard the same sort of stories (and for the same propaganda reasons). In the 1850s, Nehemiah Adams, a Boston minister, visited the South and became much impressed with slavery. He reported meetings with Southerners who wanted to abolish the interregional trade "or at least correct [it], till no wrong, no pain, should be the fruit of it which is not incidental to every human lot." And "Negro traders," he found, "are the abhorence of all flesh. Even their descendants, when they are known . . . have a blot upon them. I never knew a deeper aversion to any class of men." Traders, he seemed to have discovered, picked up only troublesome slaves or those of masters in extreme poverty; and the speculators tended to be "passionate, cruel, tyrannical men, seeking dominance in some form to gratify these instincts." As the historian Frederic Bancroft reported after reviewing a sample of contemporary works, the southern propaganda image of the trader was that of a brutal, ruthless sharper. "Imagine", he wrote,

> a compound of an unscrupulous horse-trader, a familiar old-time tavern keeper, a superficially complaisant and artful hard-drinking gambler and an ignorant,

5. H. Eastman, *Aunt Phillis's Cabin, or Southern Life as It Is* (Philadelphia, 1852; New York, 1968), pp. 213–30; B. R. Hall, *Frank Freeman's Barber Shop; A Tale* (New York, 1852), pp. 70–95; T. B. Thorpe, *The Master's House; A Tale of Southern Life* (New York, 1854).

garrulous and low politician, and you will get a conception that resembles the southern ante-bellum notion of the 'nigger trader'.

Such an image, indeed, became part of the plantation legend and the tradition of southern history.[6]

Perhaps the classic in the antebellum genre of trader stereotyping was Daniel Hundley's *Social Relations in our Southern States* (1860). Here we find the oily speculator in all his repellent features and with all of his characteristic vices. The trader, with his "grasping" instincts, was, he maintained, a "Yankee" and not a southerner in basic character. After listing a string of other southern outcasts, he resoundingly announced: "But the most utterly detestable of all southern Yankees is the Negro Trader—Speculator he delights to call himself in late years." The trader stood, according to Hundley, "pre-eminent in villainy and a greedy love of filthy lucre." He allowed that a few decent men might enter the trade, but soon even these became debauched, drunken, prematurely aged, gambling, ruthless swindlers.

The natural result of their calling seems to be to corrupt them; for they have usually to deal with the most refractory and brutal of the slave population, since good and honest slaves are rarely permitted to fall into the unscrupulous clutches of the speculator.

In oaths and "downright blasphemy" the trader's only equals were "those infidel socialists, free-lovers, and abolitionists." As for honest dealing,

Ah! Messrs. Stock-brokers of Wall Street—you who are wont to cry up your rotten railroad, mining, steamboat, and other worthless stocks—for ingenious lying [even] you should take lessons from the southern Negro Trader!

Thus, of the mendacious speculator's stock, "nearly nine-tenths" were

vicious ones sold for crimes or misdemeanors, or otherwise diseased ones sold because of their worthlessness as property. These he purchases at about half what healthy and honest slaves would cost him; but he sells them as both honest and healthy, mark you.

And in classic proslavery fashion Hundley pronounced slavery as an institution to be sound—indeed, ordained by God. The problems of slavery were few, and the abuses brought about by the trader were perhaps chief among them. Indeed, he maintained, to argue against slavery

6. Nehemiah Adams, *A South-Side View of Slavery; Or Three Months in the South in 1854* (Boston, 1855), pp. 77–78; Bancroft, *Slave Trading*, p. 368.

as a domestic institution simply because it is abused was like the socialists and free-lovers who argue against the marriage relation, because married people are always quarrelling, and running off to Indiana to be divorced. They have not the good sense to discriminate between the legitimate uses of an institution and the illegitimate abuses to which it can be subjected.

With Hundley, then, the speculator was turned from being an ideological embarrassment into being the lynch-pin of slavery's defense—the quintessential scapegoat, devoid of all honor in the South, and toward whom almost any awkward question could rhetorically be turned.[7]

A CATALOG OF CRIMES AND ACCUSATIONS

The "official" catalog of the trader's crimes included dividing those honest black families unfortunate enough to come his way, habitual brutality in dealing with slaves, trafficking in vicious, criminal, and unhealthy slaves, and general business dishonesty. From evidence in earlier chapters, we know, however, that masters, not traders, brought about the vast majority of separations, and we know that sales which broke up families were not usually made by desperate men nearing bankruptcy. The most crucial accusation—that of the trader as family wrecker—was, then, essentially no more than a propaganda ploy. Traders, acting as agents, were as much, but no more, to blame for separations than was slaveholding society in general. The presence, in southern prints and elsewhere, of the trader as prime mover in separations itself suggests—because its basis was hypocritical, self-serving ideology—that the image of the trader as outcast was there to mislead, and that behind it lay very different social realities.

This is not to say, however, that the slavemonger was not among the most accomplished in the beating and punishment of slaves, nor that his morals were especially elevated. Physical abuse would to an important extent be tempered by a professional self-interest in preserving a slave's health and saleability, but this still left much scope for brutality. How much sexual abuse of slaves by traders went on is unclear, but some references to it certainly occur in slave narratives. In one narrative Moses Roper, a slave forced to act as a trader's assistant, reported that dealers regularly forced their sexual attentions upon the most beautiful of the black women they purchased. And John Brown, another former slave, recorded that the trader Starling Finney, while

7. D. R. Hundley, *Social Relations in Our Southern States* (New York, 1860), pp. 139–40, 141, 148.

driving him southward with the rest of his coffle, supplemented his stock by stealing a girl from an old white woman, and the girl

> was then forced to get up in the wagon with Finney, who brutally ill-used her, and permitted his companions to do in the same manner. This continued for several days, until we got to Georgia, where Finney sold her.[8]

Only the wildest of traders would have indiscriminately whipped and lacerated slaves, but threats, bullying, "paddling," "hand sawing," "flopping," and otherwise chastising slaves must have been a fundamental part of the slaving business. Slave men would routinely be chained and shackled, and in selling the incentive was always there, as the speculator Thomas Williams put it, to "paddle all the crazy ones until their senses are right" and they cooperated in being sold. The speculator Ziba Oakes's letters testify to the practice of whipping slaves to make them "talk up right." Similarly, with the slave Edward, for example, Dickinson and Hill appear to have accepted the owner's instructions to whip him "a few times" to "get him to talk right." Indeed, the Dickinson letters contain many such instructions. The independent behavior of two female slaves decided the speculator J. J. Toler that he should adopt "Dr. Hall's medicine." As Toler angrily reported to his partner:

> I had [the two slaves sold] . . . but they went to putting on their complaints and they refused them and of course let them go without making a sale of them. . . . Rough talking wont do. . . . I will have to use some of Dr. Hall's medicine of North Carolina. You know what kind of medicine that is. I dont want you to sell them to anybody back there for if you do they will always brake up your sales from bad talking. They want braking and I had as well brake them as anybody.

And insurbordinate behavior from a slave woman convinced another trader that she was "the darndest nigger on occasion," and led him to explain: "I dont like whipping a sick negro though if she cuts any more capers I shall flog her severely." Punishments which would not break the skin and leave scars (marks which could damage sale) might often be favored by traders, but the slave Joe particularly annoyed McElveen, who declared: "I want to give him 100 lashes as soon as I come down as he had no cause of leaving me. He ran away from work and nothing else. Dont believe anything he tells you." Perhaps Joe was a laborer or personal servant of McElveen, and that explained the latter's recourse

8. Moses Roper, *A Narrative of the Adventures and Escape of Moses Roper from American Slavery* (London, 1840), pp. 24, 63–66; Chamerovzow (ed.), *Slave Life in Georgia*, pp. 18–19.

to a massive bout of whipping (which would have left lasting marks), rather than the use of the less damaging device of "paddling" or "moderate" whipping.[9]

The stripping and close physical examination of slaves was another charge levelled against the trader, but one which could equally be levelled against his clients. References to naked examinations are quite common both in slave narratives and in traders' letters. In one letter, McElveen reported that a slave he had just bought was "the best stripped fellow I ever examined." Another trader felt somewhat indignant over complaints concerning two slaves recently sold, and wrote to his partner that he had told the customer "to strip them and examine them, and he took them in my back room and came back and said he did not see anything the matter with them." Another examination provided the occasion for a slave's successful escape. "I bought a boy," the trader G. W. Eutsler reported, "and had him in my room and stripped him and told the man I would take him. He gave him an order to go out and get his clothing and that was the last I have seen of him"![10]

The charge that traders specialized in criminal, vicious, and diseased slaves was often made, but clearly it was based upon a propaganda tradition rather than on reality. Had criminals made up a major proportion of the vast interregional traffic, we should have to conclude that the child and young-adult population of the South (those of trading age) was so "criminalized" as to mean that the discipline of slavery was in open and permanent chaos. In reality, the notion of a trade dominated by vicious slaves was a propaganda ploy. As long as the trade was seen as a minor affair in terms of volume, the speculator could conveniently be linked to the worst minority on the fringes of society, and his traffic could even be seen as providing a police force, more or less of last resort, which would teach the worst slaves a sharp lesson.[11]

9. Williams to Dickinson, 28 June 1847, Chase Papers (AAS); Wright to Oakes, 28 Mar. 1857, Oakes Papers (BPL); Campbell to Dickinson, 8 Feb. 1850, Dickinson Papers (CHS); Toler to Ferguson, 27 Dec. 1858, Ferguson Papers (NCA); Glen to Jarratt, 4 Mar. 1832, Jarratt-Puryear Papers (DU); McElveen to Oakes, 8 Sept. 1856, Oakes Papers (BPL).

10. McElveen to Oakes, 9 Aug. 1853, Oakes Papers (BPL); Toler to Ferguson, 4 Mar. 1859, and Eutsler to Ferguson, 14 Aug. 1856, Ferguson Papers (NCA). For two of the very numerous examples from slave narratives, see L. M. Mills and Peter Johnson narratives in Blassingame (ed.), *Slave Testimony,* pp. 503–504, 507–508.

11. The claim that the trade was based to a major extent on the sale of criminals is implausible from the start, but detailed evidence against this charge comes from Virginia's official records relating to convicted slave criminals. These penitentiary records indicate that from 1816 to 1842 traders transported from the whole of Vir-

To argue that the trade specialized, not in criminal and vicious, but simply in runaways and those who were particularly troublesome would be a little more plausible, though still fundamentally misleading. Those who were exceptionally troublesome to owners might well show signs of having been sharply punished, and such signs, we know, would have tended to damage sale prices. The punishment of slaves, of course, crops up in slave narratives, planter's, and trader's records alike. In 1838, for example, J. R. Long, a trader but also a planter, recaptured one of his plantation hands and reported:

> I gave him a real whipping and hand sawing and he has been a fine negroe ever since. I told him he might run off if he chosed and I would knock out one of his jaw teeth and brand him and I intend to stick to my promise.

It seems that Long's word could be relied upon! A little later, following a whipping from his overseer, the same slave ran away but, wrote the owner, "he came home to me at knight and I branded him. He's been at work ever since and is done fine." When acting in his capacity as trader, however, Long would have been wary of picking up large numbers of slaves who were badly whipped, branded, or who had had their ears cropped or their teeth knocked out as punishment.[12]

Speculators did, no doubt, buy some slaves who showed clear signs of having been punished in such a way as to leave major scars, but the emphasis in virtually every buying advertisement was upon the need for "young and likely Negroes" in the best possible condition. McElveen was willing to consider a badly whipped slave but, as a letter to his partner showed, gave careful consideration to the market implications of scarring. He informed Oakes:

> I refused a girl 20 year old at 700 yesterday. I offered 675 for her and think it enough. If you think best to take her at 700 I can still get her. She is very badly whipped but good teeth. The whipping has been done long since.

But, typically, the advertisement of A. J. Hydrick emphasized that unmarked slaves were the priority: "NEGROES WANTED. I am paying the

---

ginia an annual average of not more than about twenty convicted slaves. Furthermore, they show that all but about 5 percent of Virginia's slave transportees were male. By contrast, we already know that in the interregional slave trade the sexes were almost *evenly balanced*. The sharp contrast between the male–female ratio among criminal transportees and that of the slave trade as a whole very strongly suggests that convicted criminal slaves can have accounted for only a very small percentage of the interregional trade. On criminal slaves see Virginia State Auditor's Papers, Item 153 (VSL); and see also U. B. Phillips, "Slave Crime in Virginia," *American Historical Review*, 20 (1915), pp. 336–40.

12. Long to Long, 16 Nov. 1838, 29 June 1839, Long Papers (NCA).

highest cash prices for young and likely NEGROES, those having good front teeth and being otherwise sound." P. H. Ellis's advertisement was similar; he sought slaves who were "young, sound, have good countenance and front teeth." And the same emphasis appeared when the trader E. W. Ferguson provided a buying agent with particulars of the type of slaves he wanted. Ferguson's note ran:

> Age from 8–22 year old. *See no scars no burn whip marks* see no lumps under throat nor rupture see ankles straight, and knees also. See the age and height and what you think they will weigh, and get the lowest cash price direct to me to Richmond. Good teeth. E. W. Ferguson, Richmond, Virginia [emphasis added].[13]

Runaways and slaves sold as punishment for "wrongdoings" certainly contributed to the trader's stock. Their misdeeds, nevertheless, would usually have been insubordination and acts against the master, rather than what the slaves themselves would have regarded as acts reflecting a debased character. We find, then, one trader reporting that he had "bought a cook yesterday that was to go out of state . . . she just made the people mad that was all. She is said to be a No.1 cook." Of another slave recently bought a trader wrote:

> I promised his owner . . . to send him out of the state. Nothing much against him but . . . [the owner] wishes him sent to the West if possible. He will run away if you give him the least chance.

Sometimes, too, traders would buy slaves who were described as still "in the woods" or "running at large." Thus, early in 1853 A. J. McElveen bought a fugitive who had just been "taken by the dogs," and later that year he wrote of another slave:

> They are one runaway which I am sure of getting. His master put out word if he come to me he would be let off. I give him until Tuesday to come to me. If he dont come in I will have the bloodhounds after him as soon as I can get them.

Even though practised runaways, then, were a part of the trade, they cannot, however, have dominated it. The sex ratio of the trade was *balanced,* but, as evidence of newspaper advertisements for runaways persistently shows, 75 percent of fugitives were adult *males*. Overall, the volume of the trade, its age and sex structure, and the trader's emphasis on "likely" slaves rule out the possibility that a specialist

13. McElveen to Oakes, 10 July 1853, Oakes Papers (BPL). The advertisements are in *Sumter Watchman* (S.C.), 18 and 25 Mar. 1857; and Ferguson's note is an undated manuscript in Ferguson Papers (NCA). On the removal of teeth as punishment and as means of identification, see also [Weld], *American Slavery As It Is,* pp. 77–85.

traffic in hardened criminals was anything more than a product of southern propaganda.[14]

The same can be said of the notion of a traffic concentrating on diseased slaves. It is true that dealers sometimes referred to "scrub Negroes," as for example when a circular of Betts & Gregory, the Richmond auctioneers, reported that "there came in this morning some scrub buyers and I hope we will be able to work them [the scrubs] off after a while."[15] The same circular, though, gave the general cautionary remark that "scrub Negroes" did not normally command a ready sale. Moreover, "scrub" seems to have been a general term for any who were not "likely"—they might often simply be middle-aged or dull-looking, rather than suffering from any ailment. And Betts & Gregory, vastly experienced auctioneers of slaves, found "scrubs" of all sorts to be a very minor and slow sale in the Richmond market. Moreover, customers usually demanded that the trader give a written guarantee, not just of title, but of soundness. The refusal of many traders, when they knew a slave to be unsound, to give a guarantee of health, suggests that bills of sale containing full warrants of soundness did provide customers with fairly valid legal guarantees against sharp practice.[16] It was, in any case, extremely unlikely that the trade could have assembled huge numbers of slaves suffering from types of physical or mental disabilities which could be both detected by the speculator and at the same time remain undetected by careful intending purchasers. Again, the charge that traders concentrated on dealing in mysteriously diseased slaves must be regarded as being significant, not for its accuracy, but for its inaccuracy and for what it revealed about the South's need to generate myths and scapegoats which would cover its massive traffic in slaves.[17]

14. Toler to Ferguson, 17 Feb. 1859, Ferguson Papers (NCA); McElveen to Oakes, 6 Mar. 1854, 26 Feb. and 9 Aug. 1853, Oakes Papers (BPL); and on the male–female ratio among runaways see Appendix 3.

15. Betts to "Edward," 31 Dec. 1859, Chase Papers (AAS).

16. On such guarantees see, for example, Browning to Boyd, 26 Dec. 1848 and 2 Jan. 1849, Boyd Papers (DU), in which Browning told his partner that giving compensation on a slave who had died was "bad but better than a law suit"; see law suit in Burton to Long, 20 Feb. 1846, Long Papers (NCA); see decision not to guarantee slave's soundness, in Toler to Ferguson, 4 Mar. 1859, Ferguson Papers (NCA); and see Bland to Mitchell, 9 Jan. 1836, Mitchell Papers (DU), in which Mitchell, a trader, "very honestly and honorably" refunded money on an unsound slave who had been fully guaranteed. See also Kotlikoff, "The Structure of Slave Prices," pp. 511–12, which emphasizes that guarantees were taken seriously in the New Orleans market.

17. An advertisement expressly calling for the purchase of unsound slaves was

MONSTERS AND NEGRO TRADERS

In beguiling visitors to the South and impressionable northern readers, the "trader-as-monster" stereotype had obvious propaganda purposes. It is significant, however, that the same sort of stereotype can also be found in conversations *within* the antebellum South, and its appearance there raises another layer of questions about its purpose and about the position of the trader. A letter by J. H. Hammond, the South Carolina planter-politician and proslavery publicist, produced just such a reference. Having been approached by his neighbor W. R. Hodgson as the possible purchaser for Hodgson's gang of fifty-nine slaves, he made an offer of $15,000, and informed the neighbor:

> I rated them at about 10 per cent under the negro trader's prices and at 10 per cent less than they would bring I think if sold separately as the trader sells. But this of course you would not think of doing nor would anyone who was not a monster—or a negro trader.

At first sight, we might see in Hammond's letter high principles and genuine revulsion against the speculator. This, though, would clearly be a mistake. From later correspondence, it is clear that the neighbor had little difficulty in disposing of the gang—and at $4,000 more than Hammond had bid. And in reality Hammond also made very numerous and extensive purchases from traders. Surviving records clearly show that the traders from whom he purchased included S. F. Slatter, Joseph Woods, Ansley Davies, H. N. Templeman (as well as Templeman, Omohundro & Co.), John W. Forward, Solomon Davis, J. Hull, Thomas Ryan, and T. N. Gadsden. And, even worse, despite his avowed revulsion against selling "separately," at least half of Hammond's recorded purchases from traders—being "separate" slaves aged from eight to fourteen years—are likely to have involved forced family separations. Indeed, as a recent biography indicates, over a thirty-year period Hammond bought 145 slaves "in gangs and as individuals from traders in Charleston, Columbia, Augusta, and Hamburg, as well as from neighbors and friends."[18]

---

found in an 1839 issue of the *Kentucky Gazette.* In his *Slavery Times in Kentucky,* p. 188, Coleman quoted the advertisement as follows: "To planters and owners of slaves! Those having slaves rendered unfit for labour by Yaws, Scrofula, Chronic Diarrhea, Negro Consumption, Rheumatism, etc., and who wish to dispose of them on reasonable terms will address J. King, No. 29 Camp Street, New Orleans." The purpose of the buyer, whether for dishonest trading or to further some medical activity, is unclear. Elsewhere in traders' correspondence and in hundreds of advertisements consulted, nothing remotely like it has been found.

18. Hammond to Hodgson, 16 Nov. 1846, 24 Jan. 1847, James H. Hammond

As Hammond's papers repeatedly show, he was a particularly astute and persistent businessman. His association of traders with monsters was no more than an attempt at blackmail for the purpose of gaining a price advantage. The letters of traders do not suggest that there was in practice any widespread problem of reluctance to deal with them. They complained of boredom, competition, bad weather, "bad" slaves, worries over prices—but not of unwillingness to do business. Indeed, from all of the traders' letters examined (running into many hundreds of items) only two pieces have been found which indicate the possibility of particular slaveholders being, for reasons principle, unwilling to sell to speculators. Firstly, in the E. W. Ferguson Papers (a substantial collection of trading correspondence) a colleague on one occasion reported to Ferguson: "I went out to the sale yesterday but they would not let a trader have the negroes." Secondly, in the R. H. Dickinson Papers, a letter of H. M. Nelson informed Dickinson, the prominent Richmond slave dealer, that, having recently bought two slaves from a local citizen, he had sent one of them to Dickinson for sale to the trade. "It has occurred to me, however," Nelson added, "that her master was possibly induced to sell her by supposing she was to come to me and not to dealers." He therefore asked that Dickinson should refrain from reselling the slave until the original master's wishes had been ascertained.[19]

At the same time, the fact that Hammond chose to use the trader-as-monster device suggests that it had some sort of resonance in the South, and that he might have had some hope at least of embarrassing his neighbor. The explanation seems to be that in order to be respectable one should not appear to be *too* willing to separate families. Slaveowners would often accept that separations brought some hardship to slaves. In the best society, therefore, one should not appear to be too willing to cause hardship. Along with this, and decisively taking precedence over it, however, went the rule that whites were the deci-

---

Papers (DU). On Hammond's purchases, see James H. Hammond Collection of Bills of Sale (SCL), Hammond Diaries (SCL) (especially April 1843 and January 1844), and correspondence between Gadsden and Hammond (from April to Oct. 1843) in James H. Hammond Papers (SCL). For documentation on Hammond's suppliers, see Appendices 2 and 4; see Goodell, *American Slave Code,* p. 40; and see Hammond's diary entry of 10 Apr. 1843 in which, without further comment, Forward, Hull, and Ryan are each listed as "trader" and as supplying him with particular slaves. The biography cited is Drew Gilpin Faust, *James Henry Hammond and the Old South: A Design for Mastery* (Baton Rouge, 1982), p. 82.

19. Eutsler to Ferguson, 14 Apr. 1856, Ferguson Papers (NCA); Nelson to Dickinson, 19 Feb. 1950, Dickinson Papers (CHS).

sion makers, and that they should in the end decide what needed to be done for themselves, their families, and their slaves. Although slaves might feel some hardship at separation, their distress was considered as in no way comparable to the sentiments and anxieties which whites could feel in their own family sphere. After all, black emotions, the proslavery argument ran, were merely temporary, excitable, or, at their more elevated, a doglike devotion to masters.[20] Without great trouble to the conscience, then, slaveowners could square their condemnation of a set of traders with their extensive sales to the trade—the key being their "knowledge" that blacks would recover from "temporary hardships," together with their confidence that as owners they could best judge the interests of the slaveholding enterprise. From this perspective, of course, any sale was possible and open to legitimization. It helped, nevertheless, even within the South to have a notional class of outstandingly oily speculators who could be ritually condemned. And if buyers and sellers were to deal honorably with traders in practice, it helped too—in fact it was a necessity—that there also be honorable traders. The logic of slavery therefore demanded that there be stereotyping of vicious traders as a class, but also that a place be made for the trader.

THE TRADER AS CITIZEN OF STANDING

If we sketch the careers of some of the traders who have appeared in this study, few if any pariahs emerge. Instead, the evidence seems clearly to be that traders, like almost any other successful businessmen, could become leaders of the local and even the wider community. The sample offered below is not scientifically selected and is not closely compared with a control group of other businessmen. It merely represents biographical information which could be gleaned for the sample of South Carolina traders discussed elsewhere in this study (see Chapter 2), together with evidence from those manuscript collections of North Carolina and Virginia speculators which have been located (and which are cited in Table 2.2). In this somewhat haphazard sample, however, the pattern is fairly consistent: trading, in itself, did not automatically lead to social ostracism, and a substantial section of the trading fraternity seems to have gained positions of real influence, respect, and leadership in the community.

A check through city ordinances and banking histories shows that several prominent Charleston (South Carolina) traders were aldermen in that city and directors of banks. Alexander McDonald, J. S. Riggs,

20. For a discussion of proslavery views on these issues, see Chapter 8.

Thomas Ryan, and Ziba Oakes (as well as A. J. Salinas, who sold large numbers of slaves and was probably a trader) were, for some part of the period 1845 to 1865, city aldermen. In addition, Ryan, Oakes, Thomas N. Gadsden, and McDonald were bank directors or vice-presidents. And whereas the banks concerned might perhaps have been partly the "pets" of traders, they were also the state's principal financial institutions.[21] The career of McDonald, one of the speculators who served both as alderman and bank director, did, it is true, end in great confusion. This, however, had nothing to do with any question that trading was harmful to business or social standing. In a court case, Eliza Coldough testified that McDonald had enjoyed

> the confidence of the public and was reputed to be a man of large means and responsible for all his engagements . . . [but that] to the great surprise of everyone, about the year 184[5] he had suddenly and clandestinely left the state and went no-one knows where, leaving a large amount of debts and little or nothing out of which they could be satisfied.

Another witness, Samuel Mayrant, gave similar testimony, observing that "up to the time of his leaving his credit was very high—His leaving took everyone by surprise".[22]

21. Except for McDonald, evidence on all of these individuals is given in Appendix 4. Alexander McDonald, with his brother Hugh, was quite clearly a trader. His advertisements, announcing "Negroes wanted. Cash will be given for any number of likely Negroes from 10 to 25 year of age" ran in Charleston papers throughout the 1830s and early 1840s. He appears repeatedly in New Orleans manifests. McDonald is known to have served as Charleston alderman in 1845; Riggs in 1859–60 and in 1865; Ryan in 1859–60 and in 1863 to 1868; Salinas in 1865; and Oakes from 1865 to 1868. See H. P. Walker (ed.), *Ordinances of the City of Charleston from the 19 August 1844 to the 14 September 1854* (Charleston, 1854); W. R. Horsen (ed.), *Ordinances of the City of Charleston 14 September 1854 to December 1 1859* (Charleston, 1859); and G. Pillsbury (ed.), *Ordinances of the City of Charleston from December 1 1859 to September 6 1870* (Charleston, 1871). The last publication indicates that records of ordinances and lists of aldermen for 1 Dec. 1859 to 12 Oct. 1865 were "lost or destroyed." Aldermanic positions held in that period are, therefore, not noticed in the present study.

Banking histories show that Ryan was a director of the State Bank of South Carolina (1857 to 1865); in 1861 he was a trustee of the Palmetto Savings Institution, and in 1865 its vice president; Oakes was a director of the South-Western Railroad Bank (1860–65); Thomas N. Gadsden, another trader, was a director of the People's Bank of Charleston (1853–55); and McDonald was a director of the Bank of the State of South Carolina (1838–45). On these banking connections, see J. M. Lesesne, *The Bank of the State of South Carolina: A General and Political History* (Columbia, S.C., 1970), p. 189; W. A. Clark, *The History of Banking Institutions Organized in South Carolina Prior to 1860* (Columbia, S.C., 1922), pp. 173, 185–86, 198, 213, 254.

22. Sumter District Equity Court (S.C.), *Green et al.* v. *McDonald et al.*, 1866, Bill 415 (SCA). See also that court's *Coldough* v. *Coldough*, 1849, Bill 347, and 1852, Bill 348 (SCA).

Of the other speculators just noted, T. N. Gadsden came from a family of particularly high repute. As the historian Frederic Bancroft wrote, in Charleston, "a community where old families of high character were numerous, few stood higher than the Gadsdens." The trader's close relatives included a bishop and a prominent lawyer, as well as James Gadsden, negotiator of the Gadsden Purchase, whose career combined the professions of soldier, planter, railroad president, and Minister to Mexico. Less is known of the trader Ziba Oakes's family, but there is no doubt that he became one of Charleston's most prominent citizens, highly influential too in South Carolina masonic circles. The Charleston City directory of 1855 shows that he was then an officer in the Most Worshipful Grand Lodge of Free Masons of South Carolina, serving on several committees, including the Charity Committee. In the same year, he was a Companion and the Grand Treasurer of the Grand Royal Arch Chapter of South Carolina Masons. Masonic connections have not always been universally popular in America and elsewhere, but in this case they do suggest, at least, acceptance within the Charleston business community.[23]

We have encountered another South Carolinian, Thomas C. Weatherly, several times in this study—advising Oakes to treat his slaves more firmly, and driving coffles to the West. *The History of Marlboro County,* first published in 1897, fails to refer to Weatherly's very extensive slave-trading activity; the failure no doubt stemmed from a longstanding southern tradition of deemphasizing the role of trading within the "peculiar institution." Since the entry for Weatherly was so favorable, though, and since slave trading was in practice the basis of his business activity, his speculative activity surely cannot have caused him serious social difficulties. The history records:

> T. C. Weatherly, so prominent in Marlboro affairs and so long one of its most popular citizens, began his business career in Clio as a salesman with Mr. McDaniel, but soon formed a partnership with Mr. J. L. McColl, which continued until he was elected Sheriff at Marlboro in 1845, when he sold out to Mr. McColl and moved to Bennettsville, in the vicinity of which place he lived until his death. He served the public and the state legislature for many years. A man of quick mind, ready action, public spirit and generous impulse, he exercised a large influence.

In fact, as well as serving as sheriff, Weatherly was a member of the state House of Representatives in the mid-1850s and mid-1860s, and a

23. On Gadsden, see Bancroft, *Slave Trading,* pp. 167–69; and on Oakes's masonic activities, see *The Charleston City and General Business Directory for 1855* (Charleston, 1855), p. 25.

member of the state Senate in the late 1860s and the 1870s. He negotiated in Washington with President Johnson, and was a leading Methodist and mason.[24]

The career of another South Carolina trader, Joseph Crews, was much more controversial. He seems almost to have fitted the southern image of the "oily speculator"—but the real controversy came, not because of trading, but because, after the Civil War, he dramatically converted from slave trader into organizer of black militias, "scalawag" Republican politician, and, it seems, racketeer. An enquiry established in order to investigate the Ku Klux conspiracy and into conditions in the South during Reconstruction turned up a great deal of evidence on the political career of Crews and, not surprisingly, this evidence shows that, as a "scalawag" politician, he was intensely unpopular in the white community. Indeed, Crews's career ended in 1875 with his death at the hands of a white lynch mob! In 1871, the subcommittee's witness Joel Foster testified that, as a politician, "Joe Crewes is understood to do a great deal of dirty work. I dont think his own party, or anybody else has much confidence in him as a man of integrity." The witness W. D. Simpson informed the subcommittee: "It is understood that he has been perfectly unscrupulous as a legislator. He has very little ability but some shrewdness."[25]

Although the enquiry heard of intense white opposition to Crews as a politician and heard strong criticisms of the standards of integrity which, before the Civil War, Crews had adopted as a businessman, no criticism was levelled against the "scalawag" specifically on the basis of his participation in the slave trade. Joel Foster, cited earlier, made no mention of Crews's slave-trading activity. Another witness, M. C. Butler, asked to name any harsh slave masters who had joined the Republicans, cited a certain "Mr. Robertson," and added: "Another is Joseph Crews; he used to be a negro-trader . . . and was not a very humane one at that." Butler, though, was interested in the inconsistency of Crews's attitude toward blacks, rather than in condemning the

24. E. B. Reynolds and J. R. Faunt, *Biographical Directory of the Senate of South Carolina, 1776–1964* (Columbia, S.C., 1964), p. 330; J. A. W. Thomas, *A History of Marlboro County, With Traditions and Sketches of Numerous Families* (Atlanta, 1897; Baltimore, 1971), p. 146.

25. Evidence on Crews appears in *Testimony Taken by the Joint Select Committee to Inquire into the Conditions of the Affairs in the Late Insurrectionary States,* 13 volumes (Washington, 1872; New York, 1968). For the testimony of Foster, see vol. 4, p. 829; and for that of Simpson, see vol. 5, p. 1315. On the lynching of Crews, see J. S. Reynolds, *Reconstruction in South Carolina, 1865–1877* (Columbia, S.C., 1905), pp. 311–13; and on an unsuccessful lynching attempt of 1871, see *Testimony,* vol. 4, pp. 1145–49.

career of slave trading which Crews had formerly followed. W. D. Simpson, a witness already quoted, testified:

> Before the war he [Crews] was a sort of merchant there [in Laurens]. Sometime before the war he failed in merchandise and became a negro-trader. There was no harm in him then, I suppose, so far as being a disturber of the peace was concerned. He was regarded as rather unscrupulous in pecuniary matters and left a good many debts unpaid; but immediately after the war he became connected with the negro element.

Simpson added that before the war Crews had not been considered respectable.

> I do not say people denounced him as a villain, but [Simpson recalled] they had little confidence in his pecuniary integrity. Crews is a curious combination. He seems a good hearted fellow, very accommodating, and would do anything for anybody nearly that wanted anything done; he would send off and do it.

Crews, truly "a curious combination," seems in the pre–Civil War period to have earned a poor reputation in his community, not because the business of slave trading itself set him at any significant disadvantage in society, but because the manner in which he conducted his merchandizing and his slave speculation raised very serious doubts about his honesty.[26]

Of the fourteen Virginia and North Carolina traders cited earlier in Table 2.2, quite detailed biographical evidence has been found on six, and limited evidence on four others. The careers of those concerned varied, but the very conspicuous success of some again indicates that trading *per se* was no bar to gaining social distinction. Several were planters as well as traders and several showed interest, during their careers, in a range of enterprises including turnpikes, merchandizing, ginning, and distilling.

Two Virginians, Francis Everod Rives and Floyd L. Whitehead, were particularly prominent in public life. From 1817 to 1820 (and possibly for considerably longer), Rives was fully and openly involved in buying and selling in the trade from Virginia to Natchez. This, clearly, did not hamper his political career, which from 1821 ran successfully for at least thirty years. He served as member of the Virginia House of Delegates (1821–1831), member of Virginia Senate (1831–36, 1848–51), and member of the U.S. House of Representatives (1837–41), as well as serving as

26. See *Testimony,* vol. 4, p. 1212, for Butler's evidence; and vol. 5, pp. 1307, 1314, for Simpson's evidence. For information about Joseph Crews, I am indebted to Adrian Nichols, formerly of Hull University.

Mayor of Petersburg, Virginia (1847–48). In addition, he was engaged in planting, in the building and management of railroads in North Carolina and Virginia, and in the development of internal improvements in his state.[27]

Whitehead, of Nelson County, Virginia, was, with his partner "Captain Loftuss," an active trader in the 1830s. Like Rives, he traded to Natchez and entered politics, though his political career was perhaps not quite so successful as that of Rives. In 1843 Richard Pollard urged that Whitehead, "acquainted with all of the voters of the county" should stand for office, and two years later a letter from Sterling Claiborne informed the trader:

> I have known you for a great length of time [in your capacities] as a citizen, as a merchant as a magistrate, as a sheriff, as a member of the legislature representing the county of Nelson in which I live, and . . . at all times and under all circumstances the public opinion has been very favorable to you.

An undated memorandum signed by members of the legislature of Virginia and addressed to President Polk recommended Whitehead for "consideration in the appointment of officers in the public departments" and added:

> Mr. Whitehead is a gentleman of great intelligence, high minded and honorable. He possesses fine business qualities, an energetic character, persevering and laborious habits and great moral worth.

It is not clear whether this sort of recommendation was simply a standard piece of lobbying for the spoils of politics or a genuine personal recommendation. Clearly, however, a trading career did not prevent the development of the most influential connections, and in 1844 or 1845 Whitehead even had discussions with the nation's President and Vice President.[28]

Another Virginia speculator, W. A. J. Finney, also appears to have been well respected and influential in local affairs. In 1865, a letter from

27. On his slave-trading activities, see contracts signed by Rives and see trading accounts in the Rives Papers (DU); on his trading profits see Table 7.1; and on his public career see archivist's notes to the Rives Papers and see L. F. Kennedy et al. (eds.), *Biographical Directory of the American Congress, 1774–1971* (Washington, D.C., 1971), p. 1613.

28. Pollard to Whitehead, 16 July 1843; Claiborne to Whitehead, 14 Nov. 1845; Loving to Whitehead, 26 Feb. 1845; legislators to Polk (no date), Whitehead Papers (UVA). On Whitehead's trading activity see Table 2.2, and for further information see Floyd L. Whitehead Papers (SHC, UVA), and F. L. Whitehead and N. Loftus accounts of slave trading (DU).

A. H. McCleish asked him to use his influence in encouraging neighbors to contribute to the provisioning of troops; two years later the president of the Lynchburg and Danville Railroad asked Finney to join the railroad committee and so to encourage the taking out of subscriptions; and in 1876 Finney's neighbor G. C. Cabell, then a Representative in the United States Congress, urged him to use his influence to get a good delegate sent from their county to the state convention. Of the other Virginia traders listed in Table 2.2 less is known. James A. Mitchell, who, in the 1830s and early 1840s (and perhaps in later years), was an active trader to the west, by 1845 at least was producing tobacco in Virginia, and in the 1850s owned land in Texas. Like several other traders and extraders, he dabbled in franchising for agricultural inventions.[29]

Of the sample of North Carolina traders given earlier in Table 2.2, William Long seems to have had the most prominent public career. In the 1830s and 1840s Long was a very active slave trader, with planting interests as well. These latter, and perhaps his trading, continued into the 1850s, and in 1853 he headed a list of some sixty members of the local Caswell County Agricultural Society. In combination with his neighbor Abisha Slade, he is credited with inventing the process which produced "bright tobacco," a curing technique which seems greatly to have benefitted local planters. In the 1860s, he founded the Border Agricultural Society of Virginia and North Carolina. Not only was he a prominent local planter; his high profile in the community extended in the 1850s and 1860s to service first as state representative and then as state senator.[30]

The North Carolina partners Tyre Glen and Isaac Jarratt, who took a great many coffles to Alabama and were fully involved in trading, were also active in planting and local politics. In 1852, the following note introduced Glen to U.S. Congressman James Brookes:

> I take this pleasure in introducing to your acquaintance Tyre Glen Esq. of this state—Tyre Glen is a gentleman of high standing among us, a genuine Whig . . . with good business habits. He visits your city upon a matter of business—and any civilities shown to him will be duly appreciated.

29. Affadavit, 27 Jan. 1863, McCleish to Finney, 28 Feb. 1865, Finney Papers (DU); president of railroad to Finney, 25 Jan. 1867, Reid Papers (UVA); Cabell to Finney, 2 Aug. 1876, Finney Papers (DU). On Mitchell, see James A. Mitchell Papers (DU) and Richard R. Reid Papers (UVA).

30. See Long Papers (NCA), especially archivist's notes, and documents dated 8 Oct. 1853 and 1 Oct. 1870.

And in the same year a supporter of Sheppeard, a local Whig, sought Jarratt's assistance, telling Glen that

> with the aid of Jarratt we can give Sheppeard a start whether he wants the nomination or not. . . . I wish you would see Isaac [Jarratt] between now and court and see what can be done for Sheppeard.

A letter of 1858 refers to Glen as "a man having much influence in . . . [his] county and state"; and various letters of the 1850s and 1860s show that Glen was on close terms with John A. Gilmer, member of the North Carolina and later of the national legislature. In 1864, for example, in a letter concerning the entry of Glen's son into the Naval School, Gilmer informed the Secretary of the Confederate Navy that the youth was "a young gentleman of high character and very respectable parentage." Glen was a man of substantial property, with interests including flour milling, textile processing, and distilling; and in 1864 he had a plantation worked by forty-two slaves. In addition, he was, during the 1850s, a director of the Yadkin River Navigation Company.[31]

About the other North Carolina traders mentioned in our sample (in Table 2.2, this is) less has been discovered. E. W. Ferguson, though, seems to have come from quite humble origins, one of twelve sons of a Scottish immigrant. He had little formal education but, mainly as a result of success in slave trading, became after the Civil War a farmer and storekeeper. In the war he had served as an army captain, and after the war three of his sons went to university and later into the medical and legal professions. The son of the trader Obediah Fields became a successful local merchant. Like many other traders, Totten and Badgett (both of North Carolina) had planting interests, Badgett, it seems coming from a family tradition of planting. And again like numerous other speculators, Totten took an interest in local investments and developments, being president of a turnpike road company. D. S. Reid (a North Carolinian not included in Table 2.2, since only fragmentary letters have been found on his trading) was a state senator and gover-

31. Jarratt to Jarratt, 11 Oct. 1840, Jarratt-Puryear Papers (DU); Moorhead to Brooke, 21 Sept. 1852, Willows to Glen, 25 Jan. 1852, Williams to Glen, 25 Jan. 1852, Fenton to Glen, 14 Apr. 1858, Gilmer to Glen, 6 Mar. 1859 and 9 Sept. 1864, Glen Papers (DU). On Glen's various economic activities, see Martin to Glen, 17 Jan. 1848; patent certificate, 28 Nov. 1855; and petition to Confederate Secretary of War, 1864, Glen Papers (DU). On the Yadkin Navigation Company, see reports to Governor Bragg, 20 Oct. 1855 and 5 Mar., 2 June, and 10 July 1858, Governor's Papers (NCA).

nor, as well as being a U.S. congressman. He also had a slave-trading partnership with his nephew Samuel F. Adams.[32]

AN HONEST CALLING TO SUPPORT MY FAMILY

Judging by the extensive traders' correspondence which has been located, the speculator's self-image tended to be that of an energetic businessman pursuing the legitimate opportunities and rewards offered by a rapidly expanding economy and slave system. Some correspondence collections deal almost exclusively with business matters, and the emphasis, rather like that of a broker following the stock market, was upon catching market trends. Added to this, the disciplining of slaves formed a constant theme. And where letters were between relatives, one finds emphasis on sacrifices made for the support of the family, and sometimes upon the adventures of travel. Quite often, the traders gave an eye to wider speculative opportunities which might complement slaving. It is not surprising therefore that several of those Virginia and Carolinas traders just commented upon became involved in a range of developing opportunities from ginning, franchising for mechanical inventions, transport improvements, to financial speculation. Some traders might have been ruthless sharpers, whereas others could appear to be insulted by occasional complaints from clients. After one such complaint, for example, the speculator McElveen reemphasized to his partner that on the health of slaves "I don't deceive no man if I am aware of the fact."[33] Overall the impression is of men whose self-image was that of roving, practical businessmen, calculating the chance of high profits against the inconveniences of rough travel and hard work. One finds no indication of guilt or of a social ostracism which should be endured or kicked against.

While fully engaged in scattering black families to all corners of the South, the speculators could, without the slightest awkwardness, write affectionately to their own families back home and assure them that

32. On Ferguson, see especially the extensive introductory notes (written by his great-granddaughter) in the Elias Ferguson Papers (NCA); on Fields see archivist's note in the Obediah Fields Letters and Papers (DU); on Badgett see letter of 17 May 1854 and archivist's note, Badgett Papers (NCA); on Totten see especially note of 24 July 1855 and archivist's note, Joseph S. Totten Papers (NCA); and on Reid see Adams to Reid, 26 Feb. 1844, David S. Reid Papers (DU). On Reid, see *Biographical Directory of the American Congress*, pp. 1596–97. On Adams's relationship to Reid, see Adams to Reid, 28 Mar. 1853, Reid Papers (NCA).

33. McElveen to Oakes, 27 Oct. 1853, Oakes Papers (BPL).

their every effort was for the benefit of their loved ones. Typical of many affectionate letters from traders selling in the Lower South was a message from Obediah Field telling his wife:

> You may look for . . . [my return] between this [late November] and Christmas as it is out of my power to say in a day or two of the time, but my dear you may rest assured that it will be as soon as possible. Kiss my dear little children and tell them their Pap will soon be home. Give my complements to mother. . . . I am yours with all the affection in my breast till death.

A letter surviving from a selling trip of 1825 again shows Fields's tenderness toward his "dear loving wife" and toward his children; and in a letter of 1834, the trader J. A. Mitchell told his children that they should be "good boys and girls" and should "go to school and learn their books" so that they would be able to "show Par how smart they have been in his absence." Mitchell, like Fields, told his wife of his great impatience to dispose of the remainder of his slave gang so that he could get home to see her and the children.[34]

The trader's double standards on the family again appeared when the speculator Samuel Logan lamented the death of his wife. "In my family sphere," he wrote, "I am utterly ruined as my children are to raise and they cannot be raised as she would have done it." A paragraph or so later, however, he could muster no sympathy at all for a slave family in his possession and informed his partner:

> I have determined to send . . . [for sale in the Lower South] my woman Fan, about 30 years old, a daughter about 10, and a boy about 6, as they are so villaneous and triffling that I can't keep them.

But his own children would need looking after, and for that he planned to buy two replacement slaves, "that is, a cook woman, and a girl that can nurse your namesake and help to take care of my other little children." Another trader, the fledgeling speculator John D. Badgett, in Georgia on a selling trip with his older brother, was keen to keep in touch with his folks back home in Virginia, and asked his father to "give my love to Mar, and all the family. Tell Mar that I want to see her very bad and that I will come home as soon as I can."[35]

Traders, it seems, might in their community take on the role of pioneer, frontiersman, and even hero, enduring hardship, enjoying

34. Fields to Fields, 29 Nov. 1822, 8 Aug. 1825, Fields Papers (DU); Mitchell to Mitchell, 10 Dec. 1834, Reid Papers (UVA).

35. Logan to Meek, 9 Nov. 1836, Negro Collection (AU); Badgett to Badgett, 12 Feb. 1860, Badgett Papers (NCA).

adventures, and all in the end for the benefit of their families. Certainly R. C. Puryear, writing to Isaac Jarratt, a trading friend, was envious that "For you the task of writing a letter is quite easy—for new and interesting scenes are constantly presenting themselves." It is true that even our traders could stray from the paths of virtue in the family sphere, and indeed Jarratt's partner Tyre Glen had been unable to join him on that slaving trip of 1832, his ailment being a "great calamity" which "the fair dame of Greensborough [not his wife!] had imparted to him." But the theme of family crops up again and again in the Jarratt letters, as when his "affectionate cousin" Betsy Ann wrote enthusiastically of his adventures and hoped that he would bring back nice presents, and later begged him "pray to send us some beaux." Jarratt, however, feared that for his cousin and his sister marriage

> is a long shot and a bad chance without a show of some negroes and beauty—both of which is lacking with Sarah [his sister] and unfortunately for you [Betsy Ann] you lack the negroes.[36]

By 1834, Jarratt had married and his wife pressed him to forsake the roving life of the speculator. "I'm afraid, my dear husband," she wrote,

> you and your friend Carson will keep up negro trading as long as you can get a negro to trade on, and when you cant get any thro the country you will carry of[f] all you can persuade at home, but one good thing Mr. C. has no wife to leave behind when he is gone.

Jarratt, though, assured her: "I have no disposition to negro trade and hope to engage in something else by which I can accumulate a little and remain with my family." Meanwhile, he wrote,

> Mr. Beverly Barksdale is here. He was married about ten days before he left home. He has some 50 negroes to sell and I have [only] 18. You complain of my absence. What do you think of the situation with Mrs. Barksdale. She cant expect him until April or May. We both [he explained] are toiling for our wives and their little ones.

Sometime in 1836 Jarratt did indeed retire to his home and farm, although debt-collecting trips were still necessary, as in February 1837 when he wrote from Alabama to his wife:

> I was candid and never will make another negro trading trip without your approbation unless a kind Providence should frown upon my labors and make it actually necessary that I should leave home to make a support for my family.

36. Puryear to Jarratt, 17 Feb. 1832; Clingman to Jarratt, 11 Feb. 1833, 20 Dec. 1833; Jarratt to sister and cousin, 29 Dec. 1833, Jarratt-Puryear Family Papers (DU).

> In that case [he concluded] I would resort to any Honest calling for the comfort of my family.[37]

From his slave-selling trips, another North Carolina speculator, T. W. Burton, frequently wrote of his restlessness to return home to his wife and family; and in 1846 he made plans to take his family, when the slaving season was over, on a vacation trip to Texas. A letter to his trading partner explained his trading plans and, more generally, outlined his concept of duty to family. "I am quite willing," he wrote, to go on the Texas vacation trip,

> and think it my duty as it will be a great schooling for my children when young. My object is pleasure in this life and not riches as I know my incompetence to take care of property if I had it. I therefore wish to be content with a competency and [shall] let my children work for themselves and earn their living and then they will be better prepared to take care of . . . [property].[38]

Traders, of course, showed the most settled complacency about the fact that their traffic was in people. This did not mean, however, that they did not feel more favorable to some slaves than to others. Indeed, a cardinal rule of slaving and of slaveholding racism seemed to be that—with the basic power foundation of racism and race hierarchy established—one could safely indulge in special favors to selected slaves, particularly to those who seemed to be especially cooperative.

A letter from McElveen to Oakes gives an example of this favoritism for particular slaves. McElveen reported:

> I have bought the boy Isaac for 1100. I think him very prime. . . . He is a general house servant . . . a first rate cook . . . and [a] splendid carriage driver. He is also a fine painter and varnisher and the boy says he can make a fine pannel door. . . . Also he performs well on the violin and other musical instruments. . . . He is a genius and its strange to say I think he is smarter than I am.

This "genius," however, seems to have been seen as an interesting curiosity rather than as a reason for the faintest doubt about the validity of slavery. On behalf of another slave, purchased a few months earlier, McElveen sent the deeply racist, but rather paternal, introduction that "the fellow may appear simple but he is got as good sense as most negroes." On occasion, he could even adopt a protective role, as when dealing with an owner's request that the slave Edward should be sold

37. Harriett to Jarratt, 29 Oct. 1835; Jarratt to Harriett, 9 Nov. 1835, 1 Dec. 1835, 15 Feb. 1837, Jarratt-Puryear Family Papers (DU).

38. Burton to Long, 19 Jan. 1846, Long Papers (NCA).

"to leave the state" of South Carolina. McElveen, however, informed his partner that

> If properly managed . . . [Edward] will be a fine boy. Do not have him punished if you can help it. He is very easy frightened. . . . He cant stand punishment or confinement. . . . If you can sell him in the city do so. His wife is there.

Another speculator, Isaac Jarratt, also flirted with a sort of paternalism, as when, on slave selling missions, his letters home would ask that he be affectionately remembered to his "people" (slaves) back home, and on a later business trip, would send greetings such as "my love to the children and Howdy to the Negroes."[39]

PROFIT AND PROSPERITY

Although T. W. Burton suggested that his aim was to store away only "a competency," and several others, "toiling for their wives and little ones," might give an impression of being men of modest means, most speculators were probably wealthy or well on their way to accumulating considerable property. It seems, in fact, that the profit rates of the trade were high by antebellum standards, and data on real and personal estate suggest, furthermore, that traders were probably in the top few percent of southern and indeed of national property owners.

Data on the profits gained by traders over the period 1817 to 1860 are summarized in Table 7.1. (Appendix 7 provides evidence on the calculations involved.) These data suggest fluctuations in profits over time, with net annual rates of 60 to 80 percent from 1817–19, 30 percent in the early 1820s, 30–50 percent in the early and mid 1830s, and 15–30 percent in the late 1840s and the 1850s. The exceptionally high profits of 1817–19 probably had much to do with the Lower South's especially rapid growth during those years, together with a brief lag in the trade's adjustment to supplying that surge in demand. The fact that the 1845–60 profit rates were generally lower than those of 1830–37 is probably, to an important extent, explained by the buoyancy of post-1844 tobacco prices in the Upper South and the consequent bidding up of that region's slave prices.[40] What is particularly significant in

39. McElveen to Oakes, 19 Jan. 1854, 7 Nov. 1853, 9 Aug. 1853, Oakes Papers (BPL); Jarratt to Jarratt, 1 Mar., 9 Nov. 1835, Jarratt-Puryear Papers (DU).

40. Some indication of profit margins can also be inferred from U. B. Phillips's data on slave prices in various markets. See Phillips, *Life and Labor,* p. 177, and see also Robert Evans,"Some Economic Aspects of the Domestic Slave Trade, 1830–1860," *Southern Economic Journal,* 27 (1961), p. 330, Table 1. On tobacco prices, see Gray, *History of Agriculture,* vol. 2, pp. 768–69.

Table 7.1. Estimated rates of profit in the interregional slave trade, 1817–60

Season or year	Firm	Route[a]	Number of slaves[b]	Trader's purchase price (in $)	Trader's sale price (in $)	Trader's crude profit	Crude rate of profit (%)	Net rate of profit (%)[c]
1817–18	Rives &	Va.–Miss.	30	11,112	21,308	10,196	91.8	79.8
1818–19	Partners		26	14,505	24,643	10,138	69.9	60.8
1822–23	Fields & Partners	N.C.–S.C.	12				36.0	30.6[d]
1832	Totten & Gunn	N.C.–Ala.	23	6,525	9,116	2,591	39.7	34.5
1833–34			37	12,693	15,340	2,647	20.9	18.1
1833			24	7,588	11,552	3,964	52.2	45.4
1834			21	7,841	11,672	3,831	48.9	42.5
1835			42	21,890	35,797	13,907	63.5	55.2
1836			26	21,991	36,170	14,179	64.5	50.8
1830	Glen &	N.C.–Ala.	9	6,042	9,650	3,608	59.7	51.9
1830	Partners		5	3,250	4,850	1,600	49.2	42.8
1830–31			59	16,832	22,148	5,316	31.6	27.5
1831–32			54	15,211	20,555	5,344	35.1	30.5
1832–33			55	17,992	25,472	7,480	41.6	36.2
1833–34			79	25,605	38,760	13,155	51.4	44.7
1833–34			22	9,520	12,721	3,201	33.6	29.2
1834–35			56	21,573	30,508	8,935	41.4	36.0
1835–36								
1836–37			29	17,905	29,043	11,138	62.2	49.0
1836–37			21	19,793	28,405	8,612	43.5	34.3
1843–44	Hughes & Downing	Kent.–Miss.	13	5,292	8,695	3,403	64.3	55.9
1849–50	Templeman &	Va.–Ga.	38	20,655	25,320	4,665	22.6	19.6
1849–50	Goodwin		26	12,595	14,685	2,090	16.6	14.4
1850–51			38	20,217	26,870	6,653	32.9	28.6
1852–53	Walker, A. &	N.C.–Al.	5	2,090	2,394	304	14.5	12.6
1853–54	A. T.		16	10,237	13,065	2,828	27.6	24.0
1854–55			13	9,740	11,780	2,040	20.9	18.2
1856–57			2	1,635	2,075	440	26.9	23.4
1856–57	Bolton & Dickens	Mo., Va., etc.–LS	664	668,474	798,966	130,492	19.5	17.0
1858–59	Owings, Charles & Robertson	S.C.–La.	34	30,186	37,192	7,006	23.2	20.2
1845–46	White &	Mo.–LS	181	81,887	107,855	25,968	31.7	27.6
1846–47	Partners	(La., Miss.,	12	5,795	6,789	994	17.2	14.9
1847–48		Tex., etc.)	29	14,731	18,679	3,948	26.8	23.3
1848–49			24	12,727	17,023	4,296	33.8	29.4
1849–50			88	50,866	68,309	17,443	34.3	29.8
1850–51			146	87,060	112,086	25,026	28.7	25.0
1851–52			19	10,922	12,883	1,961	18.0	15.6
1852–53			64	42,485	58,687	16,202	38.1	33.2
1853–54			28	23,055	27,810	4,755	20.6	17.9
1854–55			16	12,495	15,152	2,657	21.3	18.5
1855–56			62	48,832	69,859	21,027	43.1	37.4
1856–57			90	79,854	102,686	22,832	28.6	24.9

(continued on the following page)

Table 7.1. Estimated rates of profit in the interregional slave trade, 1817–60 (*continued*)

Season or year	Firm	Route[a]	Number of slaves[b]	Trader's purchase price (in $)	Trader's sale price (in $)	Trader's crude profit	Crude rate of profit (%)	Net rate of profit (%)[c]
1857–58			62	54,801	68,170	13,369	24.4	21.2
1858–59			59	51.026	71,930	20,904	41.0	35.6
1859–60			183	176,957	240,718	63,761	36.0	31.3

Sources: For Bolton & Dickens see Bolton & Dickens Record of Slaves, 1856–1858 (NYHS); and for Owings & Robertson see Anderson Equity Court (SC), *Charles* v. *Owings et al.*, Bill 325 (1861).

[a] LS = Lower South.

[b] Some traders' records cited here also included certain slaves where evidence on the buying or selling price (or both) was not given. Usually these were either small numbers "carried over" and reappearing in another account, or major lists with no price details. The omission of these slaves does not seem to distort overall results on rates of profit (though it affects volume of profit).

[c] For calculations involved in net rates, see Appendix 7.

[d] Based on letter of 29 Nov. 1822 in which Fields provided information on the sales that he had made up to that time, and in which he informed his wife that "the cost of the 12 negroes and bay mare is $2939. I think I will clear $900 on this trip" (Fields Papers [DU]).

understanding the position of the trader in the South, however, is not so much these absolute levels of profit but the comparison of traders' profits with those of other enterprises.

Profits from the trade were substantially higher than the 10 percent annual rate suggested by Robert Fogel and Stanley Engerman for slave agriculture from 1820–60.[41] At the same time, they were very close to the rates which Fred Bateman and Thomas Weiss calculated for a sample of some 2,000 southern industrial firms of 1850 and 1860.[42] The fact that rates of return seem to have been similar in slave trading and southern industry argues against any idea that there might have been a unique stigma attaching to the trade (a stigma discouraging recruitment to trading and bidding up the profits of those willing to become speculators).[43] As Bateman and Weiss argued, there might have been some disinclination among planters to become involved in industry, an activity which probably carried less status than did planting. But they

41. Fogel and Engerman, *Time on the Cross*, vol. 1, p. 70.

42. Fred Bateman and Thomas Weiss, *A Deplorable Scarcity: The Failure of Industrialization in the Slave Economy* (Chapel Hill, 1981), p. 107, Table 5.1. Bateman and Weiss, in their sample of southern industries, found rates of net profit averaging 25 percent in 1850 and 28 percent in 1860. The industries covered included the making of agricultural implements, boots, shoes, furniture, wagons, textiles, as well as metal and leather goods, flourmilling, and sawmilling.

43. Robert Evans in "Some Economic Aspects," made an early study of the possible connection between high profit rates and social status, but was only able to use very sketchy evidence on the key price and profit variables.

pointed also to the probability that poor information about opportunities and concern over the additional risks involved were strong discouragements against planters taking up industrial entrepreneurship.[44] These practical factors, and several others, must go a long way to explaining the profit differential between trading and planting. Trading involved obvious financial risks, but also brought with it real physical dangers from discontented slaves; it involved much arduous travel in all weathers, and often meant that long periods had to be spent away from home. The stereotyping of some traders as "monsters" would probably have had some influence in raising profit rates; but it is clear that in practice the South found it possible to deal "honorably" with most traders. Most successful speculators, it seems, could easily combine slaving with the enjoyment of respect and influence within their own communities.

From scattered evidence in letters and from census information, it is clear that most traders would have been among the wealthiest men in their localities. In 1859, for example, Phillip Thomas informed his partner that "Robertson of the [slave trading] firm Smith & Robertson is dead . . . [and] has left Lewis Smith his fortune of $175,000." Thomas Williams, an important slave dealer based in the Washington, D.C., area, boasted that he had made $30,000 in a few months; and Franklin & Armfield are said to have made $33,000 in 1829. In the 1840s and 1850s, J. R. White several times achieved gross seasonal profits exceeding $20,000; and over a two-year period in the 1850s Bolton & Dickens received gross profits well in excess of $130,000.[45]

More important than evidence of this sort, however, is the more systematic census data available for 1850 on real estate and for 1860 for both personal estate (including slaves) and real estate. In Appendix 4, Table A4.3 presents data on over fifty traders identified in one or both of the censuses for South Carolina in 1850 and 1860. Several traders (Allen Vance, George Seaborn, Ziba Oakes, Benjamin Mordecai, E. S. Irvine, O. B. Irvine, J. W. Ford, and T. C. Weatherly) appear as owners of property valued at some $100,000 to $200,000, which would have meant that they were in the top 0.3 percent (for the South) (and the top 0.1 percent for the nation) of free adult males holding property. Not only that, but among the forty or so traders located in the South Carolina census of 1860 the statistically average trader would, in terms

44. Bateman and Weiss, *A Deplorable Scarcity,* pp. 157–63.

45. On these profit statistics, see Thomas to Finney, 24 Dec. 1859, Finney Papers (DU); Williams and Franklin & Armfield, cited in Collins, *Domestic Slave Trade,* p. 29; and Table 7.1 of the present study.

of real, personal, or total estate, have ranked in about the top 3 or 4 percent of free adult male holders of property in the South, and would have been in an even more conspicuously wealthy position compared with such men in the nation as a whole.[46]

It is not clear whether the more common route was to enter the trade via an already established basis of family or personal capital, or to start from more modest beginnings and, through wealth gained in the trade, move toward the social and property-holding elite. Several traders appear in South Carolina's 1850 or 1860 censuses as apparently without property and, if they gave proper information to the census enumerators, might have been men starting at the bottom. Of those who did not declare any property, Charles Logan had been born in Ireland, was in1850 listed as a shoemaker without property, but in 1860 was listed as "Negro Trader" and declared $26,000 of property. H. G. Burkett appeared as an overseer in 1850, and declared no property then or in 1860 when he described himself as a farmer. W. B. Ryan and T. B. Adkins appeared in 1850 as clerks to slave traders, and again declared no property. Perhaps Logan and Burkett were cases of men of humble origins, but Adkins and Ryan were in fact both members of successful family firms which traded in slaves. A somewhat similar case was E. M. Cobb, whose family had been dealing in slaves for perhaps two decades or more, and from that family connection Cobb would no doubt have gained access to substantial cash advantages. Leaving aside those traders who might have been linked to substantial family wealth, even though not yet directly sharing in its ownership, there are those traders who seem simply to have failed to declare substantial property which they did directly own. Several who did not declare property seem to have taken a generally lax attitude toward the census and also failed to declare their occupation or their place of birth. Furthermore, when checked in slave schedules of the census, several of those traders apparently without property appear as owners of slaves.

Uncertainties about some aspects of census evidence therefore complicate the task of establishing the economic status of our sample of traders, though there seems to be no reason why traders should have been any more or less lax than other citizens in assisting census enumerators with declarations of property. Although it is difficult to establish the case decisively, one suspects that most traders began their

46. Based on comparing Table A4.3 with data in Lee Soltow, "Economic Inequality in the United States in the Period from 1790 to 1860," *Journal of Economic History,* 31 (1971), Table 7, p. 838. See also Lee Soltow, *Men and Wealth in the United States, 1850–1870* (New Haven, 1975).

careers with a base of family wealth. Whatever the trader's origins, however, the census data on property do seem to be decisive: most traders were among the wealthiest in their community, many had planting interests (as the free and the slave schedules of the census show), and most probably had close involvement with the local elite. Their high levels of property holding help to explain the prominent role which many traders took in politics and the local community.

THE NEED FOR "GOOD" TRADERS AND "BAD"

In fairly minor part, the hostile image of the trader which was so often found in southern prints and rhetoric stemmed from the fact that some speculators were, no doubt, thoroughly dishonest, vicious, and worthless by almost anyone's standards. And in part too it stemmed from regional differences of interest within the South. As we have seen in the case of Georgia, for example, old-established slaveholding sections of the state often felt alarm at slave importation into neighboring and less developed areas. Such importation brought fears of over-production of staples, overbalancing the state's race ratio, and bringing in dangerous slaves, as well as undermining the commitment of the Border South to the institution of slavery. Regional differences in attitudes to the trade and to the speculator himself no doubt to some extent existed. And, as particular areas passed from being net importers to net exporters of slaves, local changes in attitude would occur over time.

The slave Charles Ball pointed to this sort of regional difference in emphasis. In about 1805, Ball, with other members of his coffle, was taken by a speculator from Maryland to the then-frontier area of central South Carolina. There the speculator was greeted with delight by his host, a planter and innkeeper, who declared that

> any gentleman who brought such a stock of hands into the country was a public benefactor, and entitled to the respect and gratitude of every friend of the South. . . . It would be his [host's] chief business to introduce him to the gentlemen of the neighborhood, who would all be glad to become acquainted with a merchant of his respectability.

And, Ball continued,

> In the state of Maryland, my master had been called a negro buyer, or Georgia trader, sometimes a negro driver, but here, I found that he was elevated to the rank of merchant, and a merchant of the first order too, for it was very clear that

in the opinion of the landlord, no branch of trade was more honorable than the traffic in us poor slaves.[47]

There were then, to some extent, regional differences and variations over time. Low-country Georgia, when it sought to maintain control over the up-country, might be particularly sensitive to some practical (but not moral) implications of the trade. And the southern plantation legend, in slavery times and long after, tended strongly to marginalize the supposed role of the trader, to maintain that he was incidental and not fundamental to the aims of slavery. From this it was easy to create the myth that family separations were rare and the trader a mere detail within a broad, benign system. Such things could happen at the level of sectional propaganda and, just as important, could readily develop in lazy southern rationalizing and domestic myth-making. In practice, however, the antebellum South dealt with the trader daily. To have a scapegoat "evil" trader was a great convenience. But it was equally necessary, for practical purposes, that there be "respectable merchants" dealing in slaves. By making a place for such men in the life of the South—and, as we have seen, in southern society and politics at the highest local and regional level—slaveowners could readily cope with any "temporary hardships" of black family separations, and could get about the business of southern enterprise in their pursuit of personal and family advancement.

47. Ball, *Fifty Years,* p. 53.

8

Speculation and Its Impact: The Flawed Mystique of Antebellum Paternalism

THIS study has been concerned with the role of "Negro speculation" in antebellum slavery: speculative sales and family separations emerge as having been central both to the realities of the Old South and to the mythmaking in which its white citizens so lavishly indulged. Such sales tell us much about the attitudes of antebellum masters to their slaves, and about the paternal self-image which, despite those sales, the slaveholding class maintained. And speculation seems to be of central importance, too, in considering slave mentalities. This has not been directly a study of slave culture and attitudes, but I have tried, while examining masters' attitudes, to establish something of a context in which to consider slave mentalities. The evidence of the massive interregional traffic suggests that that context was usually one of deep distrust of masters and of a profound separation between the values of slaves and masters.

Trading, this study has argued, accounted from the 1810s or 1820s onward for at least 60 percent of the overall interregional movement; and those sales occurred, not because of crippling debt or the death of owners, but overwhelmingly for speculative reasons. In the antebellum South, the slaveowning class was generally willing, simply for reasons of financial advantage, to separate black families. The scale of those separations was such that one out of every five marriages of Upper South slaves would have been prematurely terminated by the trade; if other interventions by masters are added, the proportion rises to about one in three. Furthermore, the trade would have separated about one in three of the exporting region's slave children (under fourteen years) from their parents; again, local sales and other actions by masters would have raised this proportion to about one in two. And, with very intensive rates of importation into many Lower South states throughout the antebellum period, the impact on the importing states was similarly profound. Remember that the proportions forcibly separated would not have been fundamentally different if only 50 or even 45 percent of movements, not 60 percent, been allocated to the trade. And the evidence suggests that 60 percent, if anything, is an undercount rather than an overcount.

Proslavery literature and the magazines and prints of the antebellum South generally were overwhelmingly racist or protoracist—persistently arguing for innate black laziness, inferior intellectual capacity, and natural promiscuity and instability in family and sexual matters.[1] This almost universal racism could theoretically have led to one of two main outcomes—a tendency to protect "innately weak" black families and institutions, or, on the other hand, a tendency for the majority to exploit the myth that only "temporary hardships" occurred when families were wrecked or arbitrarily disturbed by masters. Despite the layers of myth which the Old South generated to make itself comfortable at home and acceptable abroad, the trade shows that the second tendency was clearly dominant. In effect, the vast bulk of the Old South's literary output on black "character," family, and "amalgamation" ingeniously constructed a framework of fable whereby masters could both separate families whenever they wished and regard themselves as paternalists whatever they did.

"AS TO THEIR HABITS OF AMALGAMATION"

Again and again, the white South's view of black character and potential began with the black's supposed natural tendency toward promiscuity and innate inability, unless under the strictest white supervision, to form lasting and loving family relationships. The journals of the South abounded with "guides for the supervision of

1. Fredrickson, after his very extensive work on the South's antebellum publications and proslavery literature emphasized the "almost universal" pattern of racist and protoracist opinion he found. See George M. Fredrickson, *The Black Image in the White Mind: The Debate on Afro-American Character and Destiny, 1817–1914* (New York, 1971), esp. pp. 56–66, 210. After working through *De Bow's Review,* Paskoft and Wilson drew very much the same conclusion from studying that major southern journal. See Paul F. Paskoft and Daniel J. Wilson (eds.), *The Cause of the South: Selections From De Bow's Review, 1846–1867* (Baton Rouge, 1982), pp. 17–19.

Negroes," and "Negro Amalgamation" formed a constant theme. A guide published in *De Bow's Review* and considered by the editor as "a practical and valuable paper for the planters" observed that on the contributor's plantation,

> beds with ample clothing are provided for them [the slaves], and in them they are *made to sleep.* As to their habits of amalgamation and intercourse, I know of no means whereby to regulate them, or to restrain them; I attempted it for many years by preaching virtue and decency, encouraging marriages, and by punishing, with some severity, departures from marital obligations; but it was all in vain.

A few months later, "A Small Farmer" wrote in the same journal: "'Habits of amalgamation' I cannot stop; I can check it, but only in the name. I am willing to be taught, for I have tried everything I know."[2]

James H. Hammond sometimes found it inconvenient to let slaves choose their own marriage partners and provided his overseer with detailed instruction on the marriages of slaves. At the same time, as we know, he was a past master at forcible family separation—and, as his wife, to her intense annoyance, knew, he had several children by at least one slave mistress (the latter being forbidden a slave husband). Even so, he could happily write in *De Bow* that family separations were rare among slaves. Those which did occur, he assured his readers, tended to be because of the slave's "perverse tendency" to link with a partner on another plantation, or came about because slaves generally preferred to be separated from their spouse rather than be parted from a master who might be migrating or changing his circumstances. And Hammond added that, of course, slave senses were "dull," but if pleasure was the absence of pain, then American slaves were very happy.[3]

Despite the massive extent of interregional trading and of other causes of forced separation, the procedure of southern writers was almost always to open with the claim that separations were rare, and then to emphasize that separations in any case brought little hardship for blacks. Chancellor Harper of South Carolina argued that blacks always lacked any real capability for domestic affection and showed "insensibility to ties of kindred." In Africa, he maintained, there had

2. A Mississippi Planter, "Management of Negroes upon Southern Estates," *De Bow,* 10 (1851), pp. 621–27; A Small Farmer, "Management of Negroes," *De Bow,* 11 (1851), pp. 369–72.

3. On Hammond see Chapter 7, above; Faust, *Hammond and the Old South,* pp. 82–88; article in *De Bow,* 8 (1850), p. 122.

been fear of parents but no love of children. And with American slaves, he went on, separations were far less keenly felt than were those of whites. In any case, the small chance of blacks being separated was as nothing compared with the risk of their being unemployed and unable to cope in a free society. The theme of the supposed cruelty and insensitivity of blacks occurred again in George S. Sawyer's treatise. Blacks, he argued, totally lacked family feeling: instead it was "lust and cruelty" and not "emotions of parental and kindred attachment" that "grew in the negro's bosom." In her novel *The North and South,* Caroline Rush took up the familiar theme that "the affections of the negro are never so strong as those of the white man. The tenderness that is but natural in the breast of a white mother, is very much lessened in the blacks." Thus, she could lament the fate of poor white mothers who, unable to provide for their children, had to send them away to the care of strangers—and all this while the long-suffering master persevered with his "lusty" and "turbulent" slaves.[4]

Thomas R. Cobb managed to recruit black "love of dance" into the medley of special pleading. He opened, following tradition, with the view that "the unnecessary and wanton separation of persons standing in the relation of husband and wife" was found "rarely if ever" under slavery. But where masters did for some reason lapse from their generations of good practice, Cobb was still ready to preempt any sympathy for the slave for, he wrote,

> The dance will allay his most poignant grief, and a few days blot out the memory of his most bitter bereavement. His natural affection is not strong, and consequently he is cruel to his own offspring, and suffers little by separation from them.

True to the tradition of this antebellum genre, he then sought to clinch his argument and the whole slavery relationship by adding that, though slaves disregarded their own families, they were capable of showing gratitude and loyalty to superiors. For blacks, in other words, slavery was comfortable and natural, but the family an excessive challenge to constancy.[5]

4. Chancellor N. Harper of South Carolina, *Slavery in the Light of Social Ethics,* p. 593, in Elliott (ed.), *Cotton is King;* Harper, in *De Bow,* 8 (1850), p. 232; George S. Sawyer, *Southern Institutes: or, An Inquiry into the Origins and Early Prevalence of Slavery and the Slave Trade* (Philadelphia, 1858), p. 222, quoted in Fredrickson, *Black Image,* p. 58; Caroline E. Rush, *The North and South, or, Slavery and Its Contrasts. A Tale of Real Life* (Philadelphia, 1852; Freeport, 1971), p. 238.

5. Thomas R. Cobb, *An Inquiry into the Law of Slavery in the United States of America* (1858; New York, 1968), pp. 245–46, 39, 35, 28.

In John H. Van Evrie's *Negroes and Negro "Slavery"* (1853), so many of the traditional propaganda pieces were deployed that we have a more or less complete manual for the misrepresentation of the slave family. Whites, we are told, because of "the elevated intellectualism of the race," displayed lofty values and a deep love of family. As for slaves, "the mother has a similar love of her offspring at an early period of its existence, possibly stronger." This intense attachment, however, arose because the black woman's "maternal instincts are more imperative, more closely approximated to the animal." Slavery, we are informed, was ordained by God and, in family capabilities, as elsewhere, was said perfectly to fit the "black temperament." A natural process of attachment and distancing was, therefore—and following God's plan—said to have evolved. "The Negro mother," Van Evrie tells us, "has always control and direction of her offspring at the South so long as that is needed by the latter." Of course, he adds, the master was the "supreme ruler, . . . the very providence of these simple and subordinate people, . . . [protecting] them in all of their rights"; but mother and child were not disturbed. We next are asked to believe, however, that slave children "like a dog or calf" quickly grew independent of their mother, and were as mature as they ever would be by age twelve to fifteen. They were still "boys," he said, but added that they would remain "intellectually boys forever."[6]

A convenient process then unfolds in Van Evrie's fable: the mother once had "boundless affection for her infants," but that attachment "grows feebler as the capacities of the child are developed; at 12 or 15 she is relatively indifferent," and eventually she "barely recognizes it." And, we are told "all of these phases . . . are in accord with the specific nature and purpose assigned . . . by the Almighty Creator." As for the husband, he mattered little, showing "a feeble and capricious love of his wife and indifference to his offspring." So far as marriage separations were concerned, then,

> Where the white husband, and certainly the white wife, might despair or die, the negro and the negress, with new partners and another marriage, are quite as happy as if they had never been separated.

After all of this, we find of course, that family separations were extremely rare, and were far less common, for example, than among "the lower orders in England." And throughout the whole process, the

6. John H. Van Evrie, *Negroes and Negro "Slavery": The First An Inferior Race, The Latter Its Normal Condition* (New York, 1853, 1861), pp. 225–43.

one person who consistently mattered for the slave was the master—since "the strongest affection the negro nature is capable of feeling is love of his master, his guide, protector, friend, and indeed Providence."[7]

The traditional Old South view of black intellectual faculties and capacity for family continued, of course, long after slavery and deep into the history of the "Solid South." In 1893 the Reverend Fletcher D. Srygley published his recollections of slavery days, remarking that in those earlier times black families "were broken up [by masters] without a moment's hesitation." As a boy, Srygley had worried over such things, believing that they brought slaves great suffering. He maintained, however, that later in life he had learned that field hands were "far too unsentimental" to worry themselves over such things.[8] Once again the dominant white group congratulated itself for supposedly showing more anxiety over the slave family than blacks themselves had. And, in the late nineteenth and early twentieth centuries, the myth that slaves had been incapable of taking the family seriously was perpetuated by the Phillips school of historians. John Spencer Bassett's book *The Southern Overseer* (1925), was a classic of this type; it reads like the writings of an antebellum planter restored to the sinister comfort of the Old South. "It ought to be remembered", he wrote, "that the Negroes themselves did not esteem marriage as the white people esteemed it." And "it is doubtful if the separations that occurred produced great distress in the minds of either party involved." His view was that "Slavery was a hard school but in it the Africans learned some good lessons." Contact with whites was often harsh; but, he maintained, *any* contact was bound to be beneficial for the blacks. The words of the overseer, he wrote,

> were apt to be severe, his epithets might be strong, his standards of justice might be crude. Negro slavery did not invite liberal ideas. The relation was primeval and the subject race was childlike. When, therefore, this uneducated white man and this child race of black men came together under the aegis of slavery there was much groping in the dark.

There was also much whipping, he added, but "it was the ordinary view that whipping was "the only thing that would do a negro good." Probably," he continued, "most of the slaves would have accepted this view in an abstract way."[9]

7. Van Evrie, *Negroes*, pp. 242–43, 230–32.

8. Fletcher D. Srygley, *Seventy Years in Dixie: Recollections and Sayings of T. W. Cask and Others* (Nashville, 1893), pp. 255–57.

9. Bassett, *The Overseer*, pp. 5, 18, 22, 16.

PATERNALISM, RACISM, AND THE SLAVEOWNER'S WORLD

The antebellum and "Solid South" opinions just outlined represented a deeply embedded white racist view of blacks and the black family connection. With such views, all things were possible. Owners could discipline slaves by threatening to sell them from their families, could look to recover runaways by searching close to the fugitive's old family, and yet could still find it possible to see black family attachments as fickle and transitory. They could separate families and still see themselves as paternalists—since they could deceive and flatter themselves with the view that only they, the whites, really worried about black families. They could readily persuade themselves that they *were* paternalists, and that separations were only incidental to the system—for in their view the whole relationship of slavery was of primary benefit to the slaves, any temporary "hardships" of separation easily being overcome. And, in any case, as J. H. Hammond told himself, a great satisfaction was that his slaves "loved and appreciated him."[10] The chief and only lasting loyalty of slaves was, supposedly, to the master and not the slave family. To have believed that the black family was really anything like as important as the white family would have meant permanent moral crisis for whites. Without that belief, the system was infinitely capable of combining a vicious program of speculation and separation with a comforting, paternal self-image for masters.

For those operating a racist system, a paternal self-image, whatever the realities of their actions, would hardly be surprising. Day-to-day racist practice might vary greatly in its manifestations and level of brutality, but racism when set down in legitimizing theory, or when consciously rationalized, tends often to speak the language of paternalism. A theory involving the "final solution" of extermination is of course a huge exception, but otherwise many racist theories talk of the "unequal talents" of different groups and the "paternal" need to keep a "weaker" group from what would otherwise be the irresistible competition of another—the need, for example, to remove Indians to the trans-Mississippi West rather than have them live "unhappily" alongside whites. In the case of planters and slavery, a sense of "burden" is often talked of, though in practice the burden would essentially be that of fear—a fear for their continuing security in an unequal system. The self-image of many planters, then, seems to have involved some notion of paternalism—although others more straightforwardly saw themselves as some sort of rough police force dedicated to keeping the hierarchy of race intact. Such differences within racism would have

10. Hammond quoted in Faust, *Hammond,* p. 104.

been reflected in the opposed stereotypes of blacks as "permanent children" or "dangerous beasts."[11]

The evidence of the slave trade, however, makes it possible to talk specifically, not just in entirely general terms, about paternalism and the practical limitations to it. One can distinguish three or four general types of slaveholder attitudes. A first category is that of the "broad paternalists" who took a wide view of their role, including in it a firmly held belief that the emotional and family welfare of slaves was more important than the convenience of masters. A second group consists of the "narrow paternalists," for whom the protection of the slave family was secondary to white convenience, but who made some effort to provide for physical needs and perhaps to limit work loads somewhat. The third and fourth categories would, for the slaves, be little different, but they can be termed "theoretical paternalists" and "supremacy policemen." By "theoretical paternalists" I mean to identify a group who used the language of paternalism as far as it occurred in proslavery arguments, but who in practice took from that framework only the idea of race hierarchy and innate white "superiority." The final category includes those not greatly inclined to trouble with self-legitimizing theory, but simply inclined toward a tough day-to-day assertion of white power. Of the categories just sketched, the first three views can perhaps be considered consensus theories based on some idea of a stable "natural order," whereas the last has stronger elements of conflict theory (with a constant need directly to assert strength so as to preserve order).[12]

These categories are not intended to be exhaustive and represent no more than a few very general types. The evidence of the trade, however, helps to make sense of them. "Broad paternalists," although figuring so prominently in the proslavery argument and in the long-sustained tradition of the plantation legend—were a distinct minority. Individual slaves, perhaps especially some domestics, might have been indulged by some owners from category two (and perhaps even categories three and four), but genuine paternalistic sacrifice seems to have been a rarity. Slaveholder and slaves were not intimately linked in a sort of extended family; for the great majority, relationships seem to have been much more distant, jarring, and lacking in mutual trust. The actions of masters in wrecking families and the low priority given to the

11. On racist stereotyping of blacks as animals and children, see Fredrickson, *Black Image*, pp. 43–70.

12. Some preliminary thoughts on such a listing were also given in Tadman, "Slave Trading and the Mentalities."

deepest of slave emotions do not suggest a system based on positive incentives, diligent workers, high morale, and accommodation within a joint economic enterprise. Slaveholder priorities and attitudes suggest, instead, a system based much more crudely on arbitrary power, distrust, and fear.[13] It is true there was, to some extent, interpenetration of white and slave culture—particularly in the outer form which slave religion took—but the general context of planter as speculator suggests only a severely limited interaction and sharing.[14] Essentially, speculators—meaning in this case slaveholders as well as traders—did not know and did not want to know enough of slave values for profound interactions to take place.

THE WORLD OF SLAVES

A fundamental yardstick by which slaves could judge masters—and, indeed, the whole system of slavery—was the black family and white attitudes toward it. As an old former slave, Jennie Hill, told her interviewer:

> Some people think that slaves had no feeling—that they bore their children as animals bear their young and that there was no heart-break when the children were torn from their parents or the mother taken from her brood to toil for a master in another state. But that isn't so. The slaves loved their families even as the Negroes love their own today and the happiest time of their lives was when they could sit at their cabin doors when the day's work was done and sing the old slave songs, 'Swing Low Sweet Chariot', 'Massa's in the Cold, Cold Ground', and 'Nobody Knows What Trouble I've Seen'. Children learned these songs and sang them only as a Negro child could. That was the slave's only happiness, a happiness that for many of them did not last.

The former slave explained that she got married when she was twenty years old, and

> then came my little babies and just before the war broke out I had three. How well I remember how I would sit in my room with the little ones on my lap and the tears would roll down my cheeks as I would ponder the right and wrong of bringing them into the world. What was I bringing them into the world for? To

13. Such comments run counter to the general accommodation theory of Fogel and Engerman in *Time on the Cross*.

14. On ideas of cultural penetration of masters into the world of slaves, and on "organic" relationships between masters and slaves, see Genovese, *Roll, Jordan, Roll*, pp. 73, 124–25, and Fox-Genovese and Genovese, *Fruits of Merchant Capital*, pp. 144–47, 138–39.

> be slaves and go from morning to night. They couldn't be educated and maybe they couldn't even live with their families. They would just be slaves. All that time I wasn't even living with my husband. He belonged to another man. He had to stay on his farm and I on mine. That wasn't living—that was slavery.

Despite all of this, however, she added that her master "was the best man that ever owned a nigger," and that "in all the 27 years I served my master as a slave I got but two whippings. That in itself speaks for the kindness of the master even though both of these whippings were for little things."[15]

Jennie Hill's story was not at all unusual. A great many exslaves reported that they had had "good" masters, but nevertheless clearly showed their hatred of slavery.[16] Such exslaves tended to judge masters on a relative scale—given that they had been slaves and had had to have masters, their master was not the worst class of master. In a sense such slaves had accommodated to the system, but this was only an accommodation through the violence of the system to them or to others. They might judge masters, for example, on something like the four-category scale outlined a little earlier. A few "good" masters might have come from category one (the "broad paternalist," who made the slave family the dominant priority), but most would no doubt have come from category two. "Bad" masters would no doubt have come from categories three and four. Even those whose own masters happened to be "broad paternalists" would most probably have been aware of the prevailing culture of speculation among masters generally, so that acceptance of the slavery system as a whole would have been only a little more likely than with other slaves. Some slaves with "broad paternalist" masters might have felt themselves genuinely to have been a part of the master's extended family, and might therefore have shown deep-rooted loyalty and affection. The great majority of "deeply loyal slaves" though, like those who "loved and appreciated" James H. Hammond, would have been a fictive white creation arising out of the needs of the slaveholder's self-image.

In the antebellum period, those specialist dealers, variously called slave traders, "soul drivers," "nigger drovers," and the like, were not the only "Negro speculators" in the South, and the slaves knew it! The predominantly speculative character of slaveholder attitudes lent itself to an underground slave culture of satirical songs and folk tales. Sale

15. Jennie Hill, narrative reproduced in Blassingame (ed.), *Slave Testimony,* pp. 589–94.

16. See Escott, *Slavery Remembered,* esp. pp. 7–12, 36–70.

and family separation facilitated the geographical growth of slavery in America and the development of economic fortunes for slaveholders, but they carried penalties for the master class too. Few economic systems actually broke up families so arbitrarily and on such a scale, so that despite the terrible power of masters, their authority, with most slaves, was only accepted conditionally. Black and white values relating to the slave family kept masters and slaves largely in separate, segregated worlds. The years of segregation began long before the age of "Jim Crow" and the ugly laws of the late nineteenth century.

APPENDICES

PRIMARY SOURCES

INDEX

Appendix 1

Estimating Interregional Slave Movements for 1790–1819

1.1. THE GROWTH RATE METHOD

Basic estimates of net interregional slave movements (given in Table 2.1) were made by use of the growth-rate method. This technique is explained in detail in Frederic Bancroft, *Slave Trading*, pp. 384–95. It starts by assuming that the decennial rate of natural increase (excess of births over deaths) was roughly uniform across the South. From this assumption it follows that if, for a particular decade, the growth rate of slaves in a particular state was *above* the southern norm for those years net *importation* had taken place. (If increase was below the norm, then exportation had taken place.) In producing Table 2.1, it was assumed for the sake of simplicity that such importations or exportations were distributed evenly over the decade concerned. On average, then, half of the natural increase of these slaves would have taken place *after* the point in the decade when they moved from one region to another. This share of natural increase will artificially inflate apparent numbers of exportations (or importations). Accordingly, divergences from expected end-of-decade totals are scaled down to allow for half of that decade's natural increase on slaves imported or exported. In order satisfactorily to advance such calculations, it is necessary to establish the basic reliability of the census data used and also the general suitability of the slave population for such analysis. These questions are addressed in Appendix 2. Appendix 1, section 1.3, will deal with the particular problem of African importations in the early years, especially 1790 to 1807.

1.2. MINOR ADJUSTMENTS OF DATA

At early periods of settlement (generally before statehood was achieved) the slave population of a few areas did not appear in the census. In a few cases, then, census data were supplemented by estimates of population levels. Thus, the Louisiana slave population of 1800 was estimated at 20,000 (see Lachance, "The Politics of Fear," p. 167); that of Florida in 1820 is estimated at 9,500 (her slaves numbered 15,501 in 1830); and Texas in 1840 was assumed to have had about 20,000 slaves (see American Anti-Slavery Society, *Slavery and the Internal Slave Trade,* p. 248). Arkansas and Alabama did not appear in the census till 1820, by which time they had slave populations of 1,617 and 41,879, respectively. They are, therefore, taken to have received, in the 1810s, totals of 1,000 and 35,500 slaves, respectively. One thousand slave importations (by the combination of trading and planter migrations) are also inferred for Florida in the 1810s.

1.3. ADJUSTING FOR IMPORTATIONS FROM AFRICA, CIRCA 1790–1819

In using growth-rate calculations for the period 1790 to 1810, special allowance had to be made for the arrival of African importations. Very active importation in those years would have boosted the decennial growth rates of the slave population in those decades, and to allow for this factor the crude growth rates of 30 percent for the 1790s and 33 percent for 1800–1809 were both scaled down to produce estimated slave natural increases of 27 percent. This figure is consistent with what seem to be the most reliable estimates of African arrivals in those years: about 30,000 for the 1790s and about 63,000 for 1800–1809 (see Curtin, *Slave Trade,* pp. 72–75; Kulikoff, "Uprooted Peoples," pp. 150, 168–69). In allocating the newly arrived Africans to particular states, Kulikoff's general assumption was adopted (that is, his calculation that new arrivals from Africa went, not to Chesapeake masters, but to buyers in the newly developing regions). The overall method for the present calculations was, first, to guess the likely share of new Africans going to particular states; next to scale down the estimated African numbers to allow for a probable 25 percent mortality among new arrivals; and, finally, to adjust the estimates of *interstate* slave movements to account for this revised total of African arrivals.[1] From this, the totals for the 1790s and 1800–1809 given in Table 2.1 were produced.

For the 1790s, it was estimated that new Africans were settled in the areas and numbers indicated: Georgia, 13,500; South Carolina, 6,500; Tennessee, 1,500; and North Carolina, 1,000. For 1800 to 1809, the following estimates were made: Georgia, 15,000; South Carolina, 14,000; Louisiana, 7,000; Mississippi, 9,000; and Tennessee, 2,250. (It is assumed that very few, if any, new Africans went to other states in these years.) The statistical impact of the African arrivals would have been reduced for South Carolina, because basic decennial growth rates indicate that in these years the low-country section of

1. For evidence of this sort of high mortality during the early "seasoning" years of new Africans, see Kulikoff, "Uprooted Peoples," p. 169; Kulikoff, "A 'Prolific' People: Black Population Growth in the Chesapeake Colonies, 1700–1790," *Southern Studies,* 16 (1977), p. 421; Michael Craton and James Walvin, *A Jamaican Plantation: The History of Worthy Park, 1670–1970* (Toronto, 1970), pp. 130–32, 172–73; and Philip D. Curtin, "Epidemiology and the Slave Trade," *Political Science Quarterly,* 83 (1968), pp. 190–216.

that state was already a net *exporter* of her own slaves (in the 1790s net exportations of some 2,000 and from 1800–1809 of some 11,000 slaves).

It is also possible that in the 1810s small numbers of African slaves were smuggled into the United States. Kulikoff's estimate for this decade is 7,000 illegal arrivals (Kulikoff, "Uprooted People," p. 152). Smuggling (after the legal trade closed in 1807) does not seem to have been on any higher scale (see Appendix 2 below) and has here been excluded from results (Table 2.1) for the 1810s.

Appendix 2

The Structure of Planter Migrations

Travel accounts, migrants' letters, coastal manifests, census data, and other sources combine clearly to indicate that planter migrations, in terms of age and sex structure, were almost completely nonselective. As Chapter 2 suggested, such migrations, on average, took from the exporting states a representative sample of that area's slave population, in crucial contrast with the very marked age-selectivity of the domestic slave trade.

Unlike almost all migrations of free people, the movement of slaves by planter migration displayed balanced sex ratios and basically unselective age ratios. Typically, planters took with them to the new lands of the West all of those slaves they happened to own. Some, immediately before leaving for the west, deliberately supplemented their stock by selective purchases (see Chapter 6); but such slave additions should, of course, be considered as part of the trade, and not as part of planter migration proper. Planters typically (see Chapter 6) moved west with a fairly small gang of slaves, established themselves, and, if at all successful, built up their stocks with substantial help from the trade.

2.1. TYPICAL MIGRATIONS

The "Memoranda and Observations" of James Asbury Tait record an experience that was probably, for our purposes, fairly typical of those who migrated with substantial numbers of slaves. Tait wrote:

> My progress in life, as to property, has been pretty much as follows: When my father and I removed to Alabama in 1818, we had about twenty-five working hands, in all about sixty in number. . . . In . . . 1820, we made that year . . . about double [the cotton] we made in Georgia, with the same force; except that our young hands were two or three years older and two or three more ten year olds put out to work. When we removed to Alabama, my number of negroes was twenty, ten or half that number working hands; my father fifteen working.

By 1835 the holding had eighty slaves, "forty of which were workers." Significantly, the Taits' migration had not been selective. They had taken *all* of their slaves to Alabama, although only about 40 percent of them were working hands. By 1853, J. A. Tait had some three hundred slaves, even though he had given many to his six children. Such a large stock was vastly in excess of growth through natural increase, and no doubt owed a great deal to the trade.[1]

In 1835, the Brownriggs migrated from North Carolina to their new plantation in Mississippi. It is clear that this exceptionally large migrant group, with ninety-one slaves, was not selective in the slaves it took. Letters from the white migrants as well as from several of the slaves recorded this exodus in great detail. One slave, Phebe Brownrigg, wrote to her mother telling her: "My master, Mr. Tom Brownrigg, starts the middle of next month with all of the people, except your sister Marg" (who, along with certain whites, was to follow the next spring). The great caravan included numerous slave children, some (probably most) of whom were carried in wagons. And, an important point, *all* of "the people" were to migrate.[2]

The use of wagons to facilitate the migration of young children (and, no doubt also, of sickly and old slaves) crops up in many sources. Basil Hall, a British traveller, came upon a migrant group with the slave "women and children stowed away in wagons." Similarly, G. W. Featherstonehaugh wrote that in the Indian country of Alabama

> We met a great many families and planters emigrating to Alabama and Mississippi to take up cotton plantations, their slaves tramping through the waxy ground on foot, and the heavy wagons containing the black women and children dragging on, and frequently breaking down. All that were able were obliged to walk, and being wet with fording streams were shivering with cold.

David Meade, a white migrant in his early fifties, probably travelled on horseback, but some of his slaves made the journey in wagons, "several little negroes" being badly shaken when their wagon overturned.[3]

Another substantial migrant was John H. Dent. When he sold his plantation in South Carolina and moved to Alabama in 1836, he "took along *all* [emphasis added] the slaves that went with the rice plantation." The planter Thomas Dabney also undertook a large and unselective migration. According to the eulogistic memoir by his daughter, the "firm but affectionate" master, shortly before migrating, gave his slaves a choice. Any who did not wish to move could try to find a purchaser so as to stay in their old locality. It turned out that only two slaves either wished to or were able to find a place locally—and these, according to the memoir, because they thought themselves too old to travel. (It is possible, though, that having children locally was a factor.) Several points

1. Tait, "Memoranda," quoted in Sellers, *Slavery in Alabama,* p. 33.

2. On the Brownriggs see Phebe Brownrigg's letter in Blassingame, *Slave Testimony,* pp. 22–23; and see the extensive Brownrigg Family Papers (SHC).

3. Hall, *Travels in North America,* vol. 3, pp. 128–29; Featherstonehaugh, *Excursion Through the Slave States,* p. 152; Still, "Westward Migration of a Planter Pioneer," pp. 319n, 324.

emerge from the Dabney case. There was no deliberate policy of age-selective migration: slaves of all ages were taken. For potential migrants generally, choice in the matter of staying or leaving was probably exceptional. Moreover, when a choice was available, it would seem that prime young slaves (being the most in demand) would usually have stood the best chance of finding a buyer and staying behind in the Upper South.[4]

Those owners who moved with substantial gangs probably took particular care in planning their migrations, but in records of such planning no reference has been found to a policy of leaving behind old slaves (or young, or those in between). John H. Burns had migrated to Louisiana in the late 1840s, taking with him "the few slaves that he owned." By 1853, he had made a trip back to South Carolina and had bought new slaves there (and no doubt he also bought on other occasions). In 1853, he was also advising his father-in-law (who planned to migrate with forty slaves) on the relative merits of overland and coastal routes, and on a great many details of migration practices. Apparently, the idea of leaving behind particular slaves on account of their ages did not form a part of their discussions. Another major migration was that of the Lides, who moved from South Carolina to Alabama in 1835. Again there is a record of very detailed planning, but again we find no mention of leaving particular slaves behind. Indeed, since the principal migrants, James and Jane Lide, were themselves aged sixty-five and fifty-seven years, respectively, when they set out, there seems to have been little likelihood of discrimination on grounds of old age! In the case of James Shackelford, intending to migrate from South Carolina to Georgia in the 1830s, careful plans were made for the work of feeble (and probably old) slaves. Shackelford was advised that

> When you arrive, the first thing to do will be to build camps for the negroes, then put as many as possible to building a warehouse . . . for provisions. . . . While about this and other buildings, that division of your force that is too feeble to work at this kind of work, may be cleaning up and burning the underbrush where you will plant.[5]

Small-scale migrations, we noted earlier, were surely far more common than the substantial movements just discussed. But the small number of slaves in the typical migrant group seems to have reflected a pattern in which most migrant slaveowners, having few slaves, took them. They did not denude existing plantations by taking prime slaves and leaving children and old slaves behind. An example of small-scale migration was reported by the exslave Sarah Fitzpatrick, who told her interviewer that "Ma' mamma's Mistus got mar'ied to a white man in Alabama named Fitzpatrick an' when she come down here

4. Dent, quoted in Sellers, *Slavery in Alabama,* p. 36; Susan Dabney Smedes, *A Southern Planter* (London, 1889), pp. 8–9.

5. Burns and Lake migrations in Wells, "Moving a Plantation to Louisiana"; Fletcher M. Green (ed.), *The Lides Go South and West: The Record of a Planter Migration in 1835* (Columbia, S.C., 1952), pp. iv–v; James Shackelford Letter (SHC).

[from South Carolina, to marry him,] she brung all o' her 'Nigger' property wid her. Dat wuz ma' mama an' her six chillun." Another small-scale migration occurred in 1784, when Samuel E. Butler moved from Virginia to Georgia with thirteen slaves—these being all of the slaves he owned. Like many other later migrants, though, over the next decade or two he greatly expanded, no doubt making heavy use of the slave trade.[6]

2.2. THE EVIDENCE OF COASTAL MANIFESTS

Coastal manifests make it clear that migrants, including some with substantial gangs, used the shipping routes to Mobile, New Orleans, Galveston, and the like for their journey. Again a strongly unselective pattern of slave migration emerges. From the collection of manifests at the National Archives, U. B. Phillips found, for example, that

> In 1831 James L. Petigru and Langdon Cheves sent from Charleston to Savannah 85 and 64 slaves respectively of ages ranging from 90 and 75 years to infancy, with the obvious purpose to develop newly acquired plantations in Georgia.

He noted, too, that in 1819 Benjamin Ballard and Samuel T. Barnes, both of Halifax County, North Carolina, sent 30 and 196 slaves, respectively, from Norfolk to New Orleans. Ballard wrote on the margins of his manifest: "The owner of these slaves is moving to the parish of St. Landry near Opelousas where he has purchased lands and intends settling, and is not a dealer in human flesh." Barnes, too, appended a note that "The owner of these slaves is moving to Louisiana to settle, and is not a dealer in human flesh." Similarly, Augustin Pugh carried seventy slaves from North Carolina—50 percent of them children, but some as old as sixty years and more—and recorded that their owner was not a slave trader.[7]

The manifests, though, give more important evidence than this. They show a profound contrast between the structure of the trade and that of planter migration. Not only that, they reveal that at the very least 73 percent (and probably rather more than 80 percent) of the slaves moving by the coastal route are attributable to the trade and not planter to migration.

Let us look at these points in a little more detail. Table A2.1 documents those individuals appearing in the manifests of the 1840s who were, beyond any doubt, important slave traders. These traders alone accounted for 73 percent of all slaves who, according to the manifests, arrived at New Orleans in the 1840s. Since several categories of unidentified trading have to be added, the actual share of coastal arrivals attributable to the trade can confidently be estimated at over 80 percent. We must add to the basic 73 percent, first, purchases by

6. Sarah Fitzpatrick's narrative in Blassingame, *Slave Testimony,* p. 639; G. M. Herndon, "Samuel Edward Butler of Virginia Goes to Georgia, 1784," *Georgia Historical Quarterly,* 52 (1968), pp. 115–31.

7. Wells, "Moving a Plantation," pp. 283–84; Phillips, *American Negro Slavery,* pp. 183, 195–96.

Table A2.1. Manifests of traders' shipments to New Orleans in the 1840s: Number of slaves

Owner or consignee	1840	1842	1844	1846	1848	Evidence documenting trader
		Baltimore (2180 slaves)				
Boudar, Thomas	9	2				Bancroft, 92n, 277n, 314
Campbell, W. L. & B. M.			42	72	188	Bancroft, 316–17, etc.
Crow, William			15	20	22	Pittman
Donovan, Joseph S.			112	299	204	Bancroft, 120–22
Harker, William			25	12		Stowe, 346
McCargo, Thomas	7		38			Sydnor, 151, 154
Purvis, James		51				Bancroft, 39, 102n
Slatter, Hope H	119	236	46	353		Bancroft, 372–74, etc.
Staples, Joshua		17				Mooney, 50
Williams, Wm. H. & T.	55		30	86	116	Bancroft, 50, 56, 58
Woolfolk, Austin				4		Bancroft, 39, 277, etc.
		Charleston (306 slaves)				
Campbell, B. M.	3					Bancroft, 316–17
Davis, Ansley	25	4				Bancroft, 93
Davis, Solomon			1	6		Bancroft, 93
Gadsden, Thomas N.	1			1		Appendix 4
Gilchrist, John M.		3				Appendix 4
Johnson, Sherman	1					Phillips, 196
McBride, Michael				1	8	Appendix 4
McDonald, Alexander	77	60	20	49		Ch. 7
Mordecai, Benjamin				2	38	Appendix 4
Oakes, Ziba B.				1		Appendix 4
Ryan, Thomas				3	2	Appendix 4
		Virginia ports and D.C. (2955 slaves)				
Apperson, G. W.			148	356	208	Phillips, 196
Barnes, G. W.	20					Stowe, 8
Beasley, Richard R.	38	15	2	79		Bancroft, 28n
Boudar, Thomas	84	1	104	94	43	Bancroft, 92n, 277n, 314
Bradley & Saunders				4		Bancroft, 309
Cochran, B. F. & James, J. D.				63		Sydnor, 154
Davis, Mark, Ben, Henry, Geo., Goodman, & So.	118	82	167	434		Bancroft, 93
Dickson, John		92	14	44		Sydnor, 154
Freeman, Theophilus	193					Stowe, 8
Goodwin, William H.	10					Ch. 2, Table 2.2
Hagan, John (& A.)	2	7	30	52	16	Phillips, 196
Johnson, Sherman	11		11			Phillips, 196
Kephart, George[a]	29					Bancroft, 51, 64n, 91–92
Lockett, Edward				15	51	Chase
Lumpkin, Robert[a]	15					Bancroft, 101–3
McCargo, Thomas	71	7				Sydnor, 151, 154
Peterson, H. F. & Smart, W. R.				34	28	Bancroft, facing 316

(*continued on the following page*)

Table A2.1. Manifests of traders' shipments to New Orleans in the 1840s: Number of slaves (*continued*)

Owner or consignee	1840	1842	1844	1846	1848	Evidence documenting trader
			Virginia ports and D.C. (2955 slaves)			
Rutherford, C. M.				16		Bancroft, facing 316
Shelton, Lewis N.				31		Chase
Tait, Bacon	1			5		Bancroft, 101, 92n
Talbott, William F.				48	58	Phillips, 196
Templeman, H. N.	3	1				Ch. 2, Table 2.2
	892	578	805	2184	982	
			Total 5,441 Slaves			

Sources: Where possible evidence identifying owner or consignee as trader refer to readily accessible sources.

Ch.: Evidence appears in the present study in the chapter cited
Phillips: U. B. Phillips, *American Negro Slavery* (Baton Rouge, 1969)
Bancroft: F. Bancroft, *Slave Trading in the Old South* (New York, 1959)
Sydnor: C. S. Sydnor, *Slavery in Mississippi* (New York, 1933)
Stowe: H. B. Stowe, *The Key to Uncle Tom's Cabin* (London, 1853)
Pittman: Letter of February 20, 1837, John W. Pittman Collection (LC)
Mooney: C. C. Mooney, *Slavery in Tennessee* (Bloomington, 1957)
Chase: Letter of February 12, 1843, Lucy Chase Collection (AAS)

Note: For the 1840s as a whole, available National Archives manifests document 13,358 slaves shipped to New Orleans by the traders listed in this appendix.

[a] = manifests give as "shipper."

individual planters returning from slave-buying trips in the Upper South. Probably more important, we must add purchases by those who were in fact traders but who have not been identified in Table A2.1. Numerous individuals, like J. Forsyth and J. R. Crane, as well as company names, like Brodie & Petty, appear repeatedly, and it is very likely that many were traders or substantial buying agents of some sort.

The impossibility of separating out all traders' lots and private purchases makes the sample of planter migrations produced from the manifests necessarily impure. It is also probable that some of the slaves not attributed to traders were in fact the personal servants of mere travellers, rather than being the property of genuine migrants. Table A2.2, nevertheless, summarizes significant results from the manifests. Row 1 indicates the typical age and sex structure of the slave population of the exporting states, and hence gives a profile of the expected composition of planter migrations. Row 2 plots the structure of the New Orleans trade as revealed by the 73 percent of slaves attributable in the manifests to known traders. The intense concentration on prime-adult males and the neglect of children is very clear. Because row 3 plots the 27 percent of New Orleans coastal arrivals not attributed to *known* traders. Row 3 is not a pure sample of planter migration, the sex ratio (at 53 percent male) does not fully reflect planter migration, and shows the residual effect of

Table A2.2. Age structure of slave population involved in planter migration, New Orleans trade sample, and other New Orleans importations

	Male (% in each age bracket)						Female (% in each age bracket)						
	0–9	10–14	15–19	20–29	30–39	40+	0–9	10–14	15–19	20–29	30–39	40+	*N*
1. Planter migration (based on structure of net-exporting area)	16.0	7.1	5.6	8.7	5.2	7.4	16.2	6.9	5.7	8.5	5.3	7.5	2,201,959
2. New Orleans slave trade (based on manifests of all known traders)	3.5	4.1	13.7	32.4	4.2	1.4	4.7	4.8	18.7	9.3	2.1	1.1	7,917
3. New Orleans manifests (excluding known slave traders of row 2)	10.5	5.4	7.4	17.0	7.3	5.6	10.6	6.2	8.4	11.0	6.1	4.5	2,921

Sources: Row 1 is based on structure of slave population of the net-exporting states as recorded at 1850 census (the 1860 census gave very similar results). Rows 2 and 3 are based on manifests recording coastal shipments of slaves arriving at New Orleans in the years 1841, 1843, 1845, 1847, and 1849.

Notes: Row 2 includes only shipments by known interregional slave traders (listed in Table A2.1). Row 3 records all shipments for these years excluding those carried by those known traders reflected in Row 2.

sugar and the trade. In particular, adult males of 20–29 are still substantially overrepresented and children are underrepresented. Despite the impurities of the sample, Row 3 is more like Row 1 than Row 2, again indicating the unselective character of planter migrations. In the manifests, then, the dominance of the trade (at least 73 percent) is clear, and the unselective character of planter migration is strongly reflected.

2.3. HYPOTHETICAL CASES OF SELECTIVE PLANTER MIGRATIONS

Planter migrations could only have been age-selective in special circumstances: (1) if those deciding to move were the owners of unusually "prime" slave gangs; (2) if migrants decided, on setting out to the west, to sell off or abandon slave children and aged slaves; (3) if "advance parties" of especially prime slaves were sent out to prepare new plantations; (4) if migrants adopted a policy of buying in extra prime slaves in preparation for migration; or (5) if there were very large numbers of dual-residence plantation enterprises (and if such establishments commonly retained old slaves and infants in the east, and sent prime slaves to the west). In practice, however, none of these hypothetical special factors disturbs the basic unselective pattern which has been proposed for planter migrations.

Let us examine the various cases in turn. The balanced sex ratio in planter migrations suggests, contrary to hypothesis 1, that slaveholders who moved were unlikely to be simply those with especially robust workforces. Owners of all types of holdings appear to have shared equally in the urge to exploit the opportunities of newer lands in the Lower South. Hypothesis 2 would itself have involved massive family disruptions equivalent to those of the trade. Moreover, there seems to have been no valid economic reason to have left infants behind. Infants and very old slaves were fairly easily moved west in wagons, and children represented an investment for the future. Even traders, the true professionals in the business of interregional migration, chose to take to the west large numbers of children, especially infants accompanied by their mothers, or youngsters just coming into working age. Although migrant planters surely cannot have had a general policy of leaving very old slaves behind, our calculations would not be significantly disturbed even by quite numerous cases of abandonment of the old.[8] Hypothesis 3, the "advance party," has initial plausibility; we can certainly establish that advance parties were quite common in planter migrations.[9] Nevertheless, the statistical significance of such a phenomenon over a given decade disappears, since, on average, the

8. For comments on the very limited statistical significance of those cases where individuals left behind were, in slave terms, very old (say over seventy years), see Appendix 3.

9. On advance parties see, for example, Wells, "Moving a Plantation"; Green, *The Lides*, p. v; Srygley, *Seventy Years in Dixie*, p. 255; Coleman, *Slavery Times*, p. 16n; Dick, *The Dixie Frontier*, pp. 55–56.

main migrant group appear usually to have joined the pioneers within a few months or a year at most.

We are left with two other hypotheses. The idea (4) that migrants, before setting out to the west, systematically prepared for their trip by buying prime young slaves is certainly valid in numerous cases and has been documented in Chapter 6. But I noted at the beginning of Appendix 2, that such purchases should properly be considered as a part of the interregional trade, and should be clearly distinguished from planter migration. As for hypothesis 5, some individuals did, indeed, own plantations in different areas—in Mississippi and South Carolina, say. Theoretically, this phenomenon could have produced selective groups of slave migrants. In practice, however, it seems for our present purposes to have been statistically insignificant, first, because such plantation arrangements seem to have been very unusual, and second because the two examples I have of migrations relating to such holdings provide very mixed evidence.[10] In 1809, Leonard Covington, unable satisfactorily to dispose of his Maryland plantation, decided to keep up that enterprise while sending thirty-one slaves to a new plantation in Mississippi. The slaves sent to Mississippi seem to have been on average about five years younger than those twenty-five who were to stay in the old country, but the difference was not great, and the two oldest slaves (both left in Maryland) seem to have been only aged fifty and forty-six years respectively. Significantly, there seems to have been no inclination to leave infants and children behind: fourteen aged nine and under were to go to Mississippi while only ten such slaves were to remain in Maryland. In 1835, James R. Polk, already the owner of a plantation in Tennessee, set up a subsidiary enterprise in Mississippi. In those slaves selected for the trip to Mississippi, there was very probably a bias toward prime young adults, but it came, not from planter migration, but essentially from a deliberate and well-documented campaign of selective purchasing undertaken specifically with the new plantation in mind.[11]

All things considered, then, only with dual-residence planters does the possibility of genuinely age-selective migration emerge. Even here, not only were dual-residence arrangements highly exceptional, but so too were genuinely selective migrations relating to them.

10. Kenneth Stampp (*Peculiar Institution,* pp. 42–43) noted that "a small number" of Virginians and Carolinians maintained a "home plantation" and a further holding in the southwest. Chalmers Gaston Davidson in *The Last Foray: The South Carolina Planters of 1860: A Sociological Study* (Columbia, S.C., 1971), p. 2, comments on the cases of the Bulls, Hamptons, Prestons, and Mannings.

11. On Covington's migration, see Nellie W. Brandon and W. M. Drake (eds.), *Memoire of Leonard Covington by B. L. C. Wailes, also Some of General Covington's Letters* (Natchez, 1928), esp. p. 54. On Polk's migration, see Bassett, *The Southern Overseer,* pp. 44, 47–48, 77, 79–80, 83, 86, 119.

Appendix 3

Calculating the Structure of the Interregional Movement

This appendix offers detailed evidence, first, on the appropriateness of survival-rate calculations (sections 3.1 and 3.2) and secondly, on the nature of the calculations themselves (sections 3.3 and 3.4). Several conditions must be satisfied before survival-rate calculations can reliably be used for the purposes of estimating movements of population.[1] In particular, I will establish, first, that there were no significant *regional* variations either in the accuracy of census enumeration or in age-specific and sex-specific mortality rates, and second, that the population was essentially a "closed" one, that is, one not influenced (in ways we cannot adjust for) by factors such as international migration, the running away of slaves, and manumission.

3.1. REGIONAL CONSISTENCY IN CENSUS ENUMERATION AND IN SPECIFIC MORTALITY RATES

First, there seems to be no reason that there should have been significant state-by-state variations in the degree of accuracy with which slaves were enumerated at censuses. The practice adopted in the principal calculations of this study—a practice of dealing with states, not individually, but according to two broad regions (the net slave-exporting and net slave-importing areas)—should, however, correct any local variations which might have existed. Somewhat similarly, this study also recognizes that the 1850s survival-rate statistics for *specific age subdivisions* within the 40+/50+ cohort are erratic (there were small numbers of slaves in these cohorts, masters were often vague about the ages of older slaves, etc.). The unreliability of the evidence on these narrow age categories (those of seventy years and over, for example) is avoided by combining those older slaves into a broad 40+/50+ category.

1. For an important discussion of the survival-rate technique, see C. H. Hamilton, "The Effects of Census Errors on the Measurement of Migration," *Demography,* 3 (1966), pp. 393–416.

What about possible regional variations in age-specific and sex-specific mortality rates? The mortality-rate requirement would not have been satisfied in the colonial period, when large numbers of Africans were imported at varying rates in different colonies, and when those newly imported slaves, on meeting an unfamiliar disease environment, displayed high mortality rates. But for the American slave population of 1820–60 the mortality-rate requirement appears to be quite satisfactorily fulfilled. There is some possibility that mortality might generally have been somewhat higher in the expanding, importing states, because of the hard work involved in clearing ground and establishing new plantations. More particularly, mortality rates might well have been above average in the highly localized sugar plantations of the importing states (that is, in southern Louisiana). But so far as survival-rate calculations are concerned, these possible variations in mortality rates would have tended to *underrepresent* the extent of the slave movement—in particular, any age-selectivity in the interregional movement—so tending to underrepresent the number of slaves apparently attributable to the trade.

3.2. EVIDENCE THAT THE SLAVE SOUTH WAS A CLOSED POPULATION, 1820–60

The idea that the U.S. slave population from 1820 to 1860 can be treated as almost completely "closed" is supported by recent demographic studies.[2] But for a detailed consideration of this question, I begin by considering the possible demographic significance of the African slave trade in this period.

Farley, Curtin, and others have pointed out that the trend in the sex ratio of the American black population seems to rule out any extensive slave smuggling into the United States after African importations were banned in 1807, and especially after 1820, the period of most relevance for my calculations. In the Atlantic trade, males typically accounted for between three-fifths and two-thirds of slaves, and the sex ratios of the North American black population of the eighteenth century showed the clear influence of these male-dominated importations.[3] By 1820, however, as censuses show, the sex ratio was almost

2. See, e.g., R. Farley, "The Demographic Rates and Social Institutions of the Nineteenth Century Negro Population: A Stable Population Analysis," *Demography,* 2 (1965), pp. 386–98; J. E. Eblen, "The Growth Rate of the Black Population in Ante-Bellum America, 1820–60," *Population Studies,* 26 (1972), pp. 273–89; Sutch, "The Breeding of Slaves," pp. 199–205; P. D. Curtin, *The Atlantic Slave Trade: A Census* (Madison, 1969), pp. 72–75; McClelland and Zeckhauser, *Demographic Dimensions,* pp. 20–21, 44–49.

3. For example, in 1701–10 the sex ratio of South Carolina's adult slaves was about 143 males per 100 females and in 1730–31 about 180:100; the ratio for North Carolina's adult black population in 1754 was about 147:100; and that for Georgia's adult slaves in 1780–81 was about 161:100. See E. B. Greene and V. D. Harrington, *American Population before the Federal Census of 1790* (New York, 1932), pp. 157, 162, 172–73; Peter H. Wood, "'More Like a Negro Country': Demographic Patterns in Colonial South Carolina, 1670–1740," in Engerman and Genovese (eds.), *Race and Slavery,* p. 154; Flanders, *Plantation Slavery in Georgia,* p. 44.

balanced (at 102 males per 100 females), and later censuses showed either a balance of the sexes or an excess of *females*. McClelland and Zeckhauser allowed for the possibility that 5,000 slaves per year were smuggled in even after 1820, on the ground that policing might have been lax.[4] There are virtually no documented cases of smuggling and no reports of unusual, unacclimatized, foreign-speaking newcomers in the slave population, so that their estimate seems to be generous in the extreme.

The assessment of colonization, a second factor which might have disturbed survival rates, seems to be relatively uncomplicated. Colonization was a formal legal process and was sponsored by societies whose officers recorded the progress of slave migration from the United States. The history of colonization is therefore fairly well documented, and its limited numerical extent has been accepted by historians. According to the statistics of the American Colonization Society's fifty-second annual report (1869), fewer than 10,000 colonists went from the United States to Liberia in the whole of the period 1817 to 1860.[5]

It also seems to be safe to conclude that slave runaways will not significantly disturb the accuracy of survival-rate calculations. Enumerations of runaways in the 1850 and 1860 censuses suggest that successful fugitives represented only a very tiny percentage of the American slave population, and since runaway rates, as officially recorded, were only a little higher in the Upper than the Lower South, most runaways would, for the purposes of survival-rate calculations, have cancelled each other out.[6] Some 75 percent of runaways were male; had running away been both common and disproportionately concentrated in one region, survival-rate calculations for interregional slave movements would have suggested an imbalance in the sexes.[7] In practice, it seems that only the slave movement to Louisiana showed a significant sex-ratio imbalance, which is explained by the specialized Louisiana slave trade rather than by any substantial number of fugitives.

The numbers of slaves manumitted appear to have been far larger than the numbers of smuggled slaves, slave colonists, or slave fugitives, but from 1820 to 1860 manumissions can have had only a very limited impact upon slave demography. According to censuses, the growth rates of the free black population in those years were so low compared with rates for slaves that, even

4. McClelland and Zeckhauser, *Demographic Dimension*, pp. 44–49.

5. See P. J. Staudenraus, *The African Colonization Movement, 1816–1865* (New York, 1961), p. 251.

6. According to federal censuses, runaway rates for the Upper South were, in 1849–50, 0.035, and in 1859–60, 0.022 fugitives per 100 slaves of population; for the Lower South they were, in 1849–50, 0.025, and in 1859–60, 0.018 per 100 (see U.S. Bureau of Census, *Preliminary Report of the Eighth Census* (Washington, 1862), pp. 11–12, 137.

7. On the sex ratio of runaways, see Gerald W. Mullin, *Flight and Rebellion: Slave Resistance in Eighteenth-Century Virginia* (London, 1972), p. 40; Blassingame, *The Slave Community*, pp. 113–14; Gutman, *Black Family*, p. 239; and D. E. Meanders, "South Carolina Fugitives as Viewed through Local Colonial Newspapers, with Emphasis on Runaway Notices, 1732–1801," *Journal of Negro History*, 30 (1975), p. 292.

allowing for the probable underenumeration of free blacks, the population cannot have been very greatly swelled by newly manumitted slaves.[8] And because of their distribution over the southern states, most manumissions cancelled each other out, as far as survival-rate calculations of slave movements are concerned. The incidence of manumission, like that of fugitives, was nevertheless slightly higher in the Upper than in the Lower South, so that manumissions would have had *some* residual effect upon my calculations.[9] But it seems that the Upper South's somewhat above average rate of manumission would have slightly underrepresented the age-selective character of the interregional slave movement, because manumission was not spread evenly over all age groups, but tended to be disproportionately concentrated among those too old to form part of the domestic slave trade.[10] In survival-rate calculations, the effect of this age distribution will be somewhat to exaggerate the rate of the Upper South's exportation of those who were above the usual slave-trading age. Overall, then, slave smuggling, colonization, and manumission are likely to have had very little impact upon survival-rate calculations of slave movements,

8. In contrast with the slave population's decennial growth rate of some 25 percent, the free black growth rate was, in the 1820s (expanded by very extensive emancipations in the North) 36.8 percent, in the 1830s, 20.9 percent, in the 1840s, 12.5 percent, and in the 1850s, 12.3 percent.

9. The *Preliminary Report of the Eighth Census* (p. 137) estimated that over the South as a whole there were some 20,000 manumissions in the 1850s, and that in 1850 the exporting states, while accounting for 64.7 percent of the South's slave population, accounted for 82.3 percent of the South's manumissions. For 1860 the corresponding statistics were 57.6 and 69.4 percent. See also McClelland and Zeckhauser, *Demographic Dimensions*, pp. 16–17.

10. According to manumission deeds, liberation usually followed long periods of service, so that most slaves on reaching freedom are likely to have been middle-aged or older. (See, for example, I. Berlin, *Slaves without Masters: The Free Negro in the Old South* (New York, 1971), p. 152; and see Tadman "Speculators and Slaves," pp. 76–79. Older free blacks were, at a much higher per capita rate than the younger age groups, supplemented by slave manumissions: for example, the composition of the free black and slave populations *aged ten years and over* in 1850 breaks down as follows (from U.S. Bureau of the Census, *The Seventh Census . . . 1850)*:

Age	Free blacks (%)	Slaves (%)
10–14	16.6	20
15–19	13.9	16.3
20–29	24.6	26.2
30–39	17.5	16.2
40–49	12	10
50+	15.4	11.2

Note: Of the free black and slave populations respectively, 27 and 32 percent were aged under ten years. This is consistent with a very low rate of supplementing of the free black population by child manumission (but a wide range of factors would have influenced the numbers of children under ten years).

Table A3.1. Interregional slave transfers, 1820–29

	Age 1820 / Age 1830							
	0–13/10–23		14–25/24–35		26–44/36–54		45+/55+	
	Male (a)	Female (b)	Male (c)	Female (d)	Male (e)	Female (f)	Male (g)	Female (h)
1. 1820 slave population of net exporting states	256,227	241,478	146,218	144,037	119,144	111,570	59,557	55,430
2. Southern slave survival rate for 1820s	0.911	0.952	0.921	0.924	0.728	0.735	0.550	0.602
3. Expected 1830 slave population of net exporting states	233,423	229,887	134,667	133,090	86,737	82,004	32,756	33,369
4. Actual 1830 slave population of net exporting states	198,701	195,415	116,264	116,738	80,479	76,207	31,259	31,870
5. Preliminary transfer totals	34,722	34,472	18,403	16,352	6,258	5,797	1,497	1,499
6. Final transfer totals	35,804	35,051	18,912	16,787	6,854	6,335	1,733	1,708

Source: Statistics are derived from U.S. Bureau of Census, *Census of 1820* (Washington, D.C., 1821) and *Fifth Census . . . as Corrected at the Department of State, 1830* (Washington, D.C., 1832).

Note: The cumulative slave population total for the exporting states in 1820 (combining row 1, columns a–h) was 1,133,661; and the exporting states' 1830 total of slaves aged 0–9 was 461,444. For slaves aged 0–9 in 1830, the estimated exportation total was 30,994.

The estimated 1820s exportation total was (combining row 6, columns a–h) 123,184 slaves, plus 30,994 slaves aged 0–9 in 1830, making a *final total* of 154,178. This suggests an overall exportation *rate* of 9.48 percent for the decade.

but (because of the age patterns of manumission) their combined effect will probably be slightly to overrepresent the role of planter migration in relation to that of the age-selective slave trade.

3.3. SURVIVAL-RATE CALCULATIONS FOR THE 1820s AND 1850s: NOTES ON THE METHOD EMPLOYED

The initial stage in my calculations was, by basic comparisons of survival rates, to separate the South into net-exporting and net-importing states.[11] The method in Table A3.1 was used both for the 1820s and for the 1850s (Table A3.2). For each age group, I first found the number of slaves present in the exporting area in 1820 who should have survived and been present in the exporting region in 1830, had there been no exportation to the Lower South. For this, the 1820 slave totals for the exporting area (columns a to h, row 1) were multiplied

11. For the 1850s, more detailed calculations were also made on a county-by-county basis *within* states; and this revealed that in those years Georgia, Alabama, and Missouri were very much "mixed states," containing (see Figure 1.1) substantial areas both of net importation and of net exportation. The incorporation of the more detailed results for these states did not affect the overall age-structure finding for the interregional movement, but did give a fuller count of that movement.

Table A3.2. Interregional slave transfers, 1850–59

	Age 1850 / Age 1860											
	0–4/10–14		5–9/15–19		10–19/20–29		20–29/30–39		30–39/40–49		40+/50+	
	Male (a)	Female (b)	Male (c)	Female (d)	Male (e)	Female (f)	Male (g)	Female (h)	Male (i)	Female (j)	Male (k)	Female (l)
1. 1850 slave population of net exporting area	185,306	189,485	166,981	167,476	278,842	277,088	192,346	187,608	113,563	116,793	163,350	165,709
2. U.S. slave survival rate for 1850s	1.043	0.972	0.927	0.958	0.899	0.872	0.759	0.785	0.808	0.783	0.642	0.628
3. Expected 1860 slave population of net exporting area	193,274	184,179	154,791	160,442	250,679	241,621	145,991	147,272	91,759	91,449	104,871	104,065
4. Actual 1860 slave population of net exporting area	172,753	164,793	133,098	136,641	202,353	196,824	125,490	130,220	82,187	83,597	96,463	96,777
5. Preliminary transfer totals	20,521	19,386	21,693	23,801	48,326	44,797	20,501	17,052	9,572	7,852	8,408	7,288
6. Final transfer totals	20,212	19,576	22,247	24,151	50,034	46,804	22,230	18,335	10,215	8,448	9,461	8,237

Source: Statistics are derived from U.S. Bureau of Census, *Seventh Census of the United States, 1850* (Washington, D.C., 1853) and *Population of the United States in 1860* (Washington, D.C., 1864).

Notes: The cumulative slave population total for the exporting area in 1850 was (combining row 1, columns a–l) 2,204,547; and the exporting area's 1860 total of slaves aged 0–9 was 752,301. For slaves aged 0–9 in 1860 the estimated 1850s exportation total was 50,469.

The estimated 1850s exportation total was (combining row 6, columns a–l) 259,950 slaves, plus 50,469 slaves aged 0–9 in 1860, making a *final total* of 310,419. This suggests an overall exportation *rate* of 10.25 percent for the decade.

by the relevant cohort-survival rates for the South's slave population (row 2). These "expected" 1830 totals (row 3) were then compared with the *actual* numbers of slaves held in the exporting region in 1830 (row 4). The difference between the "expected" and actual totals represents, for each cohort (columns a to h), the exporting area's preliminary totals of slave transfers for the 1820s.[12] These totals are given in row 5.

The preliminary totals in Table A3.1 represent those transfers who survived to 1830 and who, at the census of that year, were aged ten and older. To arrive at *final* transfer totals, we must now take account of two further groups. Firstly, we must consider those slaves who were transferred during the 1820s, but who did not live to 1830; and, secondly, we must take account of those slave children who were born during the 1820s and who, by 1830, had been transferred to the importing states.

An estimate of the number of slaves who were transferred during a particular decade, but who did not survive to its end, should ideally take into account the way in which those transfers were spaced over that decade. This is because, if the majority of movements had taken place during the second half of the decade, those slaves, after having moved, would have been subject to a lower risk of mortality than would have been the case if a majority had been transferred in the first half. A useful basis on which to judge the distribution of slave transfers during particular decades is provided by the evidence of annual slave exportations for South Carolina, a well-established exporting state, from 1830 to 1860.[13] These statistics show not only that South Carolina's out-movements were much higher in the later than in the earlier 1850s, but also, and more significantly, that there was a very close and persistent correlation between high slave prices and high rates of slave exportation. Since it is known (from statistics presented by U. B. Phillips) that U.S. slave prices tended to be substantially higher in the later rather than the earlier years of both the 1820s and 1850s, it is possible to assume that the interregional slave movement was particularly active in the latter half of both those decades.[14] In calculating final transfer totals for Tables A3.1 and A3.2, I assumed, therefore, that in both the 1820s and 1850s, slave transfers, after arriving in the importing area, were subject to an average of only some 35 percent of that decade's mortality rate.[15]

12. The term "transfer" is used here simply as a means of referring to any type of interregional movement.

13. For these annual slave-exportation statistics see Figure 5.1.

14. See prices in Phillips, *Life and Labor,* p. 177.

15. This assumption is not, in fact, critical to the pattern of results. Had I made the very different assumption that slaves (after being transferred) were subject to 65 percent of the decade's mortality, transfer-rate results would not generally have undergone any marked change. Estimated exportation rates for almost all cohorts would have fallen only fractionally, and results for those aged 0–9 at the end of the decades concerned would have fallen from the original level of about 6 percent to about a 2 percent exportation rate. Because of evidence already cited, this scaling

Fertility ratios (that is, ratios which compare the numbers of children with the numbers of women of child-bearing age) have been used in order to estimate the numbers of children born during a particular decade and transferred during that same decade. These estimates rely upon the assumption that, in slave populations unaffected by net interregional movements, there should be similar fertility ratios.[16] If, after accounting for the outmovement of a given number of slave women, the apparent fertility ratio of the exporting area falls below the southern norm, the divergence is attributed to the transfer of a proportion of the children born in that exporting area during the decade concerned. On this basis, approximate totals for exportations of children born during the 1820s and 1850s are appended to Tables A3.1 and A3.2. Ideally, these exportations of the under-tens should be scaled down somewhat, but the numbers do provide a convenient upper limit for estimating exportation rates for the under-tens.[17]

---

down of rates does not seem to be justified. If adopted, however, it would further emphasize the age-selective character of the interregional slave movement.

16. Richard Steckel points out in *The Economics of Fertility*, pp. 165, 224, that both for whites and slaves crude fertility ratios (basic ratios of children to women) were higher in the exporting than in the importing states. He suggests that with whites this happened because migrants tended to delay setting up households after arriving in the west, and mortality was higher among migrant children, and he suggests that similar factors would have operated among slaves. These suggestions, so far as slaves are concerned, do not seem to be valid. The pattern of building up some sort of economic security before setting up a family would not have applied to slaves, and for slave mothers and children the journey westward was probably not significantly more injurious to health than was their usual experience. (As Chapter 5 indicates, there also seems to be no sound basis for a claim that slave fertility was, through "slave breeding," especially high in the east.) Except for factors relating directly to slave trading (and indicated below), there seems to be no reason significantly to modify the general assumption that slave fertility ratios were similar in east and west.

17. The ratio employed for the 1850s was that of slave children under ten years to female slaves aged fifteen to forty-nine; and for the 1820s (when censuses used broader age categories) the ratio was children under ten to females aged ten to fifty-four. As an example, in order to find the number of females surviving to 1860 who would have influenced the exporting area's birth rate, I added 60,776 females to the exporting area's total of 547,282 females aged fifteen to forty-nine in 1860. These 60,776 women represented 65 percent of the decade's female exportations who were alive and aged fifteen to forty-nine in 1860, taking account of the distribution of transfers over the decade. The resulting 1860 fertility ratio for the exporting area was 8.3 below the South's average for that decade. For each fifteen- to forty-nine year old female in the exporting area's adjusted 1860 total of 608,058 slaves, I therefore assumed that there was an exportation equivalent to 0.083 children, making a total of 50,469 children aged 0–9 exported in the 1850s.

This procedure biases exportation numbers for the under-tens upward, because it incorporates the assumption that each of the women exported took with her the

We know now, for particular cohorts, the approximate numbers of slaves involved in the total interregional movement. This will be directly important for calculations in section 3.4 below. But for the immediate purpose, that of establishing an age profile of the total movement, we now need to know whether slaves of prime age (given their absolute numbers in the exporting area's population) were *relatively* more prominent in this movement than, for example, those of middle age. We need to find, not just absolute numbers, but *percentage rates* of transfer for young children, teenagers, prime adults, middle-aged, and old slaves. With this, we can compare, by age group, the relative intensity of total exportations with that which we know would have been produced purely by the trade. In this way, we can disaggregate the total movement into its trade and planter migration elements. To find percentage *rates* of transfer for the 1820s, then, we must represent final transfer totals (Table A3.1, row 6) as percentages of the relevant age-group totals found in the exporting states at the start of the decade (see row 1). Figures 2.3 and 2.4 indicate the transfer (exportation) rates for these individual age (and sex) cohorts.[18]

3.4. SEPARATING THE TRADE FROM PLANTER MIGRATION

Chapter 2 has already pointed to the overall significance of the highly age-selective pattern of exportation rates for both the 1820s and 1850s: an interregional movement heavily dominated by the trade. In this appendix I examine these exportation rates in a little more detail, and offer a fuller explanation of the conclusion I reached there.

Let us start with the data for the 1820s, and with the oldest cohorts (those aged forty-five years and over at the start of the decade). (For data see Figures 2.3 and 2.4.) The male exportation rate for this age category was only 2.91 percent, and since planter migration tended to draw at an *equal* percentage rate from all ages, this suggests that such migrations accounted for not more than

---

number of children typified by the South's average fertility ratio. We know, however, that this will exaggerate child exportations, because in the interregional trade the number of children per thousand women aged fifteen to forty-nine was (see Table 6.3) only about 624, or something like half that in the southern slave population generally.

18. Sutch ("The Breeding of Slaves," pp. 173–210) also made calculations of rates of interregional slave exportation in the 1850s. He derived these rates by comparing the decade's exportation totals (including, in fact, those who died during the decade) with the numbers of slaves from the exporting area's population of 1850 who were expected to *survive* to 1860. Since in the present study (as, in fact, in Sutch's) exportation totals are "final" numbers (and not simply transfers who survived to the end of the decade concerned) it is considered more appropriate to compare these exportations with the numbers in the relevant cohorts of the exporting states in 1850 (that is, before the effects of the decade's mortality). Similar comments apply to my calculations for the 1820s.

about a 2.91 percent exportation from *each* age group—young, old, and in between. It follows, then, that the portion of any exportation rate which exceeds the 2.91 level is attributable, not to planter migration, but to the trade.[19]

When we turn to the other end of the age spectrum, the under-tens, the conclusion is equally consistent and equally clear. We know that the exportation rate of 6.29 percent significantly exaggerates the actual exportation rate for these slaves (perhaps a 5 percent rate being more appropriate). We also know that children would have been fully represented in the planter migrations which took place. Children were easy to transport, and their inclusion was in the migrant planter's interests both as an economic investment and for plantation morale. Since we know, too, that the under-tens also made up about 18 percent of the speculators' coffles (again a matter of economic self-interest), the exportation rate attributable to planter migration would again, for the under-tens, seem to be not more than the 2.91 percent suggested by the data for the older slaves.

There is, moreover, a great deal more evidence in Figure 2.3 to support our overall conclusion about the decisive dominance of the trade. What we find, in fact, is a graduation in exportation rates (from 2.91 to 14.52 percent), with exactly the kind of pyramidal pattern which planter migration could not produce, and which we should expect from massive trading influence. We know, for example that the cohorts aged 26–44 and 36–54 were very much a part of the trade (those aged twenty-five and over made up about one-fifth of the trade), and would surely have been sufficiently robust to have participated fully in any migrations, and yet their exportation rate was only about 5.7 percent. Since this 5.7 rate is clearly one which must have been considerably swollen by trading, the exportation rate attributable to planter migration must have been markedly lower than 5.7 percent.

Overall, then, and indeed very consistently on an age-by-age basis, results for the 1820s point to a massive dominance by the trade. We can conclude that planter migration accounted for not more than a 2.91 percent exportation rate, from a total comprising the exporting area's 1820 slave population and slave children born in that area during the 1820s. This indicates that at the least 69.3 percent of the 154,000 exportations of the 1820s were by the trade.

When we turn to data for the 1850s (see Figure 2.4, Chapter 2), a similar set of comments and conclusions applies. The exportation rates for the oldest group (in this case those aged 40+/50+) again form a convenient starting point.

19. It is possible that a few very old slaves were left behind in the Upper South by planter migrants, but Appendix 2 suggests that this would have been very rare. In any case, the numbers of potential migrants of, say, sixty or seventy years and older were so small that, whether or not some were left behind, their influence on exportation rates for the broad forty years and older cohorts would have been only marginal. This point is developed more fully in note 20, which relates to the 1850s.

Exportation rates for slaves in these ages averaged about 5 percent.[20] We know, however, that at the younger end of the 40+/50+ age range, exportation rates would have been inflated by the contribution of trading. Indeed, slaves of forty years and older made up about 3.7 percent of the trade (see Figure 2.1).[21] To find the exportation rate properly attributable to planter migration, then, we must scale down the overall 4.97 percent rate for females aged 40+/50+, suggesting a rate of exportation by planter migration of not more than about 4 percent.

Data for the under-tens give strong support for this conclusion. This group not only participated fully in planter migrations, but was also an important part of the trade. Even so, the upper bound for the under-tens exportation rate was only 6.29 percent, and the actual exportation rate (from trading and migration combined) was probably not more than 5 percent. Thus the rate attributable to planter migration alone is likely to have been at the very most 4 percent, but in fact was very probably below that level.

As with the 1820s, however, it is not just data for selected age groups (like the under-tens) which indicate the decisive dominance of the trade over planter migration. It is the whole pyramid of age-selective results, with exportation rates ranging from as high as about 18 percent for prime young adults, down to about 5 percent for older slaves. The data indicate for planter migration in the 1850s an exportation rate of at most 4 percent. This, in turn, indicates that the trade in the 1850s would have accounted for at least some 61 percent of that decade's 308,000 exportations from the Upper South.

20. As in the 1820s, the exportation rate for the 40+/50+ group is not likely to have been understated by any possible tendency of planter migrants to leave behind individuals who in slave terms were very old. We have, first, no direct documentation of such a practice. Let us, for the sake of argument, assume that migrant planters of the 1850s decided to leave behind *all* of their slaves aged sixty years or more in 1860, and let us allocate a notional 10 percent exportation rate to planter migration (far higher than the 4 percent actually suggested by the evidence). This very high rate of abandoning the old would indicate that Table A3.2 understates the exportation rate for the 40+/50+ cohort generally by less than 1 percentage point. Not only does such an adjustment seem entirely excessive and inappropriate, but any slight under-representation of exportation rates for the 40+/50+ cohort is likely to have been more than counterbalanced by the effect of the relatively high rates of manumission in the Upper South. In practice, the likely net distortion is that manumission slightly raised (say by 1 percent) exportation rates for the 40+/50+ cohort generally.

21. The significance of the trade's impact within the 40+/50+ cohort can be indicated by a hypothetical example. If we assume that in the 1850s the trade accounted for 60 percent of interregional slave movements, and that about half of the trade in those older than forty years fell within the 40+/50+ cohort of Table A3.2 (columns k and l) (the remaining half falling within the 30–39/40–49 cohort [columns i and j]), the trade would have raised the exportation rate for the 40+/50+ cohort by about 1 percent.

Appendix 4

South Carolina Slave Traders of the 1850s: A Digest of Evidence

Table A4.1. Availability of newspapers for South Carolina districts, 1850–59

District	Newspaper survival[a]	Coverage[b]
Abbeville	1854–59 quite good; otherwise only 20 issues	9
Anderson	3 issues only	3
Barnwell	1 issue only	1
Beaufort	1860, 2 issues	0
Charleston	Good coverage	10
Chester	Except 1856–57, not more than 1 issue per year	6
Chesterfield		0
Colleton		0
Darlington	Mar. 1851 to Apr. 1852 quite good	2
Edgefield	Good coverage	10
Fairfield	Total of 8 issues only	6
Georgetown	1853 none; 1851, 1855, 1859 poor	8
Greenville	1851–52 good; otherwise very poor	8
Horry		0
Kershaw	Good 1850–55; otherwise poor	10
Lancaster	Generally good	8
Laurens	10–40 issues per year	10
Lexington	21 issues only	6
Marion	Quite good	8
Marlboro		0
Newberry	1858 quite good; otherwise 7 issues only	4
Orangeburg	5 issues only	4
Pickens	Quite good	5
Richland	1854, 1856 good; otherwise poor	10
Spartanburg	Good except 1852	9
Sumter[c]	Good	10
Union	Quite good 1851–52; otherwise 2 issues only	4
Williamsburg	1 issue for both 1859 and 1860	1
York	Quite good	9

[a] Newspapers are those available at the main South Carolina repository (SCL).
[b] Number of years for which at least one day's issue of a local paper was found.
[c] Clarendon, separated from Sumter in 1855, is here combined with Sumter district.

Table A4.2. Trading firms, according to district, buying slaves in South Carolina during 1850s: Outlines of evidence

Trading firm, by district	Found active	Evidence
	Abbeville	
Clinkscales, J. W., & Boozer, D. N.	1858–63	"Negroes Wanted . . . a lot of young and likely Negroes . . . between the ages of 12 and 25. . . . One of us can always be found at home, prepared to pay the highest prices for such negroes as suit us, in cash" (*3*, May–July 1858). "Clinkscales and Boozer sold 7 yesterday [at Mobile] . . . at fully $100 under the market" (WAJF, 6 Jan. 1859). Witness "saw J. W. Clinkscales in Charleston in 1863 . . . Clinkscales was at that time buying negroes." J.W.C. made trips between South Carolina and Texas in 1861 (Abbeville Equity 1868, 308). Purchases were made in the firm's name in 1860 and 1863 (P/ME).
+Gardner, W.	1860?	Abbeville census, 1860: "trader."
+Jackson, G. J.	1860?	Abbeville census, 1860: "trader."
Merrimon, L. D., & Clinkscales, J.W.	1847–56	"100 Negroes Wanted! . . . young men and women, boys and girls" (*4*, *1*, June–July, June–Oct. 1856). L.D.M. & J.W.C. were "merchants trading under the name of Merrimon & Clinkscales" (Laurens CCP 1848, 5071) were partners during 1851–54 period (Abbeville Equity 1868, 308). The firm also advertised in Edgefield and in Laurens. By 1858 J.W.C. had joined D. N. Boozer.

Sources: Newspaper sources are referred to by italicized number in the table. Complete source information appears at the end of the table (pp. 275–76).

Notes: Unless otherwise indicated (by letters *tr*, *r*), members of the firms listed appear to have bought from the public generally and then travelled to the Lower South to make sales. In general, dates given for a firm's being "found active" refer only to the date span for which direct evidence has been found. Activities probably extended over a longer period.

tr: Firm probably bought mainly through resident urban dealers rather than buying directly from the public.

r: Resident urban dealers investing in slaves and selling to traders who, in the Lower South, resold the slaves. Some of the resident South Carolina dealers listed also bought and sold on a commission basis; and some, perhaps, made occasional trips to the Lower South.

( ): Indicates the locations of traders known not normally to have been resident in South Carolina.

s: Activity might have been confined to one or a small number of trips.

+: Possible slave trading firm, described in census as "trader," "trading," or "speculator."

++: Probable or very probable slave trading firm.

(*continued on the following page*)

Table A4.2. Trading firms, according to district, buying slaves in South Carolina during 1850s: Outlines of evidence (*continued*)

Trading firm, by district	Found active	Evidence
Parks, J. T.	1858–60	"Negroes Wanted. The undersigned will at all times purchase likely negroes between 10 and 20 years" (*1,* Aug. 1858–Jan. 1859). "Will at all times be in the market . . negroes . . . ages of 12 to 25" (*1,* Aug. 1858–Jan. 1859).
Suber, J. W.	1856–57	"Wanted Immediately! 100 Negroes! For which the highest cash prices will be paid" (*1,* June 1856–Jan. 1857). Also advertised in Anderson and Laurens.
Suber, J. W., & Parks, J. T.	1855–56	"Wanted immediately 40 or 50 likely young negroes for which liberal prices in cash will be given" (*2,* Sept. 1855–Mar. 1856). See also Suber & White, and see Parks, below. (All Suber and Parks entries are, in Table 2.3, counted as one firm only.)
Vance, A.	1859	"50 Negroes Wanted . . . liberal prices for likely Negroes, both men and women, between 15 and 25 years" (*1, 2,* July–Aug. 1859).
+Waites, J. F.	1860?	Abbeville census, 1860: "trader."
White, L. J., & Mosely, T. P.	Late 1840s–1851	Abbeville census of 1850: T.P.M. listed as "speculator." Judge reports: "The evidence derived from Mosely was to the effect that before the death of White he had been his agent to traffic in the purchase and sale of negroes. . . . That after his death he continued in the business for the widow." The widow herself made some purchases (Appeals, 7 Richardson 45).
+ +Wiss, E. J.	1857–60?	Wrote to Oakes (see Charleston district) to ask whether any suitable slaves were available (ZBO, 14 Apr. 1857). Abbeville census, 1860: "trader."
	Anderson	
Berry, S. D.	1850–53	Berry "sworn saith that he went with Mr. E. M. Cobb. They had some negroes. This was in October last [1853] . . . . Mr. J. C. Cobb, E. M. Cobb and J. T. Cobb had some negroes and this deponent had some also. They had . . . between 25 and 40 negroes amongst them. They remained together a portion of the road. . . . E. M. Cobb was in the habit of backing J. T. Cobb and this deponent [S.D.B.]" (Anderson Equity 1854, 202). See Cobb & Seaborn, below.

(*continued on the following page*)

Table A4.2. Trading firms, according to district, buying slaves in South Carolina during 1850s: Outlines of evidence (*continued*)

Trading firm, by district	Found active	Evidence
+Brown, J. J.	1860?	Anderson census, 1860: "trader."
+Byrum, E. W.	1860?	Anderson census, 1860: "trader."
+Campbell, H.	1860?	Anderson census, 1860: "trader."
Cobb, E. M. (J. T.), J., & Seaborn, G.	1837–59	"They have been trading in negroes for several years" (JTH, 6 Mar. 1837). They "were partners in the business of buying and selling slaves" (Appeals, Richland Equity 54). "He stipulated with Cobb [in 1857] to deliver said slaves to Cobb's depot for slaves, in Carnesville, Georgia" (Appeals, 12 Richland Equity 234). See also S. D. Berry above.
+Owens, A. J.	1860?	Anderson census, 1860: "trader."
+Richardson, J.	1850?	Anderson census, 1850: "trader."
+Wilson, J.	1860?	Anderson census, 1860: "trader."
Wood, S. O.	1859–60	Letter from T. G. Eving, Alabama, to T. Eving, Anderson district, S.C., asks T. E. to give assistance to Samuel O. Wood, "a gentleman visiting your state and district for the purpose of purchasing slaves" (SOW, 12 Jan. 1859). J. P. Pool of Pool & Blassingame (see Greenville district) wrote that he intended to buy in South Carolina "and would like for you [Wood] to take an interest in them and you take them to sell" (SOW, 19 Mar. 1860). Wood also bought at Richmond, Va. (HD/NYPL 15 June 1860).
	Barnwell	
+Behling, E. C.	1860?	Barnwell census, 1860: "speculator."
++McKay, A. N.	1854?	Bought in low country, possibly including Barnwell district. A.N.M. wrote from Graham's Turn Out (Barnwell?) and complained to Oakes (see Charleston district) about an unsound slave bought from that trader: "If you wish I will sell him in Mississippi . . . I expect to start for Mississippi in a few days" (ZBO, 26 Sept. 1854).

(*continued on the following page*)

Table A4.2. Trading firms, according to district, buying slaves in South Carolina during 1850s: Outlines of evidence (*continued*)

	Trading firm, by district	Found active	Evidence
		Beaufort	
r	Bryan, J. (Georgia)	1859–61	J. B. advertised in Beaufort district seeking patronage for his Savannah pen: "Special attention given to the sale of Negroes, and very superior accommodations provided for them" (*5,* Sept. 1860). Also advertised: "Wanted to purchase 100 likely single negroes, for which the highest cash price will be paid" (*Savannah Republican,* Dec. 1859). J. A. Stevenson advertised: "Negroes wanted. Having commenced in the trade in Savannah, I will give the highest cash price. . . . My office is at Capt. J. Bryan's (*29,* Jan. 1861). See also Bancroft, pp. 223–24, 378.
r	Wylly, G. W., Montmollin, J. S., & Collins, T. S. (Georgia)	1853–60	Partnership arrangements among the three underwent changes; buying from Beaufort, Charleston, and low country persisted. Handbill, probably of 1853, indicated that W. & M. opened "a slave Depot" in Beaufort district, across the river from Savannah; and W. & M. would pay "highest cash prices for Negroes, either singly, in families, or in gangs" (ZBO, 7 July 1853). J.S.M. told Oakes (see Charleston district): "I would be willing to purchase [from you] a few young Negroes the season through, allowing you a reasonable profit or commission" (ZBO, 20 Sept. 1856). G.W.W.'s Savannah depot advertised in Beaufort district (*5,* Sept. 1860). See also Nipson (Charleston district), below.

(*continued on the following page*)

Table A4.2. Trading firms, according to district, buying slaves in South Carolina during 1850s: Outlines of evidence (*continued*)

	Trading firm, by district	Found active	Evidence
		Charleston	
tr	Adams, R. S., & Wicks, M. L. (Mississippi)	1853–54	1852 advertisement stated that A. & W. agents had for two months "been purchasing . . . in the old states" (Bancroft, p. 309). R.S.A. wrote from North Carolina to ask Oakes at Charleston "whether you have bought any negroes for us. . . . I have bought 80 in Richmond and Baltimore" (ZBO, 22 July 1853). A. & W. wrote: "Should we buy next summer we will probably request you to buy for us again. We have done very well with your purchases this year" (ZBO, 4 Jan. 1854). R. S. Adams was perhaps the "unprincipled" South Carolina–Mississippi trader referred to in Adams, pp. 95–96, 123–26.
r	Anker, G. V.	1855–63	Described as "G.V. Anker & Co., Brokers and general commission agents" (ALT, 22 Feb. 1860). Purchased and resold in own right. Bought at least 97 in Charleston judicial sales of 1850s (P/ME). Bought at Richmond, Va., on 21 Aug. 1858, and June–July 1860, etc. (HD/NYPL; HD/CHS).
	Austin, R.	1850s	CCD gave Austin as "Negro Trader." "Bob Austin" referred to as a trader who was willing to kidnap free Negroes (Adams, pp. 95–96, 166). Bought at least 23 slaves at Charleston district judicial sales of 1850s (P/ME). See also Bancroft, p. 183.
tr	Austin, W. W.	1856	Wrote from Georgia that slaves bought in Charleston were still unsold. Wanted 10–15 young men and girls "that will suit the market. . . . I shall go west if I buy a lot that will authorize me to go" (ZBO, 2 Oct. 1856).
++	Behn, G. W. (Texas?)	1854–56?	Wrote from Georgia informing Ziba Oakes that he wanted to buy (ZBO, 12 Dec. 1854). Wrote from Texas to recommend two traders, one from Alabama, the other from Mississippi. Hoped Oakes made profits. Enquired about slave prices and asked whether there was a vessel serving Galveston, New Orleans, and Charleston (ZBO, 6 Sept. 1856). Very probably a trader.

(*continued on the following page*)

Table A4.2. Trading firms, according to district, buying slaves in South Carolina during 1850s: Outlines of evidence (*continued*)

	Trading firm, by district	Found active	Evidence
tr	Bitting, J. A. (North Carolina)	1848–57	Traded to Alabama in 1848 (Sellers, p. 155). Told Oakes: "I would like to buy a few negroes in your market" (ZBO, 25 Oct. 1856). Wrote on his purchases and the prices he hoped to get (TG, 5 Nov. 1857).
tr	Bryan, J. H. (Louisiana)	1850s	J.H.B. informed Z. B. Oakes: "I am now in the trade [at New Orleans] as I was in Charleston, and would be happy to do some business with you in that way, between the two places . . . as fast as I sell them will remit you the proceeds to be reinvested" (ZBO, 5 May 1854; see also 12 Dec. 1856).
	Carman, J. L. (Louisiana)	1858	Received regular consignments from South Carolina, Mississippi, Georgia, Alabama, and Florida (*32*, Mar. 1858).
	+Chaplain, B.	1850?	Charleston census, 1850: "trader."
	Delap, A. (Tennessee) (also Delap, Witherspoon & Fly)	1857–59	"A. Delap & Co. [of Memphis] have just received a large stock of South Carolina and Virginia negroes at their Mart . . . and expect to receive fresh supplies every 2 or 3 weeks" (*30*, Apr. 1857). D., W., & F. bought at Charleston district probate sales, 1857 and 1859 (P/ME).
	Filor, J. (Florida)	1857?	Demanded that Oakes of Charleston replace an unsound slave and added: "I hope . . . [Oakes's cooperation in the matter] may be the means of opening a mutually advantageous business" (ZBO, 25 May 1857). Filor's name frequently appeared in manifests for Florida ports.
	Forrest, N. B., W. H., & Jones, S. S. (Tennessee, Louisiana, and elsewhere)	1857–60	Detailed description of the firm; bought in South Carolina, North Carolina, Virginia, and elsewhere (Bancroft, pp. 256–65). "500 NEGROES WANTED: I WILL PAY MORE THAN ANY OTHER PERSON, for No 1 NEGROES, suited to the New Orleans market" (*12*, Jan–Mar. 1860).

(*continued on the following page*)

Table A4.2. Trading firms, according to district, buying slaves in South Carolina during 1850s: Outlines of evidence (*continued*)

	Trading firm, by district	Found active	Evidence
r	Gadsden, T. N.	1840–60	T.N.G. arranged that S. Gasque should buy slaves in the Georgetown area and ship them to Gadsden for resale at Charleston. "Send me only prime negroes and I can do well for you" (Appeals, 2 Strobhart 324). Shipped some slaves to New Orleans in 1840s (Table A2.1). In 1853, it was stated that "Thomas N. Gadsden, as part of his business, is engaged in the purchase and sale of Negroes. . . . He provides shelter, clothing and food, for such Negroes as may be left for sale" (Appeals, 8 Richardson 180). Bought at least 33 slaves in Charleston judicial sales of 1850s (P/ME). The trader Briscoe (see Sumter district) bought from T.N.G. (ZBO, 27 Aug. 1854). The trader A. J. McElveen (see Sumter district) "Saw T. N. Gadsden up at the sale" near Sumter (ZBO, 6 Feb. 1857). Bancroft described T.N.G. as South Carolina's biggest trader of the mid-1850s. Still active in 1860 (Bancroft, pp. 167–69, 176n). Described as "mendacious" Negro Trader (Adams, pp. 65–66).
	Gilchrist, J. M.; King, J.	1845–59	"Negroes wanted. Persons wishing to dispose of slave property may obtain the highest market prices" from J.M.G. (*12,* Jan. 1845). Slave sold to "one J. M. Gilchrist of Charleston a dealer or trader in negroes" (Charleston Equity, 1847–27). Manifests for 1840s and 1850 show J.M.G. bought at least 95 slaves at Charleston district judicial sales of 1850s; and in 1851, purchases made under name Gilchrist & King (P/ME). "Gilchrist bought some also Belser [see Sumter district] bought pretty largely" at a Sumter district sale (ZBO, 2 Jan. 1854). J.K. wrote from Georgia and asked Oakes (see Charleston district) about prices compared with "when I was in Charleston in October last. I have only bought two since I saw you" (ZBO, 19 Feb. 1854). J.M.G. was active in 1859 (Bancroft, p. 176n).

(*continued on the following page*)

Table A4.2. Trading firms, according to district, buying slaves in South Carolina during 1850s: Outlines of evidence (*continued*)

	Trading firm, by district	Found active	Evidence
++	Hill, A. (Louisiana)	1854?	Wrote from Shreveport, La.: "I wish to purchase a few young negroes, girls and boys—prefer girls—from 8 to 10 years of age. Can you purchase for me. . . . The amount is not sufficient to justify a trip at present" (ZBO, 5 May 1854). Very probably a trader.
++	Limehouse, T.	1854?	Probably a part-time trader. Reported to Ziba Oakes that slaves were available in the Summerville area of Charleston district and "If you are of a mind we will buy them between us" (ZBO, 5 Sept. 1854). Also appears to have been a planter (ZBO, throughout).
r	McBride, M.	1845–63	"Negroes wanted — The highest prices will be paid for NEGROES of all descriptions and any arrangement made with the seller strictly complied with" (*12*, Jan. 1845). "Negroes Wanted . . . likely young Negroes for which the very highest market prices will be paid" (*6*, July 1850). Bought at least 47 at Charleston district judicial sales of 1850s (P/ME). Shipped to New Orleans (Table A2.1). Several references to M.M.'s trading (ZBO, 11 Feb. and 16 Mar. 1854, etc.). M.M. bought "with view to resell" (Charleston Equity case of 1856). M.M. was active 1860–1863 (Bancroft, p. 176n; P/ME, 1860–1863).
	McCargo, T. (Louisiana)	1850	On McCargo, a major trader, see Table A2.1 and see Sydnor, pp. 151, 154. Bought at Charleston district probate sale of 10 Dec. 1850 (P/ME).
tr	McKinley, J. D. (Florida)	1854	J. M. Bryant recommended J.D.M. as a man well qualified "to be connected with you in sales of negroes in Florida, in accordance with the plan you proposed" (ZBO, 6 Nov. 1854).
	Matthews, T. E. (Louisiana)	1860	"Negroes for sale. The undersigned has re-opened the well known slave Depot . . . recently occupied by John B. Smith [see below], with a likely lot of . . . [slaves]—all imported from Virginia and South Carolina. Additional supplies will be received from those states during the season" (*32*, Dec. 1860).

(*continued on the following page*)

Table A4.2. Trading firms, according to district, buying slaves in South Carolina during 1850s: Outlines of evidence (*continued*)

	Trading firm, by district	Found active	Evidence
tr	Mattingly, J. (Missouri, Mississippi)	1857	His advertisement in Missouri offered to pay "more than any other trading man in the city of St. Louis and the state of Missouri" (Bancroft, p. 140). "At Branchville last night I had escape from me a man that I purchased from Mr. White, the broker on Broad St. in Charleston" (ZBO, 15 Feb. 1857). Asked Oakes to "ship him if he is caught when you ship the others" to Mississippi (ZBO, 16 Feb. 1857).
r	Mordecai, B.	1846–60	Shipped to New Orleans in 1840s and 1850s (Table A2.1 and Manifests). Sold to traders (ZBO, 25 Dec. 1854). B.M., on buying a certain slave, undertook "that the said slave Norris shall immediately be taken beyond the limits of the state of South Carolina" (S.C. Misc., Volume 6H, p. 568). Bought at least 102 slaves at Charleston district judicial sales of 1850s (P/ME). Active in 1860 (Bancroft, p. 176n). Bought extensively and had own slave pen (Korn, pp. 172–73).
	+Newman, J.	1852?	CCD, 1852: "trader."
	Nipson, F.	1854–60	Wylly & Montmollin (see Beaufort district) arranged that "Francis Nipson of your city may purchase Negroes for us" (ZBO, 23 Mar. 1854). "Francis Nipson is said to be the illegitimate son of Montmollin and is buying negroes to ship" (ALT, 20 July 1857). Nipson active in Charleston market in 1860 (Bancroft, p. 176n). Bought at Charleston district judicial sales of late 1850s (P/ME).
r	Oakes, Z. B.	1846–63	Z.B.O. was a major dealer with very extensive trading connections. See, e.g., J. H. Bryan (Charleston), N. Vignie (Charleston), and A. J. McElveen (Sumter) entries; and see Z. B. Oakes Papers (660 items). Shipped some slaves to New Orleans in 1840s (Table A2.1). Bought at least 180 slaves at Charleston district judicial sales of 1850s and continued to buy 1860–63 (P/ME). See also Bancroft, pp. 183–84, 176n.

(*continued on the following page*)

Table A4.2. Trading firms, according to district, buying slaves in South Carolina during 1850s: Outlines of evidence (*continued*)

	Trading firm, by district	Found active	Evidence
+	Petit, G. H.	1860?	Charleston census, 1860: "speculator."
	Pickard & Cox (Tennessee?)	1856–57	J. Cox wrote from Tennessee that he wanted to buy 8 or 10. "I want to do a little trading this winter if prices will justify" (ZBO, 3 Oct. 1856). J.C. probably belonged to the firm of P. & C. who wrote from Savannah: "I want to buy 10 to 12 negroes . . . young and likely from 14 to 23. There appears to be good many negroes here but mainly in families. Mr. Wright has bought about 50." Referred to having been in Tennessee (ZBO, 7 Jan. 1857).
++	Pillow, G. P. (Tennessee)	1856?	Wrote to Ziba Oakes that, after "the character, honor, integrity and fidelity Mr. Cox [see Pickard & Cox above] has given you and from your knowledge of the market, I would rather risk your purchases than those of any agent I could send there." Wanted to buy 10–15 "likely girls 14 to 18" (ZBO, 5 Aug. 1856). Very probably a trader.
	Porter, R. W. (Tennessee)	1856	Wrote from Nashville: "I am of the opinion that money could be made between your city and this . . . a man could buy small negroes say girls from 9–14 and ploughboys and women with one or two children. . . . I am anxious to try the thing on, and if it will pay, either stay there myself or employ someone to buy for me" (ZBO, 21 Oct. 1856).
	Robinson, G. A.	1860	Robinson, of Chalmers Street ("traders' row"), Charleston, advertised to buy 500 slaves (*12*, 20 Feb. 1860, quoted in Bancroft, p. 177n).
r	Ryan, T. & W. B.	1846–63	Shipped some slaves to New Orleans in 1840s (Table A2.1). Bought at least 54 slaves at Charleston judicial sales of 1850s, and continued to buy 1860–63 (P/ME). Ryan's Mart was major vehicle of the trade, and T. & W.B.R. were still active in 1860 (Bancroft, pp. 170, 176n). Wylly (see Beaufort district) asked Oakes (see above) to find out where a runaway slave had been raised before W. bought him from T.R. Several other references to T. & W.B.R. (ZBO, 10 Apr. 1854, etc.).

(*continued on the following page*)

Table A4.2. Trading firms, according to district, buying slaves in South Carolina during 1850s: Outlines of evidence (*continued*)

	Trading firm, by district	Found active	Evidence
r	Salinas, A. J.	1851–63	Began as trader's clerk, became "commission agent" but also bought and sold in his own right. A.J.S. "was clerk with . . . [the trader T. N. Gadsden] in February 1840" (Appeals, 2 Speers 566). Advertised in Georgetown that he had removed to Charleston, where he continued in "business in the sale and purchase of negroes" (*13*, Jan. 1849). Bought at least 123 slaves at Charleston district judicial sales of 1850s, and continued to buy 1860–63 (P/ME).
++	Scruggs, F. (Alabama)	1854?	"I have recently rented a house in this city [Mobile] as a depot for the negro trade. I take the present opportunity of enquiring the prices of certain classes, the demand and your general conception of the coming season for trade. What could likely [girls] . . . from 12 to 15 be bought at, 15 to 18—men likely 20 to 15, 15 to 12 year old boys. Nice fancy young women" (ZBO, 20 July, 1854). It is not altogether clear whether Scruggs bought slaves or simply ran a "nigger jail" for the trade. But very probably a trader.
	Shelton, L. N. (Louisiana)	1859	Bought at Charleston district judicial sales, 1859, (P/ME). Was an established New Orleans trader (see Table A2.1, and see Vignie entry, below) but it is not clear to what extent he purchased in South Carolina.
+	Singleton, D.	1855?	CCD, 1855: "speculator."
	Smith, J. & J. B. (Louisiana)	1857–60	J.B.S. wrote from Richmond, referring to J.S. at New Orleans: "If you hear from or get Mr. Briscoe's Negroes you will please send them out by some ship to my brother." On Briscoe see Sumter district (ZBO, 3 Feb. 1857). J.B.S. wrote from New Orleans to Oakes: "Yours containing a list of Negroes . . . bought by my brother in your market I received by the course of a mail. . . . Let me know what the prospects are of buying negroes in your market . . . such as Jeremiah has been buying. . . . I presume you know what kind he bought?" (ZBO, 21 Feb. 1857). J.B.S. advertised Virginia and South Carolina slaves for sale at New Orleans (*11*, Jan. 1860).

(*continued on the following page*)

Table A4.2. Trading firms, according to district, buying slaves in South Carolina during 1850s: Outlines of evidence (*continued*)

	Trading firm, by district	Found active	Evidence
tr	Thomas, T. J.	1857	Wrote from Gainesville (Alabama?) that he had sold the slave supplied by Oakes. "I have had some trouble. The old woman always complains and one of the boys has had an attack of plurisy [*sic*]" (ZBO, 30 Apr. 1857).
	+Tressel, J. S.	1860?	Charleston census, 1860: "trader."
tr	Vignie, N. (Louisiana)	1857	Arrangement made for Vignie, at New Orleans, to sell slaves supplied by Z. B. Oakes of Charleston. "Since I wrote to you I have had an understanding with [Vignie] that he will make sales . . . for 3 per cent. . . . This Mr. Vignie is a French creole, a gentleman of good standing that will readily command the entire confidence of the French sugar planters. [Other arrangements with Shelton or Peterson could be made] but this arrangement with Vignie is already better. More negroes could be sold at high prices [than through other contacts mentioned]" (EL, 6 Oct. 1857). See also Bancroft, pp. 377–78.
tr	Vogue, P. (Alabama)	1857	"Having some money and wishing to purchase some negroes for my own use also some to sell again I take the liberty of writing." Wanted 15–20 (ZBO, 12 Mar. 1857).
	+Wilkinson, E.	1852?	CCD, 1852: "trader."
	Womack, J. B., & Martin, W. J. (Louisiana)	1854	W.J.M. of New Orleans wanted to buy 15 to 20 "providing I can get them at prices to suit a falling market" (ZBO, 11 May 1854). W. & M. enquired whether there were any slaves in the Charleston market. W.J.M. asked for bill of sale to be drawn up "after the same form I have all my bills of sale drawn up" (ZBO, 18 Oct. and 9 Dec. 1854). CCD, 1860: J.B.W. listed as "broker."
tr	Wright, W. (Georgia)	1854–56	Asked Oakes of Charleston to keep him informed of the market, and to send some Negroes to him in Georgia "as I intend to cross the river [Savannah] and make titles to negroes from another stall this season, it being done here frequently" (i.e., by documenting sales in South Carolina, he would evade Georgia's slave trade ban). See ZBO, 1 Oct. 1854 and see other ZBO letters.

(*continued on the following page*)

Table A4.2. Trading firms, according to district, buying slaves in South Carolina during 1850s: Outlines of evidence (*continued*)

Trading firm, by district	Found active	Evidence
	Chester	
++Houston, W.	1850?	Chester census, 1850: "trader." W.H. was perhaps "John W. B. Houston" (or a relative of J.W.B.H.) who was "doing a little [Negro] trading in Texas" (JG, letter of 1850). See also J. A. Houston (Edgefield district).
Lipford, J. C.	1856–60	"Likely negroes for sale. J. C. Lipford has a desirable lot of fine negroes, men, women, boys, girls, and children to sell low for cash" (*8*, Jan. 1856). Chester census, 1860: "merchant speculator and farming." Bought at Richmond, Va., 24 April 1858 and 19 June 1860 (HD/CHS and HD/NYPL). Probably acted as feeder to long-distance trade.
Pride, C. J.	1857–58	"Wanted 100 Negroes, men boys and girls for which the highest cash prices will be given" (*8*, Jan.–Dec. 1857). Also advertised in York district: "Wanted 100 likely young field negroes from ages 12 to 25 . . . full cash prices" (*7*, Aug. 1857–Jan. 1858).
	Chesterfield	
		No references to traders found.
	Clarendon	
		Created (1855) out of Sumter district. See Sumter below.
	Colleton	
		No references to traders found.
	Darlington	
Barnes, W. J.	1849–51	"Negroes Wanted. 18 to 20 hands wanted, boys between 12 and 25 years old, girls 12 and 18 for which liberal cash prices will be paid" (*10*, Sept. 1849). "18 to 20 young negroes from 12 to 25 years . . . cash" (*9*, Oct. 1851). W. Barnes (probably the same W. J. Barnes), writing from Georgia, asked why he had not heard from Ziba Oakes. Asked Oakes about collecting money from the trader T. N. Gadsden of Charleston (ZBO, April 1854, 27 May 1854).

(*continued on the following page*)

Table A4.2. Trading firms, according to district, buying slaves in South Carolina during 1850s: Outlines of evidence (*continued*)

Trading firm, by district	Found active	Evidence
	Edgefield	
Addison, J. A., & Warren, C.	1857	"Wanted to buy 50 likely Negroes for which the highest prices will be paid" (*4*, Jan. 1857).
Adkins, T., & Spires, W.	1850–60	"A fresh lot will be received each week" (*4*, 4 Feb. 1851). Edgefield censuses, 1850, 1860: both T.A. and W.S. listed as "slave trader."
+Coleman, N.	1860?	Edgefield census, 1860: "speculator."
Crouch, J., & Culbreath, H. C.	1856–58	C. & C. "were partners in the business of buying and selling slaves. . . . Crouch went with the negroes to the west" (Appeals, 11 Richardson 9). Most of J.C.'s estate (he died in 1858) "consisted of negroes, he being a negro trader" (Edgefield Equity 1868, 1091).
Gardiner, W. Q.	1860	Edgefield census, 1860: "slave trader."
+Harrison, S.	1860?	Edgefield census, 1860: "trading."
Houston, J. A.	1860	Edgefield census, 1860: "slave trader."
+Leonard, G. F.	1860?	Edgefield census, 1860: "speculator."
Owings, R. M., Charles, J. H., & Robertson, A. P.	1856–60	Exslave reported "Jedge Robinson [sic] he kept de nigger trade office over in Hamburg" (Georgia Narr.). A.P.R. asked Oakes about the state of the Charleston market (ZBO, 8 Aug. 1856). R.M.O. writing from Hamburg, Edgefield district, asked Oakes: "Can you sell some good negroes in your market. Is there any buyers and what are they paying. . . . It may be I will ship you some down" (ZBO, 23 Mar. 1857). The firm advertised in Charleston for 100 likely Negroes from 12 to 25 years (*12*, Nov. 1859). Advertised in New Orleans: "Will be receiving fresh supplies during the season of the best negroes that can be bought in the Virginia and Carolina markets" (*11*, Nov. 1859). Detailed information on the firm's "partnership in purchasing and selling negroes" (Anderson Equity 1861, 325). Edgefield census, 1860: R.M.O. listed as "negro trader."
Sullivan, R. H.	1860	Edgefield census, 1860: "trader." "Wanted! Twenty likely young negroes for which I will pay the market cash prices" (*4*, Aug. 1858).

(*continued on the following page*)

Table A4.2. Trading firms, according to district, buying slaves in South Carolina during 1850s: Outlines of evidence (*continued*)

Trading firm, by district	Found active	Evidence
Teague, E. F. & A. G.	1850–51	"Negroes for sale! The subscribers having purchased 15 to 20 likely young negroes for the trade, will offer them on sale day" (4, Dec. 1850–Feb. 1851). Acted as suppliers to the trade and also ran general store (4, June 1853).
+ +Watson, B. J.	1857	"Negroes wanted. The subscriber wishes to purchase 25 to 30 Negroes" (4, Dec. 1856). Probably a trader, despite lack of detail in advertisement.
	Fairfield	
+Edrington, R. J.	1850?	Fairfield census, 1850: "trader."
Hughes, D., & Randolph	1850–57	Fairfield census, 1850: D.H. listed as "speculator." H. & R. asked Oakes the prices of "No 1 likely young fellows 14–25 and young women 14–20" (ZBO, 2 Feb. 1854). H. & R. bought at Charleston district probate sale, 1857 (P/ME).
+McAlloy, J.	1850?	Fairfield census, 1850: "trader."
	Georgetown	
Christie, G. S. S.	1845–57	Had business associations with T. N. Gadsden (see Charleston district) and S. Gasque (see Chapter 7)—see Marion Equity 1847, 86. Christie vouched for man who wanted to sell a slave to Oakes (ZBO, 19 Mar. 1857). "Dickinson and Kerton are engaged in merchandising and in buying and selling negroes. . . . Kerton or Christie was Dickinson's agent" (Appeals, 2 Richardson 507).
+Coletrane, S.	1860?	Georgetown census, 1860: "trader."
"Rumney on Santee"	1850s	F. C. Adams described several traders—"Bob" Adams, T. Norman Gadsden, "Bob" Austin (on these, see Charleston district), and "Rumney on Santee." Rumney's "transactions would outshame [H. B. Stowe's] Haley." Referred to Rumney's "life on the borders of Texas — his slave traffic in the middle and southern states, . . . his cunning systems of running off free Negroes, . . . his revolting examinations of wenches, . . . his making up slave gangs." Bought in the River Santee area of South Carolina (Adams, pp. 96–98).

(*continued on the following page*)

Table A4.2. Trading firms, according to district, buying slaves in South Carolina during 1850s: Outlines of evidence (*continued*)

Trading firm, by district	Found active	Evidence
Sampson, S.	1848–50	"Negroes. The highest cash prices will be paid by S. Sampson & Co." (*13,* Oct. 1848–Jan. 1850). Also advertised to sell dry goods, etc. (*13,* Dec. 1849). Evidently a part-time trader or an agent for purchasing.
	Greenville	
Irvine, E. S. & O. B.	1847–51	E.S.I. "being at that time engaged in the purchase and sale of slaves on speculation." A woman was to be sold to E.S.I., "who would carry her entirely out of the country" (Greenville Equity 1847, 160). "Negroes. I wish to purchase a number of likely young negroes . . . cash" (*14,* Mar. 1849–Jan. 1851).
Kelly, E., & Harris	1853	"Plaintiff declined to sell to [Kelly] a negro trader" (Greenville Equity 1854, 208).
Pool, J. P., & Blassingame F.	1859–60	J.P.P. wrote to S. O. Wood (see Anderson district) from Selma, Ala.: "My partner Mr. Blassingame will remain for the week. . . . Since I saw you we have sold 6 negroes. I should like to carry out the conversation we had on the [railroad] cars relative to the trade. . . . It may be I can get a few on my arrival home [to South Carolina], if so I will buy them wright [*sic*] and would like for you to take an interest in them and take them to sell" (SOW, 19 Mar. 1860). W. A. J. Finney, a trader (see Chapter 3) sent his regards to Briscoe (see Sumter district), and Frank Blassingame (WAJF, 19 Oct. 1859).
	Horry	
		No references to traders found.
	Kershaw	
An Advertiser	1851	"Negroes wanted. Those having young Negroes for sale, from the age of 15 to 26 will find a purchaser by applying to the Wateree House" (*15,* Jul.–Oct. 1851).

(*continued on the following page*)

Table A4.2. Trading firms, according to district, buying slaves in South Carolina during 1850s: Outlines of evidence (*continued*)

Trading firm, by district	Found active	Evidence
Brown, S. N. (Alabama)	1854–59	Was already active and referring to his "old patrons" in 1852 (Bancroft, pp. 297, 381). A. J. McElveen (see Sumter district) wrote to Oakes: "Mr. Brown is here and wants nothing but what is strictly prime and says he will be here in January and is willing to join me in a lot of negroes" (ZBO, 11 Dec. 1854). Had depot in Alabama and regularly advertised that depot in Kershaw district newspapers: "Will give my personal attention to purchasing and selling slaves on commission . . . office . . . Montgomery, Ala." (*15, 16,* Sept. 1858–Mar. 1859). "New arrival of Negroes. I have just received [at Montgomery depot] . . . a large lot of Virginia and Carolina raised field Negroes" (*30,* 15 Jan. 1859).
+ +Bulger, O. L., & DeVane, P. R. (Alabama)	1854–55?	Advertised in Kershaw district: "Will attend to boarding, selling and purchasing NEGROES on commission. Office at Sanders and Fisher's old stand . . . Montgomery, Ala." (*15,* Sept. 1854–Dec. 1855). Handled slaves bought to Alabama by trader A. J. McElveen of Sumter district (ZBO, 5 Jan. 1855). No evidence that the firm itself purchased in South Carolina.
Ford, J. W.	1850	"Negroes wanted. I wish to purchase 200 Negroes, 100 men and 100 women. None need apply unless their Negroes are young and likely. For such the highest prices will be paid" (*15,* June–Sept. 1850). Probably still trading in 1857. Bought at Charleston district probate sale in 1857 (P/ME).
Page, J.	1860	"Negroes Wanted. The subscriber will pay liberal cash prices for young Negroes" (*15,* Jan.–Feb. 1860). Kershaw, census, 1860: "negro speculator."
	Lancaster	
Cureton, J. E.	1856	"Wanted to purchase, 25 likely young negroes, for which the highest cash prices will be paid" (*17,* Aug. 1856).
Ellis, H.	1859	"Negroes Wanted! The highest cash prices will be paid for single Negroes ranging in age from 10 to 30 years" (*17,* Nov.–Dec. 1859).

(*continued on the following page*)

Table A4.2. Trading firms, according to district, buying slaves in South Carolina during 1850s: Outlines of evidence (*continued*)

Trading firm, by district	Found active	Evidence
		Laurens
Dial, L. (Crews, J., agent)	1856–61	"Joseph Crews . . . used to be a Negro trader" (JSC, vol. 4, p. 1212). From about 1856 he traded in slaves with Dial. Crews "had a *carte blanche* to sign his name 'Lewis Dial, per Joseph Crews'. He carried on that [trade] up to the war" (JSC, vol. 5, p. 1314). "Negroes Wanted. I wish to purchase any number of likely young negroes for which I will pay the highest cash prices . . . Jos. Crews, ag't" (*3*, Sept. 1859).
+Johnson, L. T.	1860?	Laurens census, 1860: "trader."
Nickels, R. J., & Anderson	1858–60	R.J.N. of Waterloo, S.C., wrote to the trader W. A. J. Finney (see Chapter 3): "Me and Anderson will start to the mountains in a few days for the pirpus [*sic*] of buying some. . . . If nothing happens I will be at Montgomery by the last of February with a few slaves." Had just got back to South Carolina from Alabama (WAJF, 8 Jan. 1859). "Negroes here [Laurens] is but very high and but few to sell. We have bought a few yet, some 8 to 10. We intends buying and trying the market this fall" (WAJF, 28 June 1860). Laurens census, 1860): "negro trader."
		Lexington
Steedman, R., & Fox, W. H.	1859–60	"Negroes Wanted. We will pay the highest cash prices for young Negroes, male and female" (*18*, May 1859–Sept. 1860). Lexington census, 1860: W.H.F. listed as "negro trader."
		Marion
McLaurin & McNeal	1856	"Negro for sale. . . . Said Negro was warranted to be sound by McLaurin and McNeal, negro speculators, but she proved to be mentally and physically unsound, and was then tendered back for recantation, they refused. Now girl will be sold at their risk" (*19*, Apr. 1856).
		Marlboro
+Bingham, G.	1850?	Marlboro census, 1850: "trader."
+Brazier, J.	1850?	Marlboro census, 1850: "trader."

(*continued on the following page*)

Table A4.2. Trading firms, according to district, buying slaves in South Carolina during 1850s: Outlines of evidence (*continued*)

	Trading firm, by district	Found active	Evidence
s	Cox, R. A. & M. E.	1857	M.E.C. wrote from Marlboro to R.A.C.: "I received your letter . . . which informed me that you were in Memphis and had not sold any of the negroes. . . . You should have sold by this time . . . the expenses will take all the profits" (CF, July 3-21, 1857).
	+Hasque, T.	1850?	Marlboro census, 1850: "trader."
	+Peterkin, J. A.	1850?	(Marlboro census, 1850: "trader and clerk." J.A.P. had dispute with trader T.C.W. (on T.C.W., see below)—see Marlboro CCP case of 1850.
	+Quick, A.	1850?	Marlboro census, 1850: "trader."
	Weatherly, T. C. & J. A.	1846–59	T.C.W. bought at Richmond on 12 June 1846, 18 Nov. 1848, etc. (RHD). T.C.W. "by force of arms did take away a negro slave" (Marlboro CCP 1848, 3416). The trader E. C. Briscoe (see Sumter district) wrote: "T. C. Weatherly . . . will be out here [Port Gibson, Mississippi] this summer and [will] bring her [a slave purchased]" (ZBO, 30 Mar. 1854). J.A.W. wrote to Ziba Oakes: "The negroes I bought of you are all doing well. I have an arrangement with my bankers to send you $10,000 the first day of Dec. to invest in negroes" (ZBO, 6 Sept. 1856). A. J. McElveen (see Sumter district) wrote to Oakes: "I saw Col. [T. C.] Weatherly of Marlboro district. He is wanting to buy [slaves]." He later wrote: "I am fearful Col. Weatherly will buy [in competition]" (ZBO, 8 July 1856 and 30 Dec. 1856). J.A.W. wrote: "I returned from the South about the middle of April—made a good trip though I lost two negroes — the first I ever had to die. Write me news of trade and the state of your market" (ZBO, 4 May 1857). T.C.W. bought at Charleston district probate sale, 1859 (P/ME).
		Newberry	
	+Counts, H.	1860?	Newberry census, 1860: "trader."
	+Harris, J. Y.	1850?	Newberry census, 1850: "speculator." See also Kelly & Harris entry (Greenville district).

(*continued on the following page*)

Table A4.2. Trading firms, according to district, buying slaves in South Carolina during 1850s: Outlines of evidence (*continued*)

Trading firm, by district	Found active	Evidence
Holeman, R. B., & Tolleson, A.	1856	"100 Negroes wanted. I wish to purchase 100 likely Negroes between the ages of 12 and 25, for which I will pay fair cash prices. Persons wishing to sell will please inform Mr. Alfred Tolleson, at Spartanburg Court House, or myself at Newberry Court House" (*20*, July–Sept. 1856).
+ +Kinnard, H. H.	1856?	Dell of Florida wrote: "Mr. Kinnard never was an agent of mine and at the time he took the negroes to Charleston [he] had no claim on them" (ZBO, 1 Nov. 1856). H.H.K. wrote to Oakes that he was interested in the woman, her four children and the driver, and added "Katherine and William will suit the market except Katherine's teeth are bad." Later he added that Oakes should let him have the woman and her children at $1500 "as they are not saleable in this or the western market" (ZBO, 23 and 29 Nov. 1856).
+Suber, M.	1860?	Newberry census, 1860: "trader." See also J. W. Suber entry (Abbeville district).
	Orangeburg	
+Alorp, A.	1860?	Orangeburg census, 1860: "trader."
+Cook, W.	1860?	Orangeburg census, 1860; "trader."
Ellis, W. L.	1859	"Wanted 100 Negros [*sic*] I will pay the highest cash prices for 100 young and likely Negroes" (*21*, Mar. 1859).
+Griffin, W.	1860?	Orangeburg census, 1860: "trader."
Hydrick, A. J.	1857	"NEGROES WANTED. I am paying the highest cash prices for young and likely NEGROES, those having good front teeth and being otherwise sound . . . address Poplar P.O., Orangeburg District" (*22*, March 1857). Advertised in Sumter and apparently bought mainly in the neighboring districts of Sumter and Orangeburg.
+Louis, S.	1860?	Orangeburg census, 1860: "trader."

(*continued on the following page*)

Table A4.2. Trading firms, according to district, buying slaves in South Carolina during 1850s: Outlines of evidence (*continued*)

	Trading firm, by district	Found active	Evidence
	Manning	1850s	Stroyer (pp. 40–42) described the sale of two of his sisters and other slaves: "A Mr. Manning bought a portion of . . . [the slaves] and Charles Login [see Richland district] the rest. These two men were known as the greatest slave traders in the South." The location given—"28 miles south of Columbia" and "25 to 30 across the River" from Sumterville—places the transactions in Orangeburg district. Stroyer's date of birth (1849) and the fact that the traders used the railroad at Sumter places the sale in the 1850s.
		Pickens	
	+Fringe, J. C.	1860?	Pickens census, 1860: "trading."
		Richland	
s	Bythewood & Smith	1856	"Wanted to purchase 20 young and likely Negroes, for which the highest cash prices will be paid" (*25*, May 1856). Also acted as auctioneers and commission agents (see *25*, 1850s).
	J.M.C.	1858	"Wanted! Persons . . . having any likely negroes for sale, aged 13 to 28 years, will be called on" (*24*, Dec. 1858).
	Crowley, J. B.	1856	"Negroes wanted . . . good sound Negroes between the ages of 12 and 35 . . . cash" (*25*, June 1856).
	Forsythe, A.	1840s–1858	"I have been dealing in negroes for some time and am pretty well acquainted with their value" (Richland Equity 1850, 548). "There were a good many slavedealers in and about Columbia . . . [including] an Irishman called Forsyth" (interview cited in Bancroft, p. 244n). "On June 9 1857 . . . sold . . . to a negro trader . . . one Forsythe" (Manuscript Appeals Opinion bundles, Anderson v. Aiken, 1860). Bought at Charleston probate in 1858 (P/ME).
	++Huson, P. M.	1854–58?	Was agent of Sharp (see above, Richland district). Very probably continued to trade in his own right after 1854. S. D. Watson (see York district) advertised that he dealt in slaves in Montgomery and cited Huson as a referee as to his reliability (*7*, Feb. 1857–Jan. 1858).

(*continued on the following page*)

Table A4.2. Trading firms, according to district, buying slaves in South Carolina during 1850s: Outlines of evidence (*continued*)

Trading firm, by district	Found active	Evidence
Logan, C.	1854–60	Logan purchased slaves in 1854 and "carried them to the west and sold them . . . in Mississippi" (Richland Equity, 1858, Taylor v. Swedish Iron Co.). "Slaves wanted. . . . Highest cash prices for young and likely Negroes of both sexes" (*25,* Mar. 1856). Richland census, 1860: "negro trader." See also Bancroft, pp. 240–41; and see Manning entry (Orangeburg district).
+Rabb, J.	1860?	Richland census, 1860: "trader."
Satterwhite, J. A.	1840s–1851	"I am conversant in the value of negroes. Have been trading for some time and was in November 1850" (Richland Equity 1850, 548).
Sharp, J. M. E.	1845–54	". . . heard John Sharp say that he has applied to said J. C. Hawkins to run off his negroes . . . out of state. . . . Sharp is about going off to the west in a few days" (Richland Equity 1845, 502). "$10,000 cash in hand for purchase of negroes of either sex. Apply J. M. E. Sharp, Columbia, S.C." (*23,* Aug. 1849–Jan. 1851). Had depot at Charleston in 1853 (*6,* Jan.–June 1853). P. M. Huson testified: "Sharp, for several years previous, and up to his death had been engaged in the business of buying and selling negroes. . . . [Huson] acted as his agent [and] bought and sold negroes. . . . [Sharp] left Columbia in the fall of . . . 1854 on a trading excursion or trip westward and did not return to the state again" (Richland Equity 1856, 624).
	Spartanburg	
+Chapman, L. D.	1860?	Spartanburg census, 1860: "trader."
Owens, J.	1850	"Committed to jail . . . Henry . . . says he belongs to a Mr. James Owens, a speculator" (*20,* July 1850).
+Smith, E. P.	1860?	Spartanburg census, 1860: "trader."
+Walker, J.	1860?	Spartanburg census, 1860: "trader."
	Sumter	
++Barr, J. A.		See Cook entry, below.

(*continued on the following page*)

Table A4.2. Trading firms, according to district, buying slaves in South Carolina during 1850s: Outlines of evidence (*continued*)

Trading firm, by district	Found active	Evidence
Belser, W. S., & Myers, R. C., D. (with Belser, L. H.)	1849–57	In 1849, W.S.B. and R.C.M. "entered into a partnership in carrying on the business of buying and selling Negroes." Louisiana selling trip described; W.S.B. absconded with profits in 1850. L.H.B. had made some purchases with the firm, and continued to trade (Sumter Equity 1852, 180 new series). "Belser has agents up here [Darlington and Sumter] and is buying slaves" (ZBO, 20 Aug. 1853; see also 2 Jan. 1854, 15 Apr. 1857).
Briscoe, E. C.	1854–59	Wrote from Port Gibson, Miss.: "I landed home safe. . . . I have sold none yet on account of sickness" (ZBO, 30 Mar. 1854). Wrote from Port Gibson that he expected to get to Charleston in a couple of months to buy slaves (ZBO, 8 Mar. 1857). See also Smith reference of 1857 (Charleston district) and Pool & Blassingame reference of 1859 (Greenville district).
Burkett, H. G., & McElveen, W.	1853–54	Were "co-partners in the business and trade of buying and selling slaves" (Sumter Equity 1858, 325 new series). A. J. McElveen (see below) wrote: "Burkett met with a trader from Louisiana since he left town and from what I learn is trying to get him a lot of negroes. Sharp [see Richland district] sent him over to see Burkett" (ZBO, 29 July 1853).

(*continued on the following page*)

Table A4.2. Trading firms, according to district, buying slaves in South Carolina during 1850s: Outlines of evidence (*continued*)

Trading firm, by district	Found active	Evidence
+ +Cook, R.	1853–54?	A. J. McElveen wrote from Sumter: "I met Bob Cook here the other day. He is in private conveyance and waiting man. He says he wants to pick up some old negroes. He says he is on his way up country. Mr. Disher came in yesterday and will be here a day or two. I have just met with Mr. Barr from Alabama. He is on his way to Richmond. He tells me prime fellows are worth 1050 also he tells me Lumpkin wrote him fellows in Richmond is worth 1050" (ZBO, 9 Sept. 1854). On Lumpkin, the owner of an important "nigger jail," see Chapter 3, and see Bancroft, pp. 101–3. On Barr, see letter in which he reported from Richmond: "What southern buyers there are here say they will not pay the price" (ZBO, 11 Sept. 1854). Disher bought at Charleston district probate sales in 1853, 1858, and 1859 (P/ME). Trader in Alabama wrote 19 Nov. 1863: "I think we are bound to make money . . . judging from what negroes were selling for as we came through. Rux left yesterday for Eutaw and Bob Cook for Greensboro and Marion [S.C.]." Cook promised to bring money for Oakes, and seemed to be linked with trader Mordecai of Charleston (ZBO, 17 July 1853). Cook, Disher, and Barr were almost certainly slave traders.
Dinkins, T. J.	1849–50	"$25,000 cash to be paid for negroes from age 14 to 30" (*10*, Aug. 1849–Jan. 1850).
+ +Disher, R. W.		See Cook entry, above.
Ellis, P. H.	1857	"I desire to purchase young and likely Negroes for whom the highest cash market valuation will be given." Wanted those "young, sound, good countenances and front teeth, and who are good talkers" (*22*, Mar.–July 1857).
Hydrick, A. J.		See main entry under Orangeburg district; he also advertised in Sumter district.

(*continued on the following page*)

Table A4.2. Trading firms, according to district, buying slaves in South Carolina during 1850s: Outlines of evidence (*continued*)

	Trading firm, by district	Found active	Evidence
s	Lewis, W.	1858–59	Bought "Negroes on credit at estate sales" and sold them "in west . . . for cash" (Appeals, 13 Richland Equity 269).
	Louisiana Trader	1853	See Burkett and McElveen reference, above.
	McElveen, A. J.	1853–63	Acted as major purchasing agent for Oakes of Charleston. Bought in Sumter and neighboring districts (see Chap. 3; and see ZBO throughout). Also made at least one selling trip to Alabama. Wrote from Alabama: "I have made some sales of my poor scrubs" (ZBO, 1 Nov. 1856). Not all of his purchases were made with Oakes. Was still active in 1863. "50 young and likely negroes wanted . . . cash" (*26*, Mar. 1863).
++	McElveen, E.	1856?	Appears to have bought in small way for Oakes of Charleston, rather than being an independent trader. "Owing to ill health during last spring I was not able to take down any negroes [to Charleston] during that time, but as my health has somewhat improved, I can attend to business of that kind if I know what the prices of negroes are" (ZBO, 7 July 1856).
	Manser, H.	1846–54	A. J. McElveen (see above) wrote from Sumter: "I met Manser this evening from Richmond. He says they are [*sic*] but little doing." Later A.J.M. wrote that, in Sumter area, he and M. "have the promise of three fellows." Next month he wrote: "I think Manser is wiped out . . . two negroes ran away" (ZBO, 23 and 29 Sept., 4 Oct. 1854). Manser bought in Richmond 1846–47 etc. (RHD).
	Watson (North Carolina)	1856	A. J. McElveen wrote from Sumter: "I saw a new trader in here from North Carolina, Mr. Watson, he told me he paid 1800 for two boys in Columbia last week" (ZBO, 8 July 1856). Watson was perhaps the B. J. Watson entered under Edgefield district as a possible trader.

(*continued on the following page*)

Table A4.2. Trading firms, according to district, buying slaves in South Carolina during 1850s: Outlines of evidence (*continued*)

Trading firm, by district	Found active	Evidence
White, J. K. (or G. J.)	1854–55	A. J. McElveen wrote: "White is on his way to Alabama. . . . [He] is not willing to take any negroes that will be any trouble in getting along" (ZBO, 11 Dec. 1854). White wrote that he had not yet sold one of Oakes's slaves—"You both know it requires a man of a great deal of patience to deal in negro property" (ZBO, 25 Jan. 1855).
	Union	
+Fowler, J. W.	1860?	Union census, 1860: "trader."
	Williamsburg	
Nettles, W. J.	1860	"Negroes wanted . . . young and likely negroes . . . highest cash prices at all times" (27, Oct. 1860).
	York	
+McElveen, J.	1860?	York census, 1860: "trader."
+Sanders, J.	1860?	York census, 1860: "trader."
Watson, S. D. (Alabama)	1857–58	Advertised in York: "S. D. Watson, Montgomery, Alabama. Keeps on hand for sale, a good assortment of plantation negroes, house servants, mechanics, carriage drivers, etc. Also sells on commission at auction or private sale, and hopes for a liberal share of the patronage from his native country" (27, Feb. 1857–Jan. 1858). From the evidence of this advertisement, which ran for at least a year, Watson expected and seems to have found a significant source of slaves in "his native country," the York area.
+Wilson, J. P.	1860?	York census, 1860: "trader."

(*continued on the following page*)

Table A4.2. Trading firms, according to district, buying slaves in South Carolina during 1850s: Outlines of evidence (*continued*)

Sources: Newspaper sources are referred to by italicized number in the table.

1 *Abbeville Banner*	17 *Lancaster Ledger*
2 *Independent Press* (Abbeville)	18 *Lexington Flag*
3 *Laurensville Herald*	19 *Marion Star*
4 *Edgefield Advertiser*	20 *Carolina Spartan*
5 *Beaufort Enterprise*	21 *The Southron* (Orangeburg)
6 *Charleston Mercury*	22 *Sumter Watchman*
7 *Yorkville Enquirer*	23 *Black River Watchman* (Sumter)
8 *Chester Standard*	24 *Daily South Carolina* (Richland)
9 *Darlington Flag*	25 *Daily Carolina Times* (Richland)
10 *Sumter Banner*	26 *Darlington Southerner*
11 *New Orleans Picayune* (La.)	27 *Yorkville Miscellany*
12 *Charleston Courier*	28 *Louisville Gazette* (Ga.)
13 *Winyaw Observer* (Georgetown)	29 *The Confederation* (Montgomery, Ala.)
14 *Greenville Mountaineer*	30 *Memphis Eagle and Enquirer* (Tenn.)
15 *Camden Journal* (Kershaw)	31 *The Daily True Delta* (New Orleans, La.)
16 *Kingstree Star* (Williamsburg)	32 *New Orleans Crescent* (La.)

Traders' manuscripts: Unless otherwise stated, letters cited were directed to the individual named in the title of the relevant manuscript collection.

ALT	A. L. Taveau Papers (DU)	JTH	J.T. Harrison Papers (SHC)
CF	Cox Family Papers (SCL)	LC	Lucy Chase Papers (AAS)
EL	W. D. Ellis letter, Misc. MSS (NYHS)	RHD	R. H. Dickinson & Bro., Slave Dealers' Account Book (AAS)
HD/CHS	Hector Davis & Co., Slave Sales Record Book (CHS)	SOW	S. O. Wood Papers (DU)
		TG	Tyre Glen Papers (DU)
HD/NYPL	Hector Davis & Co., Day Book (NYPL)	WAJF	W. A. J. Finney Papers (DU)
		ZBO	Z. B. Oakes Papers (BPL)
JG	J. Graham Papers (DU)		

Miscellaneous sources:

Adams	*F. C. Adams, Uncle Tom at Home: A Review of the Reviewers and Repudiators of Uncle Tom's Cabin by Mrs. Stowe* (Philadelphia, 1853).
Appeals	Appeals case. Reference system as used in South Carolina reports.
Bancroft	F. Bancroft, *Slave Trading in the Old South* (Baltimore: 1931; New York, 1959).
CCD	Charleston City *Directory* for year indicated.
CCP	Court of Common Pleas case. Reference indicates district, year case filed, judgment roll number. These manuscript records are at SCA.
Census	Manuscript returns of U.S. census for district and year indicated.
Equity	Equity Court case. Reference indicates district, year case was filed, bill number. Records consulted are at SCA, mainly on microfilm.
Georgia Narr.	Ellen Campbell narrative, p. 223 in George Rawick (ed.), *The American Slave: A Composite Autobiography* (Westport, Conn., 1972—), vol. 13 (part 4), Georgia Narratives.

(*continued on the following page*)

Table A4.2. Trading firms, according to district, buying slaves in South Carolina during 1850s: Outlines of evidence (*continued*)

JSC	*Testimony taken by the Joint Select Committee to Inquire into the Conditions and Affairs of the Late Insurrectionary States,* 13 vols. (Washington, 1872; New York, 1968).
Korn	B. W. Korn, "Jews and Negro History in the Old South, 1789–1865," *Publications of the American Jewish Historical Society,* 50 (1961): 151–202.
Manifests	New Orleans inward manifests (NA). Very few manifests are available for the period after 1852.
P/ME	Charleston district probate and/or Master of Equity sales of slaves. Evidence from Charleston district Court of Ordinary, Inventories, Appraisals, and Sales, 1850–59 (SCA); Charleston district Court of Chancery and Equity, Sales Book of James Tupper, Master of Equity, sales, 1851–63 (SCA).
S. C. Misc.	Miscellaneous Records of Secretary of State for South Carolina (SCA).
Sellers	J. B. Sellers, *Slavery in Alabama* (Tuscaloosa, 1950).
Stroyer	J. Stroyer, *My Life in the Old South* (Salem, 1879; Salem, 1898).
Sydnor	C. Sydnor, *Slavery in Mississippi* (New York, 1933).
Table A2.1	Appendix Table A2.1, summarizing New Orleans traders and manifests for selected years.

Table A4.3. Census information on "documented" traders active in South Carolina from 1850–60 and located in the South Carolina census returns for 1850 and/or 1860

Trader and year	District	Occupation given in census	Age	Real	Personal	Place of birth	Family information	Located at census
Addison, J. A.								
1860	Edgefield	Farmer	31	4	13	—	W 1	Edgefield (V)
Adkins, T.								
1850	Edgefield	Slave trader	45	1	—	S.C.	—	Hamburg (V)
Adkins, T. B.								
1850	Edgefield	Clerk for trader	24	—	—	S.C.	—	Hamburg (V)
Belser, L. H.								
1850	Sumter	Planter	26	—	—	S.C.	—	Sumter (D)
Boozer, D. N.								
1860	Abbeville	Trader	28	—	—	S.C.	—	Greenwood (V)
Burkett, H. G.								
1850	Sumter	Overseer	34	—	—	S.C.	—	Sumter (D)
1860	Sumter	Farmer	46	—	—	S.C.	—	Sumter (D)
Clinkscales, J. W.								
1860	Abbeville	—	35	1	52	S.C.	—	Greenwood (V)
Cobb, E. M.								
1860	Anderson	Speculator	38	—	—	S.C.	W 7	Anderson (D)
Crews, J.								
1860	Laurens	Merchant	37	7	—	N.C.	W 4	Laurens (V)
Culbreath, H. C.								
1860	Edgefield	Farmer	44	4	40	S.C.	W 6	Edgefield (D)
Cureton, J. E.								
1850	Lancaster	—	24	—	—	S.C.	—	Lancaster (D)
1860	Lancaster	—	34	8	25	S.C.	—	Lancaster (D)

(*continued on the following page*)

Table A4.3. Census information on "documented" traders active in South Carolina from 1850–60 and located in the South Carolina census returns for 1850 and/or 1860 (*continued*)

Trader and year	District	Occupation given in census	Age	Real	Personal	Place of birth	Family information	Located at census
Dinkins, T. J.								
1850	Sumter	Merchant	42	1	—	S.C.	W 5	Williamsburg (D)
Ellis, W. L.								
1860	Orangeburg	—	22	—	—	S.C.	—	Orangeburg (V)
Ford, J. W.								
1860	Kershaw	Physician	42	50	100	Tenn.	—	Kershaw (D)
Forsyth[e], A.								
1850	Richland	Merchant	27	—	—	Ire.	—	Columbia (C)
1860	Richland	Merchant	39	5	40	Ire.	—	Columbia (C)
Fox, W. H.								
1860	Lexington	Negro trader	40	2	8	S.C.	—	Lexington (D)
Gadsden, T. N.								
1850	Charleston	Broker	46	50	—	S.C.	W 7	Charleston (C)
1860	Charleston	Broker	50		—	S.C.		Charleston (C)
Gardiner, W. Q.								
1860	Edgefield	Negro trader	46	—	23	—	—	Hamburg (V)
Holeman, R. B.								
1850	Newberry	—	29	14	—	S.C.	W 3	Newberry (D)
Houston, J. A.								
1850	Edgefield	Farmer	40	3	—	S.C.	W 2	Edgefield (D)
1860	Edgefield	Negro trader	51	—	10	S.C.	W 3	Hamburg (V)
Hughes, D.								
1850	Fairfield	Speculator	24	—	—	S.C.	—	Edgefield (D)
Hydrick, A. J.								
1850	Orangeburg	Planter	28	3	—	S.C.	W	Orangeburg (D)
1860	Orangeburg	Planter	39	25	50	S.C.	W	Orangeburg (D)

(*continued on the following page*)

Table A4.3. Census information on "documented" traders active in South Carolina from 1850–60 and located in the South Carolina census returns for 1850 and/or 1860 (*continued*)

Trader and year	District	Occupation given in census	Age	Real	Personal	Place of birth	Family information	Located at census
Irvine, E. S.								
1850	Greenville	Merchant	40	1	—	N.C.	W 1	Greenville (V)
1860	Greenville	Farmer	52	70	62	N.C.	W 5	Greenville (V)
Irvine, O. B.								
1860	Greenville	Physician	58	81	53	S.C.	—	Greenville (V)
Kelly, E.								
1850	Greenville	Farmer	29	—	—	S.C.	—	Greenville (D)
Lipford, J. C.								
1850	Chester	Farmer	34	—	—	S.C.	W 6	Chester (D)
1860	Chester	"Merchant, speculating and farming"	46	23	32	S.C.	W 5	Chester (D)
Logan, C.								
1850	Richland	Shoemaker	31	—	—	Ire.	—	Columbia (C)
1860	Richland	Negro trader	—	6	20	Ire.	—	Columbia (C)
McBride, M.								
1850	Charleston	Broker	32	3	—	Ire.	—	Charleston (C)
McElveen, E.								
1850	Sumter	Planter	45	0.4	—	S.C.	W 8	Sumter (D)
1860	Clarendon	Farmer	47	2	4	S.C.	W 6	Clarendon (D)
Merrimon, L. D.								
1850	Abbeville	Merchant	38	2	—	Va.	—	Greenwood (V)
1860	Abbeville	Farmer	47	13	52	N.C.(?)	—	Greenwood (V)
Mordecai, B.								
1860	Charleston	Broker	50	65	27	S.C.	W 7	Charleston (C)

(*continued on the following page*)

Table A4.3. Census information on "documented" traders active in South Carolina from 1850–60 and located in the South Carolina census returns for 1850 and/or 1860 (*continued*)

Trader and year	District	Occupation given in census	Age	Real	Personal	Place of birth	Family information	Located at census
Mosely, T. P.								
1850	Abbeville	Speculator	35	—	—	—	W	Cokesbury (V)
Nettles, W. J.								
1850	Williamsburg	Farmer	34	0.8	—	S.C.	W 6	Williamsburg (D)
1860	Williamsburg	Farmer	44	7	18	S.C.	W 6	Williamsburg (D)
Nickels, H. J.								
1860	Laurens	Negro trader	36	4	—	S.C.		Laurens (D)
Nipson, F.								
1860	Charleston	Broker	33	0.5	4	S.C.	(?)	Charleston (C)
Oakes, Z. B.								
1850	Charleston	Broker	42	4	—	Me.	W 4	Charleston (C)
1860	Charleston	Broker	53	62	50	S.C.(?)	W 3	Charleston (C)
Owings, R. M.								
1850	Edgefield	Cotton buyer	25	—	—	S.C.	—	Hamburg (V)
1860	Edgefield	Negro trader	33	2	19	S.C.	W	Hamburg (V)
Page, J.								
1860	Kershaw	Negro speculator	43	1	35	S.C.	—	Camden (V)
Parks, J. T.								
1850	Abbeville	Merchant	22	0.6	—	Ga.	W	Greenwood (V)
1860	Abbeville	Farmer	30	11	41	Ga.	W	Greenwood (V)
Pride, C. J.								
1860	Chester	Farmer	32	1	9	S.C.	W 3	Chester (D)

(*continued on the following page*)

Table A4.3. Census information on "documented" traders active in South Carolina from 1850–60 and located in the South Carolina census returns for 1850 and/or 1860 (*continued*)

Trader and year	District	Occupation given in census	Age	Real	Personal	Place of birth	Family information	Located at census
Ryan, T.								
1850	Charleston	Broker	49	24	—	Ire.	W 6	Charleston (C)
1860	Charleston	Broker	60	30	6	Ire.	W 4	Charleston (C)
Ryan, W. B.								
1850	Charleston	Clerk to Ryan, T.	27	—	—	S.C.	—	Charleston (C)
1860	Charleston	Broker	36	5	1	S.C.	—	Charleston (C)
Sampson, S.								
1850	Georgetown	Merchant	30	1	—	S.C.	W 2	Georgetown (C)
1860	Georgetown	Merchant	40	4	40	S.C.	W 6	Georgetown (C)
Satterwhite, J. A.								
1850	Richland	Merchant	43	—	—	S.C.	—	Columbia (C)
Seaborn, G.								
1850	Anderson	Farmer	52	12	—	S.C.	W 9	Anderson (D)
1860	Anderson	Farmer	62	33	58	S.C.	W 6	Anderson (D)
Sharp, J. M. E.								
1850	Richland	Merchant	33	—	—	S.C.	—	Columbia (C)
Spires, W.								
1850	Edgefield	Slave trader	28	0	—	S.C.		Hamburg (V)
1860	Edgefield	Negro trader	40	5	28	S.C.	W 2	Hamburg (V)
Steedman, R.								
1850	Lexington	Farmer	35	4	—	S.C.	W 8	Lexington (D)
1860	Lexington	Farmer	45	15	35		—	Lexington (D)
Suber, J. W.								
1850	Abbeville	Farmer	26	—	—	—	W 1	Abbeville (D)

(*continued on the following page*)

Table A4.3. Census information on "documented" traders active in South Carolina from 1850–60 and located in the South Carolina census returns for 1850 and/or 1860 (*continued*)

Trader and year	District	Occupation given in census	Age	Real	Personal	Place of birth	Family information	Located at census
Teague, A. G.								
1850	Edgefield	Physician	38	1	—	S.C.	W	Edgefield (V)
1860	Edgefield	Physician	47	3	15	S.C.	W 2	Edgefield (V)
Teague, E. F.								
1850	Edgefield	Physician	32	2	—	S.C.	W 2	Edgefield (V)
Vance, A.								
1850	Abbeville	—	43	—	—	—	W 3	Greenwood (V)
1860	Abbeville	Farmer	—	75	125	S.C.	W 3	Greenwood (V)
Warren, C.								
1850	Edgefield	Farmer	40	2	—	S.C.	W 6	Edgefield (D)
Weatherly, T. C.								
1860	Marlboro	Farmer	42	50	125	S.C.	W 7	Bennettsville (V)

Source: Information is derived from manuscript census returns for South Carolina districts, 1850 and 1860.

Notes: All traders listed in this table are documented in Table A4.2. It has not, however, been possible, from South Carolina census returns, to find information on all of the traders who are included in Table A4.2. Those traders who bought in South Carolina but were normally resident elsewhere have only rarely been located in census records. Additionally the itinerant life of most traders, both in the buying and in the selling phases of their business, made it difficult to locate in census records many of those traders who were normally resident in South Carolina.

Of the two censuses used, only that of 1860 gives information on the value of the personal estate of those enumerated. In this table (A4.3) estate values are given in thousands of dollars.

W = Indicates wife; the number following is the number of children in the trader's household. The census does not indicate family relationships, but basic relationships are assumed on the basis of the age and sex of those whites enumerated as being resident in trader's household.

V = Village

C = City

D = District (probably rural)

Information on place of birth was occasionally omitted from the census. When given, place of birth was consistent except in the cases of L. D. Merrimon and Z. B. Oakes. With Merrimon and Oakes respectively the balance of census detail makes it quite clear, however, that the same individual has been identified in 1850 as in 1860.

Appendix 5

Slave Selling and Staple-Crop Production in the Economy of the Upper South

In Chapter 5, I noted that a comparison of the economic importance of the Upper South's staple crop production and its trade in slaves required evidence on slave prices, the volume and composition of the trade, and, of course, on staple prices and production. Because censuses provide evidence on the production levels of crops for 1839–40, 1849–50, and 1859–60, my calculations were concentrated on those years.

In establishing a basis of evidence on slave prices according to age and sex, two collections of slave traders' papers (the Tyre Glen and R. R. Reid papers)

Table A5.1. Slave prices as a percentage of the average price of males aged from 16 to 29 years

	Male slaves			Female slaves[a]	
Age	Glen	Reid	F & E	Reid	F & E
0–3	14	18	10	16	13
4–7	27	30	34	26	34
8–11	48	50	55	40	53
12–15	73	80	77	60	69
16–29	100	100	100	70	82
30–39	69	90	98	50	71
40–49	30	60	72	40	47
50	19	40*	54	20*	33
55	13		38		20
60	6		25		11
65			15		5
70			7		2

Sources: Tyre Glen Papers (DU); Richard R. Reid Papers (UVA); Fogel and Engerman, *Time on the Cross*, vol. 1, p. 76, Fig. 18; vol. 2, p. 79.

Note: Where no quotation is given for a particular category, information for that category is lacking in the manuscript concerned. F & E = Fogel and Engerman. * indicates that quotation is for Reid's "50+" category.

[a] The Glen scale contains no prices for female slaves.

yield particularly valuable evidence. The Glen manuscript provides a scale of prices for male slaves of specific ages from 0 to 60, whereas the Reid scale divides slaves according to broad age categories and provides information on both male and female slave prices. These price indices, together with a scale of slave prices which Fogel and Engerman calculated, provide a substantial basis upon which to assess prices for specific age and sex groups. Evidence derived from these scales is summarized in Table A5.1 (where prices are presented according to the age categories used in the Reid scale). In that table, prices for each age and sex group are given as percentages of the prices for the most valuable broad category of slaves, that is to say as percentages of values for males aged from 16 to 29 years.[1]

Having gained evidence on slave prices according to age and sex, and (from Figure 2.1) already having a substantial basis of evidence on the composition of the trade, it is now necessary to obtain information on prices according to year. Such information is provided by U. B. Phillips's survey of price trends in several major markets (Phillips, *Life and Labor,* p. 177). That survey, it seems, was based essentially on records of court sales. This suggests that the terms of sale would usually have been credit rather than cash, so that the price levels given are likely to have been generally somewhat above those paid by traders. In the present study, calculations will be made on the basis of Charleston prices, scaled down by 5 percent to allow for the fact that Charleston price levels in those years were probably (compare Phillips's Charleston and Virginia prices) slightly, but not very markedly, above the average for the exporting group of states. Prices are then scaled down by a further 20 percent (see evidence in Chapter 3) to adjust for the trader's cash rather than credit terms.

From the several groups of evidence which have been mentioned, it now becomes possible to estimate the average value of slaves traded in the 1839–40, 1849–50, and 1859–60 seasons—that is to say, in the seasons for which censuses provide evidence on crop production levels. The Reid age-price scale is taken as a convenient basis for this calculation.[2]

1. The Tyre Glen and Reid scales are reproduced verbatim in Appendix 6. Fogel and Engerman's scale appears in *Time on the Cross,* vol. 1, p. 76, fig. 18; and certain additional information on that scale appears in *Time on the Cross,* vol. 2, p. 79. Although the Glen manuscript does not directly indicate the sex of the slaves valued, there can be no doubt that the scale is concerned with male slaves. This is, firstly, because traders routinely took males, the market leaders, as their guide in assessing price levels; and, secondly, because the age-price peaking coincides, as Table A5.1 shows, with the age concentration of the male but not the female element of the trade. (Appendix 6 also gives miscellaneous slave price information derived from Richmond slave auctioneers' circulars.)

2. In the Reid scale, the relative values of the other age groups are generally lower compared with the 16–29 age group (the most valuable age category entered in Table A5.1) than in the Fogel and Engerman scale; thus the use of the Reid statistics is not likely to cause an overestimate of the value of slaves traded.

Table A5.2. Decennial growth rates of slave populations

Decade	Growth Rate (%)		
	South Carolina	Principal net exporting states	Total U.S. slave population
1830s	3.69	-0.55	23.8
1840s	17.72	11.70	27.8
1850s	4.53	6.10	23.4

Sources: Federal censuses of 1830, 1840, 1850, and 1860.

Using the Reid scale, then, male slaves traded to cotton areas were found to have averaged 80 percent and females 56 percent of the value of a prime male *field hand* aged from fifteen to twenty-nine years. These percentages were then adjusted to take account of the participation of skilled slaves in the trade, and to account for the contribution of the especially selective New Orleans trade, so that weightings were adjusted for males to 88 percent and for females to 62 percent. Based on Phillips's prices for prime field hands, the average price paid by traders to Upper South slaveholders therefore can be estimated—in the years 1839–40, 1849–50 and 1859–60, respectively—as follows: for males, $660, $512, and $805, and for females $465, $360, and $567.

Attributing only 60 percent of transfers to speculation, the trade's exportations from the principal exporting states have already been estimated for the 1830s at 175,000, for the 1840s at 111,000, and for the 1850s at 135,000 slaves; and we know that about half of these slaves would have been male. In estimating the numbers exported in the three seasons (1839–40, 1849–50, and 1859–60) with which I am concerned, South Carolina's *annual* rates of exportation provide a valuable guide. South Carolina, as Table A5.2 suggests, exported at a slightly less intensive rate than did the principal exporting states as a whole, but her pattern of exportations (see Figure 5.1) suggests probable annual levels of exportation for the exporting states generally. The resulting exportation estimates are given in Table A5.3.[3] By combining volume and price statistics, it is, therefore, estimated that in the 1839–40 season slave traders paid $6.24

3. Statistics given in Figure 5.1 show that the 1839–40 growth rate for South Carolina's slave population was, at 1.77 percent, much higher than that state's annual average for the 1830s, but was similar to its average for the 1840s. It appears, therefore, that in 1839–40 the slave trade from the principal exporting states would have been lower than that area's estimated annual average of 17,500 slaves for the 1830s, and similar to its estimated annual average of 11,100 slaves for the 1840s. For the 1849–50 season, South Carolina's growth rate of 1.61 percent was again similar to the state's 1840s average, so that for that year (as for 1839–40) the trade from the principal exporting states is estimated at 11,100. Since the 1859–60 South Carolina growth rate of -1.94 percent was significantly below the state's average for the 1850s, the trade from the principal exporting states during the 1859–60 seasons is estimated at not less than the 1850s annual average of 13,500 slaves.

Table A5.3. Value of main staple crops and of receipts from sales to the interregional slave trade: Principal exporting states

	Tobacco	Rice	Sea-island cotton	Short-fiber cotton	Total staple crop value	Slaves traded[a]
1839–40						
Production (000 lb)	170,480	63,431	7,420	110,408		
Price ($ per 1,000 lb)	105.0	34.4	280.0	87.5		
Value (million $)	17.90	2.18	2.08	9.66	31.82	6.24
1849–50						
Production (000 lb)	145,779	165,419	6,930	135,530		
Price ($ per 1,000 lb)	47.5	32.9	260.0	116.7		
Value (million $)	6.92	5.44	1.80	15.82	29.98	4.84
1859–60						
Production (000 lb)	303,489	126,703	10,665	193,996		
Price ($ per 1,000 lb)	92.0	40.8	430.0	116.7		
Value (million $)	27.92	5.17	4.59	22.64	60.32	9.26

Sources: Tobacco prices are derived from Gray, *History of Agriculture,* vol. 2, p. 765, Figure 10; and sea-island cotton prices are from Gray, vol. 2, p. 1031, Table 43. Prices for short-fiber cotton ("middle" grade) and for rice ("prime" grade) are derived from A. H. Cole, *Wholesale Commodity Prices in the United States, 1700–1861* (Cambridge, Mass., 1938). Staple prices quoted are as far as possible monthly averages for the twelve-month period during which a particular crop would have been marketed; 1839–40 prices, for example, are based as the last four months of 1839 and the first eight months of 1840.

[a] Numbers of slaves traded were estimated at 11,100 for 1839-40 and 1849-50, and 13,500 for 1859–60 (see Appendix 5, note 3).

the principal exporting states, that in the 1849–50 season they paid $4.84 million, and in the 1859–60 season they paid at least $9.26 million.

Having estimated the value of slaves traded, the simpler task of estimating the value of crop production remains. Details are given in Table A5.3, which indicates that the value of the major staples produced in the principal exporting states was, in the crop year 1839–40, approximately $31.82 million, in 1849–50 about $29.98 million, and in 1859–60 about $60.32 million.[4]

4. Crop totals are taken from federal censuses for the years concerned, except for sea-island cotton, for which annual production totals do not appear in antebellum censuses; evidence from Gray (*History of Agriculture,* vol. 2, pp. 675–80, 731–39, 1031–32) makes estimates possible. In the principal exporting states, sea-island cotton production was concentrated in South Carolina; statistics for the state's crop of 1857–58 suggest that the South Carolina crop of 1859–60 was something over 10.5 million pounds. Because statistics on America's sea-island cotton exportations from 1805 to 1860 are available, because exportations accounted for rather more than 80 percent of production, and because South Carolina appears before the mid-1850s to have accounted for something like 70 percent of production, it has been possible to incorporate in Table A5.3 estimates of the South Carolina crops of 1839–40, 1849–50, and 1859–60.

Prices quoted for tobacco are those which obtained at Virginia warehouses, through which most of the tobacco crop passed, whereas for cotton and rice the prices are those which obtained at Charleston, a port which handled the bulk of the area's production of those staples (Gray, *History of Agriculture,* vol. 2, pp. 711–20, 723–24).

Appendix 6

Evidence on Slave Prices

Table A6.1. The Tyre Glen slave price scale (probably for early 1850s)

Pfafftown District Forsythe Co., N.C. Scale of Valuation of Slaves			
Ages Years Old	Valuation	Ages Years Old	Valuation
1	$ 100	27	775
2	125	28	700
3	150	29	675
4	175	30	650
5	200	31	625
6	225	32	600
7	250	33	575
8	300	34	550
9	350	35	525
10	400	36	500
11	450	37	475
12	500	38	450
13	550	39	425
14	600	40	400
16	650	41	375
17	750	42	350
18	800	43	325
19	850	44	300
20	900	45	225
21	875	48	200
22	850	49	175
23	825	50	150
24	800	55	100
25	775	60	50
26	750		

Source: Reproduced verbatim from Tyre Glen papers (DU; no date given).

Notes: The Glen index appears, from the price levels indicated (compare Table A6.3) and from a reference to Forsythe county—a county which was created in 1849—to date from the early 1850s. Although most of the trading evidence in the Tyre Glen Papers relates to the 1830s, it is clear that in the 1850s Glen still took an active interest in the trade (see, for example, correspondence with J. A. Bitting cited in Chapter 5, note 24).

Table A6.2. The Richard R. Reid slave price scale

Prices of different classes of negroes		
Males	50+	200
Female	50+	100
Male	40+	300
Female	40+	200
Male	30+	450
Female	30+	250
Male	16+	500
Female	16+	350
Male	12+	400
Female	12+	300
Male	8+	250
Female	8+	200
Male	4+	150
Female	4+	130
Male	1+	100
Female	1+	90
Male	birth to 1	60
Female	birth to 1	50
Mechanic		800

Source: Reproduced verbatim from Richard R. Reid Papers (UVA; no date, no signature given).

Table A6.3. Slave prices according to trade circulars and reports, 1846–61

Market	Year	Month	Source	No.1 men (19–25 yrs)	Fair/ ordinary men	Best boys (15–18 yrs)	Best boys (10–14 yrs)	No.1 women (16–20 yrs)	Fair/ ordinary women	Best girls (10–15 yrs)	Women with one or two children	Families, "fancies," "scrubs"
Richmond prices	1846	23 June	1A	550–625[a]			375–500[h]	425–475[a]		275–350[n]	Sell well	
		22 Aug.	1A	650–725[a]			425–525[h]	500–550[a]		300–275[n]	Sell well	
	1847	14 Mar.	1B	650–725				525–(?)			Sell well	
		24 May	1B	675–7(50)				525–575				
	1848	13 Nov.	2C	700–725[a]		550–600[b]	500[c]	600		425–500[c]	Sell well	
		23 Nov.	3C	700	600–650			575–600				
		7 Dec.	3C	700–725				575–600				
	1849	20 Sept.	1E	750–800			450–675[i]					
		26 Nov.	4D	850–860				580–660				
	1850	30 Oct.	1E	825–850[a]	775		375–800[l]	650–750[q]		375–650[m]	IP	
	1853	– May	1F	1150–1200			450–950[l]	800–900		425–750[m]		
		(Oct.?)	5X	1200–1300	950–1050		375–950[m]	800–1000		350–850[m]		
		12 Dec.	60	1150–1250	950–1100				850–950[e]			
	1854	23 Sept.	1H	1100–1150		850–1000	650–800[c]	900–950		525–800	950–975	
		26 Sept.	1F	1200–1250	1000–1075			900–1050[a]				
		13 Oct.	1F	950–1050[b]			450–1000[l]	950–1000[a]		400–850[m]	IP	
	1856	21 May	1I	1200–1300		850–1150	600–820	900–1000		575–850		
	1857	1 Sept.	7K	1250–1450[a]	1000–1150	1100–1200[f]	500–1075[m]	1050–1225[a]	850–1025	500–1000[m]	IP	Families/ scrubs (IP)
	1858	8 Jan.	9M	1000–1150				800–1000				
		22 Jan.	9M	1100–1200	975–1050	1000–1125	750–900[c]	1000–1050	900		1000	
		3 Apr.	9K	1250	1150			1150	1000			Fancies (SVW)
		5 May	9K	1050–1300	800–1000	1000–1150[f]	425–950[m]	900–1150	750–875	400–900[m]		
		7 May	9M	1000–1200				900–1000		450–500[o]		
		14 Aug.	12L	1200–1350	1050–1200	1050–1200	850–1050[c]	1050–1150		850–1000[c]		

(*continued on the following page*)

Table A6.3. Slave prices according to trade circulars and reports, 1846–61 (*continued*)

Market	Year	Month	Source	No.1 men (19–25 yrs)	Fair/ ordinary men	Best boys (15–18 yrs)	Best boys (10–14 yrs)	No.1 women (16–20 yrs)	Fair/ ordinary women	Best girls (10–15 yrs)	Women with one or two children	Families, "fancies," "scrubs"
		14 Oct.	9J	(?)–1350[a]			500–1150[m]	(?)–1250[a]		500–1150[m]	IP	
		20 Dec.	9L	1375–1475	1200–1300	1200–1350	900–1200[c]	1200–1300[d]			1100–1300[a]	Scrubs (I/O)
		20 Dec.	3I	1400–1500		1050–1350	850–1050[c]	1200–1350		700–1150	1250–1350	Families (RD)
	1859	12 Jan.	4O	1500–1520	1000–1100			1300–1350				
		2 Feb.	4O	1500–1575				1250–1380				
		7 Feb.	9L	1400–1525	(?)–1350	1075–(?)	850–1100[c]	1200–1300		900–1100[c]	1100–1275	
		15 Feb.	9M					1300				Fancies 1550–1680
		25 Feb.	9L	1400–1500				1250–1300[d]				Families (SW)
		26 Feb.	9L				1050–1125[j]	1200–1300				Fancies 1600
		26 Jul.	4O	1450–1525				1300–1400			1200–1300	Fancies 1325
		29 Jul.	10X	1450–1500		1250–1425	1100–1200[c]	1150–1325		1000–1100[c]		
		24 Dec.	4I	1400–1500		1350–1450	900–1300	1200–1350		900–1150	Sell well	
	1860	13 Jan.	2L	1550–1625	1350–1500			1400–1525	1250–1350		Sell well	
		14 Jan.	8I	1500–1650		1350–1450	850–1300	1350–1450		850–1300	1350–1650	
		20 Jan.	2L	1500–1600				1400–1475[d]				
		31 Jan.	2L	1550–1650				1450–1475[d]				
		26 June	4I	1550–1600		1200–1450	875–1150	1350–1400		800–1250		Families (SW)
		14Jul.	4I	1500–1600		1300–1450	900–1250	1300–1450		900–1250[c]	RD	
		20 Jul.	11N	1450–1625[a]	1100–1200		575–1275[m]	1300–1450[a]	900–1100	575–1275[m]	1250–1450	
		11 Sept.	11N	1400–1550[a]	1100–1200		400–1100[m]	1250–1400[a]	1100–1150	400–1100[m]	1300–1400	
	1861	5 Jan.	11N	900–1000[a]	750–800		275–850[m]	750–850[a]		275–850[m]		
Memphis	1849	3Dec.	1P	850–900	775–825		675–725[j]			650–700[k]	Dull	
Port Gibson (MI)	1849	24 Dec.	1P	900–950		775–850				675–750[j]		

(*continued on the following page*)

Table A6.3. Slave prices according to trade circulars and reports, 1846–61 (*continued*)

Market	Year	Month	Source	No.1 men (19–25 yrs)	Fair/ ordinary men	Best boys (15–18 yrs)	Best boys (10–14 yrs)	No.1 women (16–20 yrs)	Fair/ ordinary women	Best girls (10–15 yrs)	Women with one or two children	Families, "fancies," "scrubs"
Natchez	1849	24 Dec.	1P	950–1000								
Mont-gomery	1856	7 Nov.	13Q	1100–1400				950–1150				

Sources:

1. Harris-Brady Papers (UVA)
2. R. R. Reid Papers (UVA)
3. J. Dickinson Papers (DU)
4. W.A.J. Finney Papers (DU)
5. Cited in Olmsted, *Cotton Kingdom*, p. 595
6. J. A. Jordan Papers (DU)
7. J. W. Bond Papers (DU)
8. Dickinson and Washington Papers (DU)
9. E. W. Ferguson Papers (NCA)
10. Cited in Bancroft, *Slave Trading*, p. 117, note 52
11. D. M. Pulliam Papers (DU)
12. S. O. Wood Papers (DU)
13. Z. B. Oakes Papers (BPL)

Auctioneering and trading firms providing market quotations: (Information is derived from a trade circular unless "letter" indicated below)

A Sidnum Grady
B Hodges, Ray & Pulliam
C B. Davis/J. Dickinson (letter)
D N. B. & C. B. Hill
E Pulliam & Slade
F Pulliam & Davis
G S. Omohundro (letter)
H R. H. Dickinson, Bros.
I Dickinson, Hill & Co.
J Pulliam & Betts
K D. M. Pulliam
L Hector Davis
M Toler & Ferguson (letter)
N Betts & Gregory
O Finney & Thomas (letter)
P J. B. Moon/[J. Brady] (letter)
Q Burch, Kirkland & Co. (letter)
X Unspecified Richmond firm

Notes

Prices: Prices quoted are in dollars and, unless otherwise stated, are for field hands.
SW "Sell Well"
SVW "Sell exceedingly well just now"
RD "Rather dull and hard to sell"
IP "Sell in their usual proportations" to other classes
I/O "Inferior and old Negros rarely sell in this market to the expectation of owners"

[a] Upper price specifically relates to "Extra No.1"
[b] Quote is for lower part of age range
[c] Quote is for upper part of age range
[d] "Best black girls"
[e] "Second class and yellow girls"

Height: Where original sources do not give age or general slave type, references to height are taken as an approximate guide to age. Boys quoted as 5′3″ and over, boys as below 5′3″, and girls as below 4′11″, are taken as having been aged 15–18 yrs, 10–14 yrs, and 10–15 yrs respectively. This is based on source 1B (24 May 1847) which gives boys 5′3″ as 16 yrs; gives girls 5′3″ as 22 yrs; girls 5′0″ as 18 yrs; and girls 4′11″ as 16 yrs. Where height is used as a guide, the references which follow are used.

f 5′6″
g 5′0″–5′6″
h 4′9″–5′3″
i 4′6″–5′3″
j 4′10″–5′0″
k 4′9″–5′0″
l 4′0″–5′3″
m 4′0″–5′0″
n 4′5″–4′7″
o 4′0″

Appendix 7

Estimating the Profits of the Trade

Chapter 7 included an interpretation of the rates of profit gained by traders. "Crude" rates of profit were simply taken to be the difference between the trader's buying and selling prices for slaves. The rates of "net profit," however, took account of a series of expenses, including costs of travel and subsistence, wages for any hired hands, interest payments, losses through the death of slaves, and the cost of discounting promissory notes. This appendix outlines the evidence used to convert crude rates of profit into net rates.

Direct evidence on the expenses of transporting slave gangs and of putting them up for sale in the Lower South has been found for five of the consignments included in Table 7.1. Of these five, the expenses for the Hughes & Downing consignment are given in the most detail, these expenses including food, clothing, medical costs, jail fees, and several charges for river transportation. Basic expenses of this type were, for the five consignments just mentioned, equivalent on average to 4.7 percent of the price which the trader initially paid in acquiring those slaves; and this 4.7 percent ratio between the basic expenses of trading trips and initial purchase price will be assumed to have been roughly typical of the trade.[1]

The burden of wage payments to hired assistants seems usually to have been slight. Indeed, except for firms which traded on a very large scale, assistants

1. As well as Hughes & Downing's basic expenses of $257 on slaves purchased for $5,292 (expenses being 4.9 percent in this case), Totten & Gunn had 8.8 percent basic expenses on their 1833–34 consignment; Glen had 6.2 percent expenses on his first lot of 1836–37; and Templeman & Goodwin expenses at 1.4 and 4.0 percent on the two lots for which we have data. Expenses of the same order are suggested in "The Expence of Travelin with negros," a manuscript at Duke University Library describing a trading trip which James A. Mitchell made from Virginia to Natchez in 1834. The manuscript did not indicate the purchase price of the slaves concerned (and for that reason this consignment is excluded from Table 7.1); but it is clear that the slaves sold in Natchez for about $30,000, with Mitchell on the outward journey incurring expenses of $570, and incurring a further expense of $113 on his return journey to Virginia. Mitchell's expenses were principally on charges for being ferried across rivers, and on food and clothing for his slaves.

seem, if hired at all, to have been employed only for brief periods. In 1834, for example, Jarratt & Glen hired Richard J. Cook as assistant for the supervision of a coffle, and Cook's note of 2 December 1834 records: "Received of Jarratt and Glen $45.50 in full for my services from the time I left home being 25 days coming out and allowing 16 days for going home. Wages $25.50. Expenses money home $20." Somewhat similarly, a letter of January 1860 from Phillip Thomas to his trading partner Jack Finney noted that a certain Calhoun had been hired at $21.13 per week to assist in disposing of a slave coffle in Alabama. In the event, Calhoun proved unsatisfactory and was dismissed, but he would in any case have been employed at most only for the two or three months during which the Alabama slave market was most active. Trading firms which operated on a large scale would often have employed one or more buying assistants on a permanent or semipermanent basis, and one such assistant was hired by Joseph Meek and his partners at $550 per year. Such a salary would, however, have amounted to less than the purchase price of a single adult slave, and it is clear that Meek and his partners handled some 150 or more slaves per year. Even with large trading firms, therefore, expenditure on wages is likely to have been the equivalent of no more than 1 or 2 percent of the purchase price for the season's slaves.[2]

Interest on borrowed capital would usually have been a more significant expenditure. In their study of the economics of slavery, Conrad and Meyer examined antebellum interest rates and, drawing from contemporary chronicles, concluded that "it was obvious that southerners and northerners alike considered 6–8 percent a reasonable . . . asking price for loans." They found, however, that in 1836, a year of exceptional speculation, interest rates soared to the highly unusual level of 20 percent.[3] It is not clear what proportion of trader's purchases were made with borrowed capital and what with ploughback profits, nor is it clear whether loans were usually made for periods of as long as a year; but except in a very few years, interest payments appear to have been equivalent to rather less than 6–8 percent of the price which traders paid for their season's slaves. Interest payments at the rate of about 6 percent are therefore assumed, except in calculations for the exceptional year of 1836, when a rate of just under 20 is inferred.

Deaths of slaves and life insurance on slaves (when it was used) would have imposed further financial burdens upon the trader. In some cases, though, especially when slaves were bought with a written guarantee of their good health, traders would have been reimbursed for slave losses. Moreover, only a

2. Cook note, Jarratt–Puryear Papers (DU); Thomas to Finney, 19 Jan. 1860, Finney Papers (DU); and Haynes to Meek, 22 Apr. 1836, Negro Collection (AU). On "implicit" wages of the principals of trading firms, see Chapter 7.

3. Conrad and Meyer, "Economics of Slavery in the Ante-Bellum South," p. 101, and p. 102, Table 3.

very small percentage of slaves traded would have died while in the trader's possession or shortly after sale by the trader. Costs to the trader through slave deaths, through slaves escaping, and through insurance on slaves are, therefore, in an average season, likely to have been equivalent to not more than 1 or 2 percent of the purchase price for the season's slaves.[4]

Other expenses incurred by the trader would have included unpaid debts owed by customers, but most sales, as we know, were for cash or "good cashable paper," and such losses would not usually have undermined profits dramatically. There would also, it is true, have been expenses when traders decided to cash their "paper" before it had matured, but the case of Pascal & Raux suggests that such outgoings would have been on a minor scale.[5] Bad debts and the discounting of paper were probably more or less compensated for by the trader's ability to turn over a part of his capital more than once during a given trading season. (The protracted business of selling would usually have meant, though, that only a small percentage of capital could be reinvested in the same season.) Again, traders would have incurred certain expenses in

4. Since they would have directly affected profit and loss calculations, traders' accounts (where they give full price details) could hardly omit numbers of slaves who absconded or who were lost to the trader through death (before he sold them). Only one escapee appears, however, and deaths were two for Totten & Gunn, three for Bolton & Dickens, two for Owings & Charles, thirty for White and partners, and none for the other traders' lots listed in Table 7.1. This suggests an average, for runaways and deaths combined, of only 1.5 percent of slaves purchased. Given the relatively short time the slaves were usually in the trader's possession, a percentage of this order is perhaps not surprising.

5. The Pascal accounts are fragmentary and do not seem to allow rates of profit to be satisfactorily calculated, but they do give some valuable evidence on expenses (including the discounting of promissory notes) as a percentage of the basic purchase price of the slaves concerned. One entry indicates "general expenses" on 146 slaves "shipped at different times from Oct. 1834 to March 25 1835." The purchase price of the slaves was $70,338. Expenses were:

House rent, marketing, medical etc	$3,811.12
Commission and brokerage	1,132.17
Mortgage certificates	55.50
Discount on sundry notes	602.32
Passage and clothing	2,606.50
Cash paid on sundry postages	27.50
	$8,235.11

See Pascal Papers (HLH). Such expenses represent 11.7 percent of the basic purchase price, and discounting on notes amounted to a very tiny fraction of those costs. The account did not refer to any costs through interest charges, and such charges might have raised overall costs by perhaps 6 percent or so. Allowance would then be needed for bad debts, for turning over a proportion of capital more than once in the season, and so on—but the result would probably be broadly in line with the rates of expense estimated in this study.

accommodating their slaves prior to departure. But usually they left the slaves with their Upper South owners until shortly before departure for the Lower South; and when traders did acquire slaves at some considerable time before shipment, expenses could be offset by working the slaves or by hiring them out.

Considering the various items of expenditure which have been mentioned, only very approximate estimates of net profit seem justifiable. It seems probable, though, that, in most years, expenses would together have been equivalent to some 15 percent, and perhaps a little less, of the price which traders paid for their slaves. Expenses of this order have been assumed except for 1836 when (because of high interest rates) a 27 percent ratio of expenses to the trader's basic purchase price for a slave has been inferred.

Appendix 8

Calculating the Proportions of Upper South Slaves Forcibly Separated from Parents or Spouse

8.1. CHILDREN TRADED AWAY FROM PARENTS

These calculations (and those for marriage separations, below) are based upon rates of exportation by the trade which Chapter 2 established for the 1850s. They assume that about 60 percent of interregional movements were accounted for by trading. And, as Chapter 2 indicated, the percentage of the Upper South's slave population exported in that decade was similar to or a little below that for 1820–60 generally (see Chapter 2, note 37).

The procedure adopted in calculating the trading away of children from their parents can be illustrated by taking the example of children aged eight to eleven (inclusive). First, the census was consulted in order to gain an estimate of the number of slaves aged eight to eleven who were found in the Upper South in 1850. Table 6.3 (Chapter 6) was then consulted to find the percentage of the trade which was made up of slaves of those ages who had been forcibly separated from their parents. Since Chapter 2 estimated the overall volume of the trade (in the 1850s) at 184,991 slaves, it was then possible to calculate the numbers of eight- to eleven-year-olds traded separately from their parents. Those numbers were then compared with the number of eight- to eleven-year-olds present in the exporting states in 1850. It was assumed that the number of such slaves in that area would have been fairly constant over the 1850s. As with other estimates in this appendix, the results given are intended only as broad indications of likely proportions.

8.2. THE SEPARATION OF SPOUSES BY THE TRADE, ACCORDING TO AGE OF PERSON SOLD

Table A8.1 attempts to plot the cumulative chance that an Upper South slave, from the time he or she entered marriageable age until late-middle age, might be separated from a spouse by being sold in the interregional trade. The results given, particularly because mortality data might have significant imperfections

Table A8.1. Estimates of the proportions of Upper South slaves traded from the partners of their first marriage: Mid and late antebellum period

	Males (by age at the beginning and at the end of the decade)					Females (by age at the beginning and at the end of the decade)				
	5–9 15–19	10–19 20–29	20–29 30–39	30–39 40–49	40–49 50–59	5–9 15–19	10–19 20–29	20–29 30–39	30–39 40–49	40–49 50–59
1. Proportion of cohort traded in a typical decade	.093	.139	.076	.050	.004	.104	.129	.058	.032	.000
2. Proportion of cohort married or previously married	.010	.300	.800	.950	.950	.090	.750	.950	.950	.950
3. Weighting to allow for death of spouse over previous decades	.972	.889	.737	.578	.425	.913	.757	.593	.458	.332
4. Weighting to allow for death of spouse in current decade (allowing for half of the decade's mortality rate)	.986	.958	.915	.892	.868	.956	.915	.892	.886	.862
5. Proportion *not* traded from spouse in current decade (row 1 × row 2 × row 3 × row 4)	.999	.964	.959	.976	.999	.992	.933	.971	.988	1.00
6. Cumulative proportion *not* traded from spouse[a]	.999	.963	.924	.901	.900	.992	.926	.899	.888	.888
7. Cumulative percentage chance of being traded from spouse[b]	0.1%	3.7%	7.6%	9.9%	10.0%	0.8%	7.4%	10.1%	11.2%	11.2%

[a]Multiply row 5 columns 1 × 2 × 3 × 4 × 5 for cumulative male data according to increasing age. Multiply row 5 columns 6 × 7 × 8 × 9 × 10 for cumulative female data according to increasing age.

[b]Convert row 6 into row 7 by taking result in each column of row 6 from 1.0, and multiply by 100.

(see below), are intended only as broad indications of probable patterns. The calculations in Table A8.1 began by estimating (see Chapter 2, note 37) the proportions who would have been traded from the base populations (male and female) of Upper South slaves across successive decades (that is, with increasing age). To find the proportion of each age group at risk of separation, weightings were then added for three factors—the proportion of slaves who would have married by the time of being traded; the percentage of those married who should be discounted because they would already have been widowed in previous decades; and, finally, the proportion of those who before being traded (but in the same decade as they were traded) lost a spouse through that spouse's death. These proportions (rows 1 to 4), when multiplied together (row 5), should yield estimates of the proportions of particular age groups *not* traded away from a spouse (row 6), and traded from a spouse (row 7).

Certain notes should be appended to these calculations. (a). The typical age at first marriage was taken to be, for females, about nineteen years and for males about twenty-four years (see Chapter 6, note 28).

(b). If the overall share of the trade (as against planter migration) had been estimated at only 50 percent (a very unlikely hypothesis) or (more probably) at 70 percent, the results would not have been greatly different from those given in Table A8.1. Table A8.4 (which assumes that trading accounted for 60 percent of interregional movements) attributes to the trade about 20 percent of all of the family separations of Upper South slaves, but if trading had been attributed 50 or 70 percent of movements, the trade's share of separations would have been 17 percent or 23 percent, respectively.

(c). The estimates of levels of mortality according to age are based upon survival rates derived directly from census data. In Chapter 2, such survival rates were used to estimate levels of interregional population movement, and there they presented no serious problems. Any errors in the quality of census enumeration were likely to have been cancelled out in the interregional comparisons made (see Appendix 3.1). Demographers are, however, quite justifiably wary about taking any particular survival (and hence mortality) rate as being entirely reliable. Some slaves might have been missed by enumerators, some ages might have been inaccurate, and, most important, inaccuracies might have tended to be more frequent for one age group than for another.[1] For the particular purposes of Table A8.1, the problems posed by such inaccuracies are, however, not likely to create fundamental distortions. Many of the calculations rely on *cumulative* patterns, so that inaccuracies from one census to another would tend to be balanced out in the long run. Moreover, the notoriously unreliable data for the under-fives are wholly avoided in this table, and data for the fives-to-nines are of only minor significance.

8.3. HYPOTHETICAL PROPORTIONS OF MARRIED SLAVES (ASSUMING NO FORCED SEPARATIONS BY MASTERS) WHO WOULD HAVE DIED

On a similar basis to the previous table, Table A8.2 estimates, across successive ages, the cumulative chance that an Upper South spouse would die. Row 1 plots the proportion of each age group who would have been ever married: row 2 plots (from census-survival rates) the proportion of each age group who would have died during the decade concerned; and row 3 multiplies these (according to age group) to produce estimates of the preliminary proportion of each age group who would have been married and would have died and left a widow or widower during that decade. Row 4 converts these into preliminary results for the cumulative proportions who would have been ever married and have died leaving a bereaved spouse. Calculations in section 8.5 will combine male and female risks and so estimate proportions of marriages broken.

1. See, for example, Paul Demeny and Paul Gingrich, "A Reconsideration of Negro-White Mortality Differentials in the United States," *Demography,* 4 (1967), pp. 820–21. For a critical and original essay on mortality rates see also Meeker, "Mortality Trends of Southern Blacks, 1850–1910."

Table A8.2. Hypothetical proportions of the Upper South's married slaves (assuming no forced separations by masters) who would have died: Mid and late antebellum period

	Males (by age at the beginning and at the end of the decade)					Females (by age at the beginning and at the end of the decade)				
	5–9 15–19	10–19 20–29	20–29 30–39	30–39 40–49	40–49 50–59	5–9 15–19	10–19 20–29	20–29 30–39	30–39 40–49	40–49 50–59
1. Proportion ever married, by age indicated	.010	.300	.800	.950	.950	.090	.750	.950	.950	.950
2. Weighting for own group's mortality rate	.073	.101	.241	.192	.265	.042	.128	.215	.217	.312
3. Preliminary proportion of cohort dying and leaving widow or widower (row 1 × row 2)	.001	.030	.193	.182	.252	.004	.096	.204	.206	.296
4. Preliminary cumulative proportion of cohort dying and leaving widow(er)[a]	.001	.031	.218	.360	.522	.004	.100	.283	.431	.599

[a]Calculate by converting entries in row 3 into proportions not dying and leaving widow or widower (.001 becomes .999 etc.). Then multiply revised data as in Table A8.1, note a. Convert results into proportion dying and leaving widow(er).

Table A8.3. Comparing causes of the separation of spouses: Upper South slaves in the mid and late antebellum period

	Proportion *not* separated, according to factor									
	Husband dying or removed (by age at end of decade)					Wife dying or removed (by age at end of decade)				
	15–19	20–29	30–39	40–49	50–59	15–19	20–29	30–39	40–49	50–59
1. Motality rate as factor	.999	.969	.782	.640	.478	.996	.900	.717	.569	.401
2. Interregional trade	.999	.963	.924	.901	.900	.992	.926	.899	.888	.888
3. Combination of mortality rate and interregional trade[a]	.998	.933	.723	.577	.430	.988	.833	.645	.505	.356
4. Combination of force (all types) and mortality[b]	.998	.916	.694	.547	.409	.984	.800	.610	.476	.337

[a]Row 1 × row 2.

[b]Row 1 × revised row 2 (see Chapter 6 for basis of revised weighting to include local sales and nonmarket forcers).

8.4. COMBINING SEPARATIONS FROM TRADING, HYPOTHETICAL RATES ESTIMATED FOR DEATHS, AND OTHER FACTORS

Table A8.3, by multiplying the probability of *not* being traded with that of a married slave *not* dying (rows 1 and 2), gives estimates of the combined chance of *not* being traded from a spouse and *not* dying and leaving a surviving spouse. These estimates will be refined in section 8.5. Row 4 goes further and includes interregional trading, mortality, local sales, and nonmarket factors. This cal-

Table A8.4. Cumulative proportions of Upper South slaves with marriages broken: Mid and late antebellum period

	Factor considered							
	Not separated from spouse[a] (by average age at end of decade)				Marriage broken[b] (by average age at end of decade)			
	M24 F19	M34 F29	M44 F39	M54 F49	M24 F19	M34 F29	M44 F39	M54 F49
1. Mortality (hypothetical level of effects) (i)	.969	.782	.640	.478	.940	.630	.411	.232
(ii)	.970	.805	.642	.485	6.0	37.0	58.9	76.8
2. Interregional trade (i)	.963	.924	.901	.900	.934	.845	.809	.799
(ii)	.970	.915	.898	.888	6.6	15.5	19.1	20.1
3. Mortality and trade combined (i)	.933	.723	.577	.430	.878	.533	.333	.185
(ii)	.941	.737	.577	.430	12.2	46.7	66.7	81.5
4. Mortality, trade, and all forced separations (i)	.916	.694	.547	.409	.852	.493	.298	.164
(ii)	.930	.710	.545	.400	14.8	50.7	70.2	83.6

Notes: M and F indicate male and female

[a]The top line (i) in each row of columns 1 to 4 gives proportions for males; the bottom line (ii) in each row for these columns gives those for females.

[b]The top line (i) in each row of columns 5 to 8 gives proportions not broken; the bottom line (ii) in each row of these columns gives percentages broken.

Columns 1 to 4 give a revised version of results in Table A8.3. The revision gives estimated data for specific ages. For example, it converts results for males aged 20–29 directly into results for males aged 24. These data are set against those for women who were 5 years younger; in this way possible spouses are paired.

Columns 1 to 4 illustrate two alternative combinations of risk, these being the chance of either (a) a husband being forcibly removed from a wife or losing a wife through death or (b) a wife being forcibly removed from a husband or losing a husband through death. Columns 5 to 8 attempt to combine the risks involved in (a) and (b), and seek to show the total chances of family breakdown according to age and to a particular factor or combination of factors. To combine these risks, multiply entries (i) and (ii) for a particular age combination in columns 1 to 4 (e.g. males 24 and females 19) and for a particular factor or combination of factors in rows 1 to 4 (e.g. row 1, mortality). This produces, according to the age combination and factor(s), entries in columns 5 to 8. In the case of males aged 24 and females aged 19, the suggested chance of not having had a marriage broken by death is .969 × .970 = .940, or 6 percent.

culation is made by giving an additional weighting to row 2, and then multiplying as before. The basis of the weighting for local sales and nonmarket transactions is given in Chapter 6.

8.5. ESTIMATING RATES OF MARRIAGE SEPARATION

So far estimates have been made, in isolation, for the impact firstly of removal of a husband and secondly of removal of a wife. By combining the probabilities of husbands *not* being separated and wives *not* being separated, we can remove certain overcounting and produce estimates (by age and cause) of *marriages* broken. Since males seem, on average, to have been about five years older than females at the time of their first marriage (and we are here concerned only with first marriages) we should not simply link males and females of the same age.

Table A8.5. Rates of slave exportation or importation according to region and state, 1820–29

	Percentage exportation or importation rate (by age, 1820/1830)							
	0–13/10–23		14–25/24–35		26–44/36–54		45+/55+	
	M	F	M	F	M	F	M	F
Net exporters								
All net exporters combined	14.0	14.5	12.9	11.7	5.8	5.7	2.9	3.1
Delaware	23.2	32.7	64.6	56.3	55.4	42.5	25.2	24.4
Kentucky	4.0	1.7	13.6	13.2	4.7	5.3	1.7	0.4
Maryland	19.9	24.2	33.4	31.1	17.1	18.1	9.9	13.8
North Carolina	13.6	12.2	19.2	14.5	0.5	2.3	+0.9	+0.9
South Carolina	5.1	3.7	0.2	+3.9	4.7	1.4	3.6	1.2
Virginia	20.6	23.2	10.6	14.0	5.8	7.3	2.3	3.5
Net importers								
All net importers combined	47.0	42.5	34.7	29.6	15.7	16.0	10.5	12.1
Alabama	114.7	122.0	79.2	90.5	54.8	61.3	66.6	78.2
Arkansas	165.9	193.2	52.5	57.8	67.1	54.1	6.4	6.3
Georgia	12.4	10.5	7.6	11.2	6.7	5.9	2.2	3.3
Louisiana	64.4	60.2	54.5	24.2	8.2	7.7	6.9	10.2
Louisiana (sugar area only)	173.9	126.9	132.0	74.6	47.8	37.9	36.9	29.0
Mississippi	64.7	68.3	60.5	54.3	13.5	18.6	21.9	13.7
Missouri	86.7	108.5	45.3	59.7	39.0	49.4	10.9	20.8
Tennessee	25.0	30.7	20.2	17.7	21.3	18.7	9.7	11.0

Note: The rates indicated give the net exportations (or importations) of slaves for each cohort as a percentage of that cohort's start-of-decade population of slaves.

M = male; F = female.

+ = apparent net importation for a cohort, within a context of the state's overall net exportation.

Data for Table A8.4 were therefore developed by making certain adjustments to results in Table A8.3. The basis is the age of slaves at the *end* of the notional decades in question. Males aged twenty to twenty-nine at the end of the decade are taken, on average, to have been representative of twenty-four-year-olds (and similar assumptions were made for other age groups). This process was repeated for females, but in their case proportions traded (dying, etc.) were plotted on graphs (not reproduced here). From these graphs, it was possible to derive intermediate readings for ages nineteen, twenty-nine, and so on—and in this way a basis was achieved for combining, for example, males of average age twenty-four with females five years younger.

8.6. RATES OF SLAVE EXPORTATION OR IMPORTATION ACCORDING TO REGION AND STATE

In order to help provide a background for considering the impact of the trade—and more particularly separations—upon different areas, Tables A8.5 and A8.6 indicate percentage rates of exportation and importation by state (and according to particular decades). The calculations are based on the same survival-rate method as in Chapter 2.

Table A8.6. Rates of slave exportation or importation according to region and state, 1850–59

	Percentage exportation or importation rate (by age, 1850/1860)											
	0–4/10–14		5–9/15–19		10–19/20–29		20–29/30–39		30–39/40–49		40+/50+	
	M	F	M	F	M	F	M	F	M	F	M	F
Net exporters												
All net exporters combined	10.9	10.3	13.3	14.4	17.9	16.9	11.6	9.8	9.0	7.2	5.8	5.0
[a]Georgia	4.2	1.5	3.2	2.8	6.5	4.7	4.4	2.9	1.1	0.5	1.7	1.3
Kentucky	10.8	10.7	12.4	15.3	22.1	24.8	16.9	12.0	9.3	5.3	5.5	7.1
Maryland	15.2	14.7	10.6	16.2	26.8	26.2	25.5	19.6	16.1	14.0	11.5	10.6
North Carolina	6.0	6.3	14.3	18.2	14.7	13.5	8.1	8.0	7.6	7.0	+2.4	+3.5
South Carolina	15.3	14.0	13.2	14.1	20.1	15.7	9.8	8.6	9.0	8.1	8.8	9.0
Tennessee	6.6	4.7	10.8	11.6	15.7	13.2	12.4	8.9	9.9	8.0	+1.9	+0.2
Virginia	9.0	9.5	15.8	17.7	20.6	21.8	9.5	8.5	7.6	5.0	8.2	5.5
Net importers												
All net importers combined	25.2	23.1	30.7	33.1	42.0	39.3	22.8	19.1	16.5	13.8	13.6	12.7
[a]Alabama	-1.0	0.0	1.6	4.6	6.0	6.1	3.1	1.9	-0.6	1.3	-0.1	1.0
Arkansas	82.7	72.6	96.2	103.0	111.3	104.3	58.4	57.1	61.2	59.8	50.3	49.8
Florida	26.0	26.7	27.7	26.8	38.9	34.4	20.0	17.8	23.1	20.4	12.7	14.7
Louisiana	6.3	2.0	18.4	21.7	51.0	41.1	20.9	12.4	8.9	2.4	5.3	4.1
Louisiana (sugar area only)	-4.7	-10.8	10.1	4.9	45.8	27.1	23.1	16.0	12.2	1.9	-8.2	-4.7
Mississippi	9.4	7.1	11.0	19.3	26.6	27.9	10.8	5.7	4.1	0.3	8.0	5.8
[a]Missouri	6.4	9.4	7.0	4.1	-4.4	-6.7	-11.6	-3.4	2.4	7.1	3.6	3.9
Texas	147.3	143.2	160.4	165.1	159.5	150.0	110.9	106.0	102.6	96.4	87.4	79.5

Note: The rates indicated give the net exportations (or importations) of slaves for each cohort as a percentage of that cohort's start-of-decade population of slaves.

M = male; F = female.

\+ = Apparent net importation for a cohort, within a context of the state's overall exportation.

\- = Apparent exportation within a general context of importation.

[a] Net results for "mixed states" which combined (in 1850s) major sections of exportation with major areas of importation.

Primary Sources

I. UNPUBLISHED PRIMARY SOURCES

American Antiquities Society, Worcester, Massachusetts (AAS)
Lucy Chase Papers
R. H. Dickinson & Bro., Slave Dealers Account Book (1846–49)
Atlanta University, Georgia (AU)
Negro Collection
Boston Public Library (BPL)
G. W. Barnes Papers
Ziba B. Oakes Papers
Chicago Historical Society (CHS)
Hector Davis & Co., Slave Sales Record Book
Richard H. Dickinson Papers
Duke University, Durham, North Carolina (DU)
J. W. Bond Papers
Archibald H. Boyd Papers
Joseph Dickinson Papers
Dickinson and Washington Papers
Obediah Fields Papers
William A. J. Finney Papers
Tyre Glen Papers
James Graham Papers
James H. Hammond Papers
William H. Hatchett Papers
Jarratt-Puryear Family Papers
John A. Jordan Papers
James A. Mitchell Papers
D. M. Pulliam Papers
David S. Reid Papers
Francis E. Rives Papers
Austin L. Taveau Papers
F. L. Whitehad and N. Loftus Accounts of Slave Trading
Samuel O. Wood Papers
Houghton Library, Harvard University, Cambridge, Massachusetts (HLH)

Paul Pascal Papers

Library of Congress, Washington, D.C. (LC)

John W. Pittman Papers

Lewis C. Robards Papers

Missouri Historical Society, St. Louis (MHS)

J. R. White Account Book, Chinn Collection

National Archives, Washington, D.C. (NA)

Manifests of Slave Shipments, Record Group 36, Bureau of Customs

United States Census Bureau, Manuscript Census Returns for 1850 and 1860, Free and Slave Schedules for South Carolina

New York Historical Society (NYHS)

Bolton & Dickens Record of Slaves, 1856–58

W. D. Ellis Letter, Miscellaneous Manuscripts

New York Public Library (NYPL)

Hector Davis & Co., Day Book

H. N. Templeman Account Book

North Carolina Department of Archives, Raleigh (NCA)

Badgett Family Papers

Elias W. Ferguson Papers

William Long Papers

North Carolina Governors' Papers: E. B. Dudley (Governor, 1836–41), T. Bragg (Governor 1855–59)

Stokes County List of Taxables, 1830–37

Joseph S. Totten Papers

South Carolina Department of Archives, Columbia (SCA)

Anderson District Court of Ordinary: Inventories, Appraisals, and Sales book, 1850–56

Bills of Sale, South Carolina Secretary of State's Office

Charleston District Court of Chancery and Equity, Sales Book of James Tupper, Master in Equity, 1851–63

Charleston District Court of Ordinary: Inventories, Appraisals, and Sales, 3 ms. volumes, 1850–59

Court of Common Pleas Judgment Rolls, South Carolina Districts (c. 1845–70)

Equity Court Bills, South Carolina Districts (c. 1845–70)

Miscellaneous Records of Secretary of State for South Carolina

Loose Legislative Papers, Petitions, Box 4

South Carolina Historical Society, Charleston (SCHS)

Louis D. DeSaussure Papers

Hutson-Lee Collection

Alonzo J. White, List Book of Negroes for Sale, c. 1855–63

South Caroliniana Library, University of South Carolina, Columbia (SCL)

Cox Family Papers

Louis D. DeSaussure Papers

Edward S. Hammond Papers

James H. Hammond Collection of Bills of Sale

James H. Hammond Papers
James Spann Papers
Southern Historical Collection, University of North Carolina, Chapel Hill (SHC)
Brownrigg Family Papers
T. C. Hanson, Miscellaneous Letters, Addition
James T. Harrison Papers
Isaac Jarratt Papers
Quitman Family Papers
James Shackelford Letter (typed copy)
Templeman & Goodwin Account Book
A. & A. T. Walker Account book
Floyd L. Whitehead Papers
Sumter County Sheriff's Office, Sumter, South Carolina (SCSO)
J. C. Rhame Sheriff's Sales Book, 1852–56
H. Skinner Sheriff's Sales Book, 1848–52
Alderman Library, University of Virginia, Charlottesville (UVA)
Grinnan Family Papers
Harris-Brady Papers
S. & R. F. Omohundro Slave Sales Book
Palmore Family Papers
Richard R. Reid Papers
Edward D. Tayloe Papers
Floyd L. Whitehead Papers
Virginia State Library, Richmond (VSL)
Virginia State Auditor's Papers, Item 153

II. PUBLISHED PRIMARY SOURCES

In footnotes, wherever publication details cite more than one edition of a book, the first citation refers to the original date of publication, the second to the edition actually consulted.

Antebellum Novels and Related Materials

Most of the novels listed below are available on microfilm in the *American Fiction* series issued by Research Publications, Inc., New Haven, Conn. (1967–75).

[Anon], "The Queen's Dream: A Sequel to *Uncle Tom's Cabin*," *DeBow's Review,* 15 (1853), pp. 95–105.

[Anon], *The Yankee Slave-dealer, or, An Abolitionist down South. A Tale for the Times* (Nashville, 1860).

Adams, Francis C., *Uncle Tom at Home: A Review of the Reviewers and Repudiators of Uncle Tom's Cabin by Mrs. Stowe* (Philadelphia, 1853).

Bulfinch, Stephen G., *Honor; or, the Slave Dealer's Daughter* (Boston, 1864).

Bennett, Martha H., *Anti-fanaticism: A Tale of the South* (Philadelphia, 1853).

Chase, Lucien B., *English Serfdom and American Slavery, or Ourselves as Others See Us* (New York, 1854).

Criswell, Robert, *Uncle Tom's Cabin, Contrasted with Buckingham Hall, the*

Planter's Home, Or a Fair View of Both Sides of the Slavery Question (New York, 1852).

Eastman, Mary H., *Aunt Phillis's Cabin, or Southern Life As It Is* (Philadelphia, 1852; New York, 1868).

Flanders, G. M., *The Ebony Idol, by A Lady of New England* (New York, 1860).

Georgian Lady, "Southern Slavery and Its Assailants; by a Georgian Lady," *DeBow's Review,* 15 (1853), pp. 486–96.

Hale, Sarah J., *Liberia; or, Mr. Peyton's Experiments* (New York, 1853).

Hall, Baynard R., *Frank Freeman's Barber Shop; A Tale* (New York, 1852).

Page, John W., *Uncle Robin in his Cabin and Tom Without One in Boston* (Richmond, 1853).

Randolph, J. T., *The Cabin and the Parlor, or, Slaves and Masters* (Philadelphia, 1852).

Rush, Caroline E., *The North and South, or, Slavery and its Contrasts. A Tale of Real Life* (Philadelphia, 1852).

Schoolcraft, Mary R., *The Black Gauntlet: A Tale of Plantation Life in South Carolina* (Philadelphia, 1860).

Stowe, Harriet B., *The Key to Uncle Tom's Cabin; Presenting the Original Facts and Documents Upon Which the Story is Founded* (London, 1853).

Stowe, Harriet B., *Uncle Tom's Cabin, or, Life Among the Lowly* (Cleveland, 1852; London 1853).

Thorpe, Thomas B., *The Master's House; A Tale of Southern Life* (New York, 1854).

Vidi [pseud], *Mr. Frank, the Underground Mail Agent* (Philadelphia, 1853).

Antebellum Treatises on Slavery and the South

American Anti-Slavery Society [Weld, Theodore D.], *American Slavery As It Is: Testimony of a Thousand Witnesses* (New York, 1839).

Andrews, Ethan A., *Slavery and the Domestic Slave Trade in the United States, in a Series of Letters Addressed to the Executive Committee of the American Union for the Relief and Improvement of the Colored Race* (Boston, 1836).

Blanchard, J., and Rice, N. L., *A Debate on Slavery Held in the City of Cincinnati on the First, Second and Sixth Days of October 1845, Upon the Question Is Slaveholding in Itself Sinful, and the Relation between Master and Slave, a Sinful Relation?* (Cincinnati, 1846; New York, 1969).

Cairnes, John E., *The Slave Power: Its Character, Career and Probable Designs* (London, 1862).

Cobb, Thomas R., *An Inquiry into the Law of Slavery in the United States of America* (1858).

Elliot, E. N., *Cotton is King, and Pro-slavery Arguments: Comprising the Writings of Hammond, Harper, Christie, Stringfellow, Hodge, Bledsoe, and Cartwright* (Augusta, 1860).

Executive Committee of the American Anti-Slavery Society, Eds., *Slavery and the Internal Slave Trade . . . Being Replies to Questions Transmitted by the British and Foreign Anti-Slavery Society* (London, 1841).

Goodell, Rev. William, *The American Slave Code in Theory and Practice: Its Distinctive Features shown by its Statutes, Judicial Decisions, and Illustrative Facts* (London, 1853).

Hundley, Daniel R., *Social Relations in Our Southern States* (New York, 1860).

Hurd, John C., *The Law of Freedom and Bondage in the United States* (Boston, 1858–62; New York, 1968).

Jay, William, *A View of the Action of the Federal Government in Behalf of Slavery* (New York, 1839).

Jay, William, *Slavery in America or an Inquiry into the Character and Tendency of the American Colonization and American Anti-Slavery Societies* (London, 1835).

Torrey, Jesse, *The American Slave Trade; or An Account of the Manner in which the Slave Dealers take Free People from Some of the United States of America, and Carry them Away, and Sell them as Slaves in Other of the States* . . . (London, 1822, with preface by William Cobbett; reprinted Negro University Press, Westport, Conn., 1971, and originally published as *A Portraiture of Slavery in the United States* (Philadelphia, 1817).

Van Evrie, John H., *Negroes and Negro "Slavery": The First an Inferior Race, The Latter Its Normal Condition* (New York, 1853).

Slave Narratives

Ball, Charles, *Fifty Years in Chains; or, The Life of an American Slave* (New York, 1858).

Brown, William W., *The Narrative of William W. Brown: A Fugitive Slave* (Boston, 1847; Reading, Mass., 1969).

Chamerovzow, L. A. (Ed.), *Slave Life in Georgia: A Narrative of the Life, Sufferings, and Escape of John Brown, A Fugitive Slave, Now in England* (London, 1855).

Douglass, Frederick, *My Bondage and Freedom* (New York, 1855; Dover reprint, New York, 1965).

Grandy, Moses, *Narrative of the Life of Moses Grandy, late a Slave in the United States of America* (Boston, 1844).

Northup, Solomon, *Twelve Years A Slave: Narrative of Solomon Northup, a Citizen of New York, Kidnapped in Washington City in 1841, and Rescued in 1853 from a Cotton Plantation Near the Red River, in Louisiana* (Auburn, 1853).

Rawick, George P. (Ed.), *The American Slave; A Compositive Autobiography,* 19 vols. (Westport, Conn., 1972).

Roper, Moses, *A Narrative of the Adventures and Escape of Moses Roper from American Slavery* (London, 1840).

Stroyer, Jacob, *My Life in the South* (Salem, 1879; Salem 1898).

Travel Accounts

Adams, Nehemiah, *A South-Side View of Slavery; Or Three Months in the South in 1854* (Boston, 1855).

Buckingham, James S., *The Slave States of America* (London, 1842).

Featherstonehaugh, George W., *Excursion Through the Slave States, from Wash-*

ington on the Potomac to the Frontier of Mexico; With Sketches of Popular Manners and Geological Notices (New York,1844; New York, 1968).

Hall, Basil, *Travels in North America in the Years 1827 and 1828* (Edinburg, 1829).

Ingraham, Joseph H., *The South-West, by a Yankee* (New York, 1836).

Olmsted, Frederick L. *The Cotton Kingdom* (ed. Arthur M. Schlesinger; New York, 1953).

Stirling, James, *Letters from the Slave States* (London, 1857).

Tower, Philo, *Slavery Unmasked: Being a Truthful Narrative of Three Years' Residence and Journeying in Eleven Southern States* (Rochester, 1856).

Newspapers and Periodicals

The list below gives the main South Carolina newspapers consulted (mostly 1845 to 1860 issues) at SCL.

Abbeville Banner
Abbeville *Independent Press*
Beaufort Enterprise
Camden Journal
Charleston Courier
Charleston Mercury
Chester Standard
Columbia Daily Carolina Times
Columbia *Daily South Carolinian*
Darlington Flag
Darlington Southerner
Edgefield Advertiser
Georgetown *Winyaw Observer*
Greenville Mountaineer
Kingstree Star
Lancaster Ledger
Laurensville Herald
Lexington Flag
Marion Star
Orangeburg *Southron*
Spartanburg *Carolina Spartan*
Sumter Banner
Sumter *Black River Watchman*
Sumter Watchman
Yorkville Enquirer
Yorkville Miscellany

Non-South Carolina newspapers and periodicals consulted (mostly 1845 to 1860 issues) included those listed below. The location of the copy used is indicated by the abbreviation in parentheses.

Augusta Chronicle and Georgia Adveriser (SCL)
De Bow's Review (New Orleans; UH)

Louisville Gazette (Georgia; JCL)
New Orleans Daily Crescent (Louisiana; BL)
Niles's Weekly Register (Baltimore; issues for 1811–28; UH)
Richmond Enquirer (Virginia; BL)
Savannah Republican (Georgia; SCL)
Virginia Patriot (Independence, Va.; BL)

Directories and Almanacs

Charleston City Directory for 1852 (Charleston, 1852).
The Charleston City and General Business Directory for 1855 (Charleston, 1855).
The Charleston Directory Containing the Names of the Inhabitants, A Subscribers' Business Directory, Street Maps of the City and an Appendix (Charleston, 1859).
Miller's Planter's and Merchant's Almanac (years 1850–60).

United States Censuses and Other Federal Materials

The *Sixth Census* (1840), cited below, includes valuable summaries of the population information given in the five earlier decennial censuses.

DeBow, J. D. B., *Statistical View of the United States . . . being a Compendium of the Seventh Census* (Washington, D.C., 1854).
United States Bureau of Census, *Census for 1820* (Washington, D.C., 1821).
United States Bureau of Census, *Fifth Census . . . as Corrected at the Department of State, 1830* (Washington, D.C., 1832).
United States Bureau of Census, *Sixth Census . . . as Corrected at the Department of State in 1840* (Washington, D.C., 1841).
United States Bureau of Census, *The Seventh Census of the United States: 1850* (Washington, D.C., 1853).
United States Bureau of Census, *Agriculture in the United States in 1860* (Washington, D.C., 1862).
United States Bureau of Census, *Preliminary Report of the Eighth Census* (Washington, D.C., 1862).
United States Bureau of Census, *Population of the United States in 1860* (Washington, D.C., 1864).
United States Bureau of Census, *The Statistics of the Population of the United States . . . Ninth Census* (Washington, D.C., 1872).
United States Congress Joint Select Committee, *Testimony Taken Before the Joint Select Committee to Inquire into the Conditions and Affairs of the Late Insurrectionary States*, 13 vols. (Washington, D.C., 1872; New York, 1968).

South Carolina Official Publications

South Carolina's *Reports and Resolutions*, cited below, are available for the years 1830 to 1860 (and for certain earlier years) at the South Caroliniana Library. This material, for 1837 onward, is available on microfilm in W. S. Jenkins, *Records of the States of the United States of America: A Microfilm Compilation* (Washington, D.C., and Chapel Hill, 1949).

General Assembly, *Reports and Resolutions of the General Assembly of the State of South Carolina* (Columbia, 1839–1860).

Horsen, W. R. (Ed.), *Ordinances of the City of Charleston 14 September 1854 to December 1 1859* (Charleston, 1859).

Pillsbury, G. (Ed.), *Ordinances of the City of Charleston from December 1 1859 to September 6 1870* (Charleston, 1871).

Richardson, J. S. G., *Reports of Cases at Law Argued and Determined in the Court of Appeals and Court of Errors of South Carolina* (Columbia, 1867).

Richardson, J. S. G., *Reports of Cases in Equity Argued and Determined in the Court of Appeals in Equity and Court of Errors of South Carolina* (Columbia, 1868).

Strobhart, James A., *Reports of Cases Argued and Determined in the Court of Appeals and Errors of South Carolina on Appeal from the Courts of Law* (Columbia, 1850).

Strobhart, James A., *Reports of Cases in Equity Argued and Determined in the Court of Appeals in the Court of Errors of South Carolina* (Columbia, 1850).

Walker, H. P. (Ed.), *Ordinances of the City of Charleston from the 19 August 1844 to the 14 September 1854* (Charleston, 1854).

Edited Documents and Miscellaneous

American Anti-Slavery Society [Thompson, Mortimer], *Great Auction of Slaves, at Savannah, Georgia, March 2nd and 3rd 1859* (New York, 1859).

Catterall, Helen T. (Ed.), *Judicial Cases Concerning American Slavery and the Negro,* 5 vols. (Washington, D.C., 1926–37).

Dodge, N. S., *A Charleston Vendue of 1842* (New York, 1867).

Donnan, Elizabeth (Ed.), *Documents Illustrative of the History of the Slave Trade to America,* 4 vols. (Washington, D.C., 1930–35).

Ferrand, Max (Ed.), *The Records of the Federal Convention of 1787,* 4 vols. (New Haven, Conn., 1911).

Green, Fletcher M. (Ed.), *The Lides Go South and West: The Record of a Planter Migration in 1835* (Columbia,S.C., 1952).

Phillips, Ulrich B., Commons, John R., et al. (Eds.), *A Documentary History of American Industrial Society,* 11 vols. (Cleveland, 1910–11; New York, 1958).

Index